A History
of STONE & KIMBALL *and*
HERBERT S. STONE & COMPANY

A History of
STONE & KIMBALL
and
HERBERT S. STONE & CO.
with a Bibliography of Their Publications

1893-1905

BY SIDNEY KRAMER
Preface by Frederic G. Melcher

Chicago · NORMAN W FORGUE · Illinois
m c m x x x x

COPYRIGHT 1940, BY NORMAN W. FORGUE

TO
ALL MY TEACHERS

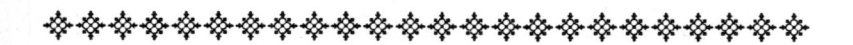

Preface

THE DETAILED and documented history of a publishing house is an interesting and significant record, the importance of which will become increasingly recognized as time goes by. Dr. Kramer's careful study gives us an insight into what book publishing really is: it pictures for us the reading interests of a rapidly changing decade, and it brings close to us a brilliant pair of young men who, while yet in their twenties, created a publishing house which blazed like a comet across a startled booktrade.

Herbert Stone and Ingalls Kimball had taste in literature and in bookmaking, a flair for list building, and a driving enthusiasm. Entering into the field when American business was at an ebb and book publishing was facing, in addition, the problem of adjusting itself to changes brought about by the new copyright law, they stepped forward confidently, almost gaily, and did the seemingly impossible. They found ways to publicize and distribute books while their office was still a college dormitory, drew great names to an unknown imprint, searched out new artists for book design and illustration, and made Chicago a name in current book publishing.

Such a story is worth the telling and the details are important to have in print, for the records of publishing houses are all too quickly lost. When historians of our cultural life try to recreate the past, they have book titles as the data of past publishing seasons, but few records of the creative, explosive force that put these books into motion—that caused them to change taste, mould opinion and influence events.

We should have more histories of publishing houses done with the painstaking competency of this.

FREDERIC G. MELCHER

Contents

Preface by Frederic G. Melcher	ix
Introduction	xv

HISTORY

I. The First Year in Cambridge	1
II. The Chap-Book and Its Contemporaries	25
III. Stone & Kimball: Chicago and New York	56
IV. Herbert S. Stone & Company: Chicago and New York	95
V. Notes for Students and Collectors	138

BIBLIOGRAPHY

I. Publications of Stone & Kimball: Cambridge, Chicago and New York, 1893-1897	195
II. Publications of Herbert S. Stone & Company: Chicago, New York and London, 1896-1905	252
III. Publications of Way & Williams Reissued by Herbert S. Stone & Company	357
IV. Printings Made for Copyright Purposes Only by Stone & Kimball and Herbert S. Stone & Company	359
V. Privately Printed Books Produced Under the Supervision of Stone & Kimball and Herbert S. Stone & Company	361

TABLES

I Chronology of Stone & Kimball, 1893-1897	xxi
II Chronology of Herbert S. Stone & Company, 1896-1906	xxii
III Publishers' Devices	193

List of Illustrations

Figure		Facing Page
1	From the Harvard College Class Albums: H. S. Stone and H. I. Kimball, 1894, M. E. Stone Jr., 1897, H. G. Rhodes, 1893	24
2	Bliss Carman: Drawing by Dawson Watson, From The Chap-Book, September 1, 1896	25
3	Portrait of Kenneth Grahame; and a Letter assigning American rights to "The Golden Age"	55
4	From Files of Stone & Kimball: Letter from "Fiona Macleod" and Postcard from William Sharp	56
5	Harold Frederic: From the original pen drawing by Fred Richardson	94
6	Offices of Herbert S. Stone & Company: Drawing by Frank Hazenplug	95
7	George Ade and John T. McCutcheon: 1900	137
8	Beardsley's illustrations: "The Masque of the Red Death" and "The Murders in the Rue Morgue"	138
A	Bookplate designed by H. S. Stone	149
B	Theodore Low DeVinne's "Horrible Example"	152
9	Covers of the first publication of Stone & Kimball	159
10a	"Stone & Kimball's First Book"	160
10b	Stone & Kimball's Own Favorite Book	160
11	Some early bindings for Stone & Kimball	161
12	Hamlin Garland's first publication with Stone & Kimball	162
13	From "Main-Travelled Roads": Vignette by H. T. Carpenter	163
14	Border by Aubrey Beardsley	164
15	Border by Pierre la Rose	165

16a	Border and lettering by Martin Mower	166
16b	Border and lettering by the Author	166
17	Binding by T. B. Meteyard	167
18	Volume I, Number 1	168
19	Chap-Book cover by Claude Bragdon	169
20	"In Russet & Silver": Typography by H. S. Stone	170
21	"In Russet & Silver": Binding by Will H. Bradley	171
22	Two Bindings designed by H. S. Stone	172
23	Two Bindings designed by Bruce Rogers	173
24	Series bindings for Stone & Kimball	174
25	Edition bindings for Stone & Kimball	175
26	"Grip": Title designed by H. I. Kimball	176
27	"Grip": Text page	177
28	"Episcopo & Company": Typography by H. S. Stone, Ornament by Frank Hazenplug	178
29	"Love's Dilemmas": Typography and ornaments by Will H. Bradley	179
30	Early bindings for Herbert S. Stone & Company	180
31	Later bindings for Herbert S. Stone & Company	181
32	Binding design by Blanche McManus	182
33	Stone editions of Shaw	183
34	Shaw's Portrait and Plays	184
35	"G. B. S. Recommends"	185
36	Stone's Best-Seller	186
37	A First Novel by Wardon Allan Curtis	187
38	Poster by John T. McCutcheon for George Ade's "Pink Marsh"	188
39	Poster by J. C. Lyendecker for The Chap-Book	189
40	"Irish-American Bar" by Toulouse-Lautrec: Poster for The Chap-Book	190

Introduction

THE PLAN OF THIS BOOK is simple. The Bibliography, although prepared first, is presented last, as documentation and reference material. It is preceded by a group of thirty-two plates illustrating bindings, decorations, title-pages, and types used in the books and magazines of Stone & Kimball and Herbert S. Stone & Company, and the posters designed to advertise the publications. The History, illustrated with portraits and reproductions of autographs, is largely a running account of the publishing adventures of Herbert Stuart Stone, Hannibal Ingalls Kimball and Melville E. Stone Jr., between 1893 and 1905. Chapter II contains some analysis of the most important creative literary venture of these men—*The Chap-Book*. Chapter V, "Notes for Students and Collectors," is addressed to those curious about the place of the firms in publishing history, and mentions the rarer Stone imprints. It contains also some details about the construction of the Bibliography, that may be useful to those who will use it. Cross-references to bibliographical entries have been avoided in the History and illustrations, but are plentiful within the Bibliography. The Index was done by Miriam Kramer, a steadfast friend of the manuscript during five years of its life.

It would be ungracious to publish a work of this sort without acknowledging that it is a composite of one's own endeavours and those of many others. This is not to avoid responsibility for error or mistaken judgment; the final draft of both History and Bibliography have been composed altogether privately. But in the beginning, six years ago in New York City, these studies owed much to the friendly interest of Mr. Frederic G. Melcher of R. R. Bowker Company, and Messrs. Hellmut Lehmann-Haupt and Roger Howson of Columbia University. In 1938, a draft of the History was accepted as a doctoral dissertation in the Graduate Library School of the University of Chicago, where my work was directed by Professor Pierce Butler, and advice was received from other members of that faculty. At all times I have been offered the fullest cooperation of the Kimball and the Stone families, and of their many friends. The generosity of Herbert Stuart Stone Jr. in turning over to me his bibliographical notes and of Elizabeth Stone Goodridge in making available her brothers' family correspondence is especially appreciated.

The many published researches used are cited in the footnotes and bibliographical entries: a general thanks is here made to the authors and publishers who permitted quotations to be made. The unpublished studies of Professor Virginia Robie, Mr. Ralph Fletcher Seymour, and Mr. Robert Moore Limpus; correspondence and interviews with Mrs. W. J. Calhoun, Mrs. Mary Kimball Hail, Mrs. Laura Kimball Covell, Mrs. Kathryn Kimball Cohû, Mr. W. J. F. Dailey, Mr. Clarence Holmes, Mr. Will Bradley, Mr. H. C. Chatfield-Taylor, Mr. Wallace Rice, Professor Robert Morss Lovett, Mr. Edward H. Dodd, Jr., Mr. Walter and Miss Mary Benjamin, Mrs. Gertrude Hills, Miss Margaret Rhodes, Mr. John Alden Carpenter, Miss Edith Franklin Wyatt, Miss Mary Prindiville, and Mrs. Cecil Clark Davis have been invaluable.

For counsel received I am grateful to Miss Carolyn Wells, Mr. Frederick Coykendall, Mr. H. M. Lydenberg, Mr. Mitchell Kennerley, and Professor Mary M. Shaver of New York; Mrs. Flora V. Livingston, Mr. Sidney A. Kimber, Mr. B. R. T. Collins, Mr. David T. Pottinger, and Mr. Pierre la Rose of Cambridge; Mr. Charles E. Lauriat and Mr. William Dana Orcutt of Boston; Dr. George Parker Winship of Charles River; Mr. Carl P. Rollins of New Haven; Drs. H. B. Van Hoesen and L. C. Wroth of Providence; Mr. Norman H. White of Central Village; Mr. Hartley I. Saunders and Mr. John A. Plugge of Washington; Miss Dorothy Colman, Mr. Walter Walden, Mr. H. E. Fleming, and Mr. Ben Abramson of Chicago. At the Lakeside Press so many have been helpful that I will thank them all in the person of Mr. T. E. Donnelley, its Chairman. In Evanston there is Mr. T. W. Koch; in Oak Park Mr. W. J. Kirk and Mr. Raleigh Morgan; in Hinsdale Mr. and Mrs. Robert Hamill and Mr. Frederick J. Schulte.

The staffs of the many libraries used have been uniformly helpful: thanks are due to Mr. Valta Parma, Mr. George A. Schwegmann, Mr. L. C. Smith, and Mr. Julian Leavitt of the Library of Congress; Miss Isadore Gilbert Mudge, Miss Bertha Frick, and Miss Janet Bogardus of the Columbia University Library; Miss Ruth Granniss and Mr. George L. McKay of the Grolier Club; Mr. R. W. G. Vail of the American Antiquarian Society; and the reference and curatorial departments of the New York Public Library, Harvard College Library, and the Newberry Library.

Finally, I believe the reader will be as grateful as the writer, to the publisher, Mr. Norman W. Forgue, and his editor, Miss Virginia Mills, for care taken in production; and to those four of my friends (each already mentioned) who have gone over the proofs.

SIDNEY KRAMER

Chicago, October 25, 1939

A History
of STONE & KIMBALL *and*
HERBERT S. STONE & COMPANY

CHRONOLOGY OF HERBERT S. STONE & COMPANY, 1896-1906

1896 Firm of Herbert S. Stone & Company formed to continue *The Chap-Book*. Stone's summer and fall booklists include works by Richard Le Gallienne, Arthur Morrison, Gabriele D'Annunzio, George Ade, and H. C. Chatfield-Taylor.

1897 Stone contracts to be authorized American publisher of plays, criticism, and novels of George Bernard Shaw. Sales office opened in New York, in charge of Melville Edwin Stone.

1898 Harrison Garfield Rhodes, editor, leaves to work in England. *The Chap-Book* dies during the Spanish-American War. *The House Beautiful*, published by Stone since 1897, now edited by Herbert S. Stone.

1899 The big year of Herbert S. Stone & Company; they are temporary successors to the publishing house of Way & Williams, founded in Chicago, 1895; issue fifty original publications.

1900 George Ade's *Fables in Slang* and other books successful. Melville Stone concentrates on sales, Herbert on business management. New York office closed.

1901 George Barr McCutcheon's *Graustark* a best seller; Stone experiments with cheap reprints of earlier publications.

1902 *The Story of Mary MacLane* a literary sensation; McCutcheon's romantic novels continue popular.

1903 The booklist weakens, but circulation of *The House Beautiful* grows; Virginia Robie now assistant editor.

1904 Only four new books published.

1905 Lucy Monroe, chief reader of manuscripts, leaves. Only one book issued, and this with imprint of *The House Beautiful*.

1906 Booklist of 200 titles sold to Fox, Duffield & Company of New York—later Duffield & Company, and as Duffield & Green purchased in 1934 by Dodd, Mead & Company.

CHRONOLOGY OF STONE & KIMBALL
1893-1897

1890 Herbert Stuart Stone, *aetat.* nineteen, and Hannibal Ingalls Kimball, sixteen, enter Harvard College. Both join the daily *Crimson*, Stone on the editorial side, Kimball on the business.

1891 Kimball acquires printing and advertising contract with the *Harvard Monthly*, and attempts to draw other undergraduate publications into similar arrangements.

1892 Stone writes, illustrates and publishes (with his younger brother Melville Edwin Stone), *Chicago and the World's Fair: A Popular Guide;* compiles bibliography of American first editions.

1893 Firm of Stone & Kimball formed; Fair Guide reprinted under advertising contract; *First Editions of American Authors,* with introduction by Eugene Field, published from Cambridge. Stone's Fair Guide, revised, published from Chicago. Imprint "Cambridge and Chicago" used December 1893, on first complete list, which included books of Eugene Field, Hamlin Garland, Joaquin Miller, and Kenneth Grahame.

1894 Herbert Stone and Ingalls Kimball, with Bliss Carman, begin *The Chap-Book* in May, from Brattle Square in Cambridge. In August, magazine and book business moved to Chicago.

1895 The big year of Stone & Kimball; publish many important American and foreign books, some of which sell well. Collected edition of Poe completed; books published in four different series; Kenneth Grahame's *Golden Age* appears. *The Chap-Book* sets off poster and pamphlet movements.

1896 Kimball purchases book business and moves to New York; magazine stays with Stone in Chicago. *The Daily Tatler* published November 7-21, edited by Kimball and Carolyn Wells.

1897 Stone & Kimball liquidated: 104 books had been published. Kimball enters printing business in New York, with The Cheltenham Press.

Chronologies

TABLES I AND II

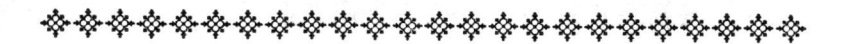

CHAPTER I

The First Year in Cambridge

HERBERT STUART STONE and Hannibal Ingalls Kimball Jr. were members of the class of 1894 in Harvard College, and began to publish books together in the course of their junior year. Stone was the older by three years; he was born in Chicago, May 29, 1871, the first child of Martha (McFarland) and Melville Elijah Stone. Early in 1888, M. E. Stone retired from the editorship of the *Chicago Daily News,* which he had founded, and took his wife and children to Europe. Herbert accompanied the family on their travels about the continent, and completed his secondary education at the Château de Lancy near Geneva and under tutors at Dresden. The family returned to the United States in the fall of 1890 in order that the oldest son might enter college. Of his years at Harvard, Herbert wrote in a class report fifteen years after: "I devoted myself, while in college, chiefly to languages and literature. I think I studied nine different languages without learning very much of any one. I took no part in athletics, debating, or religious work, but was an editor of the *Crimson* for three years."

Herbert Stone's memory was not inexact, even though he exaggerated for comic effect. By actual count, from the official transcript furnished by the Dean of Harvard College, Herbert Stone had eleven courses—in seven foreign languages —Greek, Latin, Semitics, German, Spanish, Italian and French. He was constant to at least one foreign tongue, taking advanced courses in French as well as English literature, and spending much time at the student club La Conférence Française. When the French novelist and journalist Paul Bourget visited the United States in 1893 and 1894, he reported with much delight that some students at Harvard College had an unusual knowledge of contemporary French literature.[1] Stone was one of those students, for he related in a letter to his family the capture of Paul Bourget for a luncheon in Memorial Hall.

The free elective system, then at its apogee under President Eliot, doubtless served to develop the catholicity of taste which Herbert Stone exhibited as a publisher. One clear influence from academic life must be mentioned—"Fine Arts 3 and 4." Like others of Charles Eliot Norton's students, Stone acknowledged the importance of these courses in the history of art, as an enlarging influence in all fields of spirit and taste. He wrote in *The Chap-Book* of June 15, 1898, on the occasion of Professor Norton's retirement:

> Professor Charles Eliot Norton is not a favorite, for the moment, or more would have been said of his retirement from the active position of lecturer on the Fine Arts at Harvard. Only those who know Harvard realize what this means to the University, and through its graduates to the outside world. It is perhaps too much to say that Professor Norton has been the dominant influence in Cambridge; the place is too big for that. But for many years he has come nearer than any other single personality to embodying the many curious qualities which we call vaguely the "Harvard Spirit." One never felt quite sure whether Professor Norton influenced the university or whether it was that by a wonderful sensitiveness he had come to be the spirit of the university made concrete.

[1] Paul Bourget, *Outre-Mer* (Paris: Alphonse Lemerre, 1895), Vol. II, pp. 107-8.

Objection to such broad generalizations as this will be made by every man who has lived in Cambridge. Part of Harvard's independence consists in each man having his idea of what Harvard really is; and rarely did any one agree thoroughly with Professor Norton. He has been called by every class un-American, reactionary, a kind of Ruskin manqué. Hundreds of men took his courses, in Fine Arts III and IV, which were ostensibly on the history of ancient and medieval art, without ever consciously listening to what was said. But the lectures would not keep inside the lecture room. They were in the whole atmosphere of the place; they formed a kind of background to which the new student learned to fit his life. A kind of mental aristocracy, a fastidiousness, an assumption that beauty and delicacy were things it was not effeminate to love, a vigorous and unyielding independence of judgment, a democracy of feeling which comes rather from a feeling that there are inequalities that can be bridged than from any conviction of equality, an emphasis constantly laid on manners, with the idea that in the end this meant morals as well—all these were various phases of thought which as found in the Harvard undergraduates were directly traceable to Professor Norton. They talk a great deal about the "atmosphere" of Harvard. It can never be quite the same without Fine Arts III and IV.[2]

Although Stone had none of the courses in the practice of art, he had been sketching since childhood. During a college vacation, he made better than acceptable drawings of the buildings set up for the first Chicago World's Fair, which were published in 1892 with his own descriptive text. During a busy life he continued to draw, even venturing, in his thirties, to oil painting. His book-plates are exceptionally good (see p. 149, Fig. A); and his sketch for the *Harvard Crimson* "shingle" is still in use.

Stone's best grades as an undergraduate were won in the English literature and creative writing courses. One example of his writings, as a junior, was mentioned in a letter to his family of January 29, 1893: "In one of our English courses,

---

[2]Compare these remarks with those of Daniel Gregory Mason, "At Harvard in the Nineties," *New England Quarterly*, March 1936, Vol. IX, pp. 63-65; and George H. Chase, "The Fine Arts," in *The Development of Harvard University Since the Inauguration of President Eliot* (Cambridge: Harvard University Press, 1930), p. 131; Charles Moore, in *Dictionary of American Biography*.

[Barrett Wendell's "English 11-12"] we are called upon to write eight connected themes during the second half-year. In the place of that Harrison Rhodes and I are going to write a play. We have drawn up our plot and submitted it to the English department for approval and we expect to begin on it soon in earnest. In style it comes near being like one of Ibsen's than like anything else. It is somewhat similar to 'Margaret Fleming,' that is, in kind, but they are not at all alike in plot. This is rather a stupendous undertaking but it will be excellent practise and will be an interesting experiment. The whole English department is in league with us and we expect to write a good play or know the reason why." "Old Wine: A Comedy in One Act" was completed in the spring of 1893, and soon submitted to commercial producers. Apparently the only production was one given in 1896 by the pupils of Anna Morgan at the Powers Theatre in Chicago. "The performance," Miss Morgan said in *My Chicago,* "was largely attended and much appreciated by their numerous friends." The typewritten copy, deposited for copyright at that time, is not now available at the Library of Congress.

Publishing became the business of Herbert Stone's life by intention, we infer from his early start in, and his constancy to, the production of books and magazines. The choice of profession came easily to the son of a newspaper editor who was also a book collector and a patron of authors. M. E. Stone furnished advice as well as material encouragement throughout the early years of his son's career. In addition to his work on the *Crimson* editorial staff, Herbert Stone acted as college correspondent for metropolitan newspapers, and held summer jobs on Chicago papers. His first venture in publishing was a species of journalism. Having spent most of the long vacation of 1892 in Jackson Park, Chicago, where the construction of the Columbian Exposition was under way, he collected his notes and sketches into a *Popular Guide to Chicago and the World's Fair*. This five-cent pamphlet bore neither author's nor publisher's name on its title-page, but was copyrighted in the name of H. S. Stone on September 26, 1892. It was printed by Donohue & Henneberry of Chicago for a "company" consisting of the author-illustrator and his younger brother Melville Edwin.

When Stone returned to Cambridge in the fall of 1892, he was already at work on another and more important compilation. It was probably in connection with the *First Editions of American Authors* that Herbert Stuart Stone came to be intimate with Hannibal Ingalls Kimball, although the two had been acquainted since freshman days and were both on the *Crimson*. The latter owned the typewriter used by Stone in the preparation of his lists of first editions (based largely on the collections of Harvard College Library). Kimball developed an interest in the work and after having assisted Stone for a few months, suggested the formation of a partnership to publish the book. The offer was accepted, Kimball soon also taking over M. E. Stone Jr.'s share in the *Popular Guide*. Stone wrote to his family late in January 1893, concerning his new partner: "He is an excellent business man and I am sure he will make money for himself and me—if he gets half a chance."

Kimball's business reputation rested on a coup made as a sophomore of seventeen. He approached the editors of the august *Harvard Monthly* with an offer to pay the printing bills during the year 1891-1892, if he were permitted to solicit and retain payment for advertisements. Robert Morss Lovett, then a senior and the editor-in-chief, remembers that year as a financial success both for the magazine and the entrepreneur. Kimball also tried to draw *Advocate* and *Lampoon* into the scheme. He was Business Manager of the daily *Crimson* in his own senior year, writing for his class report of 1909: "At Harvard, attained no distinctions of any kind, unless the establishment of *The Chap Book,* while still an undergraduate, may have been considered as a distinguished performance. Was business manager of *The Crimson,* and it was under my business management that the paper began being actually printed in Cambridge, instead of in Cambridgeport. The first extras were also issued under my administration, one having been made at Springfield at the time of the Yale game of 1893, and being for sale on the street before the crowd reached the station. More papers would have been sold had we won the game."

Kimball, when asked if he had tried any plans for making money during his college course, wrote to Professor E. K. Rand, permanent secretary of the Class of 1894, on a report blank for the twenty-fifth anniversary publication: "Yes. Slews of them." Other extra-curricular activities included membership in the Camera Club and Conférence Française. His work in course showed less eclecticism than Stone's. There were eight language courses—Latin, German, Spanish and French; seven in English, five in history, four each in mathematics and the physical sciences, two in political economy, "Philosophy 1" with Palmer, Royce and Santayana, and Norton's course in Fine Arts.

Hannibal Ingalls Kimball Jr., born April 2, 1874, in West Newton, Massachusetts, the youngest child and only son of Mary (Cook) and H. I. Kimball, came by a bent for business as naturally as Stone for editing. Kimball Senior was a man of many enterprises, who left New England and the family trade of carriage building to become southern manager of the Pullman Company, settling in Atlanta. "During the ensuing twenty years he was prominent in the business life of that city. When the Georgia legislature in 1867 voted to transfer the state capitol [sic.] from Milledgeville to Atlanta, Kimball purchased an abandoned opera house and converted it into a building suitable for temporary use as a state house and sold the structure to the legislature as the state capitol in 1868. Kimball also provided buildings and grounds for the Georgia agricultural fair in 1870 and in the same year erected the H. I. Kimball House, for a generation one of Atlanta's most noted hotels. During the same period he was actively engaged in promoting railway construction projects, being at one time president of nine different railroad companies and the builder of Atlanta's first union railway station. Later he established the Atlanta cotton factory, which did much to stimulate the development of cotton manufacture in the South, and as director general of the International Cotton Exposition held in Atlanta in 1881 he organized and carried that enterprise through to a successful conclusion. He also played an important part in arranging for the International Commercial convention in Atlanta in 1885 and was prominently identified with many other public enterprises in that city."[3] In 1893, while temporarily resident in Chicago, H. I. Kimball Sr. acted as Chairman of the Board of Judges of the Department of Manufactures and Liberal Arts of the World's Columbian Exposition. His son served as personal secretary, and when the board presented the father with a watch, it was requested that it should be left to the son.

Ingalls Kimball (as he preferred to be known in later years) began his education in the South, continuing at the New Church School in Waltham, Massachusetts. He also attended the Newton High School, but deciding to enter college early, left in 1889 to be privately tutored for a year. Most of his school and college vacations were spent in travel; the first of several trips abroad was made alone at the age of fourteen. His oldest sister, Laura Kimball Covell, informs us, in recent correspondence, that: "My brother was quite musical, playing a violin in a concert at the age of five. He soon got away from that, and took up gardening, selling

---

[3]Information received October 7, 1936, from James T. White & Company, publishers of *The National Cyclopedia of American Biography*.

the products. Later he took up photography, and at the age of twelve, photographed a graduating class of the Boston University. As a boy, Mr. Kimball was always more interested in work than play. He had no training for printing, and showed no special interest in it at that time. But was interested in merchandising and advertising. Succeeded in having the railroad put his ad as a photographer on their local timetable, also made posters himself and tacked them on the telegraph poles."

Professor Robert Morss Lovett, whose years in Cambridge overlapped Stone's and Kimball's by two, and who was settled at the University of Chicago when the publishing business arrived on Dearborn Street, recalls that both men early exhibited characteristics of their temperament. Stone was deliberate and thoughtful even as an undergraduate—Kimball impetuous and dynamic. Associates of Kimball in college and later refer to him as "a vibrant personality"; "possessed of great energy"; "a colorful, almost bizarre character; versatile, lovable, humorous, notably a salesman"; "Mr. Kimball's brain was at least three years beyond his physical growth."[4]

"Herbert Stone," writes a contemporary British publisher, "was a man whom to know was to like, a fellow of infinite charm. He loved books, he loved life." Other interesting glimpses of Stone's character and attitude towards his business are given by two artists who worked with Stone,[5] but as Lucy Monroe Calhoun, who was associated with him for seven years, wrote the author on October 21, 1937, from her present home in Peking: "It is a large order to describe a man like Herbert Stone. In many ways, in his publishing, in

[4] W. J. F. Dailey in a letter of October 8, 1937; Royal Cortissoz in an editorial tribute after Kimball's death, New York *Herald Tribune* for October 18, 1933; C. H. Holmes in *Fortieth Annual Report of the Secretary*, Class of 1894 Harvard College (Cambridge, 1934), p. 107; W. B. Covell in a letter of December 29, 1937.

[5] Grant Richards, *Author Hunting, by An Old Literary Sportsman* (New York: Coward-McCann, Inc., 1934), p. 127; Claude Bragdon, "The Purple Cow Period," *Bookman*, July 1929, Vol. LXIX, pp. 476-77; Ralph Fletcher Seymour, "This Far," unpublished autobiographical manuscript, 1936, pp. 26-28.

his dress, in his manner, and even in his outlook on life, he was a martinet. But intellectually he was much bigger than that. It cramped his style, though, and prevented him from making a fortune out of his work. He was an exquisite, and it was that side of the making of books that he most liked. He had great originality of taste, and he enjoyed bringing before the public unknown or neglected works of talent."

The respective activities of the partners seem to have been distinct, at least in the beginning, when Stone always referred to Kimball as the "business manager" and to himself as in charge of relations with printers and authors. The first problem of the firm was the guidebook to the World's Fair. Herbert Stone, at the end of the summer of 1892, had secured an understanding with the steamship line which ran between downtown Chicago and the exposition grounds to the south, that his alone, of the many official and unofficial handbooks, was to be sold on their docks and boats. Samuel T. Clover (then on the staff of the *Herald,* later editor of the *Chicago Evening Post* and publisher of newspapers on both coasts) was to have looked after the Chicago sales. The steamer concession met opposition from W. B. Conkey & Company, publishers of the official guidebook; Clover was much out of town; and in the end Stone Senior footed a bill of $250 for the printing of 10,000 copies before his sons had much return from sales. After Kimball took over the share of the younger Melville Stone and offered to finance a new edition, a Chicago agent was acquired. The first letter head of the firm read: "Stone & Kimball, Publishers, Cambridge; L. D. Atwater, Agent, 2526 Calumet Avenue, Chicago."[6] Letters of Herbert Stone soon complain of not hearing from Atwater, and also indicate that the concession was probably not retained.

[6]*The Lakeside Annual Directory of Chicago* for 1892 listed an "L. Duane Atwater, stenog. 425 Phenix bldg. H. Morgan Park." In 1893 "L. D. Atwater, agt. H. 2526 Calumet av." This Atwater does not appear in earlier or later directories. Calumet Avenue was then a fashionable address, but the residents of No. 2526 are not listed in the contemporary *Blue Books.* The site is now occupied by a clinic of Mercy Hospital.

9

One good stroke of business accomplished with the *Guide* was the sale of a hundred thousand copies to the Plymouth Rock Pants Company, who were among the largest and most sprightly advertisers of the day, as we have recently been reminded by F. P. A.[7] "The Plymouth Rock people" as they were delicately referred to in the correspondence of Stone & Kimball, placed their famous slogan "Do You Wear Pants?" on the back cover of a special printing of the guidebook, which had the title *Chicago and the World's Fair: A Popular Guide,* but allowed Stone & Kimball to sell space inside to other advertisers. A few thousand additional copies were printed for Stone & Kimball, without advertisements, except for one of their own on the back cover. On all of this Stone & Kimball made a profit of $600, which probably went into the printing of 10,000 copies of a revised edition, published with the imprint "Chicago: Stone & Kimball" and called *The Terra Cotta Guide: Chicago and the World's Fair.* This was to have been ready for the official opening of the Fair on May 1st, 1893, but as the partners were still busy with school and the preparation of *First Editions of American Authors,* publication was delayed until August 22, only six weeks before the exposition closed.

The Terra Cotta Guide included an amusing "Word in Advance" in which Herbert Stone stated his purpose to "Let others tell all the world and his wife what they ought to know. We shall rigidly confine ourselves to telling them what they want to know, and leaving everything else out." The text, high-lighting the Fair in a lively and readable manner, was amplified over the 1892 text, especially concerning "Art at the Fair." The illustrations were the pleasant line drawings which Stone had made in 1892, and a few sketches by John T. McCutcheon, reproduced from the Chicago *Daily News.* Others added were a dubious advantage, having been hastily selected from stock half-tones.

[7]Franklin P. Adams, "Advertising Poetry," *The New Yorker,* September 11, 1937, pp. 54 ff.

It is tempting to make a great deal out of Stone & Kimball's connection with the greatest of all American fairs. If one were to judge only from the official lists of books and pictures shown at the Fair, it can be said that there is little knowledge the partners could have added in those galleries to what they had seen at home, in Cambridge, or in Europe. The boys had had unusual opportunities to develop their literary and artistic tastes, through parentage, education, and travel. Yet there was something ineffable about *the* Fair, which can hardly have failed to charm Herbert Stone and Ingalls Kimball.

The World's Columbian Exposition of 1893 not only presented old-world civilization in a dramatic manner to millions of Americans, but was also the starting point for important native developments in such fields as architecture, city planning and lighting. The plan and execution of the World's Fair were symbols of Chicago's desire to be known as a city of quality as well as a town of size and wealth. It was made the scene, in the summer of 1893, of congresses of artists, authors, and scholars. Frederick Jackson Turner's startling paper on "The Significance of the Frontier in American History," was delivered at a Columbian exposition historical congress, it will be remembered. Less important, but amusing and interesting in its day (and even yet) was the semi-serious debate between realistic and romantic writers of American fiction, carried on in Chicago that summer. The affair began in a "Sharps and Flats" column, Eugene Field attacking his glum friend Garland, and through him Howells. Mary Hartwell Catherwood, Field's "Queen of Western Romanticism" had her say in the column, as did Garland; Field closed with an imaginary conversation in a Russian railway train between Garland and Tolstoi. Field's attack was really directed at W. D. Howells, as Garland's mentor.[8]

[8]Field's and the others' views expressed in "Sharps and Flats," are abstracted by Charles H. Dennis, "Girding at the Realists," in his *Eugene Field's Creative Years* (Garden City, New York: Doubleday, Page & Company, 1924), pp. 130-36.

The Columbian Exposition attracted people who wrote and made pictures for a living, for an official daily, a *World's Fair Puck,* dozens of illustrated periodicals and hundreds of brochures and books were produced; Stone's *Guide* was an immediate response to the publishing opportunities which it offered. In the end, we can say that Stone and Kimball doubtless chose Chicago as a permanent place of business because there was little competition in book publishing, and because their families lived there; but that the incidence of the Fair gave additional impetus to their career.

"The Saints and Sinners Corner" owed nothing to the World's Fair. The congregation of book collectors which met in George M. Millard's department of rare books at McClurg's Wabash Avenue bookshop, had been named and discussed by Eugene Field in his column since 1889. The librarian William Frederick Poole and the ministers Gunsaulus, Bristol and Stryker were the principal characters in Field's whimsical accounts of collecting exploits. Dennis calls the rest of the company "merely a sort of Greek chorus," yet there were regular and occasional attendants who have written of the importance in their lives as bookmen of the actual meetings and Field's fictionized versions. One may mention Francis Wilson, Harry B. Smith, Roswell Field, George Doran, Frederic Goudy, and include Melville E. Stone and his sons.

The Corner is not mentioned by name in extant letters of Herbert Stone, but the names of its actual and its spiritual leaders—George M. Millard and Eugene Field—do appear in connection with the conception, preparation and publication of the checklist of *First Editions of American Authors.* We find him writing from 23 Hastings Hall on February 9, 1893, to his father in Chicago: "On Monday the Prospectus for my book will be out and I shall send you some copies. Could you find time to have a little talk with Mr. Millard (or have Mr. Field do it) and see if they will not take a certain number of copies of the book. My prospectus will tell you all about it. I will give McClurg the usual 10 per cent jobbers commission besides 25 per cent regular commission on a $1.25 book—and should like to have them take charge of the Western sales. Will you see what arrangements of that sort can be made—and you will greatly oblige me. I am working hard on the thing and I should like to have it succeed." About the 25th of the same month, he wrote to his mother: "The book-sellers here tell me that Mr. Field's name will sell the whole edition. Has father the time to go to McClurg's and speak to Mr. Millard about taking 300 copies and charge of all the Western sales? I know he is very busy and think perhaps he will not feel like doing this. In that case, never mind. I have written to Mr. Millard myself, but I thought that father's interest would be so much more likely to interest Mr. Millard. But I do not want father to feel forced to do business for me as well as for himself. He has been very good already and I am truly grateful."

Eugene Field had remained on the friendliest terms with the man who brought him to Chicago, even after Melville E. Stone left his connection with the *News*. The *Second Book of Verse* first appeared in a limited edition, printed by Field's favorite printers, John Wilson and Son at The University Press in Cambridge, with the imprint: "Chicago: Published by Melville E. Stone, 1892." The friendship extended also to Stone's children; one of Field's loveliest lyrics, "The Sugar Plum Tree," was dedicated, when she was a child, to the present Mrs. Malcolm Goodridge. Herbert Stone's copy of William Blades' *Books in Chains* bore this autograph verse by Field:

> *What though they bound their books in chains—*
> *They'd have their trouble for their pains.*
> *We'd rend all chains those books to own,*
> *And draw a draft on Father Stone!*

Dec. 1892   E. F.

When this presentation was made, Herbert Stone was well along in his work of bibliography, for he had written to his family on October 4, 1892, from the *Crimson* office: "I am now engaged in cataloguing what books I have and in diving frantically into the glorious library we have here." Yet there is a legend already printed that the compilation of the list of first editions was Field's idea, suggested at this Christmas vacation of 1892. Gathering all available information, the connections seem to be as follows:

Herbert Stone had inherited the germ of bibliophily from his father and as a youth his tastes were fostered by Eugene Field through gifts and advice. When the family returned to the United States from Europe in 1890, Herbert began a Field collection and in its progress discovered that there were no lists useful to the collector of Field or indeed of any American author, and decided to supply the need. With Kimball's help, which began in the winter of 1892-1893, *First Editions of American Authors* was compiled. These are the facts as they were told by Herbert Stone to W. J. F. Dailey, onetime advertising manager of Stone & Kimball, and by Mr. Dailey to the present writer.

Field's interest in the work was natural and constant, but there is no hint in the preface which he was asked to write, that he was the prime mover in the project. Indeed, Field was not Herbert Stone's first choice, for it was mentioned in a letter from Cambridge in January 1893, that: "I telegraphed on Saturday to Mr. Field to see whether he would be willing to write a short introduction for my book on First Editions. I think his name would be useful and I should gladly send him a checque for his trouble. I have not yet heard from him but fear he will not find it agreeable. If I knew Col. Higginson a little better I should have asked him but as it is, I hardly like to."

With these reservations, we introduce Ingalls Kimball's comments on the history of the book, from his inscription made when Eugene Field's large paper copy of the book was presented by the late Leonard Mackall to the Grolier Club:

> This book was "written"—in so far as it may be said to have been written at all—mainly from the title pages of the first editions themselves, at the college library when Herbert Stone and I were at Harvard. The lists there prepared were typewritten in my bedroom and sent to the authors or their heirs for correction. The proofs, in galley, also were sent to these people. The book came out in the spring of our junior year, the suggestion for making it having come from Eugene Field at Christmas time when Herbert was in Chicago. There were three editorial copies of the large paper edition, one to Stone, one to Field, and to me. This one was signed by Stone.
>
> INGALLS KIMBALL,
Of Stone & Kimball,
>
> New York, March 6, 1927

Whether the original idea was Field's or Stone's, the creation of the *First Editions* was a landmark in the increasing attention of American collectors to American literature. The first bookseller's catalogue devoted solely to American authors had been issued less than ten years before, by Leon & Brother of New York, in 1885. Although Stone's list was neither as careful as P. K. Foley's *American Authors 1795-1895,* published four years later, nor as full as the more recent compilations on *American First Editions* begun by Merle Johnson, it has its value today. A number of early political and religious figures not found in later lists are included, and the nature of the choices in general is an interesting reflection of the collecting tastes of the nineties. Eugene Field's "Ad Lectorem," which describes his collecting friends and their special interests, and includes an amusing dialogue between Plato and Ximenes on the value of first editions, has been often reprinted. How well the publishers had gauged a need was shown by the quick sale, for the large paper edition of fifty copies, advertised by a prospectus mailed to collectors and dealers during February and March, was oversubscribed, and the small paper edition of five hundred went out of print soon after publication.

The ephemeral form and content and the manner of distribution of the *Guide* permitted Stone & Kimball to announce as their "first book," *First Editions of American Authors*. This is indeed the first bound volume published by Stone & Kimball, and by virtue of the delay in issue of the revised edition of the *Guide,* the first work to bear this name on a title page. Therefore, especially as the existence of Herbert Stone's *Guide* has not been known outside his family, the *First Editions* has been termed by bibliographers "Stone & Kimball's First Book."[9]

As possibilities—not all realized—appeared for the sale of the *Guide,* and as orders for the *First Editions* began to come in during the spring of 1893, a future career in publishing seemed alluring. At Kimball's suggestion, it was decided to plow back any profits into the production of other books. Possibly their resolve was strengthened when W. Irving Way, after he had received the prospectus for *First Editions,* suggested to Melville Stone that his son would be an agreeable partner for a publishing business in Chicago. Herbert was flattered by the older man's offer, but was satisfied to stay with his classmate. Way, incidentally, maintained a friendly interest in the young firm's productions, featuring their work in the articles on book design he wrote for *Inland Printer* and other magazines during the next few years. His own venture in book publishing, begun in 1895, with the financial assistance of Chauncey Williams, was absorbed, but only temporarily, by Herbert S. Stone & Company in 1899.

There were sources for interesting manuscripts close at hand in 1893, once the decision to build a publishing business was made. Stone, first through his father and later directly, approached Eugene Field and Hamlin Garland for manuscripts. He was especially anxious to have Eugene

[9] See the article of that title by Leonard L. Mackall, in New York Herald Tribune *Books,* November 12, 1933, p. 34.

Field's next book of poetry, writing: "I have some ideas for the prettiest book of poetry that America has seen for some time." Stone & Kimball were promised two prose works by Field. One of these, *The Holy Cross and Other Tales,* was actually published in December 1893. The edition of *A Sentimental Life of Horace,* however, mentioned as "In Preparation" by Stone & Kimball in the first notice of the firm in *Publishers' Weekly,* September 9, 1893, is a "Ghost." Field had planned a biography of Horace as preface to *Echoes from the Sabine Farm,* the Horatian translations by Roswell and Eugene Field first published in 1891 by Francis Wilson. The actor and bibliophile wrote of Field's intention in his introduction to the 1891 Scribner edition of *Echoes:* "It is my belief that as he thought upon the matter it grew too great for him to handle within the space he had at first determined, and that tucked away within the recesses of his literary intentions was the determination, nullified by his early death, to write, *con amore,* a life of Quintus Horatius Flaccus."

Hamlin Garland's books were the rock on which the firm was securely founded. In the spring of 1893, Mr. Garland, still working in Boston, mentioned in a letter to M. E. Stone his problems concerning publication. This was forwarded to Herbert, who replied to his family on March 9, 1893: "The thing about Mr. Garland's letter that attracted my attention first and preeminently was his remarks about his two books. I wish I had enough of a 'pull' to get a chance at publishing them myself. I would see that they were as prettily gotten out as any books in the country. But I suppose Mr. Garland would hardly wish to have a new firm take hold of the thing—much less a boy. But I believe I could make the thing succeed as well as any of his books and as for the illustrating—I could get the artists perhaps better than he. I wish I could do it—I should like nothing better." Although at first Garland wrote from Boston to Cambridge that he felt Stone

& Kimball's "facilities inadequate for doing the work of distributing the books," he became reconciled to the notion of having two boys publish for him. This decision is recorded in the second of his autobiographic chronicles: "Having cast in my lot with Chicago, it was inevitable that I should ally myself with its newest literary enterprise, a business which expressed something of my faith in the West. Not only did I turn over to Stone the rights to *Main Travelled Roads*, together with a volume of verse—I promised him a book of essays—and a novel."[10]

The verse was *Prairie Songs*, the essays *Crumbling Idols*, and the novel *Rose of Dutcher's Coolly*. Another volume of stories, *Prairie Folks*, was published by Stone & Kimball in 1895 from the types of an earlier edition. The author was extravagantly pleased with the appearance of these books; especially with the designs of H. T. Carpenter for *Main Travelled Roads* and *Prairie Songs*, and with the symbolic design of three cornstalks the publishers gave their bindings. Great pains were taken in the production of these books. *Main Travelled Roads* was reset for the Stone & Kimball edition not once but twice. The first printing, by the Craig Press of Chicago, was not satisfactory and it was redone by Wilson in Cambridge, according to unpublished Garland letters. Special circulars were made up and careful advertising begun. Although he did not relish their slow sales, Garland remained with the firm until Stone & Kimball was liquidated in 1897, and his books taken over by Macmillan. The author at this time called himself a "Jonah" to his publishers, who had included Arena in Boston, Appleton in New York, and Schulte in Chicago, as well as Stone & Kimball.[11] Garland also brought them from "The Hights" in Oakland, the manuscript of Joaquin Miller's utopian prose romance *The Build-*

---

[10] Hamlin Garland, *A Daughter of the Middle Border* (New York: The Macmillan Company, 1921), pp. 24-25.
[11] Hamlin Garland, *Roadside Meetings* (New York: The Macmillan Company, 1920), pp. 397-98.

ing of the City Beautiful. This was included with two Garland titles, in the Stone & Kimball fall list of 1893, which, incidentally, appeared too late in the season for the Christmas trade. The first account of their program which appeared in the trade press, includes, in addition to a list of titles, some interesting details.

In spite of the unsettled condition of finances and the apparently unpropitious time for starting new companies, a publishing firm has been founded this summer which promises much. Messrs. Stone & Kimball of Cambridge and Chicago, promise to do great things, especially in the West. Their first aim, after the worth and truth of a book is assured, is to give it a beautiful setting, and the new firm is preparing to bring out books which will astonish most American bookbuyers by the mere beauty of manufacture. They are using the best papers in the market—Dutch, English and American—are decorating their books with designs by the best artists in this country and England, and are printing and binding their books at the leading establishments in the country. Aims such as these are at least new to Chicago and the West. The ambition of this new firm is, in short, to attain to the ideal realized by Messrs. Elkin Mathews and John Lane, of London. What these are doing in the way of original book-making in England Messrs. Stone & Kimball intend doing in America.... They will make a specialty of large-paper editions, another new departure for a Western firm.

In Cambridge, where most of the books are made, are the headquarters and the main distributing point; in Chicago, the office in the Caxton Building is under the general management of Francis J. Schulte. In its very beginning the firm of Stone & Kimball aims to take a place, not among the largest, but among the best publishing houses in the country.[12]

The Chicago connection with Mr. Schulte was more a friendly gesture than a business arrangement, he revealed in an interview at his home in Hinsdale in the winter of 1937. Mr. Schulte had been publishing for several years, specializing in Western authors, when in the spring of 1893, his firm was embarrassed by the suicide of Horace O'Donoghue, a

[12]*Publishers' Weekly*, September 9, 1893, Vol. XLIV, p. 311.

well known Chicago printer, and a friend whose notes Mr. Schulte had endorsed. Frederick J. Schulte & Company had to be abandoned, and while it was being re-established (to endure only a short while) as the Schulte Publishing Company, Mr. Schulte at the request of Stone's father, looked after the Chicago end of the young firm.

An early notice by a Chicago critic, herself later associated with Stone, made much of a connection with the English firm of Elkin Mathews and John Lane, and reviewed in advance *Pagan Papers* by Kenneth Grahame, as the first example of collaboration with the Bodley Head.[13] The spring and summer of 1894 brought more importations, the most interesting being a collected edition of John Davidson's poetic dramas, and a play in verse by W. B. Yeats, both volumes decorated with Beardsley designs. It was one of John Lane's pleasant boasts that he had placed an American edition of every book he had published.[14] Since 1889 American houses the country over had imported the editions of Elkin Mathews & John Lane, but from 1893 to 1896 (when The John Lane Company was established in New York), the house which got first choice was Copeland & Day, whose imprint appears on the title of *The Yellow Book*. These Boston contemporaries had been strengthening their English lines while Stone & Kimball were making the best of their family and school connections, and their publication program, first announced in *Publishers' Weekly* of December 2, 1893, consisted solely of editions of English authors. (Their first publication had been a privately issued and anonymous edition of *The Decadent*, by Ralph Adams Cram, with decorations by his architect partner Bertram Grosvenor Goodhue). Stone & Kimball observed in *The Chap-Book* of October 1, 1894, that *Songs from Vagabondia* by Carman and Hovey,

---

[13]Lucy Monroe, "Chicago Letter," *The Critic*, November 11, 1895, Vol. xx (New Series), p. 310.

[14]J. Lewis May, *John Lane and the Nineties* (London: John Lane, The Bodley Head [1936]), p. 158.

was "the first original publication of Messrs. Copeland & Day of Boston." Later they were competitors for the same manuscripts: for instance, Stephen Crane's *Black Riders* (Copeland & Day, 1895), and Gabriele D'Annunzio's *Episcopo & Company* (H. S. Stone & Co., 1896).

This company's rivalry with Stone & Kimball, however, was of the friendliest kind. Herbert Copeland made a business trip to New York during the summer of 1894 in company with Herbert Stone and Bliss Carman. The latter's poetry appeared on both their booklists, and Carman was also for its first two months an editor of *The Chap-Book*. Copeland & Day supported Stone & Kimball's magazine with advertising from the first number almost to the last.

Stone & Kimball, in hunting books for their spring list of 1894, flushed Cambridge for an American "nest of singing birds," comparable to The Bodley Head's. There were the poets of *The Harvard Monthly,* which, wrote Robert Morss Lovett "represented a high ambition in those days. The brilliancy of the first board of editors, Alanson Bigelow Houghton, George Santayana, George Rice Carpenter, and others, and of their immediate successors, George Pierce Baker and Bernard Berenson, was a recent memory. It was the only undergraduate publication admitted to Poole's Index."[15] Stone & Kimball published books by Santayana and Hugh McCulloch and single poems by these and others, including William Vaughn Moody. It has been suggested that a collection of poems by Moody, which was submitted for consideration by Stone & Kimball in 1894, may have been issued by them or another publisher before 1900.[16] It would be well to consider the complete text of the letter which gives rise to this hypothesis. This document is now in the collection of Mr. John T. Winterich.

[15] Robert Morss Lovett, Introduction to *Selected Poems of William Vaughn Moody* (Boston: Houghton, Mifflin Company [1931]), p. xvi.
[16] David A. Randall, "American First Editions," in *New Paths in Book Collecting* (New York: Charles Scribner's Sons, 1934), pp. 206-8.

My Dear Mr. Stone:

It seems to me, in view of what you say in your note of the 18th and of what Mr. Kimball has told me, that it would be wise to postpone the publication of the verses indefinitely. Business considerations aside, I think the book will gain by waiting, and I should be glad of the extra time to mature some things which I have long had in mind—Perhaps then no present agreement had best be made—I will ask you to return the mss. and in the fall—if it still seems to our advantage—we can look it over together in the form it may then have assumed. Thanking you for your trouble in the matter, I remain

Very truly yours
23 Hilton Block   William Vaughn Moody
January 21/1894.

From a letter written to Robert Morss Lovett on February 5, 1894:

Stone and Kimball... are getting out volumes of verse for Mac and Santy [Hugh McCulloch and George Santayana] and have even approached *me* with harp and psaltery, though so far I have had grace from God to resist their blandishments...[17]

Neither Professor Lovett nor any other of Moody's friends and colleagues has ever referred to a miscellany published before the *Poems* of 1901. One might add also that there is no record of entry in the Copyright Office of such a collection under Stone & Kimball's or William Vaughn Moody's names, between 1894, when publication was first discussed, and 1901, when publication was made by the Houghton Mifflin Company.[18] No Stone & Kimball edition of Moody's poems exists, and it is not likely that the *Poems* were issued by another publisher, even privately or anonymously, before 1901.

[17] As edited by Daniel Gregory Mason, in *Some Letters of William Vaughn Moody* (Boston and New York: Houghton Mifflin Company, 1913), p. 15. The complete text is not now available.

[18] Moody's first book was *The Masque of Judgment: A Masque Drama*, published by Small, Maynard & Company of Boston in 1901; his "Ode in Time of Hesitation," included in the *Poems* of 1901, had been previously printed in *The Atlantic Monthly* for May 1900, and in the small volume *Liberty: Poems Inspired by the Crisis of 1898-1900* (Boston: The James West Company, 1900).

Literary gossip and the pleasant critical reception their first books had received, now brought Stone & Kimball to the attention of the mandarins of literature. In December of 1893, Louise Chandler Moulton summoned them to see if they were really only "a couple of undergraduates at Harvard" as she had heard from her Boston publishers, Roberts Brothers. "We had a delightful evening," Herbert wrote home, "talked of all the literary people from the author of the Pentateuch down. She is going to edit a book of poems for us—which I think will be very good. We are having lots of fun these days over our ages. Mrs. Moulton had thought from my letters that I was about 35 or 40... If we haven't money, we have friends and are constantly get[ting] new ones. Why—only a few days ago—a very clever young novelist Gilbert Parker—came to us—*on the recommendation of Edmund Clarence Stedman*. It was in itself the greatest compliment we have had... So you see we are steeped in literature... But it is hard work to attend to college and the work too and I am continually getting warnings from the office that I must stop cutting...."

Making books is a full-time activity, and the academic work of the student-publishers naturally suffered. Stone would have dropped out of school in favor of the business even in his junior year had it not been his family's desire that he take his degree. At the end of January 1894, Herbert Stone and Ingalls Kimball seem to have been threatened with suspension. But a letter of January 28 from Stone to his family reported that some professors were sympathetic: "They have... agreed to treat both Kimmie and myself as foot-ball men and let us off as easily as they can. They are in perfect sympathy with our work and one of them was good enough to say... that this was the first piece of real enterprise connected with Harvard College. You know the faculty is trying to do away with the prevalent idea that Harvard is not practical and so they are mighty glad to have us here. We are doing some little campaigning and to say the least, the whole faculty is very much interested to see what we are going to do."

This crisis passed and the boys were properly registered for spring courses in 1894. Another one came with *The Chap-Book;* Herbert Stone later said that *The Chap-Book* was continued "despite a threat from the Harvard faculty that if it was not discontinued they could not be graduated."[19] The "threat" must have been only a warning that class work was suffering, for there is no record of disciplinary action on the part of the college. However, Herbert Stone resigned from college on April 16, 1894, returning in 1896 to complete his course work and receive the A.B. Ingalls Kimball remained in college through June 1894, but had not at that time sufficient credits for the degree. He hoped for some years later to be able to return, but his father's sudden death and his own early marriage made it impossible.

[19]In conversation about 1905, with Herbert E. Fleming, reported in his *The Magazines of a Market Metropolis,* p. 798.

Herbert Stuart Stone, *1894*    Hannibal Ingalls Kimball, *1894*

Melville E. Stone Jr., *1897*    Harrison Garfield Rhodes, *1893*

FIG. 1. *From the Harvard College Class Albums*

FIG. 2. *Bliss Carman*
Drawing by Dawson Watson From The Chap-Book,
September 1, 1896

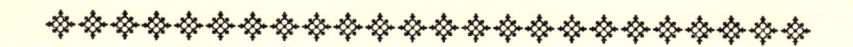

CHAPTER II

The Chap-Book and Its Contemporaries

When on May 15, 1894, the first number of *The Chap-Book* was issued from Cambridge, Stone & Kimball had the means to move from the limited, however interesting, circle of family and friends into the mainstream of American life. As one looks back, the four years' life of the magazine is seen as part of an historical movement in arts and letters, with antecedents and parallels in this country and others, and an influence of its own, manifested by swarms of imitators. It is worth observing, therefore, that at the time of its founding there was only an immediate and practical objective seen by the editor, Herbert Stuart Stone writing to his family in May 1894: "To speak plainly the *Chap-Book* is no more nor less than a semi-monthly advertisement and regular prospectus for Stone & Kimball." And in bidding farewell to its readers on July 15, 1898, *The Chap-Book* stated: "It was at first intended as scarcely more than an attractive kind of circular for advertising the books published by the house. But the instant attention which it attracted induced its publishers to continue."

Both the price (five cents) and the size (7-1/2 x 4-1/2 inches), were small. This evidence of light-heartedness in a magazine of serious intentions, the reminiscent flavor of the title and simple typography, perhaps contributed as much to the success of the magazine as anything it had to say.[1] For printing history, *The Chap-Book* has also the adventitious interest of presenting the early advertisements of such men as D. B. Updike, who took a full page in the first number to announce that he was preparing an edition of the *Altar Book;* of Bruce Rogers, featured as a designer for Stone & Kimball, Way & Williams and J. M. Bowles, whose *Modern Art* was a consistent advertiser; of Thomas B. Mosher with his reprint series; and the gay announcements of Frederic W. Goudy who, when he was setting *The Chap-Book* in type at The Camelot Press, Caxton Building, Chicago, proclaimed "Private printing in limited editions especially solicited. Prices Reasonably High"; and in a later number encouraged readers to "Send for The Black Art: A Homily, By D. B. Updike, sent free to any address. Daintily printed on English hand-made paper. We make a specialty of work requiring more care than most printers will give."

The twelve numbers of the first volume (ended November 1, 1894, all printed by Graves & Henry, Cambridge; publishers' imprint changed from "Cambridge & Chicago" to "Chicago" alone, with Number Eight, August 15, 1894) had very much the character of a house organ. Delicate hints of the interest of the firm's productions were inserted, and many of the authors whom they had, or were intending to publish, were represented. Bliss Carman, who had had experience on *The Independent* and *The Literary World,* came to assist in editing during the first two months, and later contributed critical essays on Gertrude Hall, William Sharp and Gilbert Parker; Carman's poetry is discussed by his friend and countryman, Charles G. D. Roberts. Percival Pollard, then doing newspaper work in Chicago, published five lyrical "Dreams of Today." The environment of Boston and Harvard is re-

[1] Earnest Elmo Calkins, "The Chap-Book," *The Colophon,* April 1932, Part x.

flected by poetry from Ralph Adams Cram, Richard Hovey, William Vaughn Moody and Louise Chandler Moulton; and prose from Charles T. Copeland, Louise Imogen Guiney, T. W. Higginson, Pierre la Rose and Herbert Small. Ingalls Kimball, in writing of his friend Bertram Goodhue, left a few interesting words on the surroundings in which *The Chap-Book* was born: "Goodhue, if my memory serves, was one of the little group which included C. G. D. Roberts, Bliss Carman, Harrison Rhodes, Herbert Stone and myself, who sat around an old oil cloth covered table at the Holly Tree Coffee rooms in Cambridge one evening in May '94 waiting for the first sheets of the *Chap Book* to come from the printer."[2]

The office of the firm in the old Brewer's Block on Brattle Square, was another congenial meeting place. Clarence H. Holmes, a classmate who joined Stone and Kimball in the spring of 1894, as, he says, "a sort of a handy man around the office," wrote: "There was a mélange of business and amusing goings on. Any afternoon there were likely to drop in artists and authors from Boston, contributors to the 'Chap-Book,' or merely admirers of that new and surprising publication. They added an 'air' but did not help solve business problems. In those days there was a self-styled group of 'Visionists,' who took themselves not too seriously. The name was about as far as they progressed, I think. Bliss Carman, Charles G. D. Roberts, Harrison Rhodes, Bertram Goodhue (whose widow 'Kimmie' was to marry many years later), and others were members. Some one or two of them were likely to be found of an afternoon in the 'Chap-Book' office."[3] Eight years after Herbert Stone and Ingalls Kimball had formed their partnership, and five since it was broken, Kimball sent to Stone a Christmas poem by Bliss Carman,

[2]Ingalls Kimball, *Book Decorations by Bertram Grosvenor Goodhue* (New York: The Grolier Club, 1937), p. [4].

[3]Harvard College, Class of 1894, *Fortieth Annual Report of the Secretary* (Cambridge, 1934), pp. 107-8.

which had been produced at the Cheltenham Press, with this delightful inscription:

    H. S. S.
    Once we were Visionists!
                     I. K.

The "Visionists" were but one of the informal groups of young Boston bookmen of the nineties. Others were "The Pewter Mug Associates," whose meetings at the Bell-in-Hand and other taverns, Mr. Melcher tells us, "drew Bruce Rogers, Bertram Goodhue, Jim Bowles, Willard Small, Wolfe, and Lamson."[4] The "Procrastinatorium" is also mentioned by Ralph Adams Cram in his comprehensive account of those years and of "that original and vivacious group of individuals that, for the ten years between 1890-1900, made life for me so notably worth living. Most of us were assiduously engaged in literary composition, both prose and verse, some of which—notably of course that of Carman, Hovey and Lou Guiney—was achieving publication, my own early indiscretions 'The Decadent' and 'Black Spirits and White' having been perpetrated at that time, the one published by Copeland and Day, the other by Stone and Kimball. This crusade for the improvement of the craft of bookmaking was a very significant showing of the buoyant temper of the time. Three firms, made up of members of our crowd,—Copeland and Day, Small, Maynard and Co., and Stone and Kimball,—were the leaders in this..."[5]

Of all of this, Stone & Kimball were a part only in their beginning. We cannot know, except by comparison of dates and contents, how much the founders of *The Chap-Book* were influenced by the periodicals in which the hopes of these active young men had previously found expression—*The Knight Errant* and *The Mahogany Tree*. The earlier of these,

[4][Frederic G. Melcher], "Four Brilliant Years," *Publishers' Weekly*, January 13, 1934, Vol. cxxv, p. 132.
[5]Ralph Adams Cram, *My Life in Architecture* (Boston: Little, Brown and Company, 1936), pp. 84-85.

The Mahogany Tree of 1892, was, Mr. Cram says, "fathered by a cluster of Harvard undergraduates... It was a purely literary affair without any particular claims to typographical distinction, but its content was very sympathetic to our Boston faction and naturally, therefore, the two groups promptly coalesced..." *The Knight Errant*[6] was a quarto, handsomely printed on handmade paper, and intended to be a quarterly, although the first of its four numbers was issued in April 1892, and the last not until October 1894. Edited by Cram and Goodhue, with the cooperation of F. H. Day, Herbert Copeland and F. W. Lee, it was somewhat ponderous in its concern with abstract esthetics and impossible politics, and made much of a point that "the present separation of pictorial and literary art is unwarrantable and unwise." Perhaps the nearest approach in America to Herbert Horne's *Hobby Horse*, it is valuable for its wealth of decoration by Goodhue, in which the young architect first exhibited his talent for typographic design. But its manner was not that of *The Chap-Book,* which in regretting its demise, classed *The Knight Errant* among the "humorous papers."[7] If we must have local antecedents for *The Chap-Book,* one may call attention to the similarities in typographical style between *The Chap-Book* of 1894 and *The Harvard Advocate* (both were printed by Graves & Henry in Cambridge); as well as to a like editorial arrangement.

The tone of *The Chap-Book* as well as of the ephemeral intellectual products which stemmed from it, was primarily personal. While they, like the established critical journals, discussed general tendencies, it was always by way of individuals and actualities. This approach was pervasive in all periodicals of the American nineties, and was indeed the manner in which the new cheap periodicals of S. S. McClure

---

[6]The full title was *A Quarter-Yearly Review of the Liberal Arts called the Knight Errant; Being a Magazine of Appreciation.*... Printed for the Proprietors at the Elzivir Press, Boston, A.D. MDCCCXCII.
[7]Editorial note, August 15, 1894, with reproduction of the masthead designed by Bertram Goodhue for *The Knight Errant.*

and Frank Munsey, by substituting intimacy for the impersonality of the standard monthlies, were reaching new highs in mass distribution. The one history of American magazines which has covered the period of the nineties, in discussing this very point, remarks: "In the history of American thought they [the dinkey magazines] are ... of considerable importance, but to the history of the American magazine they contributed chiefly one more factor in the growth of the personal note at the end of the century."[8]

The manner of speech of *The Chap-Book*, as well as the essential psychological difference between optimism and the "subtilizing refinement"[9] of the leading English writers of the first years of the decade, differentiated it from *The Yellow Book*, with which it was popularly associated then and later. Percival Pollard once stated that the parents of *The Chap-Book* were *The Yellow Book* and *The Butterfly*, a pocket periodical of London. As a matter of exact record, the first series of the latter magazine, ten numbers from May 1893 to February 1894, passed unnoticed by the editors of *The Chap-Book*. No work of the men who made *The Butterfly*—L. Raven Hill, Manuel Sime and Edgar Wilson—ever appeared in the American magazine. Herbert Stone wrote to his Chicago office from London, May 17, 1898, when he first met this group of artists: "I think some of their stuff would do the *Chap-Book* a world of good and I hope to get it cheap." Probably the exciting advent of the Bodley Head's quarterly, which listed Copeland & Day as co-publishers, had something to do with Stone & Kimball's desire to have a

---

[8] Algernon Tassin, *The Magazine in America* (New York: Dodd, Mead and Company, 1916), pp. 357-58.

[9] The phrase is Arthur Symons', in his essay, "The Decadent Movement in Literature," *Harper's New Monthly Magazine,* November 1893, Vol. LXXXVII, p. 858; quoted from Robert Moore Limpus, "American Criticism of British Decadence," unpublished Ph.D. dissertation, Department of English Language and Literature, University of Chicago, 1937, p. 12. This work examines in valuable detail the prevailing moralistic tone of American literary criticism, and the mild reaction of the *Chap-Book* brood. See also Holbrook Jackson, *The Eighteen-Nineties* (London: Grant Richards, 1913), pp. 29-36 and *passim.*, for analysis of the characteristics of the English literary decadents.

magazine of their own, but the correspondence in time of issue is too close,[10] and the difference in content too great, to permit *The Chap-Book* to be called a mere reflection of *The Yellow Book*.

It is noteworthy that in the first volumes of *The Chap-Book* the English contributions are less important than the French material. True, Oscar Wilde and Aubrey Beardsley are favorite subjects of comment, and some Beardsley drawings intended for Stone & Kimball's edition of Poe are printed. There was direct representation, however, of Verlaine's verse in French, and in translation by Gertrude Hall. An article on his "Mes Hôpitaux," by Anatole France, is translated from *La Plume;* Stéphane Mallarmé appears both in the original and Englished by Richard Hovey. The French influences flowed most directly into *The Chap-Book* through Harrison Garfield Rhodes, its assistant editor from September 1894 to July 1898. Rhodes was also chief reader for Stone & Kimball until April 1896 and for Herbert S. Stone & Company until July 1898, when he went abroad as business representative for various American magazines and correspondent for New York and Chicago newspapers. In London he also acted as agent for Herbert S. Stone & Company. After his return to the United States he became a successful playwright, remembered for his dramatization of *Ruggles of Red Gap*. Rhodes was also the author of numerous magazine articles, of which the best, reminiscences of American cities and his own childhood and education, appeared in *Harper's Magazine* during the twenties. The most popular of his books was a guide to Florida, where he had a home in Daytona Beach. Harrison Rhodes was especially respected by his contemporaries as a critic. Finley Peter Dunne, for instance, rejected Eugene Field's help but sought out Rhodes in Chicago when he was selecting the newspaper articles which

---

[10]The first number of *The Yellow Book* is dated April 1894, and, according to a note in *The Bookman* of September 1896, reached America on April 12th, 1894. *The Chap-Book's* issue of May 15, 1894 was made up during April and was available in May.

went into his first book, *Mr. Dooley in Peace and in War*.[11] Anthony Hope Hawkins, after meeting Rhodes for the first time, described him in a diary as "Decidedly notable, less grim than represented, strong, a dreamer, a touch of the Gascon, engrossed in his work, impatient with the views imposed on others by their work, an attractive as well as an interesting person..." Their friendship formed at Tring in 1899 was longlasting. One of the last vacations Sir Anthony enjoyed was spent motoring through Italy "with Hal Rhodes."[12] Rhodes himself died in England in 1929 after years of ill health.

To return to his years as assistant editor of *The Chap-Book* and his knowledge of French literature, it should be noted that Rhodes had spent the year after his graduation from Harvard in 1893, studying and travelling in France. In Paris he met the Symbolist editors and authors, including Verlaine and Mallarmé, who later addressed to M. Harrison Rhodes a long letter concerning Arthur Rimbaud (printed May 15, 1896 in *The Chap-Book*). These people Rhodes (and later Stone) met through the mediation of Stuart Merrill. Merrill, an American educated in France, achieved distinction both as a French poet and as an interpreter of French literature to readers of English. He was to translate and furnish an introduction for *Poems of the Symbolists* as the first volume in the "Green Tree Library" of Stone & Kimball, and the volume was announced in the 1894 *Publishers' Trade List Annual*. This work was not completed

[11]Personal advice from Mr. and Mrs. Robert Hamill of Hinsdale, where Dunne and Rhodes read the manuscript in 1898. Anna Farwell De Koven's reminiscent *A Musician and His Wife* of 1926, refers to Herbert Stone as the publisher of the first Dooley book. He and Rhodes had planned the publication, which was actually issued in 1898 by Small, Maynard & Company of Boston. Dunne wrote in his Introduction to the posthumously published *Mr. Dooley at His Best:* "I recall that Eugene Field, who was 'reading' for a Chicago publisher, was one of the first to suggest making a book of Dooley's sayings. I wouldn't let him do it. My ambition lay in another direction. I wanted to be a great publisher. In time I became a publisher. But I never heard the word great applied in my case."

[12]Quotations and references in Sir Charles Mallet, *Anthony Hope and His Books* (London: Hutchinson & Co. Ltd. [1935]), pp. 111, 213.

and was never published, according to M. L. Henry's biography and bibliography of Merrill.

After Stone in the summer of 1895 visited Paris and wrote home that he had "nothing to do beyond reading a few manuscripts," the French material begins to drop off. But before that time there had been so much representation of French poetry in *The Chap-Book* that M. René Taupin, the authority on Franco-American poetic connections, discusses it at length, early in his discussion of how French symbolism penetrated into America:

L'année 1895 est celle où l'Amérique s'est le plus intéressée aux écrivains français. Il faut attendre jusqu'à 1914 pour voir un tel intérêt s'élever au sujet d'une littérature étrangère. C'est l'année où l'on discute si violemment les idées de Nordau, c'est l'année où paraît le *Bookman* de Peck, et c'est à partir de cette année-là qu'on va voir paraître une foule de petites revues révolutionnaires imitées des revues symbolistes françaises et consacrées pour la plupart à la propagande française.

La première et la plus importante de ces revues fut le *Chap Book*. ... Parmi les collaborateurs se trouva représenté presque tout le groupe des «symbolistes» américains: Richard Hovey, Bliss Carman, C. G. D. Roberts, Archibald Lampman, Duncan Campbell Scott et Gilbert Parker. Il y avait encore, avec George Santayana et Eugene Field, des poétesses connues: Louise Moulton, Louise Imogen Guiney et Gertrude Hall qui venait de traduire Verlaine. Les tendances communes de ces écrivains assuraient au *Chap Book* un caractère personnel qui manquait aux grands périodiques.

Pour bien marquer l'originalité de la revue, Bliss Carman donna aux premiers numéros l'apparence de ces almanachs ou «chapbooks» que les colporteurs vendaient autrefois aux gens des campagnes. Les premiers numéros manifestaient les tendances révolutionnaires des collaborateurs et leur enthousiasme pour la littérature française...

La revue se tenait au courant de la peinture et elle faisait la critique des expositions aussi bien que des livres français; elle reproduisait des croquis d'artistes français; des portraits de Rimbaud et de Mallarmé par Valloton (qu'on retrouve dans *Le Livre des Masques*) et des dessins déja parus dans des revues françaises, surtout dans *La Plume*...

Car le *Chap Book* était en rapport avec les revues symbolistes dont il s'est sûrement inspiré. Les éditeurs envoyaient leur revue à la *Plume,* au *Magazine International,* à *l'Ermitage,* qui n'aimaient pas leurs poèmes; «des vers, beaucoup de vers, c'est la partie faible, il faut l'avouer».[13]

The Chap-Book, as we shall see, later pursued an equivocal attitude towards the literary products of the end of the century in France, as in England, but its appreciation of the prints of French artists was constant. Among the decorators of the first two volumes were F. A. Cazals, Eugène Grasset, J. F. Raffaelli, Alexandre Seon, and F. Valloton; later volumes also included work by Andhré des Gâchons and Georges Pissaro. Henri de Toulouse-Lautrec was not represented by any prints in the volumes themselves, but he was the only foreign artist selected to do poster work for *The Chap-Book.* Oddly, although the editors thus exhibited their admiration for Lautrec, they never mentioned the appearance of the poster in their columns, as they did the American posters made for them. Possibly Lautrec's colored lithograph—one of the best examples of this period in his work—was intended to attract readers for the American review only in France and England, where Lautrec's posters were much admired and imitated. There are two states, one of a hundred proofs before lettering, and the second (Fig. 40), with lettering indicating the scene as "Irish and American Bar, Rue Royale," and its purpose of advertising "The Chap-Book." The poster was printed at the "Imprimerie Chaix" and also bears the legend of the "Affiches Artistique de LA PLUME, 31 Rue Bonaparte, Paris." According to contemporary authority *The Chap-Book,* "voulant varier sa manière, s'est adressé à la revue *la Plume,* à Paris, qui lui a fourni, en juillet 1896, une affiche de la main de M. Lautrec; c'est une scène de moeurs dans un bar."[14] According to Gerstle Mack, the "Irish and

---

[13]René Taupin, *L'Influence du Symbolisme Français sur la Poésie Américaine* (Paris: Honoré Champion, 1929), pp. 32-34.
[14]M. La Fargue, "Etats-Unis (Amérique)," *Les Affiches Etrangères Illustrées* (Paris: G. Boudet, Editeur; C. Tallandier, Libraire, 1897), p. 180.

American Bar" was Lautrec's favorite. Ralph, the bartender, is shown with two coachmen; the fat one, who appears in other Lautrec pictures, drove for Monsieur de Rothschild. The costumes of the men suggest John Bull and Uncle Sam.

THE POSTER PERIOD

The cult of the artistic poster at the end of the last century originated in France, where Jules Cheret first demonstrated the possibilities of the color lithograph applied to the ancient art of outdoor advertising.[15] Because of the standing of the artists who took up this work—Forain, Grasset, Mucha, Steinlen, Toulouse-Lautrec—the product had a natural interest for collectors as well as advertisers. The making and collecting of the picture-size poster became a cult which spread from France to England, Germany, and the United States.[16] There was a collectors' interest in this country as early as 1889, signified by an *Exposition d'Affiches* at the Grolier Club.[17] In that and succeeding years several popular magazines issued occasional designs by Eugène Grasset of Paris and Louis Rhead of London and New York. The movement, however, did not become naturalized until Edward

---

[15]The hoarding has a history of its own; what is meant here are small designs in which illustration, decoration, lettering and color as well as the "message" are conceived as a unity. The best historical treatment of the general subject is in Ernest Maindron, *Les Affiches Illustrées* (Paris: H. Launette & Cie., 1896). E. McKnight Kauffer, *The Art of the Poster* (London: Cecil Palmer, 1924) and Charles Matlock Price, *Posters* (New York: George W. Bricka, 1913), are retrospective international surveys of the small artistic poster. Better representation of the work for Stone & Kimball and other American firms during the nineties will be found in contemporary works such as Charles Hiatt, *Picture Posters* (London: George Bell and Sons, 1895); *The Modern Poster* (New York: Charles Scribner's Sons, 1895); Edward Penfield and Percival Pollard, *Posters in Miniature* (New York: R. H. Russell and Son, 1896); *Les Maîtres de l'Affiche* (5 vols.; Paris: Imprimerie Chaix, 1896-1900). *Les Affichés Etrangères Illustrées* (Paris: G. Boudet, Editeur; C. Tallandier, Libraire, 1897) is especially valuable for details of the development in America, in an article by M. La Fargue. A brief survey of the same events is given by Henry Collins Brown, *In the Golden Nineties* (Hastings-on-Hudson: Valentine's Manual, Inc., 1928), pp. 201-4, from information contributed by H. L. Sparks, the greatest American collector of posters.

[16]See Brander Matthews, "The Pictorial Poster," *Century*, September 1892, Vol. XXII, pp. 755-56, for details of the introduction into America of the new technique in poster-making.

[17]After 1895, when a great international show was held in Boston, most American cities held poster exhibitions, often at the public library. In Chicago, posters were shown at the University's Quadrangle Club; see the *Catalogue of an Exhibition of American, French, English, Dutch and Japanese Posters,* from the collection of Mr. Ned Arden Flood (Chicago, 1897).

Penfield began, in April 1893, to make simple and effective 'miniature' colored posters for *Harper's Magazine*. His pioneering series brought forth pictorial designs for other periodicals, then for books, newspapers, and the theater, and finally for advertisers of merchandise all the way from bicycles to narcotic cures. The inevitable slump from overproduction came about in 1898.

Stone & Kimball had used a printed poster to announce their *Terra Cotta Guide,* and when Will Bradley was asked by them to decorate *When Hearts Are Trumps,* a decorative poster was also commissioned. *The Chap-Book* series of posters, begun by Will Bradley and continued by Frank Hazenplug, Claude Bragdon, E. B. Bird and J. C. Lyendecker, ranked with the best American work. The designs were appreciated here, analyzed in Paris, and bought in London. Many of the gay lithographs, with their use of impressionist color and the flat perspective of the popular Japanese prints, are completely satisfying as pictures—one wonders if they were not too good in themselves to be effective in selling something else. Herbert Stone encouraged the fad by word as well as deed, writing for the *Chap-Book* issue of October 1, 1894, an appreciation of Penfield's work, and for that of December 1, 1894, one on Will Bradley with reproductions of his early work for the Chicago publications *Vogue* and *Inland Printer.*

The editors of *The Chap-Book* treated their pictorial placards as objects of separate interest, beginning with a notice in the masthead of issues after January 15, 1895: "Owing to the demand for Chap-Book posters, the publishers have reserved a few copies for collectors, at fifty cents each." Within a few months, their magazine and book posters were advertised individually in almost every number, the last list of December 1, 1896 including fourteen *Chap-Book* posters and other designs created for Stone & Kimball. The business in posters became a considerable part of the commerce of the concern, Stone & Kimball even importing French posters made for others, and advertising them for sale. The definitive list of importations, in the issue of October 1, 1895, totals one hundred and fifty-six, with all the contemporary masters represented—the highest prices being asked for long runs of Cheret, Grasset, and Lautrec. Although *The Chap-Book* did not advertise posters for separate sale after 1896, they were made for the books of Stone & Kimball and Herbert S. Stone & Company until 1902.

THE PAMPHLET PERIOD

On May 1, 1895, the last number of its first year and second volume, *The Chap-Book* was able to report, in a booklet expanded half again in contents and advertisements from the twenty-four page issue of May 15, 1894, "average circulation for three months, 12,206." The first numbers, as announcements of the publishers and booksellers' advertisements indicate, had gone out of print at once, and, Faxon reported in his bibliography, "were in demand by collectors at from 20 to 50 times the original issue price of five cents a copy. All sorts of little magazines were soon on the news-stands, competing for a part of the *Chap-Book's* favor. They were, with few exceptions, easily distinguishable by their appearance as well as by their names, which were apparently carefully chosen to indicate the ephemeral character of the publication." By this time in 1895 there were enough pamphlet magazines to constitute a movement which flourished until 1896 and had a slight renaissance in 1900. The editors of *The Chap-Book* began to comment with wonder at the new periodicals which were made in its size, emulated its typography, copied its illustrations, or rivalled its literary content, in efforts to express their own editorial individuality and to draw on the discriminating class of readers and collectors which *The Chap-Book* had found. Gelett Burgess, in bringing his own *Lark* back to earth, wittily summed up the meaning of these adventures, which H. L. Mencken later called "the pianissimo revolt of the nineties."

In 1895, the "Chap Book" had already begun its successful career as the American leader of the remarkable literary revolution that made the year typical of the vagaries of the "end of the century" madness. Suddenly, without warning, the storm broke, and a flood of miniature periodicals began to pour over the land. The success of the "Chap Book" incited the little riot of Decadence, and there was a craze for odd sizes and shapes, freak illustrations, wide margins, uncut pages, Jenson types, scurrilous abuse and petty jealousies, impossible prose and doggerel rhyme. The movement asserted itself as a revolt against the commonplace; it aimed to overthrow the staid respectability of the larger magazines and to open to younger writers opportunities to be heard before they had obtained recognition from the autocratic editors. It was a wild, hap-hazard exploration in search of a short cut to Fame; it proposed to carry Prestige by storm.

But that war is almost over now, and the little wasplike privateers that have swarmed the seas of journalism are nearly all silenced; the freak fleet has disarmed, but who knows how many are missing. Not a port but gave help to the uprising and mustered its volunteers in the fight against Convention. It was a tea-pot tempest that made them and wrecked them, and yet, when the history of the Nineteenth Century Decadence is written, these tiny eruptions of revolt, these pamphleteering amateurs cannot remain unnoticed, for their outbreak was a emancipation from the dictates of the old literary tribunals. Little enough good has come of it that one can see at present, but the sedition is broached, and the next rebellion may have more blood to spill.

The Lark itself was certainly the most delightful of *The Chap-Book's* contemporaries, and would be famous if only because it began with the famous rhyme of "The Purple Cow."[18] Of all the odd periodicals which collectively expressed dissatisfaction with the literary order of things, *The Lark* is the best expression of the unforced gaiety which was a principal ingredient of most American ephemerals, and which is in such sharp contrast with the seriousness of the

[18] See Carolyn Wells, "What a Lark," *The Colophon,* Part VIII (October, 1931), pp. [8], for intimate discussion of its collaborators, and excellent reproductions.

majority of esoteric periodicals abroad.[19] *The Chap-Book*, conscious of all its foreign brethren, was in especially close touch with the Paris group of young men's papers. The "Notes" in the issue of March 15, 1895, begin:

> This is the age of esoteric magazines, published for the few, "The Remnant," as John Eglinton calls them in that little book that comes from Whaley, in Dublin.
>
> The conservative man thinks these periodicals the apotheosis of foolishness, and the fulcrum of the logroller.
>
> Dear conservative! The gods give him joy. Some of the rest of us enjoy them.
>
> Paris has long witnessed the triumph of the apparently unread. Apparently only, for the illuminate read. There is *La Plume*, vigorous and incorporated, *L'Ermitage, Le Mercure de France, La Revue Blanche*. There was, perhaps is now, a *Revue Jeune*. Perhaps most wonderful, there are in Paris enough people who love legends and fairy tales to support *Le Livre des Legendes*, edited by Jacques des Gâchons, a charming poet, and filled with dainty flower-sprinkled picturings by his brother Andhré.
>
> At Brussels thrives *La Jeune Belgique,* and at Ghent appears a curious brochure on folk lore called *Wallonia,* read so far as I know by one person only in this country, Prof. Child, of Harvard.
>
> Holland possesses *Der Nu van Strak,* and Germany, characteristically, has an annual, the new *Musen-Almanach.*
>
> In England, not to speak of *Hobby-Horses* and *Yellow Books,* there is at Birmingham *The Quest;* at Oxford the suppressed *Chamelion,* organ of Oscar, *Le bourgeois malgré lui,* as Whistler calls him; while at Edinburgh some of the younger Scots are to start *The New Evergreen.*
>
> Here we commence only. Mr. Mosher, of Portland, knowing the eagerness of the public to glut its maw with periodicals, and its conscientious aversion to the classics, has decided to trick it into reading the good things of literature. The little *Bibelot* is to give us monthly reprints from rare editions. Already I have seen some Blake poems, some of John Payne's translations of Villon, and the promise of much in coming numbers.

---

[19]This is carefully discussed in Limpus' Chicago thesis, pp. 128-30. Osbert Burdett, *The Beardsley Period* (New York: Boni and Liveright, 1925), Chapter IX, and Holbrook Jackson, *The Eighteen-Nineties* (London: Grant Richards, 1913), Chapter II, have valuable analyses of the mood of the English *fin de siècle* periodicals. A fairly full list of them is given by E. L. Casford, *The Magazines of the 1890's* (Eugene: University of Oregon [1929]), p. 39.

Claude Bragdon introduces his reminiscent article on the period by detailing some of its characteristics:

> The Purple Cow Period of American letters is synchronous with *The Yellow Book* Period in England, that is, it corresponds to what is now referred to jeeringly by the Younger Generation as "The Gay Nineties." And in sober truth this is not such a bad title, for the most characteristic literary products of that particular decade were inspired far more by the play-spirit than those of today. The era found perhaps its most acute expression in certain periodically issued, small, and for the most part short-lived, brochures or broadsides referred to in the slang of the day as the Dinkey Magazines, each of which expressed the attitude and point of view of an individual or of a group. In the aggregate they can be characterized as "young," devouringly egocentric and self-assertive and either good-naturedly or bitterly critical of one another. They constituted a sort of metaphysical Fleet Street, extending from coast to coast.[20]

The pocket periodicals which had the longest lives, had least in common with *The Chap-Book*—Elbert Hubbard's *Little Journeys* (1894-1903), and *Philistine* (1895-1915); T. B. Mosher's *Bibelot* (1895-1914); and the small magazines of sensational short stories, like *The Black Cat* of Boston (1895-1903). *The Bibelot* derived directly from the eclectic publications with which "The Portland Pirate" had begun, in 1891, his publishing career, and Stone & Kimball were always polite to Captain Mosher. Hubbard they abhorred, greeting *Little Journeys* with the pleasant comment that "Mr. Elbert Hubbard...writes in a spirit of bland contentment with the commonplace worthy of the 'Ladies Home Journal' at its best...and as to his literary style, 'ça n'existe pas.'" *The Philistine* was welcomed with "It has his usual overwhelming dullness and paucity of idea, while the style has all that deftness which we have learned to know as peculiarly his own, a delicacy of touch as of a hippopotamus

---

[20]Claude Bragdon, "The Purple Cow Period: The 'Dinkey Magazines' That Caught the Spirit of the 'Nineties,'" *Bookman*, July 1929, Vol. LXIX, p. 475.

on a tight rope or a Nordau forging *vers de societé.*"²¹ The editors obviously felt that Elbert Hubbard was vulgarizing the literary meaning of the pamphlet revolt, just as Bernard Shaw felt that Hubbard's books were only parodies of Kelmscott books.

We are fortunate in having an almost complete list of the phantom periodicals of the nineties, begun in 1897 and revised in 1903 by the late F. W. Faxon.²² With keen perception, he seized the unusual opportunity offered by his business of periodical service to libraries, to make a contemporary record of this abortive cultural revolt. Mr. Faxon wrote in the introduction to the revised bibliography: "Hardly any one now collects these publications, and unless the names, and the dates of their births and deaths are somewhere recorded, no future collector will ever be able to obtain accurate information concerning this large, somewhat useless, but very interesting class of periodicals. This then is our excuse for the following attempt at a bibliography." From the first list we see that ninety-eight had already appeared and almost as many had died by June 1, 1897. From the second, which included a few earlier publications, some British journals, and the small short story magazines, that 209 had been published by 1903.

It requires only a few titles from his lists and elsewhere to indicate both the wide dispersion of these little magazines and enough of their individual contents for our purposes. Reading from Northeast to Southwest, there was *Truth in Boston; The Fly Leaf,* Boston organ of the distinguished critic Walter Blackburn Harte from December 1895 to April 1896. In nearby Springfield *Bradley, His Book* was published for nine months in 1896. In New York there were *The Cri-*

---

[21]*The Chap-Book,* April 15, 1895, Vol. II, p. 446; July 1, 1895, Vol. III, p. 159. *The Philistine* returned the compliment in divers ways, including the advertisement, in its issue of January 1897, of back numbers of *The Chap-Book* at two for a cent.
[22]Frederick Winthrop Faxon, "A Bibliography of Ephemeral Bibelots," *Bulletin of Bibliography,* June 1897, Vol. I, pp. 21-23; " 'Ephemeral Bibelots,' " *Ibid.,* April 1903—January 1904, Vol. III, pp. 72-74, 92, 106-7, 124-26.

terion and *M'lle New York,* both militant and exciting in their independence.[23] *John-A-Dreams* was published in New York, with drawings and early writings by Booth Tarkington. There was also *The Daily Tatler,* a separate story for a later chapter, the organ of Ingalls Kimball during the time he was sole owner of Stone & Kimball.

Moods, A Journal Intime, appeared quarterly in Philadelphia with work by John Sloan, who was then being discovered simultaneously by *Inland Printer,* Copeland & Day and *The Chap-Book.* Washington's ephemeral was a *Bauble; Events* occurred in Wheeling, West Virginia; *The Alkahest* in Atlanta. Texas had *The Fad* in San Antonio and *Brann's Iconoclast,* removed from Chicago to Waco via Austin, where a weekly edited by O. Henry is supposed to have begun under the same name.[24] Kansas City was very prolific, with *The Baton, The Lotus, Pierrot,* and *Poster Lore,* one of several miniature magazines devoted to the parallel cult of miniature posters. Others were *The Poster* of New York and *The Echo* of Chicago. *The Kiote* came from Lincoln, Nebraska, and *Lucifer's Lantern* from Salt Lake City, Utah. Chicago's best were *Four O'Clock,* interesting for its illustrations, and *The Blue Sky Magazine,* well printed by T. W. Stevens and A. C. Noble.

Looking backward over four decades, we can see not only that Stone & Kimball's *Chap-Book* set off a literary rocket of pamphlet periodicals during the financial depression of the nineties, but that like increases in the number of ephemeral publications have continued to mark important economic and cultural changes. The pamphlets are bibliographical evidence, if we did not have an abundance of other types of testimony, that there were people the country over, who had things to say, pictures to show, and ideas of typography

---

[23]Both were staffed with noteworthy writers, *The Criterion* having Pollard, Vance Thompson, W. S. Harte, and Bliss Carman; *M'lle New York,* edited by Thompson, featured illustrations by Thomas Fleming and T. E. Powers, and writings on music and art by James Huneker.
[24]Fanny E. Ratchford, "The Rolling Stone," *The Colophon,* June 1934, Part XVII, p. [1].

that they felt were not being expressed through the channels for publication then in existence. That none established themselves permanently does not deny the importance of our first "little magazines," and of *The Chap-Book* in setting their form and tone.

Bibliographical and critical data on ephemeral periodicals since 1900 are incomplete, but there are enough to show that outpourings of little magazines have twice since the nineties accompanied crisis periods in American development.[25] The second and third groups have been parts of a progressive series, in certain obvious ways. The first group was individualistic to the point of back-biting, and, competing for the favor of the general public as well as of the knowing, helped to kill each other off. Again important for historical comparison is the fact that the best of the pamphlets—*Chap-Book, Lark, M'lle New York, Criterion, Bibelot*—were distinctly internationally minded.

The second group, scattered between 1912 and 1929, but with essential characteristics derived from a few periodicals begun just before the war, included several magazines which, through subsidy or editorial intransigeance, continued for considerable lengths of time. There was a strong Chicago orientation, but many of the '1912' magazines were intense peripatetics, like their editors and contributors, who included the pre- and post-war literary exiles. If they called themselves "Little Magazines" it was to emphasize their appeal to a select audience, and to adopt the phrase of the moment —the "Little Theater" was strong in 1912. Typography and illustration were no longer major concerns, and these publications of literary groups, like *The Little Review,* tended to concentrate on a particular literary form, critical approach, or technical method.

---

[25]Exactly how close and how significant is the connection between lows in the business cycle and the florescence of non-commercial literary periodicals, is an exacting problem for the student of publication trends. That such publications are nowhere regularly recorded will make it only a little harder.

Most of the third group, children of the 1929 depression, have thrown individualism and art for art's sake overboard; many define themselves into recognizable political groups; all favor a simple prose. They have few international associations, occasionally are nationalistic, and are usually the product of regional groupings of authors. No less than the earlier groups, however, "directly or indirectly they reveal a strong ferment in American literary life and foreshadow to some extent the dominant characteristics of the literature that is coming."[26]

TOO SUCCESSFUL

The range of activity contemplated for *The Chap-Book* was indicated in its first number: "The Chap-Book will have at least one signed review in nearly every number, besides several short notices, and literary essays. In addition to this, the Chap-Book will contain poems and occasional short stories by both well-known and unknown writers." This was restated on February 15, 1896, when the price of *The Chap-Book* was raised to ten cents a copy, two dollars a year: "The editors hope by this means to make it a better representative of the younger writers, not only of this country, but of England and France as well. It will make its readers acquainted with the cleverest of the young men, and renew their knowledge of many of the older. It also hopes to bring to public notice hitherto unknown authors, and to be a distinctly literary periodical, with the highest standard of taste and judgment." Since the magazine even in the first number had contributions from established as well as new writers—and rightly, if it was started to assist Stone & Kimball's book business—it was favorably received by conservative magazines and daily newspapers. Among the press notices reprinted in the second issue of *The Chap-Book,* one from the New York *Tribune* was quite discerning: "It is to be the

[26]Robert Cantwell, "The Little Magazines," *New Republic* July 25, 1934, Vol. LXXIX, p. 295. This is a valuable study of fifty new magazines issued in the first six months of 1934.

medium of communicating to the public all that is most modern and aggressive in the Young Man's literature. It is to contain book reviews, literary essays, poems and short stories, and, as this first number shows, illustrations in the fearful and wonderful style of young Mr. Beardsley. The cleverest thing in the number is a little sketch by Maria Louise Pool—a bit of work whose motive, so far from bristling with modernity, is as old as it is pathetic."

One has only to leaf through the hundred numbers issued twice a month between May 15, 1894 and July 1, 1898, to see that *The Chap-Book* never became dull, though the high level of the early issues was not maintained. In time the conservative minority of contributions became a majority, and the editors, as their financial cares increased, could not supply the light-heartedness which had made their "Notes" such good reading. The preceding section on "The Pamphlet Period" has shown how *The Chap-Book's* initial success was a signal for enterprising young writers to become their own publishers. The founders of *The Chap-Book* had judged only too well the temper of their time—their success was eventually their undoing. Since many of the literary men who could not or would not publish in the newspapers, the standard monthlies, or the new cheap magazines issued pamphlets, there was soon too much leadership among the young rebels and not enough substance. It is generally conceded that although the time was exciting there was no plethora of perfectly matured young writing talent at work in the American nineties;[27] Stone & Kimball were aware of what

---

[27] Percy H. Boynton opens his discussion of "The Temper of the 1890's," in *Literature and American Life* (Boston: Ginn and Company [1936]), p. 710, with: "It may have been an accident in time or it may have sprung from a consciousness that a century was ending, but the 1890's, like several other tenth decades, were more than averagely eventful and provocative. In the literary stratum of the English-speaking world the passing of a generation of writers was enough to give pause. Within a few years of 1890 came the deaths of Arnold, Ruskin, Morris, Carlyle, Tennyson, Browning, as well as Emerson, Longfellow, Melville, Lowell, Whitman, Whittier, Holmes, Mrs. Stowe . . . Hamlin Garland, young Western upstart, might discredit the torchbearers in his essay on "Crumbling Idols," but the public could see no evident successors nor any clear promise of them. The leaders of the next generation were either silent or unheard . . ."

there was, and reached out for it. Contributions were sought from writers as different as Woodrow Wilson and Frank Norris.

In the short story, Hamlin Garland, who wrote for *The Chap-Book,* had already produced his best realistic work. Stephen Crane, forging his way to approval as a journalist in the East, and as a novelist abroad, sent only poetry. Ambrose Bierce, no longer young in years, but still too grimly shocking for the *Century, Atlantic Monthly, Harper's* or *Scribner's* of the time,[28] never appeared in the magazine, although a new edition of his *Tales of Soldiers and Civilians* was scheduled for publication by Stone & Kimball in 1894.[29] On the other hand, they did have heavy representation from the local-colorists, and the short story of New England character was a constant filler of *The Chap-Book* from beginning to end. The stories by "Octave Thanet," Maria Louise Pool, and others (also collected in the booklists of the firm) were craftsmanlike. They were, however, the work of people whose reputations had already been made and who were acceptable even to the most conservative editors. Among the longer stories contributed to the magazine, we soon see the beginning of the trend to historical romance which swamped the country at the turn of the century. Stone & Kimball's specialists were Clinton Ross and F. Frankfort Moore.

In the first booklists of Stone & Kimball and in the early numbers of *The Chap-Book* were included almost all the important poets that showed themselves in the United States before 1900.[30] But Richard Hovey and Bliss Carman had their books of vagabond verse published by Copeland & Day,

---

[28]Thomas Beer, *The Mauve Decade* (New York: Alfred A. Knopf, 1926), p. 224.

[29]In *Publishers' Trade List Annual* (New York: Publishers' Weekly, 1894). No copy of this edition has been found, and it is not recorded in Vincent Starrett, *A Bibliography of Ambrose Bierce* (Philadelphia: The Centaur Bookshop, 1929).

[30]Edwin Arlington Robinson, originally a member of the class of 1895 Harvard, left Cambridge before Stone & Kimball was founded there. His verse never appeared in *The Chap-Book,* where *Children of the Night* was reviewed on January 15, 1898. The caption "The Promise of Fame," indicates the editors' opinion of this poet; it was one of the most favorable early reviews received by Robinson. See Charles Beecher Hogan, *A Bibliography of Edwin Arlington Robinson* (New Haven: Yale University Press, 1936), pp. 136-37.

and Hovey's historical and patriotic poems found easy acceptance with magazine editors nearer him in the East. William Vaughn Moody, who came to teach in Chicago in 1895, a year after Stone & Kimball had moved there from Cambridge, favored *Harvard Monthly*. Santayana's shorter pieces were also being published there, although Stone continued to put the philosopher's verse into books until 1899. The names indexed under the heading "Poetry," from the third volume onwards, exhibit a strenuous effort to discover new poets, and reading the verse contributions, one can see that poets were not required to conform to a house style. This reaching after little-known names, coupled with an absence of censorship in poetry, were unusual editorial policies for American magazines a generation ago, as Harriet Monroe's career illustrates. *Poetry* was founded in 1912 as a place where poets might freely have their say, for her own experience had taught her

what a desperate fight for recognition poets had to make, and make mostly in vain, through the score of years before 1912. A correspondence with *Hampton's Magazine* may be cited to illustrate this point. The editor commented on the "distinction of the verse which you have been publishing in other magazines," and asked me to submit some to *Hampton's,* adding, "We prefer lyric stanzas and verses of a rather informal type."

But the lyrics I submitted came back promptly, the editor explaining: "The verses we print are rather of the progressive, uplift type, the kind that Kipling might do if he were writing in this country. Anything more graceful and delicate is unbecoming to the contents of our magazine."

My grief over being unbecoming to Hampton's was modified by a smile or two, but other magazines were equally unhospitable. This niggardly attitude of publishers and the public toward poetry was emphasized by so many rejections that by 1910 I had well-nigh ceased sending poems to periodicals.[31]

The later volumes of *The Chap-Book* included verses from such people as John Vance Cheney, Louise Imogen Guiney,

[31]Harriet Monroe, *A Poet's Life* (New York: The Macmillan Company, 1938), pp. 188-89.

Madison Cawein, Josephine Preston Peabody and Father John B. Tabb, but were overbalanced by contributions from such adherents to established forms as Richard Burton and E. C. Stedman, and workers in the simple sentiment of Ella Wheeler Wilcox.

The Chap-Book made no exciting discoveries among American meditative essayists—as *The Yellow Book* had of Max Beerbohm and Kenneth Grahame among the British. Walter Blackburn Harte, whose *Meditations in Motley* was published in Boston the year Stone & Kimball's magazine was founded, first published his own periodical and then tried to collaborate with Elbert Hubbard. By the fifth volume, only two years after its beginning, *The Chap-Book* had to turn to the reminiscent essay. Alice Morse Earle's "Curious Punishments of Bygone Days," later collected as an early book publication of Herbert S. Stone & Company, was very good of its kind—but very little different from the historical *pastiches* of the big magazines. A year earlier our little magazine had discovered its ancestry, commissioning the English antiquarian John Ashton to write on "Chap-Books" for the opening number of the third volume (May 15, 1895), old woodcuts and modern imitations being used as illustrations. The thorough critical essay, especially the close analysis of a writer's new work[32] or the study of tendencies and schools in foreign literatures,[33] that had made the first volumes of *The Chap-Book* so distinctly valuable, was continued only intermittently.

Harry Thurston Peck, who founded *The Bookman* in 1895, under the aegis of Dodd, Mead & Company, took a great deal of wind out of *The Chap-Book's* sails. Here was a big magazine with big money behind it, also dedicated to the principle of literary hospitality. It would seem simple jeal-

---

[32]See Hjalmar Hjorth Boyesen, "Ibsen's New Play," February 1, 1895; Louise Chandler Moulton, "The Man Who Dares," [John Davidson] February 15, 1895; Lilian Bell, "With the Procession," [Henry B. Fuller] June 1, 1895.
[33]The last of these was William Sharp, "A Note on the Belgian Renascence," December 15, 1895.

ousy that made Peck the subject of much criticism for "vulgarity" in *The Chap-Book,* did one not see in *The Bookman's* notes and literary criticism, along with praise for Stone & Kimball's typography and admiration of their publicity methods, many unmerited innuendoes on the immorality of their productions.[34] Even Stone & Kimball's posters[35] and book illustrations were piously disapproved.[36]

Herbert Stone and Harrison Rhodes were thus badgered into impolitenesses in their erstwhile gay and chatty editorial comment, while the columns of literary criticism were taken over by Hamilton Wright Mabie, Brander Matthews and Maurice Thompson—no mean names but ones perfectly familiar to readers of avowedly conservative critical journals. Perhaps the last of these, later the author of "Alice of Old Vincennes," should not be classed with two genuine scholars,

[34]Compare the notes on the "Chap-Book Teas," and the advance notices of Mrs. Reginald De Koven's *A Sawdust Doll* and H. C. Chatfield-Taylor's *Two Women and a Fool* (*Bookman,* April 1895, p. 156), with the review of these two volumes (*Bookman,* May 1895, pp. 265-66), where the latter work, a harmless study of infatuation, is termed "as gross a piece of pseudo-realism as we have yet seen in American fiction with any pretence to that title. It is a pity if this is indicative of the way the new literary currents are tending in the West; one must lament to see real ability and cleverness prostituted to such degrading ends. For Mr. Chatfield-Taylor... has considerable wit, a modicum of wisdom—of a worldly cynical sort, it is true—and much wickedness. But it all has a Dead Sea fruit taste, and the apple of lust and lies, so inviting to the eye, is rotten at the core and turns to ashes in the mouth. It is an insult to one's moral sense to be expected to find any interest in the liaison of a Bohemian artist with a music-hall beauty, and to enjoy the confessions of a slave of passion's whim. Messrs. Stone and Kimball deserve credit for their excellent artistic taste in the mechanical portion of these books, but one could wish that they had not sullied the lustre of their growing literary reputation with the responsibility of at least one of them."

[35]See Louis J. Rhead, "The Moral Aspect of the Artistic Poster," *Bookman,* June 1895, pp. 312-14, which defends Beardsley against imitation by "Western artists who cannot draw the figure, and who hide their defects under the mantle of his quaint and original style. The editor of a certain journal wrote to a publisher asking whether it was the English B or the American B who designed a poster seen on the stands—a question hardly flattering to either artist." This same article, after attacking Cheret for "lewdness... abandoned license and wild madness," concludes: "No, the moral aspect of the artistic poster, then, is that it may be, if done well, an important factor in the community, and it is best, to begin aright, with high ideals and aims, to educate, ennoble, and make men and women think of life not as a silly dream, but as earnest and sublime."

[36]Reviewing Gertrude Hall's translations of Verlaine in the Green Tree Library, *Bookman* of June 1895, p. 350, says of Henry McCarter's pictures: "The illustrations it is not possible to commend. One of them, facing page 11, is frankly indecent, but we object to it less on that account than because the indecency is wholly without excuse in the lines which it professes to illustrate. The others are harmless, but sometimes unintentionally comic." The censured plate is not a good picture, but certainly not a dirty one.

for in one essay on style, he managed sneers at writers as diverse as Meredith, Verlaine, Mallarmé, Le Gallienne, Sharp, Zangwill, Whitman, Crane, Lang, Haggard, James and Stevenson.[37]

The critical outlook of the editors could be no clearer than the times. Taupin said well, in his comment on the premature aging and death of the magazine: "Il avait vécu la vie ordinaire des idées littéraires de son epoque." To begin with, Carman, Stone and Rhodes were never sympathetic to Hamlin Garland's "veritist" version of realism, although they published his theoretical essay and the early imaginative works which exemplified it.[38] Towards Zola, towards William Dean Howells in his own writings and his championship of Tolstoi, they were tolerant rather than approving. But the other end of the spectrum from realism and social criticism—the concentration on style and all the rest that we crudely term art for art's sake—became anathema to the general in the spring of 1895. Oscar Wilde's unsuccessful prosecution of the Marquess of Queensberry for libel, which ended with his own arrest on April 6, 1895 and conviction on May 25th, seemed to justify temporarily the identification of all writers in "decadent" styles with moral degeneration, which had just brilliantly but superficially been achieved by Max Nordau in his volume *Degeneration*. The editors of *The Chap-Book* never joined the universal condemnation of Wilde's writings which followed his trial, and soon after bravely defended the free circulation of ideas:

Recent newspapers have brought the information that the authorities of the British Museum have withdrawn from circulation

[37] Maurice Thompson, "The Art of Saying Nothing Well," *The Chap-Book*, July 1, 1896, Vol. v, pp. 148-51.

[38] See Hamlin Garland, *Roadside Meetings* (New York: The Macmillan Company, 1930), p. 276 ff., especially his report of the conversation with Herbert Stone which led him to "put aside economics." After experiencing poor returns from his early crusading books, "when Herbert said, paternally, 'You started right, Mr. Garland, but you've gone wrong,' I listened meekly. He went on: 'You're a bit of the preacher where you should be only the artist. The *Arena* was all very well once, but you need a different kind of publishing now. You must write for the *Chap-Book* and forget your cause.'"

all books written by Mr. Oscar Wilde. For this performance there has been applause on all sides. It has been hailed as a most righteous judgment and a noble act of justice. Preachers have approved, moralists have commended, the Prevention of Vice people have been loud in their praises and now the critics also come in with their cheers. For most of these there is the old excuse of utter and growling ignorance and on that score one must—we suppose—forgive them. In the present instance, however, it is cowardly and small. They have struck a man when he is down. They have kicked a body when life was nearly gone and they found pleasure in doing it—they—the erudite, the honest, the just critics ...

If there ever was in any of Mr. Wilde's writings literary merit and beauty, which may perhaps originally have led the Museum to purchase the works, the same merit and beauty still exist and will continue to exist. Once and for all, a book printed and given to the public has a life wholly its own and independent of the fortunes of its author. Even should we discover that Shakespeare himself had committed sins against a dozen decalogues, it would not alter by one hair's breadth the wonder of his poetry. This is a far cry, but the question is one of principle and justice and not of the values at stake. The performance of the curators of the British Museum is an act of bigoted and blind fury. It is narrow-minded and indiscriminating. One must protest.

Yet as time went on *The Chap-Book* developed its own taboos, calling attention to hidden perversities in Aubrey Beardsley's drawings; confessing that it was "glad for the change" which carried *The Yellow Book* from "strong drink to tea"; denouncing as "notorious for his immoral pose," Arthur Symons, editor of *The Savoy;* condemning the publisher of this magazine, Leonard Smithers, as "publisher of the avowedly erotic"; making a long attack on *L'Ymagier,* termed "blasphemous" in its devotion "to the reproduction of old religious prints and to the exploitation of certain moderns who produce scrawls on religious subjects." One of the editors even declared that such an example of "the ever-recurring outrages to decency and good taste which I see in books and on the stage," as the May Irwin—John C. Rice kiss shown in "The Vitascope, a sort of magic lantern which reproduces movement," called "for police interference."

The English contributions are the strongest side of *The Chap-Book* after its third volume; the second had seen Kenneth Grahame, Edmund Gosse, and Israel Zangwill admitted. British representation grew ever larger after the magazine and its editor were flatteringly well received by London authors and editors, especially William Sharp, Douglas Sladen and Henry Harland. The establishment of an English edition of *The Chap-Book,* in connection with John Lane, and the opening of a London branch to publish books were considered during Stone's London visit of 1895. At that time Robert McClure, already in close touch with the British literary market as representative of his brother's magazine, was appointed London buying agent for Stone & Kimball. Thus John Davidson published his best ballads in *The Chap-Book,* often before they were issued in England. Even after Robert Louis Stevenson's death at the end of 1894, there was a supply of his books for the firm and newly discovered articles for their magazine. H. G. Wells was on the list with a short story and a novel, both in his first vein of scientific romance, while Arthur Morrison was favored among British realists. George Bernard Shaw is not represented by any direct contributions, but *The Chap-Book* published an interview with Clarence Rook, in the issue of November 1, 1896, which remains an essential source on his first twenty London years. This was accompanied by a "counterfeit presentment" of Shaw by Max Beerbohm, one of six "Chap-Book Caricatures" of literary folk made by him. The drawings did not reproduce well in small size, but no size of type could diminish the charm of "the incomparable Max's" essay on dandyism, written for, and printed in *The Chap-Book* during Beerbohm's visit to America in the company of his actor brother, Sir Herbert Beerbohm Tree. Beerbohm's literary parodies, "A Christmas Garland," had their first run in *The*

Chap-Book of December 15, 1896, sixteen years before they were collected in a book.

Although the advertising pages fattened, and circulation grew from the "12,206" of the end of the first year and second volume to a high of 16,500 copies in the spring of 1896,[39] the tiring of *The Chap-Book* was obvious when it was enlarged to twelve by eight and a half inches, the conventional size of English literary reviews like the *Athanaeum* or *Academy,* with the fifth number of Volume VI (January 15, 1897). As *The Chap-Book* had run on from its first number, and especially after Herbert Stone became the sole owner on May 1, 1896, it had given less and less display of its own publisher's books. In the large size it made such a serious effort to be an impartial critical journal, that it omitted to review Stone publications. Its function as trumpet for an individual booklist was gone, while other publishers' books were often so sharply reviewed that much book advertising was withdrawn. A final failing, reported by Herbert E. Fleming after an interview with Herbert Stone in 1905 was that "no effort to secure a list of annual subscribers was made. 'If we had secured such a list, the *Chap-Book* would be alive today,' says Mr. Stone. 'Newsstand sales fluctuate. A list is needed in order to get advertising in off-years.'"[40]

Circulation as well as advertising dropped sharply in the year and a half of the full-size magazine. Its readers must have been shocked when *The Chap-Book* grew up. One great attraction was lost when pictorial covers, colored prints as supplements, woodcut illustrations and humorous vignettes were eschewed. While cult magazines talked of the necessity for discussing artistic tendencies in connection with literary developments, *The Chap-Book* had actually exhibited the

[39] According to a trade circular issued during the course of Volume v. Comparable figures for other literary periodicals, as reported in Ayer's *American Newspaper Annual* 1896, are: *Bookman* 1096, *Critic* 5500, *Nation* 11,009. For standard monthlies: *Harper's* 165,000 and *Scribner's* 85,000. For low-priced monthlies: *Munsey's* 480,000 and *McClure's* 166,666.
[40] Herbert E. Fleming, *Magazines of a Market-Metropolis: Being a History of the Literary Periodicals and Literary Interests of Chicago* (Chicago, 1906), p. 803.

work of the contemporary artists of London, Paris, and Chicago along with its printing of contemporary writing. Pictures were not only printed in the magazine, but the editors had held regular displays of original drawings, paintings and posters at their offices. Various expedients were tried to keep the magazine alive: a drive for subscriptions with tuition scholarships in selected colleges as prizes; fiction supplements; a political stand. When Harrison Rhodes, the editorial mainstay of the firm, left to work in England, Melville E. Stone Jr., in charge of the Chicago office while his brother was abroad, felt there was no point in continuing. *The Chap-Book* died in the midst of the Spanish-American War, for which it had exhibited no enthusiasm. The cover dated July 15, 1898, included only a final folio of farewell, in which the magazine's career and influence were reviewed and the announcement made that it was being merged into the fortnightly Chicago *Dial*. Chicago writers, like H. C. Chatfield-Taylor, H. B. Fuller and Wallace Rice regretted its passing, for it was still the most liberal and wide-awake general journal being published in Chicago. Mary Abbott, writing in the Chicago *Record* on this occasion, said:

> From the offices of Herbert S. Stone & Co.'s publishing-house has arrived the really sad tidings that the Chap-Book no longer exists. With its subscription list, right to its name and good will, it has merged into the Dial, and according to its old owners is translated to another and a better sphere, the Dial being, as they nobly and disinterestedly affirm, the "best purely critical review in America." But this is a matter of opinion. And the merging of the younger periodical has many voices to deplore it...
>
> But the publishing firm came to the wise determination to confine itself to the publishing business. The demand of the public has increased for newspapers with its interest in the war, but has declined in fashionable literature. What the Duke of Wellington said of himself and Sir Robert Peel might be said of most literary reviews of the general character of the Chap-Book: "I have no small talk; Peel has no manners." But the Chap-Book has had both small talk and manners. It was fashionable and a luxury.

As for there being a larger demand for magazines of the type of the Dial, it is hard to see exactly what the demands of literary Chicago are. The question is not whether the readers of the Chap-Book will change their tastes with their removal along with the good will and fixtures. The publishing business of Messrs. Stone & Co. will certainly be benefited by this consolidation of purpose. The firm has shown taste, judgment and discrimination in its selection of manuscripts and authors. It has mounted its books with dignity and beauty. Now that it has all its time to give to this, its legitimate calling, there will be even better results. The public will miss the Chap-Book, but congratulates the publishing business.

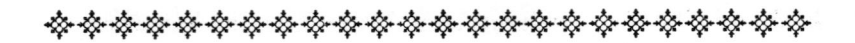

CHAPTER III

Stone & Kimball

CHICAGO AND NEW YORK

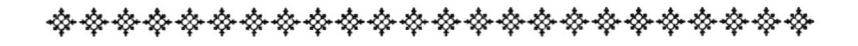

CHICAGO: 1894-1896

THE FIRST YEAR of the publishing partnership of Herbert Stone and Ingalls Kimball ended with their leaving college to make a business out of an avocation. Their trumpet was *The Chap-Book,* in its first three years one of the most effective publicity devices ever invented by an American book publisher. It was necessary, in reviewing the magazine's career, to refer to books published by Stone & Kimball and Herbert S. Stone & Company between 1894 and 1898. In general, the editorial policies concerning books were similar to those of the magazine. The bibliographical record indicates that Stone & Kimball's selection of books during the years 1894 and 1895 was as timely as *The Chap-Book's* articles had been, and that like the magazine, the booklist was moderately successful financially. At least one new printing was required for twenty-five of the first fifty books.

Stone & Kimball did overreach themselves in their desire to supply the needed collected edition of the works of Edgar Allan Poe, tying up a considerable proportion of their working capital in an expensive and show-selling set. The editors,

Edmund Clarence Stedman and George Edward Woodberry, were gentlemen of distinction whose reputations and years of work in the field were worthy of the substantial advances they received. The ten volumes were supplied with lengthy introductions and annotations, carefully printed at the University Press and richly illustrated with reproductions. Illustrations were commissioned from the popular painter Albert Edward Sterner, and an extra series was ordered from Aubrey Beardsley for the large paper edition. The partners visited collectors and members of the Poe family to borrow prints of old portraits and engravings. The paper was ordered by S. D. Warren & Company of Boston, and was the first to bear a special Stone & Kimball watermark. This was the first machine-made paper produced with a real deckle edge, reports Mr. W. J. F. Dailey, then production manager for Stone & Kimball (and, he adds, "the only Yale man to have part in this history making episode in American publishing"). The manufacturers of the paper unfortunately have no record of exact details, but the recollections of the printer and the binder of this edition all jibe with Mr. Dailey's belief that Stone & Kimball worked out the plan for running deckle-edged paper on Fourdinier machines, for edition work.

Herbert Stone had discovered, during his first stay in Paris, that Poe had a tremendous vogue in France. Believing that American taste was a reflection of European, he planned the production of a fine new edition. The plan struck fire at once with Stedman, who had already written a biography of Poe. He called on George Edward Woodberry, who already had reputation as a textual critic. At the beginning of their career as publishers Stone & Kimball produced what is still the scholar's standard edition of Poe. Unfortunately, however, they had neither a "subscription department" nor that standing with libraries which was necessary to sell a definitive edition, intended, as the prospectus states, "alike for the librarian, the student and the book lover."

It is not known now how many copies of the Poe were printed at the first run, but there were enough left in 1897 to supply the second-hand market with thousands of odd volumes, and enough unbound sheets to make it worthwhile for Herbert S. Stone & Company to buy the copyright at the dismantling of Stone & Kimball in October 1897. Even in these hands there were no complete reprintings, although Messrs. Scribner, who acquired the edition in 1903, have used the plates repeatedly and even found it possible to sell a new large-paper, large-type printing of the same text. The heavy capital investment was made even more slowly recoverable by the printing of an additional two hundred and fifty sets on handmade paper for sale at $50. Ninety-seven large paper sets were in the stock of Stone & Kimball purchased and remaindered in 1897 by the late Isaac Mendoza. Stone & Kimball were led into overestimation by the success of their first limited and large paper editions—*First Editions of American Authors,* Field's *Holy Cross,* Garland's *Main-Travelled Roads* and *Prairie Songs,* Miller's *Building of the City Beautiful,* Santayana's *Sonnets,* and Carman's *Low Tide on Grand Pré* all sold out their limited issues. There were four other titles issued in special as well as trade formats before the deluxe Poe. After the completion of the set, only two books had special limited editions—Watson's *Father of the Forest* and Stevenson's *Vailima Letters.*

If it is not wise for a beginning publishing house to rush into the market for collected editions, neither is it necessary for them to buy up the most popular author in the world. Stone & Kimball were not imprudent when, in the spring of 1894, they seized an opportunity to become American publishers of Robert Louis Stevenson's new books. Their arrangements for the American publication of Stevenson's books were made with Charles Baxter of Edinburgh, man of business for R. L. S. since 1887, when "Having promised Messrs. Scribner the control of all his work which might appear in America, he shortly afterwards, in sheer forgetfulness, sold the serial rights of his next story to Mr. McClure. Nobody could have been more sincerely or deeply distressed over the matter than Stevenson himself, and, fortunately for his peace of mind, nobody seems ever for one instant to have thought him capable of any act of bad faith. But it must have been as much of a relief to every one concerned, as it was very greatly to his own advantage when shortly afterwards he handed over the disposal of his writings to the management of his old and trusted friend, Mr. Charles Baxter."[1]

"Stevenson was a man who hated to change publishers worse than anything and he would never have agreed to let the story [*The Ebb Tide*] go to a new and young house until there had been a financial inducement," reads a letter from Herbert Stone to his father. The personal letters preserved by the family, and the business correspondence now in Harvard College Library, together with bibliographical evidence, tell the complete story of Stevenson's and Baxter's relations with Stone & Kimball and something of the effect of the big purchase on the internal history of the firm. To let Herbert Stone continue, in April 1894:

Things are going on beautifully: we have been doing very well and have sold many books, but we are continually handicapped by a lack of capital. A week ago we got a cablegram from Robert Louis Stevenson's agent offering us the "Ebb-Tide" his new novel, for $2900. We had been thinking of the thing for some time: they wanted $3000. When this cablegram came, we were crazy. For a while we thought the thing was out of the question: Kim could not get much money and I told him I refused to ask you to put up the whole amount. Finally after a long council of war with Ned and a discussion as to just how you felt about things, I got Kim in a corner and made him a proposition that we divide the firm into three parts: of which I was to own two and he one. I told him frankly that I was doing it with the idea of a place for Ned when he got out of college. At first Kim would not listen to the

[1] Graham Balfour, *The Life of Robert Louis Stevenson* (New York: Charles Scribner's Sons, 1906), II, p. 39.

thing and then he demanded a right to buy back his share as soon as he got the money. That I could not refuse: it would not have been fair but I insisted that he must buy it back within three years or before Ned graduated or he would forfeit the right. This he agreed to and in consideration of the 2/3 and 1/3 arrangement and to pay him for the share I bought for Ned. I agreed to buy the Stevenson story myself and to give it to the firm: that is, I practically gave Kim $750 for 1/6 interest in the firm on condition that he turn the money back immediately for the firm's uses. This I thought to be quite fair and Ned and I both thought you will think it a wise move and would be willing to help me out.

So we cabled to Stevenson that we would take the story. He replied that we could have it provided we paid on the delivery of the mss. That we agreed to and the result is that I must have $2900 inside of a fortnight. I am hoping that Father will soon be home and so the matter can be settled easily. I suppose he is now on the water or I should have cabled to him for advice. However I spoke to him before he left and he then seemed to think the book was a wise investment. From my point of view, it is the finest thing in the world. It will give us a splendid standing. And the best part of it all is that we have first option on everything else that Stevenson does. I insisted on this and they finally consented.

The agreement Baxter drew up for this book and those that followed was expensive for Stone & Kimball, peculiar, and so complicated that even Scotsmen (Baxter and Graham Balfour, Stevenson's cousin and official biographer) later found difficulty in keeping the terms straight. As I understand the documents, Stone & Kimball had first refusal of all Stevenson material to be published in book form in the United States. If they permitted Baxter to set the advance against royalties (15, later 20, per cent), they had to accept the offer, or Baxter was free to offer it elsewhere. If Stone & Kimball preferred themselves to set the price and royalties for the specific book offered, Baxter was free either to accept their offer or to throw it into open competition. Once Stone & Kimball had agreed to publish a Stevenson book, they were committed to advance royalty payment on delivery of the manuscript, and to stipulated quarterly payments in addition. The quarterly payments were balanced against the yearly royalty statement, made the first of February, and any additional royalties were then due June first. There were to be no refunds by Baxter and each title was a separate account.

The Ebb Tide: A Trio & Quartette by Robert Louis Stevenson & Lloyd Osbourne, was published by Stone & Kimball from Chicago & Cambridge on July 15, 1894. The list price was $1.25 for a handsomely decorated (by T. B. Meteyard) binding on a tolerably well-printed book (see Fig. B and pp. 151-3 for T. L. DeVinne's opinion of its typography). The novel, which was actually written by his stepson and only revised by Stevenson, had already appeared in America in *McClure's Magazine,* between February and July 1894. The book sold perhaps as well as could be expected: four printings of probably 1500 apiece were made for Stone & Kimball in 1894 and 1895.

As in the case of Poe, Stone & Kimball were using the long view towards a permanent position in the publishing world. They could hardly have anticipated, when they paid an advance of $2900 against 15 per cent royalty for the American copyright of *The Ebb-Tide,* and were granted an option on all future works from the Scottish writer's pen, that the literary idol of the English-speaking world would at last succumb to consumption at Vailima in the South Seas, before the year was out. The news of Stevenson's death on November 28, 1894, had just reached America (a memorial meeting was held in New York on January 4) when on January 18, 1895, Stone & Kimball issued *The Amateur Emigrant: From the Clyde to Sandy Hook,* which described Stevenson's steerage passage of 1879. Because of its autobiographical content, the book did well. The entire first edition was sold on the day of publication, and three other impressions were made by April 15, 1895.

Macaire: A Melodramatic Farce by Robert Louis Stevenson and William Ernest Henley, originally written and privately printed in 1885, appeared in *The Chap-Book* during May 1895 and was put out separately late in June. There is no record of a Stone & Kimball reprint. *Vailima Letters: Being Correspondence Addressed by Robert Louis Stevenson to Sidney Colvin, November, 1890—October, 1894,* a two volume work, was copyrighted by Stone & Kimball on October 23, 1895 and sold by them in an ordinary cloth-bound edition as well as an edition on Dickinson handmade paper. There were also ten extra-special copies on Japan paper put up in morocco, which were not for sale. Up to May 7, 1896, Stone & Kimball had sold 2846 sets of the small paper edition and 55 large paper, reporting royalties due Baxter of $1304.10. On that day, as we shall see, Stone & Kimball were forced to transfer their Stevenson copyrights to Charles Scribner's Son, authorized American publishers of Stevenson's earlier works and of the first collected or "Edinburgh" edition, edited by Sidney Colvin, and begun under the direction of Charles Baxter, in November 1894. A fifth Stevenson title was being printed (*Weir of Hermiston*) and a sixth held by option (*St. Ives*) when this change was made.

To return to the change from the equal partnership in Stone & Kimball necessitated by the purchase of *The Ebb-Tide*—we do not know from the documents whether a balanced partnership between Herbert Stone and Ingalls Kimball was ever restored before they parted company in May 1896, but it is clear that the Stevenson purchases put Kimball at a disadvantage, and was a cause of the friction which two years later led to the dissolution of the firm.

The turn of the year 1895 brought also the shock, personal in its implications, of the untimely passing of Eugene Field. Field's interest brought Stone & Kimball books to the attention of the potent "Saints and Sinners Corner"; his future books were promised to his publishing *protégés;* and he tried to bring the books of other newspaper men, including Finley

Peter Dunne, to them. Herbert Stone felt, and *The Chap-Book* expressed, deep loss in the death of a rare spirit as a friendly adviser.

These opening paragraphs have made the situation of Stone & Kimball as Chicago publishers in 1894 and 1895 seem rather desperate. On the contrary, even if the background was charged with business danger, the foreground of the picture was altogether gay and prosperous. On the tenth of August 1894, Herbert wrote his parents from Cambridge, that they were

in the midst of moving. Clarence Holmes leaves this afternoon for Chicago and nearly all the furniture has gone already—so I am surrounded by mussiness and dust... Shall probably settle down somewhere near here to watch the Poe—which progresses steadily —though somewhat slowly. Business is really pretty good: the Ebb Tide is going splendidly and we have sold nearly 3000 copies in a month. Hearts are Trumps is in its second edition: the City Beautiful is going into its third edition. The Lover's Diary, Santayana's Sonnets and Pagan Papers are all going into second editions within a month—so I am gratified. As soon as we get a good bookkeeper we shall begin to show profits—I think—worth the while. I am glad we are going to be in Chicago where I can consult with Father about things. I hope you will take a house somewhere on the north side and go to housekeeping for the winter. Rents are low and I want some place where I can entertain people a bit: the business demands it.

Many entertainments were held at Stone & Kimball's offices in the Caxton Building, still standing on lower Dearborn Street, but then more than now at the center of the printing and publishing trade of Chicago. There were regularly held public readings of manuscripts, book and picture exhibitions, "Chap-Book Teas" and Vaudevilles. Here they met the Chicago literati not already known to their families. "I first met Herbert Stone soon after his return from college, when the firm of Stone & Kimball was just beginning and they gave a cabaret show in their offices," writes Lucy Monroe Calhoun.

Her sister Harriet also attended, and soon after received a copy of Maeterlinck's plays in "The Green Tree Library," with this inscription:

> "Presents endears absents"
> says Lamb.
> To
> Miss Harriet Monroe
> with the compliments of
> Herbert Stuart Stone
> Her Birthday
> MDCCCXCIV

Perhaps the occasion to which Mrs. Calhoun has referred was "The Chap-Book Music Hall" of December 20, 1895. The Kimball family has preserved an illustrated program, which indicates the participation of local amateur talent. The newspaper clipping accompanying the cheerful document states that "The Caxton Building last evening was the scene of an elaborate and highly successful affair... Back of the seats the sawdust-strewn floor held small round tables, from which was served during the performance sausages, oysters and beer. The ladies who presided at the tables were Mrs. H. I. Kimball, Misses Dexter, Peck and Margaret Abbott... At the close of the performance a supper was served."

Those interesting people whom Rhodes, Kimball and Stone did not meet at their own parties (continued through the Eldridge Court days) they met at "The Little Room." Chicago artists and writers had been meeting Fridays from four to six in studios at the Fine Arts Building, since 1893. The title for these aggregations was taken from Madeleine Yale Wynne's story of that title: her "Little Room" had the habit of disappearing and reappearing at intervals. Most regular in their attendance were Ralph Clarkson (usually the host), Harriet and Lucy Monroe, Clara Laughlin, H. B. Fuller, Edith Franklin Wyatt, Lorado Taft, Irving and Allen Pond, and Madeleine Yale Wynne herself. These folk also gave parties and produced plays and burlesques—those who didn't write them acted them. After 1897, 'Ned' Stone, as Melville Edwin Stone Jr. was always known in Chicago, was a star comic playwright and producer, but before then 'Hal' Rhodes, Herbert Stone and 'Kim' were largely contented to be players. Reference has already been made to the production of *Old Wine,* which Rhodes and Stone had written as undergraduates, by Anna Morgan. Miss Morgan and her students were actually in the nineties and early nineteen-hundreds the leading producers of 'serious' contemporary drama, in this country. She shared the advance-guard interests of Stone & Kimball, and gave the first American performance of plays by Ibsen, Maeterlinck, Yeats, and Shaw, all of whom had been introduced to the American reading public by Stone. There were other clubs where membership was valuable in one way or another to the Stone publishing staff. The Press Club (founded by Melville E. Stone Sr.) brought them in touch with working newspapermen like Opie Read, Stanley Waterloo and Will Payne; The Chicago Club gave them solidity; The Saddle & Cycle jollity; The Cliff-Dwellers a place to lunch visitors. Herbert Stone in 1895 was a founder[2] of the Caxton Club, where as a member of the Council and the Publication Committee, he worked with such other publishers as W. Irving Way and Chauncey L. Williams, booksellers like George M. Millard, printers like Thomas E. Donnelley, librarians like John Vance Cheney and collectors like George Merryweather and John H. Wrenn. Herbert was also a charter member of The Duodecimos, that interesting printing club whose organization provided, "Probably to insure against undesirable provincialism, members residing in any city or town, at time of election, were limited to four. There was to be neither clubhouse nor...'designated place

[2]The other fourteen founders were George A. Armour, Edward E. Ayer, Charles J. Barnes, John Vance Cheney, Augustus N. Eddy, James W. Ellsworth, George Higginson Jr., Charles L. Hutchinson, George M. Millard, George S. Payson, Martin A. Ryerson, W. Irving Way, Chauncey L. Williams, and John H. Wrenn.

of habitation'... of the club. Nor were its imprints to bear any such designation."[3]

The dramatization of their appearance in Chicago was great fun for Ingalls Kimball and Herbert Stone, and made their Chicago years a permanent part of 'the higher life in the Mid-western metropolis.' Their exploits are invariably cited whenever, from then till now, 'Chicago's position as a literary centre' is reviewed.[4] The entertainments probably helped to bring manuscripts where, as in the cases of H. C. Chatfield-Taylor and Anna Farwell DeKoven, Chicago's social and literary worlds overlapped. Yet there are implications in the memoirs of some writers now better known than most on Stone & Kimball's list that the publicity attending the descent on Chicago made the publishing house seem more splendid than approachable. Hamlin Garland, speaking of Stone, Kimball and Rhodes, records that "... when, of an afternoon these three missionaries of culture each in a long frock coat tightly buttoned, with cane, gloves and shining silk hats, paced side by side down the Lake Shore Drive they had the effect of an esthetic invasion, but their crowning audacity was a printed circular which announced that tea would be served in their office on Saturday afternoons... Culture on the Middle Border had at last begun to hum!"[5]

[3]Thomas A. Larremore, "The Duodecimos," *New York Herald Tribune Books*, March 14, 1937, p. 29. The articles were continued the two succeeding Sundays, in the column "Notes for Bibliophiles," edited by Leonard L. Mackall. Mr. Larremore names the six founders: Eugene Field, Edmund H. Garrett, Paul Lemperly, Herbert Stuart Stone, W. Irving Way and Francis Wilson; and the six invitees: Judge Ben T. Cable, Edward Stratton Holloway, Frank Easton Hopkins, Francis M. Larned, the Reverend Jahu DeWitt Miller and Leon H. Vincent. Mr. Larremore presents also, intimate details of their publication program.

[4]As for instance by Henry B. Fuller, "The Upward Movement in Chicago," *Atlantic Monthly*, 1897, Vol. LXXX, pp. 544-45; Samuel Putnam, "Chicago: An Obituary," *American Mercury*, August 1926, Vol. VIII, p. 420; Lloyd Lewis and H. J. Smith, *Chicago: The History of Its Reputation* (New York: Harcourt, Brace and Company, 1929), pp. 231-32; Fred Lewis Pattee, *The New American Literature, 1890-1930* (New York: The Century Company, 1930), p. 30; Albert Parry, *Garrets and Pretenders: A History of Bohemianism in America* (New York: Covici Friede Publishers, 1933), pp. 93, 181 and *passim;* Burton Rascoe, *Before I Forget* (New York: Doubleday, Doran & Company, Inc., 1937), p. 317; M. S. Mayer, "Chicago: Time for Another Fire," *Harper's Magazine*, November 1938, Vol. CLXXVII, p. 566.

[5]Hamlin Garland, *A Daughter of the Middle Border* (New York: The Macmillan Company, 1921), pp. 24-25.

Edgar Lee Masters calls Stone & Kimball "a snobbish publishing house," with which members of the Little Room were more or less allied; and states that he "had cast his fortunes with the Press Club Crowd." But he also records in his autobiography, that Stone was not willing to issue his first *Book of Verses,* which came to their hands in 1898 by the accident of Way & Williams' failure.[6] No one else cites rivalry between members of the Press Club and the Little Room or Stone & Kimball. If there was any snobbishness involved, it was an inverted form, stemming from members of the working press who banded together as self-conscious proletarians, in the Whitechapel Club. And many Whitechapel boys, like George Ade, George and John McCutcheon, Eugene Field, Wallace Rice, were also members of the Little Room and published with Stone & Kimball. Mr. Ade, Mr. John McCutcheon and Mr. Wallace Rice all speak with respect of Ingalls Kimball and of Herbert Stone, whom Claude Bragdon has called "a truly democratic spirit." It can be said that no publisher of their own generation is remembered with more affection by American authors. Even their transitory connection with Cambridge and Boston has left its record in the literary biography of that region; while they are so frequently mentioned in the biographies and memoirs of writers who worked in Chicago in the nineties that it would be surprising to find them omitted from one such literary log. Even many members of later generations of Mid-Westerners find it necessary to cite the firm's career as a living influence in the city's cultural life. A considerable album could be made of quotations from these reminiscences and critical comments, some containing direct observations or evaluations, others mere acknowledgements, at second-hand, of a tradition.

To turn from Stone & Kimball's relations with local authors to the effect of their work on readers, "A Reader in the Eighties and Nineties" (William Allen White, in the *Book-*

[6]Edgar Lee Masters, *Across Spoon River* (New York: Farrar & Rinehart [1936]), pp. 251, 336-37.

man for November 1930), remembers that *The Chap-Book* was "circulated in a thousand country bookstores and a thousand country towns across America. We have positive evidence of Stone & Kimball's impact on the area within Chicago's influence. Earnest Elmo Calkins speaks for others of his generation of Mid-Westerners when he says: "In the early nineties, while I still lingered in Galesburg Illinois, writing a column of gossip for the local daily paper and putting most of it in type myself, I was agreeably titillated to find on the periodical counter of the bookstore a tiny magazine with an engaging title, THE CHAP-BOOK. My heart leapt up like Wordsworth's when he saw the rainbow. I bought it and came back to buy its successors, and have not been the same man since."[7]

To let two famous American printers speak: First, Frederic W. Goudy:

> Someone has written that occasionally it is given to a young man to embark upon a joyous adventure, with tentative ideas as to goal, and yet presently to make an enduring mark. Ingalls Kimball, while a student at Harvard in the early '90's had developed a passion for the fashioning of good books, and with his classmate, Herbert Stone (son of Melville Stone), another enthusiast, he founded the publishing firm of Stone & Kimball; together they embarked upon just such an adventure from which flowed a lasting and far-flung unforeseen influence.
>
> It was while I was operating the Camelot Press that I came to know Herbert S. Stone and Ingalls Kimball. While still students at Harvard, they had begun the publishing of a slender fortnightly magazine called *The Chap-Book*. The first volume was printed May, 1894, in Cambridge, Mass. It met with so much success that the publishers left Harvard, came to Chicago and through the introduction to them by my erstwhile friend and book-lover, the late W. Irving Way, I became the printer of the second volume. *The Chap-Book* was an innovation in magazine format and contents. The publishers, no doubt, had been strongly influenced by the work of another young publishing firm, Copeland

[7]"The Chap-Book," *The Colophon*, April 1932, Part x, p. [1].

& Day, who, in turn, were following closely the beginnings of what we now speak of as the revival of printing in England.

Mr. Ernest Elmo Calkins says that the magazine wrought in him a transformation; it was to me an inspiration as well as a transformation. In the offices of Stone & Kimball I met a number of writers and designers. As I was becoming more and more interested in design, I recall the thrill that was mine on being introduced to Tom Meteyard, the English artist, who had just designed for Stone & Kimball the cover for Stevenson's *The Ebb Tide,* and he showed me his drawing for it. He knew Stevenson personally, he said, and Richard Hovey, and Bliss Carman, and other well-known Boston literary celebrities. It was at this time I first met Hamlin Garland, a contributor to *The Chap Book. The Chap Book* brought to my notice the work of Aubrey Beardsley, William Sharp, Percival Pollard, T. B. Hapgood and others.

All these inconsequential contacts helped to broaden my field of study and strengthened my wish to know more of the work of those men whose names represented so much of idealism for me. Later, I did come to know more or less intimately such men as Bruce Rogers, D. B. Updike, Bertram Grosvenor Goodhue, Bliss Carman, Alfred Pollard, Sir Emery Walker and many others.[8]

Mr. Will Bradley in his youth designed many posters for *The Chap-Book,* two books of verse (*When Hearts Are Trumps* by Tom Hall and *In Russet and Silver* by Edmund Gosse) for Stone & Kimball and one book of short stories (*Love's Dilemmas* by Robert Herrick) for Herbert S. Stone & Company. On August 5, 1938 he wrote from his home in Short Hills to the author:

Replying to yours of the nineteenth: I do not recall having designed the cover for "Love's Dilemmas"—but may have. I was living at Geneva at the time. For "Russet and Silver" I designed a cover and mailed it on an early morning train. Returning to my home, on the Fox River between Geneva and Aurora, I saw a russet hillside with leafless trees clean-cut against a silver sky. The title for the volume was suggestive of the poems having been written late in life—the earliest volume, as I recall, having been titled "Scarlet and Gold." The poetical significance of an autumn

---

[8]Frederic W. Goudy, An Introduction to *A Bibliography of the Village Press* by Melbert B. Cary, Jr. (New York: The Press of the Woolly Whale, 1938), pp. 13-14.

hillside, together with the so obvious composition and color scheme, made me hurry back to the telegraph office and wire Mr. Stone not to use the design already sent, that I would go in on the noon train with a new drawing. This was back in the days of youthful enthusiasms—enthusiasms stimulated by contact with Herbert Stone. He was one of the finest men I ever met—an artist's friend, a *young* artist's friend, of a type far too rare. He came into my life at just the right time—for me. I have no way of expressing my appreciation of the luck which brought my drawings to his attention and gave me the boon of his gentle and understanding guidance... I later knew Mr. Kimball in New York—where at the Cheltenham Press, he carried the book traditions, acquired in his association with Mr. Stone, into commercial printing. I look upon Herbert Stone as having brought to the publishing house its finest traditions—typographical. The early commercial printing, patterned on that of the books of Stone & Kimball, of the Cheltenham Press, was so far beyond that of any other commercial printing establishment as to have been in a class quite by itself—unsurpassed and only rarely equaled up to the present time...

The simon-pure historian does not admit the validity of fiction as source material, nor does the philosopher of aesthetics or the literary critic admit the truism that art imitates life. But so seldom is a mere publisher included as cultural background in historical fiction, that we can say that the drama of Stone & Kimball has become part of the Mid-Western legend. So Carl Van Vechten, recreating fictionally the intellectual life of an Iowa town in the mid-nineties, identifies his youthful hero as a superior student by detailing his books, which included "John Gabriel Borkman in Wm. Archer's translation, recently issued by Stone & Kimball in Chicago," and says of the hours which he spent with his favorite teacher: "They bent over numbers of Stone and Kimball's new Chap-Book, sitting side by side, Gareth particularly attracted by some sketches by an unknown writer named Max Beerbohm, because, as Gareth quickly ascertained, this Max was a brother of Beerbohm Tree and had visited America in his company. Lennie finding more pleasure in Henry James' novel, *What Maisie Knew*, which was still running in these pages."[9]

The substance to the legend is that Stone & Kimball were actually publishing in 1894 and 1895 many books of immediate appeal and lasting value, in more consistently attractive editions than any American trade publisher had thought it worth while to attempt. Mr. Melcher, who in the nineties, was a bookseller in Boston, remembered that, for these reasons, "By 1895, the firm's books were watched for everywhere." Other retired and active booksellers in Boston, New York, Cleveland and Chicago, have given like information in the course of this study.[10]

In January 1895, a good American bookseller would have had in stock these books issued by Stone & Kimball at the end of the preceding year: Stevenson and Osbourne's *Ebb Tide;* Gilbert Parker's *Pierre and His People;* Norman Gale's romantic prose and poetry; and Edmund Gosse's poems *In Russet and Silver,* designed by Will Bradley. Certainly also the first volumes—Sharp's *Vistas,* Maeterlinck's *Plays* translated by Richard Hovey, Ibsen's *Little Eyolf*—in "The Green Tree Library," which the publisher's announcement called: "A series of books representing what may be called the new movement in literature. The intention is to publish uniformly the best of the decadent writings of various countries done into English and consistently brought together for the first time." If he had any trade with intellectual radicals, the bookseller might have a few copies of Hamlin Garland's

---

[9] Carl Van Vechten, *The Tattooed Countess: A Romantic Novel With a Happy Ending* (New York: Alfred A. Knopf, 1924), p. 104.

[10] The late Andrew McCance, of Smith & McCance, Boston, wrote on October 8, 1937, "as we all know Stone & Kimball revolutionized the making of books—even today collectors are still hunting for Stone and Kimball imprints." Conversations with the late Isaac Mendoza, in 1936 and 1937; with Mr. W. H. Cathcart, in 1937 librarian of the Western Reserve Historical Society, and onetime manager for Burrows Brothers; and Mr. Richard Laukhoff, bookseller, who collected Stone & Kimball and Copeland & Day books as good examples of American printing even before his arrival in this country in 1895. Mr. William R. Hill, the longest-established bookseller in Chicago, in conversations during 1935. See also William J. Flynn, "A Bookseller Looks Back," *Publishers' Weekly,* April 22, 1933, Vol. CXXIII, p. 1331.

critical essays, *Crumbling Idols;* but Mr. Garland's work before *A Son of the Middle Border* in 1917 always attracted more comment than purchases.[11] The bookseller would soon be receiving consignments of Stevenson's *Amateur Emigrant,* first published in January 1895 but written in 1879 and 1880 as an account of his first passage to America; and his play *Macaire* written with W. E. Henley in 1884. H. C. Chatfield-Taylor's *Two Women and a Fool,* with illustrations by Charles Dana Gibson and admirable typography and binding, was on the *Bookman's* best seller list for six months after its January publication, and, writes Mr. Chatfield-Taylor, "probably because of its title, it led the sales in Salt Lake City for almost an entire year."[12] He might venture a set or two of the collected Poe, now completed in ten volumes. Later in the year he would order Verlaine's *Poems* translated by Gertrude Hall and a collection of Belgian short stories translated by the Scottish Mrs. Wingate Rinder, both 1895 issues in "The Green Tree Library." Likely choices would be one or another of the five books of William Sharp (two as "Fiona Macleod") published by Stone & Kimball, and some copies of the Canadian tales of the almost equally prolific Gilbert Parker. June brought *The Golden Age* of Kenneth Grahame, in buckram and lettering of gold. "The English Classics," bound from imported sheets, appeared in 1895, with well-printed and edited editions of Congreve's *Plays,* Johnson's *Lives of the English Poets,* and Walton's *Lives of John Donne, Tristram*

[11]Mr. Garland's most successful early work was *Main Travelled Roads,* which went into its tenth thousand in the hands of its original publisher, B. O. Flower of *The Arena,* Boston, between 1891 and 1893. Stone & Kimball's edition had no great success, but the volume was reprinted after 1898, when Macmillan took over its production. It is an interesting instance of the generally slower pace in publishers' publicity and the public reception of solid thought, a generation ago, that Garland's *Crumbling Idols,* in its time a revolutionary critical document, appealing for American themes in all art forms, should never have been reprinted by any publisher since its first edition by Stone & Kimball in 1894. Perhaps the savor of his summing up of the meaning of Impressionism, Ibsenism, Realism in fiction, and Walt Whitman evaporated in the periodicals where the essays were first published. Walter Hines Page, editor of *The Forum* in 1893, assured Garland that one of his articles "had brought forth nearly a thousand editorial comments, commendatory and otherwise." See Hamlin Garland, *Roadside Meetings* (New York: The Macmillan Company, 1930), p. 251.
[12]Letter of September 27, 1937.

Shandy and James Morier's *Hajji Baba.* Two series of original works were started by Stone & Kimball in 1895: "The Carnation Series," which ran to five volumes, and "The Peacock Library," designed by Frank Hazenplug, attaining only two. The year was weaker in Stone & Kimball poetry than 1893 or 1894, but there were two slim volumes from William Watson, and Richard Hovey's *Marriage of Guenevere.* To top the Christmas trade, Stevenson's *Vailima Letters* in two volumes, and picture books by Walter Crane, in pamphlets at a quarter each or three bound together at a dollar were popular.

There were only three books issued in 1896 with the imprint "Chicago: Stone & Kimball," the last the most important piece of fiction published by the firm as a partnership —*The Damnation of Theron Ware.* Set in Harold Frederic's native Mohawk Valley of New York, the novel now convinces more by its *mise-en-scène* than by its plot and characterization, but Ernest Sutherland Bates, writing in the *Dictionary of American Biography,* calls it Frederic's masterpiece, in which the author "transcended the limitations of his era and produced a work of enduring value. In his study of spiritual deterioration, which enjoyed a *succès de scandale* owing to the fact that its shallow hero is a Methodist minister, Frederic was the first to lay bare a fundamental weakness of American character in its tendency to rely on a purely verbal moral idealism." Frederic was then living in England, where he had been correspondent for the *New York Times* since 1884. Heinemann's edition (titled *Illumination*), winning praise from Gladstone, was an immediate success. Its progress in America was slower, but the use of Gladstone's recommendation and the enthusiastic reception by younger writers overcame critical neglect. Booth Tarkington in his reminiscences of the nineties, *The World Does Move,* records a conversation with a friend:

"I'm going to take you Tarkington to a dinner at the Lantern Club," he said. "Irving Bacheller's the toastmaster; Steve Crane's

a member and he knows Harold Frederic. Has anybody ever written a better novel than Frederic's *Damnation of Theron Ware?*"
"No, it isn't possible to write a finer novel."

The volume went to 20,000 in the hands of Stone & Kimball; 55,000 more were printed before 1906 by Herbert S. Stone & Company, including an edition of 25,000 distributed by Grosset & Dunlap; and *The Damnation of Theron Ware* has remained in print since 1908. The "Modern Library" edition, Boni & Liveright, had a valuable preface by Robert Morss Lovett.

The firm's business was expanding early in 1896; on March 1st, Stone & Kimball moved from third floor offices in the Caxton Building to a larger suite on the tenth floor. At the same time, a New York sales office was opened in the Constable Building at 139 Fifth Avenue. Kimball moved to New York to take charge. A month later, the partnership was suddenly dissolved. As Ingalls Kimball, thirty-five years after, recalled the circumstances for Frederic Melcher: "The rapid expansion had begun to worry the firm's backers and particularly the father of the senior partner. He reiterated his demand for more liquidation of investments, as many titles meant a good deal of capital tied up. To Kimball, laboring with sales in New York, this urgency seemed unwarranted by the prospering state of the list. On the spur of the moment he wired to Chicago an offer for taking over the Stone interests, and Stone accepted." Mr. W. J. F. Dailey, who was with Stone & Kimball from August 17, 1894, the day their Chicago office opened, until the split, then with Herbert S. Stone & Company until 1904 when he rejoined Ingalls Kimball at The Cheltenham Press in New York, added these details in a conversation with the present writer during September 1938: A buy or sell offer was made by M. E. S. Sr. in Chicago. Kimball agreed to buy—for $20,000 including *The Chap-Book*. 'Kimmie' came to Chicago and then made a hurried trip South, reappearing in a week with $10,000. This was accepted as sufficient for the book business, but Herbert kept

The Chap-Book and soon after launched into the book business as Herbert S. Stone & Company.

The Chicago newspapers regretted "the end of one of the most artistic enterprises that ever thrived in this city." The *Daily News* continued: "The small beginning grew to large proportion, because the originators never varied from the rigid standard. The little magazine passed all expectation. The firm printed three of the four important novels brought out last year by Chicago writers.[13] Its lists comprise more than 100 volumes, many editions of which attracted national and international mention. The press of the firm was getting to class with the established houses in the east. It is all over now as far as the original plans are concerned, and the two men will try to win more fame along separate lines, the business manager and the plant going to New York, and the editor and his hopes remaining in Chicago."

NEW YORK: 1896-1897

New York papers made no furore over another book publishing house. The venture did not start with good omens, even for Ingalls Kimball, who, as he told Mr. Melcher, had little money, and had to ask his printers and his paper makers to be his bankers. Luther C. White is supposed to have brought in some capital, as well as training in accountancy, when he joined with Kimball in 1896. An estimable character, who later held state office in Vermont and did important work in the reform of Federal prisons,[14] White had at this time no experience in publishing. Kimball had the help of an efficient office manager, W. J. Kirk, now with Steel Sales Corporation, who had begun his business life as office boy for Stone & Kimball in the Caxton Building. He had also volunteer as-

---

[13]Actually four novels by writers living in Chicago were published by Stone & Kimball in 1895—Lilian Bell, *A Little Sister to the Wilderness;* H. C. Chatfield-Taylor, *Two Women and a Fool;* Hamlin Garland, *Rose of Dutcher's Coolly;* Mrs. Reginald De Koven, *A Sawdust Doll.* Harper's published in the year 1895, H. B. Fuller, *With the Procession.*

[14]*National Cyclopedia of American Biography* (New York: James T. White & Company, 1931), Vol. XXI, pp. 282-83.

sistance for a year from a young Harvard graduate who was considering publishing as a career, and a possible investment in Stone & Kimball. However, Arthur Harlow in 1897, chose printing and later art: his print shop in Radio City is now known to all collectors. Mr. Harlow reports that his chief duty with Stone & Kimball was the liquidation of the stock of the Anglo-American publishing house of J. Selwin Tait & Sons, purchased in 1896 as a speculation in remainders.

Ingalls Kimball in his capacity as business manager of the original firm had had range to develop his taste for selling things, and had also, to judge from the imaginative typography of the New York Stone & Kimball books, gone a long way in training himself for his next career as a designer of printed advertising. The New York Stone & Kimball books almost outshone in typography the books of Herbert S. Stone & Company of Chicago, but Kimball did not know authors and their agents in the intimate way that Stone did, as editor of books and magazine publications. This is especially true of foreign writers. There is no record of Kimball having been in Europe between 1893 and 1897, while Stone spent the summer of 1895 in London and Paris, on business. Robert McClure, appointed English agent for the firm in 1895, after 1896 worked for Herbert S. Stone & Company, not Stone & Kimball. There were misunderstandings in '96 and '97 based on incomplete recollection or imperfect recordings of arrangements with writers, and some authors showed irritation at having horses changed for them in midstream. The correspondence with William Sharp in his proper person and as "Fiona Macleod" illustrates both points.[14]

[14]This is now held, almost in its entirety, by the Henry E. Huntington Library in San Marino, where it was read and abstracted for me (with the permission of Huntington's Librarian) by an old friend, Mr. Samuel E. Thorne, Law Librarian of Northwestern University. According to a list prepared by L. H. Smith of the Department of Manuscripts, Henry E. Huntington Library and Art Gallery, there are 18 letters from William Sharp to Herbert S. Stone, 6 from W. S. to Stone & Kimball, 3 to H. Ingalls Kimball; 7 letters from "Fiona Macleod" to H. S. S., 6 to H. I. K., 2 to Stone & Kimball, 2 assignments to the firm and 2 notes concerning the works of "Fiona Macleod"; 7 letters from H. I. K. to "Fiona Macleod"; 6 from H. S. S.; 8 letters and 3 statements from "Fiona Macleod" to the firm of Stone & Kimball.

On June 22, 1896, Kimball had to write from New York to Fiona Macleod:

> In answer to yours of June 9th, *The Washer of the Ford* has been copyrighted but not yet on the market. The details necessitated by my purchase of Stone's interest have made it impossible for me to gain an absolute knowledge of all the points in his department... Thus I knew nothing of your former letter to which you were awaiting a reply, nor can I find any letter in our files to which an answer has not been sent. As a matter of fact, I know nothing of the advance of £25 that was due on publication, but that you shall have as soon as the book is on the market, and when I return to the city I will look up the Sin Eater account and send you a draft. It is embarrassing to me to lay things at Stone's door but the facts unfortunately are as they are...

There was no great amount of money involved either for publisher or author(s). Two of the six Sharp volumes could not be copyrighted in the United States and the payment for *Vistas* to William Sharp was only fifty copies of the "Green Tree Library" edition, whose design Sharp much admired. £10 was paid for the entire American rights to *Pharais*, Fiona Macleod altering the text slightly from the already published English edition. Miss Macleod received only nominal advances against 15 per cent royalties for her two collections of short stories, *The Sin-Eater* and *The Washer of the Ford*. William Sharp's largest payment was the £100 advance royalty, paid on delivery of the manuscript of *Wives in Exile: A Comedy in Romance* to Stone & Kimball, who had commissioned the work. These low payments had to prevail in spite of the fact that Sharp was in these years at the height of his literary productivity and fame, under two names and on two continents, for neither Sharp nor his "cousin" were "good sellers" in American bookstores. Sharp had contributed several articles, including an excellent critical essay on the contemporary Belgian writers, to *The Chap-Book*, which devoted the issue of September 15, 1894, to a "Sharp Number." This had a photograph, a birthday verse written to Edmund Clarence Stedman, and appreciations of Sharp's work by many other friends whom he had made during visits to America. When he came again to New York in 1896, a trip, he said, "to be spent chiefly in transacting business with publishers," Kimball sent the "ship-news reporter" for *The Daily Tatler* to interview Sharp. The reporter was John D. Barry, onetime dramatic critic, and now known as newspaper columnist.

What is most interesting in the correspondence, which it is hoped can shortly be published in full, is the opportunity it affords for the study of William Sharp's "cousin Fiona Macleod." When William Sharp, under a compulsion which, his wife's *Memoir* indicates, had exhibited itself even in youth,[15] began in the summer of 1893 to write the Highland fantasies which he published as *Pharais* under a woman's name a year later, he kept the secret from all but his family and most intimate friends. Two acquaintances, the poet Richard Le Gallienne and the scholar Grant Allen, appear to have been the only contemporaries not in the know, who guessed the identity of the brilliant "Fiona Macleod." He kept up the deception with his American publishers, writing to Stone & Kimball in his own hand and referring to Fiona as a third person (see Fig. 4b) and as Fiona Macleod writing a disguised hand (Fig. 4a). When Herbert Stone visited London in the summer of 1895, Fiona vanished to her highlands; when Ingalls Kimball wrote that he would like to settle business matters with her in person, Fiona answered on January 20, 1897, that it will be "impractical for me to see you when you are in Great Britain for I am going to Italy immediately and when I return in late spring or early summer I will go to Glasgow to sail to the Hebrides. I am hardly ever in London,

---

[15] "... I remember he told me that rarely a day passed in which he did not try to imagine himself living the life of a woman, to see through her eyes, and feel and view life from her standpoint, and so vividly that 'sometimes I forget I am not the woman I am trying to imagine.' " The time was 1881, when Sharp was settling to an editorial career in London. Quoted from *William Sharp (Fiona Macleod)* A Memoir Compiled by his Wife, Elizabeth A. Sharp (New York: Duffield & Company, 1912), Vol. I, p. 82.

rarely in Edinburgh, though it has been convenient to have my letters addressed there." If Ingalls Kimball or Herbert Stone ever suspected that Fiona Macleod's works were written by William Sharp, there is no hint of it in their letters.

Fiona was surely womanish in her demands on the publishers. She wanted *The Sin-Eater and Other Tales and Episodes* to be published both in Edinburgh (by Patrick Geddes & Colleagues, of which William Sharp was Literary Director) and in New York on October 15, 1895—but on October 14 Herbert Stone had to cable Sharp that complete proofs had not been received in time and American publication could not take place before November 1st. Concerning her next book (and last publication with Stone & Kimball), *The Washer of the Ford: Legendary Moralities and Barbaric Tales,* there was a similar delay. Fiona Macleod had promised the manuscript for January 1896, but on April 4th of that year, wrote Herbert Stone that she was only then sending the opening pages of *Washer of the Ford* and that the remainder would go by next mail. And she hoped that Stone & Kimball could bind sheets and perhaps "nominally" sell copies, by *May 1st, 1896,* when Geddes planned to publish in Edinburgh. Even hastily put together, *The Washer of the Ford* was not able to be deposited for American copyright before June 12, 1896. Miss Macleod once berates Stone & Kimball for slow publication and slow payment, but the next letter is twelve pages of satisfaction with the contracts offered and "courteous treatment," and expressing "perfect confidence in the firm's good faith."

William Sharp, on the other hand, wrote to the firm and to its members individually, with the same graciousness and understanding he displayed in all his relations with other editors, publishers and authors. He delivered manuscript and proof on time, made only reasonable requests for advance payments and pressed for money politely. One of his letters, which has remained in the hands of the Stone family, deserves quotation, for its content, warmth of friendship and epistolary style:

24th January/96   Rutland House—Greencroft Gardens
                       South Hampstead, London

MY DEAR HERBERT:
   This is merely a hurried line, a chronicle of woe!
1) When I was in Edinburgh a few days ago, I found Miss Macleod ill, and though now convalescent unable to be at work. She says she cannot now let us have *The Washer of the Ford* till the middle of March: tho' can promise it by then. So that renders publication till beginning of May infeasible: but we hope to issue *then*.
2) On my return I went to see Mrs. Wingate Rinder, and found *her* ill also, and more seriously: inflammation of the bowels. However, she too is now better, and hopes to be up out of bed in three days or so. But *The Shadow of Arvar* cannot now come to us till about the same date—namely mid-March: and even that can't be taken for granted until next week.
3) As to W. S.— he admits he is a culprit: and that he is not so far on towards "finis" in *Wives in Exile* as he had hoped. But apart from the trouble connected with Mrs. Sharp's break-down and going to Italy, and the extra strain thrown on me, and having her work to do for her—I too have been very far from well. Moreover, I have been under a great strain of anxiety and suffering of another kind, as to which I can only hint to you, thus: but now [paper cut out] and anxiety are almost over. Still—with the delay, and with all involved, I must ask you to wait for *Wives in Exile* till well on in February. I am going to do nothing else now till it is finished, and at last can work at it again with verve and pleasure. Believe me, the delay is wise. The book will be all the better for it. There is an interpolated story—episode in the latter portion of it, "*The Man of Two Minds,*" or *The Woman of Two Natures* which, for one thing, I want to rewrite.
   I hoped to have had a cable from you about Ernest Rhys's book and, as I wrote on January 4th (about new books by Rhys, Mrs. Wingate Rinder, and myself—and also a proposal by Mrs. Sharp). [The next paragraphs in red ink.]
   In the faint hope that this blood of my crucified patience may better attract your attention I write to say that I have never

yet received the "Gypsy Christ" you say in your last were sent a month ago, nor have I seen a copy of that book—though a week or two ago I had a very nice letter from Mrs. Moulton about it.

DO SEND SOME COPIES FORTHWITH, OR I SHALL DAMN YOU EVERLASTINGLY.

Affectionately yours
WILLIAM SHARP

The Stevenson matter, of less psychological interest but of high financial significance, came to a head shortly after Ingalls Kimball took over the complete administration of the affairs of Stone & Kimball. The opening of the present chapter discussed the terms of the contract under which the firm published four of Robert Louis Stevenson's books, beginning with *The Ebb-Tide* in the summer of 1894. The Stone & Kimball editions were now uniformly printed, bound in green polished buckram and advertised together "The Later Works of Robert Louis Stevenson." Stevenson's negotiators and Stone & Kimball ran into difficulties in the winter of 1895-1896, especially over royalty payments on the *Vailima Letters*, which were published in October 1895, and over the exercise of Stone & Kimball's option on *Weir of Hermiston*, the important novel which R. L. S. left unfinished at his death. The story of one almost-publication, of another unfinished novel, *St. Ives: A Story of the Napoleonic Wars in Spain*, is simpler than the other, and can be disposed of first. This is referred to in the Stone personal correspondence as having been purchased for £300, and announcements of its forthcoming issue were made both by Stone & Kimball in their trade announcement for 1894-1895, *Concerning the Books of Stone & Kimball*, and in the literary press.[16] Apparently the price was to be paid on delivery of the manuscript, which was never handed to Stone & Kimball; the work was eventually published by Charles Scribner's Sons in the United States.

[16]See for instance the magazine *Book Buyer*, published by Scribner's, February, 1895.

Weir of Hermiston became a bone of contention because Mrs. Stevenson asked Graham Balfour to handle the disposal of the manuscript. Ignorant of the terms of Baxter's 1894 agreement with Stone & Kimball, he placed the book rights of *Weir* "with Scribner's on 20% royalty with £500 advance. It is certainly a direct violation of the terms of the agreement and I shall hold Balfour and Baxter rigidly to your contract with them," wrote Robert McClure from London to Herbert Stone in Chicago, on September 7, 1895.

After an involved correspondence, remarkable both for hard feeling and good will, between Stone & Kimball and Balfour, Baxter, McClure and presumably the Scribners, an official tender of the manuscript was made by Baxter to Stone & Kimball:

11. 11. 95
6 Staple Inn
Holborn Bars, London E.C.

Dear Sirs,

As Executor of the Late R. L. Stevenson and in pursuance of my agreement with Messrs. Stone & Kimball I hereby offer to them through you as their agent, the copyright of the unfinished story Weir of Hermiston said to amount to 43,000 words (which number is not guaranteed) at the sum of eight hundred pounds Sterling.

This offer is conditional on my concluding an arrangement with the Magazine known as Cosmopolis for serial publication on 1st January 1896, in which event proof sheets will be supplied and your clients will be bound to copyright the book in the United States on that date.

The date of publication will not be before 20th May 1896, and the price shall be payable on the date of book publication in America.

I am yours truly
A. BAXTER

Messrs. S. McClure & Co (Lt)
Hastings House
Norfolk Ct.

Kindly remind Messrs Stone & Kimball of the £500 payable on publication of the Vailima Letters.

Robert McClure's covering letter of November 12th, to Herbert Stone, added:

My dear Stone:

Weir of Hermiston. I enclose two letters from Baxter, which will supplement and explain my cable to you of this date. *Cosmopolis,* as you have doubtless learned, is the name of a new International Quarterly to be published in London, Paris, Berlin and by someone in America. It is to contain about 300 pages, 1/3 to be set up in French, 1/3 in German, and 1/3 in English. Fisher Unwin is to be the English publisher. The backers apparently have plenty of money, and they have offered £1000 for the serial rights of this story, which they intend to publish in three numbers. The price here will be 2/6, and, I suppose, 50 cents in America. I cannot believe that it will achieve a large circulation in any country, and I do not think that the serialization of the story in its pages will tend in the least to diminish the value of the book. I should explain to you that Graham Balfour has retired from the management of the Stevenson business, and that the affairs are once more in Baxter's hands. Baxter's first price for the American bookrights was £900., but, at my urgent request, he reconsidered the matter, and, as a result, has named £800. for American book copyright. I think that this is still high, but I do not doubt for one minute that Scribners would cheerfully give as much, or even more.

The price was eventually lowered to £650, accepted by Baxter on November 26, 1895; and the date of May 20, 1896 set for book publication in America and England (by Chatto & Windus). As proofs from *Cosmopolis* were received, Stone & Kimball had the material set in type. There exist three of these part issues, received for copyright January 4, February 6 and March 5, 1896. Printed by the Lakeside Press, they include the material through page 231 of the book as published—by Charles Scribner's Sons on May 20, 1896, and printed for them at the Norwood Press.

The reason for the change in publisher and printer is clear —on March 7, 1896 Stone & Kimball in Chicago refused to accept a sight draft for £250 drawn on them by Charles Baxter, Edinburgh, February 24th. This was a balance due on *Vailima Letters.*

During February 1896 Stone & Kimball had had the expense of moving their Chicago office and of opening a new one in New York; in March and April the dissolution of the firm took place. Money was tight for the new owner, and a check to Baxter sent during April, turned out to be an overdraft. Baxter promptly protested and Kimball cabled the sum to McClure, who placed it in Baxter's hands on May 1, 1896.

The care Stone & Kimball took to preserve their American copyright by having the pamphlet part printings made all came to naught. Kimball, having met his obligations, now felt it wiser to give up the ghost. He turned over to Charles Scribner's Sons his Stevenson copyrights, including the printed but unpublished *Weir of Hermiston* and the option on *St. Ives*. He informed Baxter of this transfer in a formal letter of May 7, 1896, enclosing final royalty statements. Thus ended the Stevenson chapter in the history of Stone & Kimball—it had brought them more worry than glory.

The thirty-six books published by Stone & Kimball between May 8, 1896 and July 3, 1897 indicate an editorial approach differing from the original program. Contracts already made were concluded by the publication of books of John Davidson, "Fiona Macleod," Maeterlinck, Santayana (revised and enlarged edition of the *Sonnets* originally published in 1894), Ibsen, Clyde Fitch and Maria Louise Pool. Several new authors were added, whose work matched the pattern already made by Stone & Kimball—one may mention H. G. Wells' *Island of Dr. Moreau,* Carolyn Wells' first book, *The Sign of the Sphinx,* and John D. Barry's first novel, *Mademoiselle Blanche.* The tendency, apparently already in 1896, away from imaginative toward informative books, was continued in the last eighteen months of Stone & Kimball. Only sixteen of the one hundred and four of the firm's book publications are classifiable as other than fiction, poetry, drama, or essay. Six books in non-belles-lettres categories occur during the administration of Ingalls Kimball. Two travel books: *The Thlinkets of Southeastern Alaska* by anthropologists Frances Knapp and Rheta Louise Childe, and *The Yankees of the East* by journalist William Eleroy Curtis. One biographical work: Samuel Johnson's *Lives of the English Poets*, reprinted in "The English Classics." A book of charades *The Sign of the Sphinx*, by Carolyn Wells. One story for boys by Robert Overton, *Friend or Fortune?* And a book of reference, *The College Year-Book for 1896-97*. The desire to give solidity to the list is understandable; so also is the quest for a best-seller, evident in the publication of light— even insignificant—works of popular authors. Nothing of Marie Corelli's, it is safe to say, would have come from the Stone & Kimball firm while it stood on two legs. Other books —*James, Grip, With the Band*—while not altogether without merit, were probably purchased only because they could be had cheaply.

Kimball was in a desperate hurry, for soon after the University Press accepted his long term notes in 1896, Mr. Melcher related, "the old Wilson ownership of the University Press at Cambridge changed, and Herbert White took over the business. 'Mr. White insisted,' Kimball explained to us a few years ago, 'that the notes be changed to negotiable form, and soon after, in August, 1897, when this was done he forced payments which meant liquidation to meet the obligations.' The capital stock of the firm was $75,000. Luther C. White was at this time secretary and treasurer; the assets were given as $71,563 and the liabilities $32,690. In October of that year all rights and stock were sold, and Mr. Kimball turned to the printing business."

Kimball was granted time to publish between November 7 and 21, 1896, *The Daily Tatler*. This expresses his real literary interests perhaps better than the books of his last days as a publisher. Edited by the publisher and Carolyn Wells, this, the only daily paper published for profit in the United

States and devoted exclusively to literary and artistic topics,[17] excites not only by its novelty, but by the quality of its content. There were poems, articles, interviews, reviews, by and about such notables of the time as Edmund Gosse, Sadakichi Hartmann, Richard Hovey, W. D. Howells, Brander Matthews, Maurice Maeterlinck, Clinton Scollard, William Sharp, Walter Damrosch, Moritz Rosenthal and Frederick Macmonnies. Miss Carolyn Wells in her autobiography writes:

> My connection with the short-lived Tatler was one of my most thrilling experiences.
> This little daily paper was published by the Chicago firm of Stone and Kimball, but Mr. Ingalls Kimball was in charge of the New York office, and it was there the enterprise was carried on.
> The office was beautiful, with real stained glass windows and aesthetic furnishings that gave joy to the visitor.
> One day when I was there Mr. Kimball and I were lamenting the lack of really original sin in the imitative periodicals of the day, and we concluded that the only completely unbeaten track was that of a literary daily.
> The impossibility of the thing attracted us; the increasing difficulties lured us on, and by some superhuman effort on our part *The Daily Tatler* appeared on the following Saturday. It was a small eight-page affair, entirely literary, and delightful in every way.
> Now literary periodicals are usually weeklies or monthlies, and few editors of such know anything of the soul-harrowing rush of a daily. For two weeks we lived by the instantaneous process and then gave up the ghost.
> The nicest thing about *The Tatler* was its staff, a mob of gentlemen who wrote with ease, while I occupied the early English editorial chair and giggled at the funny things that were said. It was all in the magic Nineties, and everybody was clever and quick of understanding.
> Richard Hovey, of blessed memory, was the jibe maker, and he stalked the floor and outwhistled Whistler in his gentle art. All books sent in for review were marked with the official stamp,

---

[17]Newspapers printed for charity fairs in nineteenth century America were largely literary in content. A separate study and bibliography of these is under way.

which was the paw of the office kitten and a purple ink pad. Our deepest perplexity each morning was whether to sell that day's issue as a paperweight or to sell a paperweight with it—the decision resting on the voice of the New York press of the day before.

Nor did *The Tatler* die of inanition. Always sold out before the uptown stands were reached, it proved, however, too great a strain on the time and energies of the staff, who discovered that to rise at six o'clock every morning is a sad grind and without its due reward in fun.

So the thirteenth day saw the final edition of what was doubtless the only daily literary paper ever attempted.[18]

The Daily Tatler was an important venture—the last flare from Stone & Kimball. It loses little of its heady quality by being read forty-three years after the event. Further, it is an accurate index to the cultural life of New York City in mid-November of 1896, as it was skilfully used by Thomas Beer in *The Mauve Decade*.

No publications were issued after July of 1897. Financial atrophy had already set in: beginning in March of that year, twenty-seven assignments of copyright were made, chiefly to Norman H. White, owner of the Boston Bookbinding Company, and brother of Herbert H. White, who was running the University Press. S. D. Warren & Company, paper merchants, held the set of Poe; the University Press, the originals of unpublished drawings made by Beardsley for the limited edition of the Stone & Kimball Poe, and *The Damnation of Theron Ware*. These dealings cannot be interpreted as part of the trading in authors which was a continuous feature of the activities of Stone & Kimball,[19] but mean what assignments of stock and accounts receivable mean in any business—the beginning of the end. Gilbert Parker only left them for Appleton's, who produced his greatest success, *The Seats of the Mighty* in 1896, because he found royalty

---

[18]Carolyn Wells, *The Rest of My Life* (Philadelphia: J. B. Lippincott Company, 1937), pp. 174-75. See also her "Post-Mortem Statement," *The Chap-Book*, February 1, 1897, Vol. VI, pp. 251-52.

[19]A letter from Mr. W. J. F. Dailey of October 8, 1937, refers to "gambling in manuscripts" as a regular activity of the firm.

payments slow. Surely Kimball would not have transferred *Wives in Exile,* which had been specially commissioned from William Sharp, to the new Boston firm of Lamson, Wolffe & Company, if he had not been pressed. Though the book had been copyrighted as early as March 1897, it was never actually published, but sold as sheets. The successful *Golden Age* was also sold separately at this time to another publisher —to Mitchell Kennerley, acting as manager of the newly opened New York office of John Lane. The sum paid for plates and contract in this case is said to have been a thousand dollars. Hardly a high price, but there were only a few titles as easily translatable into cash.

Before the final disposition of the business was made, Kimball offered it to the Stone firm for the sum of its debts, according to a telegram of September 15, 1897, from Herbert Stone, in Boston, to Melville E. Stone Jr., in Chicago: "Offered Stone and Kimball business for its debts twenty thousand dollars six months time granted by creditors it is a great bargain and requires no cash consult with father and wire me Jamestown at once." But the Stones decided to buy the individual copyrights they desired at the public sale, which took place on October 21, 1897. Hamlin Garland, who attended as an interested party, has described the scene in his *Roadside Meetings* of 1930, but even more vividly in the manuscript diary on which his printed account is based:

> I have just returned from a sheriff sale of the books of Stone & Kimball. A rather melancholy affair. The walls of the pretty office dismantled—the furniture in disorder. The dust moving over all.
> The sheriff a consequential little Dutchman was bustling about seeing that the goods were marked.
> Few salesmen from department stores and second hand stores assembled like birds of prey—unclean—sordure of fall.
> Kimball "the corpse" kept up a cheerful show and laughed with Mr. Stedman, Mr. Woodberry and myself with apparent insouciance, alluding to us as "Chief Mourners." A lot of attor-

neys were there to protect the interests of the leading creditors and authors.

The clerks looked dismally on as the people crowded through the small rooms and thumbed the books which were set aside in lots.

Everything went absurdedly low as they always do at such a sale. The most of the buyers were too ignorant to know the names of the books and were there to buy any book at 3c to 5c. It was not a cheerful scene.

Mr. Stedman said to Mr. Woodberry and myself "If we could but contrive to have Kimball's insouciance put up at auction we would all be paid in full."[20]

He smoked his pipe and shook hands with the sorrowful authors quite unmoved by the affair—apparently. It may have been a brave show merely.[21]

Isaac Mendoza of the Old Ann Street Bookstore, New York, was the largest buyer of bound stock, and Herbert S. Stone & Company bought practically all printed sheets and plates. There was some conflict over the copyright of the works, quickly adjusted by attorneys for the new publishers and for protesting creditors,[22] for the wholesale disposal of the volumes purchased was continued by Stone as well as by Mendoza. The late Mr. Mendoza, Charles E. Goodspeed tells us, encouraged him to enter the book business and the first stock of Goodspeed's Book Shop on Beacon Street in Boston, was liberally salted with Stone & Kimball remainders, purchased from Mendoza. The opportunity to buy attractive Stone & Kimball imprints at twenty-five cents and odd volumes of the Poe set at fifty cents was appreciated by "the ladies of Beacon Hill and the Back Bay," he says.[23] Thus the

[20]The ten volume set of Poe, edited by Stedman and Woodberry, sold very slowly, as we have noted elsewhere. The advance payments on account of royalty had been made promptly on publication, at least to E. C. Stedman, who in a letter to H. I. Kimball, March 27, 1895, acknowledged the receipt of two hundred and fifty dollars as a last installment in this advance payment.
[21]Hamlin Garland, "Literary Notes," Unpublished Manuscript, 1897, p. 17.
[22]See *Publishers' Weekly*, October 30, November 6, November 30, 1897, Vol. LII, pp. 701, 733, 777, 807.
[23]In "How Goodspeed's Began," Foreword to *Catalogue 250* of Goodspeed's Book Shop, Incorporated (Boston, 1935), pp. ii-iii; and again in *Yankee Bookseller; Being the Reminiscences of Charles E. Goodspeed* (Boston: Houghton Mifflin Company, 1937), pp. 18-19.

dispersal of Stone & Kimball was not altogether an ill wind. Besides this incidental encouragement to two good booksellers, the list of Herbert S. Stone & Company was consolidated and strengthened,[24] and Kimball himself made a prompt success with The Cheltenham Press.

The Cheltenham Press, actually an office for the design of printed advertising, and still doing business on Fifth Avenue, was started by Kimball in the house in Greenwich Village which he then shared with Mitchell Kennerley. This was one of the earliest, if not the first, of our contemporary firms of advertising typographers. Many original advertising ideas came from this shop, Kimball always demanding a free hand, as in the case of the first Rogers Peet newspaper advertisements, whose style is followed today. The products of advertising are ephemeral, however, and Ingalls Kimball is remembered as a book typographer for the design of the Stone & Kimball books of 1896 and 1897, of the *King Edward Prayer Book,* and of several charming pamphlets by his friend Bliss Carman, Robert Louis Stevenson and others, issued privately from the Cheltenham Press between 1897 and 1917, when Kimball left the organization.

The name "Cheltenham" will live on for generations in the supreme advertising typeface "Cheltenham Old Style," which was designed in 1900 and 1901. Mr. Alan H. Gamble of the present Cheltenham Press Staff, has given the most exact information on its production, in a letter printed in the January 1937 issue of the periodical PM:

I came to the The Cheltenham Press in 1900, when Cheltenham type came into being and I saw all of the various stages of its development.

A fact, which does not seem to be generally known, is that Cheltenham Old Style was originally designed as a Linotype face.

Ingalls Kimball, the head of The Cheltenham Press, was definitely commissioned by Mr. Phillip T. Dodge of the Mergenthaler

---

[24]Herbert S. Stone & Company also acquired from the first consignees, the Poe edition and *The Damnation of Theron Ware,* and may be considered virtual successors to the business of Stone & Kimball.

Linotype Company to design a book face for the Linotype which would have great legibility and which also would set considerably closer than any other Linotype face.

Mr. Kimball, in accepting this commission, retained the Foundry production rights and after the design was completed, because of new principles involved, secured patent rights.

The right to produce Cheltenham Old Style in the United States was sold by Mr. Kimball to the American Type Founders Company and they produced the face several years in advance of the Mergenthaler Linotype Company.

I well remember the first specimen sheet which came to us in 1902 from the American Type Founders Company—eleven point body was the only size shown on the sheet.

When the Mergenthaler Linotype Company produced the type, we prepared for them an explanatory pamphlet entitled: "The Designing of This Face of Type"—which set forth the principles involved upon which patent rights were secured. As far as I can find out the only copy extant is in the New York Public Library.

Your article fails to mention the part that Bertram Grosvenor Goodhue, the well known architect, had in the production of Cheltenham type.

Mr. Kimball could not draw, so it was a natural sequence for him to turn to Mr. Goodhue, his friend of long standing, to make the working drawings of the various characters in Cheltenham Old Style.

The fact that Mr. Goodhue did make the actual drawings has led many to believe, erroneously, that he was the designer.

Kimball had in Chicago impressed a future great printer—Frederic W. Goudy. In New York he became an intimate of Walter Gilliss, craftsman extraordinary. It is little known, as another communication to PM (July 1936) discloses, that Ingalls Kimball was actually associated with the Gilliss Press. Mr. James A. Anderson writes of the Gilliss Press at the turn of the century:

Interesting people came and went—artists, authors, book-collectors, editors, publishers; the list is a long one, with many well-known names. Ingalls Kimball was one, a slim young man with a shock of curly hair, and a flair for shocking people. At college he and his friend Herbert Stone had started a successful publishing business. Stone went back to Chicago, and became an important book publisher. Kimball settled in New York, and founded the Cheltenham Press. With his friend the architect Goodhue he designed Cheltenham Old Style type—one of the high spots in type history.

He carried on an enormously successful advertising business. He was chock full of ideas, good ones, new ones, money-making ones; he could afford to make the first item of every estimate: $50 for his own fee. He dealt in ideas, and had a staff of competent artists, but his "Press" was only a few cases of type. He gave out the presswork and much of the composition to other printers; the more difficult bits were apt to go to Walter Gilliss, who had printed his first catalogue. A strong friendship sprang up between the two men, and for a while Kimball was Vice-President of the Gilliss Press; on his resignation the present writer took that place.

What Ingalls Kimball always felt his most important work, was yet to be accomplished when he left printing in April 1917 to become President of the National Thrift Bond Corporation. Here, in a field far removed from his twenty-five years in publishing and typography, Kimball invented the "baby bond," as a means of investment for low-income groups. His oldest sister and his brother-in-law, Mr. and Mrs. W. B. Covell have informed the present writer in letters and in conversation, that "Mr. Kimball felt the Thrift Bond was his best work, and was greatly disappointed when he had to give the name &c. up to the government at the time of the war. He felt, that while it helped the government at that time, it would have helped the people for all times."

It was a natural step from Mr. Kimball's work providing investment facilities for wage-earners to then consider the insurance problems of the same groups. After Ingalls Kimball joined the Metropolitan Life Insurance Company in 1921, he became their first Director of Group Annuities. The librarians who organized the American Library Association group annuity plan, for instance, consulted with Mr. Kimball.[25] At

[25]Information received December 1938 from Mr. Keyes D. Metcalf, present Director of Harvard College Library.

the time of his death (October 16, 1933, at Mt. McGregor, New York, after an illness of several months), Ingalls Kimball was recognized as an outstanding authority on industrial pension plans, through his work and the many articles which he wrote on this and allied subjects in his later years. Earlier he had contributed extensively to newspapers and magazines on his business of printing and on his hobby of collecting sporting prints. In 1908 he compiled an interesting account of *The First Ten Years of the Cheltenham Press;* wrote after the war a small volume on *Thrift in France* (New York: "La France," 1919); and later edited, with a memoir, The Grolier Club publication, *Book Decorations by Bertram Grosvenor Goodhue.*

Memorials to Ingalls Kimball were printed in the insurance magazines, the printing and publishing trades journals and in his Harvard Class Book. Perhaps the best brief memoir was written by a friend of forty years standing, Royal Cortissoz, in the editorial columns of the New York *Herald Tribune* for October 18, 1933.

It is sometimes given to a man to embark in his youth upon a joyous adventure with only tentative ideas as to his goal and yet presently to make an enduring mark. This was the fortune of Ingalls Kimball, who, while still at Harvard in the early '90's, developed a passion for the fashioning of good books. When, with his Classmate, he founded the firm of Stone & Kimball, and started publishing, they had between them a vast store of ambition and enthusiasm. Out of it came volumes admirably illustrating the passion aforementioned. But from it there flowed also an influence at which they could have hardly guessed.

Kimball's conception of the making of a good book embraced a resolution to know how as to the last practical detail. He made himself a master of typography and *format,* a designer who had knowledge as well as taste. He could give a collection of poems the proper investiture, and he could devise the dress that The New Republic still wears. His repute rests perhaps most conspicuously upon his contribution of the Cheltenham font to the American press, but it really had broader foundations. Foremost among them was just his feeling for beauty, and the important point here was his application of it to the trade book. There was nothing 'precious' about Kimball's art. He had none of the foibles which so often handicap the production of the book printed at 'a private press.' Stone & Kimball's books, well printed in graceful type on excellent paper, lightly touched in design, agreeable to look at and to handle, were made to be sold at a reasonable price—and to be read. They remain to this day so many charming memorials to an enlightened ideal.

It is hard to part with 'Kim,' as his friends loved to call him. Possessed of great energy, gay, witty, altogether endearing, he filled a niche that was peculiarly his own, and to which it was inspiriting for those who knew him to repair. He turned from the printing press to finance. He immersed himself in the dry science of economics. But 'Kim' was never dry. He was always sensitive, ebullient, vital, the very soul of happy companionship. To lose him is to lose a comrade who veritably made the world about him brighter and sweeter.

FIG. 5. *Harold Frederic*
*From the original pen drawing (9¼ x 6¾ inches), by Fred Richardson;
printed April 15, 1896 in* The Chap-Book, *in greater reduction*

FIG. 6. *Offices of Herbert S. Stone & Company*
Drawing by Frank Hazenplug

CHAPTER IV

Herbert S. Stone & Company

CHICAGO AND NEW YORK

1896-1900: A BALANCED BOOKLIST

IN THE BREAK WITH Ingalls Kimball of April 1896, Herbert Stone was left only *The Chap-Book,* Harrison Rhodes remaining in Chicago as assistant editor. The London agent, Robert McClure, also remained affiliated with Stone, who before the end of the year had a booklist of seventeen titles. The first books published by Herbert S. Stone & Company, came from *Chap-Book* authors—Richard Le Gallienne, *Prose Fancies: Second Series;* Arthur Morrison, *A Child of the Jago;* F. Frankfort Moore, *The Jessamy Bride;* Maria Louise Pool, *In Buncombe County;* Alice Morse Earle, *Curious Punishments of Bygone Days,* illustrated in woodcut style by the staff artist, Frank Hazenplug; *Essays from the Chap-Book,* and a like collection of *Stories,* with title-pages lettered by Claude Bragdon and pictorial bindings by A. E. Borie and Bragdon. The most important American and foreign books included on this first list were, respectively: *The Land of the Castanet,* travel sketches by H. C. Chatfield-Taylor; and Gabriele D'Annunzio's *Episcopo & Company,* his first appearance in English translation. The translator, Myrta Leonora Jones of New York, had, as the bibliographical entry indicates, a hard time finding a taker for the manuscript, and the published edition was reviewed as "sickly twaddle" and "a horrible tale, fortunately short."

Herbert Stone and Harrison Rhodes never rejected a manuscript because it was "too realistic," and concerned themselves only with the artistic intention and literary values of the manuscripts submitted. They had published, for instance, Hamlin Garland's studies of the effects of economic stress on Mid-Western farmers, and Harold Frederic's novel of the decay of religious faith in up-State New York. In general, it may be said that the documentation of American rural life had been proceeding for several decades in American magazines and books. In the nineties we began to have local-colorists of the city, reporters and columnists for metropolitan dailies, whose work, while not always specifically humorous in intent, was usually taken lightly by the great public.[1] One may mention Richard Harding Davis's "Gallegher" and "Van Bibber" stories, published respectively as books by Scribner's in 1891 and Harper's in 1892, and Edward W. Townsend's "Chimmie Fadden," also reprinted from New York papers and distributed by Dodd, Mead & Company. Stone published *Checkers* by Henry M. Blossom and *One Forty Two* by Henry M. Hyde, and beginning in 1896, issued the masterpieces in this genre of George Ade, whose "Stories of the Streets and the Town" had been appearing regularly since 1890 in the Chicago *Record,* usually illustrated by his fellow Hoosier, John T. McCutcheon. Herbert Stone suggested that Ade make a volume of these sketches, and Ade's first book, *Artie,* reprinted with revisions, from his newspaper columns, and with the accompanying drawings, was published in September 1896. Mr. Ade's intent was to be a realist, an observer, a recorder of the slang and the manners of the common man of the big city. His columns and the first volumes compiled from them (*Artie,* 1896, *Pink Marsh,* 1897, *Doc' Horne,*

[1] Fred Lewis Pattee, "The New Journalism," *The New American Literature* (New York: The Century Company [1930]), pp. 57-63.

1899) were welcomed as satire by thousands of readers, and as something "incomparable" by a few (see Mark Twain's letter to William Dean Howells concerning *Pink Marsh,* under the bibliographical entry). Mr. Ade was only labelled a 'funny man' when with *Fables in Slang,* published as a book late in 1899, but dated 1900, he happened to use capital letters to drive home his modern use of the ancient fable form.

Most of the books published by Stone in 1896 and the three succeeding years exhibit special care in their typography, presswork, paper and binding. It is noteworthy that the most attractive books designed either by Herbert Stone or Ingalls Kimball were done when they were running separate firms—doubtless there was a rivalry between them in this matter which has left us with several dozen of the most attractive trade editions ever published in America. The Stone list, in its emphasis on typography and belles-lettres, was started on the same basis as the original Stone & Kimball. Perhaps there was a greater flavoring of English writers, whom Stone met on their home ground in 1895, 1897 and 1898, and a little less from continental authors, whom he did not meet. We have already observed, in the story of *The Chap-Book,* how the interest in French letters died down. The Maeterlinck and Ibsen plays held by Stone & Kimball were again acquired by Stone in October 1897, but M. Maeterlinck's favored English translator, the American poet Richard Hovey,[2] died in 1900, when "the Belgian Shakespeare" had added only one more work to his roster of poetic

[2]One of the earliest projects of Stone & Kimball was the publication of Maeterlinck in translation. A letter of Herbert Stone's, dateable about March 20, 1893, says: "We are thinking of publishing another book—a translation of a French play by Maurice Maeterlinck but nothing decisive has been done thus far." Presumably they had been discussing the matter with Richard Hovey, who translated four plays of his friend Maeterlinck and furnished an essay on "Modern Symbolism and Maurice Maeterlinck" for the second issue in "The Green Tree Library," 1894. Herbert Stone's copy of this edition (sold at auction in 1918) had an inserted note by the author: "I hereby certify that this translation of my works is the only one authorized by me for America. 1895. Maurice Maeterlinck." Maeterlinck contributed a preface (in French) to the second series of plays translated by Hovey, published in 1896, which included with three others, *Pelléas and Mélisande.*

dramas.[3] Ibsen wrote only one more book before his death in 1906, *When We Dead Awaken,* published in "The Green Tree Library" during 1900.

The mantle of Ibsen as dramatist of ideas fell on George Bernard Shaw[4] and the first American publisher of Shaw's plays was Herbert Stone of Chicago. Before going on to discuss the arrangement of 1897, by which Stone published between 1896 and 1901 Shaw's first three volumes of plays, two novels, and a volume of criticism, one must remark that it was from Chicago that Shaw conquered America. In 1896, *The Chap-Book* published Clarence Rook's interview, introducing Shaw as a personality to America. The first American performances (often private or amateur) of Shaw's plays were, before the advent of The Theatre Guild, as often given in Chicago as in New York. *Arms and the Man* (1894), *The Devil's Disciple* (1897), and *How He Lied to Her Husband* (1903) were seen first in New York,[5] but more important works, such as *Candida* (1899) and *Caesar and Cleopatra* (1901), were given their first American performances by the pupils of Miss Anna Morgan.[6] Herbert S. Stone & Company, in the years they published Shaw, were also his agents for authorization of performances; Miss Morgan had to apply to them for permission to give the two plays just mentioned;

[3]*Aglaviene et Selysette* (Paris: Mercure de France, 1896); See Francis Ambrière, "Essai de Bibliographie," in Auguste Bailly, *Maeterlinck* (Paris: Firmin-Didot, 1931), p. 198.

[4]"*The Quintescence of Ibsenism* (1891) is Shaw's masterpiece in the field of literary criticism. . . .
    In Ibsen, Shaw recognized a kindred spirit. . . .
    To Ibsen, 'The ideal is dead; long live the ideal!' epitomizes the history of human progress. . . .
    When Shaw began his work on *The Saturday Review* he was the author of four plays, three of them strongly influenced by Ibsen. . . . The literary side of the mission of Ibsen in England he felt, was the rescue of that unhappy country from its centuries of slavery to Shakespeare. The moral side of Ibsen's mission was the breaking of the shackles of slavery to conventional ideas of virtue. Shaw's iconoclastic slogan in *The Saturday Review* was 'Down with Shakespeare. Great is Ibsen; and Shaw is his prophet.'"—Archibald Henderson, "The Drama Critic," *Bernard Shaw: Playboy and Prophet* (New York: D. Appleton and Company, 1932), pp. 312-14.

[5]C. L. and V. N. Broad, *Dictionary to the Plays and Novels of Bernard Shaw* (New York: Macmillan and Company, 1929), p. 210.

[6]Archibald Henderson, "The Shavian Movement in America," *Bernard Shaw: Playboy and Prophet* (New York: D. Appleton and Company, 1932), pp. 397-98.

likewise Hart Conway in presenting for the first time in America (1903) Shaw's *You Never Can Tell*.

Not least important, it was in Chicago in 1903 that Archibald Henderson decided that a lifetime spent propagandizing for Shaw might be as valuable as one spent teaching the higher mathematics, as the first paragraphs in his definitive work on Shaw inform us:

> More than a quarter of a century ago, when I was doing research work in mathematics at the University of Chicago, a friend of mine, Maude Miner, a gifted teacher of expression, urged me with great enthusiasm to attend a performance of a hilarious comedy, *You Never Can Tell*. It was by a virtually unknown author, one Bernard Shaw. The play was presented by the amateurs of the Hart Conway School of Acting. At this time, Shaw was not wholly unknown in the United States, for his novel, *Love Among the Artists,* published by H. S. Stone in Chicago, had found a small number of mildly interested, but rather mystified readers; and Richard Mansfield had produced and taken into his repertory, with some success, "the anti-romantic" comedy, *Arms and the Man,* and had subsequently taken New York by storm in *The Devil's Disciple,* thereby enabling Shaw to retire from journalism and settle down as an established playwright and (incidentally) as a prosperously married man.
>
> When the curtain rose...I felt immediately electrified, as though immersed in a bath of cosmic rays which at that time had been discovered, not by the scientists, but by Bernard Shaw alone...
>
> After a year's reading of Shaw's own writings, and the gathering of such little information as was obtainable about the man himself, I arrived at the momentous decision to make known to the world my "discovery" of a neglected genius!

Stone's relations with Shaw seemed perfectly happy between 1898 and 1903. Certainly they were started well in England under the bland guidance of Shaw's young publisher, Grant Richards. In his words:

> To return to Shaw. There was a new firm in Chicago—Stone and Kimball—who were more forward-looking and who had keener insight into reality and a surer hand on what was happening in the

art of letters than almost any of their older rivals. Kimball I never met. (Herbert Stone was a man whom to know was to like, a fellow of infinite charm.) He loved books; he loved life. In later years Elliot Holt reminded me of him. A young man, he threw himself into publishing with zest, and he had no small share in founding the tradition which has made the comely American book today as fine as anything that is produced in this country or on the Continent. Herbert Stone was over here in that 1897; he read Bernard Shaw, and he succumbed. Shaw wrote to me on August 7 from the Argoed, Penallt, Monmouth, that "before leaving town" he had "applied" his "mind to business for a day. Among other matters I considered our American project; and I came to the conclusion that Stone and Kimball's offer is good enough as such business goes. If you like to close with them without looking any further do so. S. and K. are as keen as any Americans on my work: we shall do no better with Putnam, as far as I can judge." So Herbert Stone's firm was to introduce Shaw to the United States. The arrangement lasted for a few years; but the upshot bore out Shaw's cheerful habit of predicting bankruptcy for any publisher rash enough to put him on his list. The Stone firm crashed;[7] and their Shavian successors persisted in pursuing Shaw's claims in a Jarndyce lawsuit in which the assets were entirely swallowed up by the costs.[8]

After recounting the amount of work required from printer and publisher over the proofs of *Plays Pleasant and Unpleasant,* by Shaw's fierce enforcement of the typographic rules he had learned from William Morris, Grant Richards quotes *in extenso* the letter in which Shaw finally decided to let his books go to the firm which he still thought of as Stone & Kimball. The letter is reprinted by permission of Mr. Shaw, who adds: "All I remember of this business is that there was a long lawsuit which Brentanos won. Presumably Stone had to pay the costs. Anyhow it cost me nothing."

[7]Richards here confuses the passing of Stone & Kimball in 1897 with the sale of Herbert S. Stone & Company, a solvent firm in 1906, to Fox, Duffield & Company.
[8]Grant Richards, *Author Hunting* (New York: Coward-McCann, Inc., 1934), pp. 127-28. The printed text has a footnote expressing the author's surprise (as of 1934) in finding Putnam mentioned as a possible publisher for Shaw; the paragraph preceding the one quoted above, refers to Richards' difficulties in finding the first American publisher for Shaw's plays, and to later English experiences which finally led Shaw to hire publishers on commission. On the "Jarndyce lawsuit," see p. 136.

The Argoed, Penallt, Monmouth
28th August 1897

This letter of yours comes well, Grant Richards, from a man who has been bounding idly up the Jungfrau and down the Matterhorn to an exhausted wretch who, after a crushing season, has slaved these four weeks for four hours a day at your confounded enterprise. I have sent three plays to the printer, transmogrified beyond recognition, made more thrilling than any novel; and he has only sent me proofs of one, of which it has cost me endless letters and revises to get the page right, to teach him how to space letters for emphasis, and how to realise that I mean my punctuation to be followed.

I had no idea of the magnitude of the job. Anything like a holiday is out of the question for me. Must I endure in addition the insults of a publisher for whom I am preparing, with unheard-of toil, a gigantic Triumph? Read *Mrs. Warren;* and then blush for your impatience if you can.

Stone and Kimball's offer, as described to me in your letter of the 9th Apl. (doubtless negligently and lazily composed before going up the river) mentioned neither the price nor the royalty after 10,000 copies. The latter I assume to be 20%; the former not less than 75 cents at least. A princely affluence will accrue to S. & K. on these terms; but I desire to make the fortune of one American publisher in order that I may spend the rest of my life in plundering all the others!

Shall I draw them an agreement? If they prefer to do it themselves, warn them that I wont assign copyright, but simply give them exclusive leave to publish in the U. S. for 5 years.

yrs, overworked to madness
G. Bernard Shaw

The last paragraph of the letter contains the joker[9] in the contract which was the basis for Shaw's suit, in 1906, to recover the American copyright of his books from Fox, Duffield & Company—but that is part of the aftermath, and the

---

[9] Such a clause as license to print for only five years is rare in American publishing. Even in England in the nineties, limitations in time on a publisher's license to print (under royalty agreement) other than for the legal length of copyright, were not common. Such limiting clauses in contracts are nowhere mentioned in Stanley Unwin's *The Truth About Publishing* (Boston and New York: The Houghton Mifflin Company, 1927). See especially in contradiction, Chap. IV, "Agreements," p. 70.

present history of Herbert S. Stone & Company has not yet reached the high tide.

In 1897, besides contracting for the books of Shaw (the first of which, the two volumes of *Plays Pleasant and Unpleasant,* were not published until April 18, 1898), Herbert Stone also became the publisher of the works of the American mental and physical hygienist, Horace Fletcher. There is a concise account of Fletcher's varied career by George Harvey Genzmer, in the *Dictionary of American Biography:* "In 1895 ... a life-insurance company declined to accept him as a risk, and Fletcher realized suddenly that he was fifty pounds overweight, harrowed by indigestion, and subject to frequent illness. He tried several cures without result, consoled himself with the New Thought, and—imbued with the American business man's idea of 'service'—wrote two books, *Menticulture, or The A-B-C of True Living* (1895) and *Happiness as Found in Forethought Minus Fearthought* (1897), to spread his gospel of health and happiness. Traces of the New Thought stuck to his doctrines until the last, but his recovery of his normal exuberant good health he attributed to the simple procedure of chewing his food thoroughly. . . . He himself was one of the best-natured and least fanatical of reformers; he enjoyed the good things of life and was publicly seen taking second helpings of turkey. . . . In America 'Fletcherism' and 'fletcherize' became current words. . . . Though his doctrines were not new or entirely true, his work and influence were on the whole beneficial. . . . During the War of 1914-18 he engaged in welfare work in Belgium, teaching the refugees to make the most of their scant rations. He died of bronchitis in Copenhagen (1918) worn out by his zeal for the welfare of others." On October 2, 1897, Herbert S. Stone & Company published uniformly bound in pea-green cloth as "The Menticulture Series," Fletcher's first two books on nutrition. Others were published in 1898 and 1899, with such startling titles as *What Sense? or Economic Nutrition* and *Glutton or Epicure?*

Horace Fletcher was a good friend of the firm, sending from his travels greetings like the following:

Gruss aus Weimar!   Eisenach Jany 30th 1898
To MESSRS HERBERT S. STONE & CO.
1030 Caxton Building
Chicago, Ill., U.S.A.
Dear Friends:

  Just received your letter of Jany 15th forwarded from Wiesbaden and am much pleased of course to hear of good prospects for "Men"—You can be assured that if Menticulture becomes a fad it will become a fact as it is natural Christianity and must grow. With a suitable preface "Happiness" will lead in the end and do more solid good. The letters I have recd.

                                           Sincerely yours
                                           H. F.

Did you see R. M. F.'s notice in "Lights and Shadows" column of Jany 8th?

  Some other American books of the year 1897 were George Ade's *Pink Marsh,* Clyde Fitch's *Smart Set,* and a satirical romance of young life in Greenwich village, titled *Phyllis in Bohemia,* with fitting illustrations in sepia tints by Orson Lowell, and a charming binding by Frank Hazenplug. The authors are given as L. H. Bickford and Richard Stillman Powell. The former was a real person and a Denver newspaperman; the latter was a pseudonym for Ralph Henry Barbour, since renowned as the author of books for boys. British books published in 1897 by Stone included: *Maude: Prose & Verse,* a piece of juvenilia by Christina Rossetti, posthumously published with an introduction by her brother William; *Flames,* the first of several novels from Robert Hichens; *One Man's View,* by Leonard Merrick; Charles Benham's romance, *The Fourth Napoleon;* and *What Maisie Knew,* on an English theme by Henry James.

  A long awaited event came to pass in July 1897 when Melville Edwin Stone Jr., directly on his graduation from Harvard, entered the firm as junior partner. One would think from the manuscript evidence that, as in the case of his brother, the younger Stone was never in perplexity over the choice of a career. At eighteen he had participated in Herbert's first adventure as an author and publisher in 1892, and a place in the firm had been reserved for 'Ned' as early as 1894. He spent his summer vacations while in college 'on the road' for Herbert S. Stone & Company, and on April 13, 1897 'Herb' wrote 'Ned' a long letter concerning their common plans for Herbert S. Stone & Company. Yet we are informed by his sister Elizabeth, younger by five years, that her brother Melville had planned to enter medical school and that during the summer of 1897 he was persuaded by father and brother that he was needed in the book business.

'Ned' Stone brought to Herbert S. Stone & Company something of the youthful insouciance and taste for exaggeration which Ingalls Kimball gave to Stone & Kimball. Stone was one of the most popular and active men in his Harvard Class of '97. He was an editor of *Crimson;* a contributor to *Advocate* and *Monthly;* a member of D.K.E., Zeta Psi, Signet, O.K. and Institute of 1770. He was President of the Hasty Pudding Club and wrote the play for 1897, *The Flying Dutchman,* which had music by John Alden Carpenter. The two collaborated again in 1900, on the operetta *The Little Dutch Girl,* produced at the Potter Palmer home by Herbert Stone, who designed the settings and costumes. Of other Chicago productions, Anna Morgan wrote: "We had several notable burlesque performances on my stage, largely under the management of Melville E. Stone, Jr. One was given on Saturday evening, May 23, 1903. The program announced that 'the unparalleled Stock Company of The Little Room will appear for the first, last and only time in an unparalleled etcetera performance of "Little Room," a moral play done in moral English from the mediaeval, that is, out of respect to twentieth century conventions.' The actors were Franklin H. Head, Chatfield-Taylor, Ralph Clarkson, Melville E. Stone

Jr., Wallace Rice, Hugh Garden, William Morton Payne, Karleton Hackett, Lucy Monroe and Marjorie Benton Cook. A note on the program stated that after the performance an attempt would be made to restore the appetites of such of the audience as had remained in Mr. Clarkson's studio to which was added the admonition 'Eat and drink, for tomorrow we may not feel like it.' "

The stage was one of the younger Stone's abiding interests. Like Herbert and their father, his acquaintance with playwrights and actors was wide—Clyde Fitch, Francis Wilson, the Otis Skinners, the Hernes, the Barrymores, Cissie Loftus —were close friends with one or another of the Stones. 'Ned' was not permitted the time to write his history of the American stage, but collected important materials, such as playbills, which he left to Harvard College Library. He drew royalties, he wrote for a Class Report, "as part author of two plays, *Brewster's Millions* and *Graustark*." The Class Book article written about him by Carl Hovey, is far and away the best biography, and with permission, is quoted here:

Any one who knew Ned Stone will feel disappointed by any ordinary treatment of his life. Ned lived through his imagination to such an extent that he deserves to be portrayed through the medium of art rather than by setting down what are commonly called cold facts. His life would have furnished a subject for George Meredith, Barrie, Locke, or Galsworthy; in fact, for any of the finer novelists who give us, as no one else can, portraits of extraordinary human beings. Even as a boy in college, as a Freshman, Ned was altogether out of the usual. He must have impressed himself upon each of his classmates differently. I can only give my own impression which was that he stood apart from the crude world of warm personal ambitions, acid antagonisms, and far from humorous judgments which make up at all times so much of undergraduate psychology. Ned was a perfectly poised—I had almost said perfectly dressed—person; for he looked like a gentleman of leisure, always ready to go anywhere or enter any company; he had wit and sympathy, of which few of the rest of us had developed the smallest amount at that stage, and he understood very well what was going on in the world outside. Along with this social equipment, there constantly flowed in him a natural spring of human sympathy. The special way that Ned felt his relationships with others was just another proof of his unusualness. He was not thinking of what he could get out of others, nor so much of what he could tell them, although he did like to set them right when he saw the chance, because he hated to see any of his convictions as to the way things should be done violated; but he was genuinely interested in their points of view, in what kind of men or boys they were and where they got off. Ned loved to size-up people even in those days, to place them, and to know them. I might have said simply that he was friendly. It may sound like little, but friendliness when it is extended to people you barely know is really one of the rarest traits, as it is one of the most lovable. Perhaps it was Ned's friendliness which made him so much loved.

I did not have any sort of daily contact with Ned in college, only knew him enough to feel, as so many others did, that he was there and that he made the place different by being there. I mean he made the place more friendly, more interesting, because his viewpoint was not the every-day, undergraduate viewpoint. Some years later I went to work for him on the staff of the *Metropolitan Magazine*, which he controlled, and from that time on until he went to California, I saw him under all kinds of circumstances, in situations which brought out his humorous and clever side, and in various trials, some of which were of a severe sort. It seemed to me then that he was precisely the same Ned Stone that he had been in college. Nothing had changed him, nothing had been added to him. He started out in his youth full-fledged, with a personality very strongly developed, and he remained to the end a personality that aroused interest and inspired love and admiration as in the early days in college. In a sense he stood still. Ned did not, it seems to me, develop and advance to the point where, in a professional or business way, he made that impression on the world which his personality entitled him to make. I think this was because he was very fine. He always seemed more interested in having things done right and in accordance with his feeling of what was fine than in advancing his own position. As the publisher of a popular magazine he was effective in one way and ineffective in another. He was more than effective, he was gifted and wise, and superbly able in his choice of stories that had a sure human appeal, that displayed, moreover, the working of a vigorous talent. In this respect he followed no rule, played no favorites, was little influenced by what other people thought. But when it came to constructive operations, to the publishing of serious articles, he was often the Quixotic idealist. We undertook at one time a Gargantuan series to cure poverty. Just that. We were by publishing magazine articles to put an end to poverty in the whole world. Ned was very keen about this. Yet if any other magazine publisher had undertaken it in the way he did, I can fancy the witty things Ned would have said at his expense. I always remember his smile when I showed him a copy of a paper that was put out on the largest scale under the name of *Ridgeway's Weekly*. It had for a motto in large type "For God and Country." I must say I was a bit impressed by such a high-sounding slogan. Ned was sitting at his desk, without his coat and with his sleeves rolled up, the way he always sat; he smiled his delightful smile and remarked, "Sort of a boola-boola motto, isn't it? Let's make it 'For God and Country and Ten Cents.'" But he didn't see anything funny in our own fatuous attempt to cure poverty by writing articles about it. At another time he went after Roosevelt in a vain attempt to stand that gentleman on his head. We printed a lot of articles, under the title, "Mr. Roosevelt, Please Answer." In these articles, which Ned got up himself, were asked all the damning questions which a cool and decidedly hostile critic could ask of a public character who was in the habit of cutting sharp corners whenever he thought it was time to do so. The only point about the series (which did not get anywhere) that is worth making is that it showed Ned's predilection for trying to set things straight and in accordance with his convictions as to how people should act. Later on this passion for reform found a much fuller and freer expression during the war when, as Mr. LaFarge writes from Altadena, Ned used up far more personal energy than he could spare in pleading the case of disabled soldiers and in attacking those who did not have the loyal feelings about the war. It is sad to think how he exhausted himself, how he could never bear to spare himself once he got started. His capacity for forgetting his own physical weakness—I mean the weakness produced by the disease which eventually caused his death—was shown after his brother Herbert was drowned on the *Lusitania*. I remember seeing Ned at the Harvard Club in New York while he was struggling with the difficulties of settling his brother's estate. He looked terribly ill; his face was almost gray instead of being a natural color; but he never mentioned himself, only talked about the war and about the things he had to do to straighten out his brother's affairs.

I have been led to write about Ned as a publisher because that is the way I knew him best. In everything he did there was something which revealed his personal character, so perhaps this part of his life will serve as well as another. And I must not forget to mention, in this connection, one of the things which gave him the keenest pleasure. This was to score a magazine beat, comparable in effect with a news-gathering beat in the daily field. His mind was always working on the possibility of getting ahead of all his fellow publishers by some clever piece of foresight and vision. I think his best talents lay right in this direction. In proof of it is the story which the *Metropolitan* published exposing Dr. Cook at the very time when Dr. Cook was being treated as a hero by Europe and America, having wreaths draped about his willing neck by—I think it was—the Danes, as a reward for discovering the North Pole. Ned began to pooh-pooh the whole affair. He said Cook was a faker, that he never went to the Pole, and that he was going to prove it. He had the boldness to print an article denouncing Dr. Cook as a faker and to do this simply on the strength of a set of calculations which proved that, taking Dr. Cook's own story, he could not possibly have made the journey in the way he said he made it. To publish that story took first-class nerve. At the time the article was sent to press not a word of suspicion had crept into the newspapers. Before the magazine could be brought out with it, the exposure of Dr. Cook did begin in other quarters, but that doesn't in the least lessen the courage with which Ned carried through his attack. Ned's nerve was equal to anything, as I know from having seen him deal with angry creditors at times when the magazine was short of funds. When Ned took the *Metropolitan* it was in a low state. He began to build it up, but it cost money to do so. When he didn't have the money, he went ahead just the same, and I can still see the president of the paper company coming into Ned's office prepared to close down the whole works unless he instantly received a check for thirty or forty thousand dollars. It seemed to make no difference to Ned that, instead of having thirty or forty thousand, he was overdrawn at the bank. That is to say, he received his visitor in the pleasantest fashion, offered him a cigarette out of a beautiful cigarette-case, and proceeded to charm him in a perfectly natural manner until the man was quite willing to let Ned take his own time about the payment. Nevertheless, one doesn't carry on under such difficulties without personal strain, and I am sure Ned paid the price; the carrying out of a large undertaking with inadequate financial backing was undoubtedly one of the causes to be counted in Ned's physical breakdown. But was he ever anything but cheerful? He was more than cheerful; he was delightful. I am sure that he enjoyed life, too, all through this period and in his own special way. The life of the theaters and restaurants, the romances that were always just around the corner in a city like New York, were a constant fascination to Ned's temperament. He never forgot to be keenly interested in people. There is no interest, perhaps, which yields such a steady enjoyment.

After he gave up the magazine because of his ill health, Ned went to live at Mt. Kisco in a charming house which he rented from John Hunt, '96. I often used to see him out there reading, strolling about through the woods, or sitting in the sunshine and getting fat. "This kind of fat is no good," he used to say, "but I have to put it on." Also he slept out of doors constantly, and said one day, "I always hated it, and now I find that the medical profession thinks that cold-air sleeping for my trouble isn't the thing, so I shall be the last man who ever did it."

A summary of Ned Stone's life from A. A. Sprague reads as follows:

"Melville Edwin Stone, Jr., was born in Chicago, Ill., Nov. 3, 1874, and prepared for college, after his early schooling in Chicago, at Phillips Academy, Andover, Mass. He received the degree A.B. from Harvard after having been in college 1893 to 1897. He married, Oct. 27, 1900, in Chicago, Lucretia Hosmer, who died Aug. 3, 1901.

"After his graduation Ned lived in Chicago, until the beginning of 1906, when he moved to New York City. During this time he had been a partner in the book publishing firm of Herbert S. Stone & Co., and was actively engaged in the business. His wife died in 1901, less than a year after their marriage. After moving to New York he remained in the publishing business, first as general manager of the *Associated Sunday Magazines,* and later as president of the Metropolitan Magazine Company, and editor of the *Metropolitan,* a monthly magazine. This latter work he was compelled to abandon during the summer of 1911, on account of ill health— lung trouble having developed. He spent six months in the Adirondacks and improved to such an extent that he was allowed to go to Bedford Hills, New York. There he devoted his time to writing. Ned had written many articles for magazines and was part author of two plays, "Brewster's Millions," and "Graustark," from which he drew royalties. From 1911 to 1915 he did little beyond attempting to get well, with many ups and downs.

"In the spring of 1915 he felt he had regained his strength and health, and was on the point of getting back to work, when a relapse put him back to where he had been four years before, and again his cheerful, patient pursuit of health. During this time he had been living in Switzerland, Arizona, and California.

"Nobody knew Ned Stone except to love him, and the longer the friendship, the deeper the affection. He always did his part, and frequently more than his part, and he is sadly missed at every reunion."

Mr. LaFarge, who lived near Ned at Altadena, Cal., writes about him in a way to show that up to the last minute of his life Ned was perfectly unflagging, both in his efforts to stir up the public mind and in his enjoyment of talk and leisure. He looked and felt well—he was the same Ned Stone in all the essentials that we used to meet in the Yard in the old days of the class of ninety-seven—they used to talk late into the gentle California night, with plenty of Scotch and cigars ready at a side table for the guest, and all went on pleasantly and sociably until without any warning life ended for Ned.

C. H.

The part Melville E. Stone Jr. played in his brother's publishing enterprises is not as clearly documented as his later work on the *Metropolitan Magazine;* his personal letters have not been preserved with the completeness of Herbert's; and no associate in the Chicago days has written a complete account of his work. From what Mrs. Calhoun, Miss Robie, Mr. Kirk and Mr. Dailey have told the writer, together with the references in his brother's letters, we can say that his energy and inventiveness were completely appreciated by the staff and by Herbert Stone.

The end of the year 1897, then, found Herbert S. Stone & Company established in Chicago and New York. A small office had been opened the preceding February, in the Constable building at Fifth Avenue and 18th Street. An aggressive new business manager was selling two magazines, thirty-six new book publications and forty-two older books selected from the stock of Stone & Kimball. And business was good, as Herbert Stone's letters make us understand, the only pressing liabilities being small sums owed British authors as royalties on books previously published by Stone & Kimball. "I am establishing relations with a lot of people whom the Kimball business alienated and I hope before long to get the debts over here all paid up ... Just now it is embarrassing to meet—at dinner—a man to whom you've owed £17 for over a year." (Herbert Stone's letter to his family from London, July 25, 1898.)

In the spring of 1898, the firm moved into new Chicago quarters at 11 Eldridge Court, recently a carriage house back of the old Willoughby residence on Michigan Avenue, but rebuilt and redecorated in such wise that the book-trade journal was able to say, "Judging from its counterfeit presentment, Herbert S. Stone & Co. may certainly be congratulated upon having one of the most artistic publishing houses in the United States, as well as upon being so blessed with the needful means that they can afford to educate the public, even by their office buildings, in such taste as will in time bring them sure reward." A drawing by Frank Hazenplug (Fig. 6) shows the exterior, but there remain no photographs of the interior, decorated by Eugene Klapp, first editor of *The House Beautiful*. The color scheme was red and black, with fireplaces everywhere. The offices had a charm remembered not only by those who worked there, but by the writers and artists who met there—to name a few—Wallace Rice, John T. McCutcheon and George Ade. Miss Virginia Robie writes: "The Eldridge Court building remodelled from a stable marked a new era in publishing houses. Enclosed by a high picket fence and further screened by a hedge of sunflowers, it made a bright spot of color in the changing world of Michigan Avenue, Wabash and Twelfth Street. Architecturally, it belonged to the gabled, turreted and steepled school popular in Chicago in the nineties and not unsightly, well covered with ivy and woodbine. Within were brick floors, deep yellow walls, dark green woodwork, a huge fireplace, built-in settles, and rows and rows of books. Vacant spaces were filled with the posters of Beardsley, Bradley and Penfield. On office walls hung signed sketches and rare autographs."

More than twice as many books (36) were published in this year as were issued in 1897 (16), but the number of magazines was reduced to one, with the departure of Harrison Rhodes and the passing of *The Chap-Book* in July 1898. *The House Beautiful,* now edited as well as published by Herbert Stone, made steady progress, but because of its field of specialization, was almost without influence on the Stone book-list. Several books were made up of articles previously printed in this magazine by "Oliver Coleman," pseudonym of Eugene Klapp: the first of these, *Successful Houses* appeared late in 1898. There were three juveniles, the handsomest being a book of *After-Supper Songs,* by Elizabeth Coolidge; three biographies; three volumes of critical essays, including Shaw's *Perfect Wagnerite;* his *Plays;* and *Some Verses* of Helen Hay (now Mrs. Payne Whitney). Two historical works were: an illustrated news account of the Spanish-American War and J. Holland Rose's substantial *Rise of Democracy,* in "The Victorian Era Series," which Stone began this year to import from Blackie & Son of Glasgow. A posthumous work of Sir Richard Burton's on *The Jew, The Gypsy and El Islam* was also imported, and *The New Economy,* by Laurence Gronlund, Danish-American socialist, was printed in Chicago. Stone published in 1899 one book each in the fields of hygiene, religion, and travel; also *Etiquette for Americans,* by "A Woman of Fashion," and *How To Play Golf,* by H. J. Whigham, Chicago newspaperman and American Amateur Champion in 1896 and 1897.

Fiction retained its predominance in the Stone booklist, fifteen books coming from three foreign and twelve native authors, but none of the pieces were distinguished, although they included Harold Frederic's posthumous *Gloria Mundi* and Will Payne's *The Money Captain,* based on an intimate knowledge of Chicago traction finance. Mr. Payne was financial editor of the Chicago weekly *Economist* at this time. The small proportion in 1898 of foreign fiction, which usually ran to half the total in this division of the Stone lists, was probably due to Herbert Stone's holding off other contracts for a month during his spring trip to London, while he discussed a "Great Fiction Scheme" with Grant Richards. The reference in Herbert Stone's letters from London at this time are obscure, and nothing materialized, at least in connection with his firm. Grant Richards has not yet given details, as he promised in *Author Hunting:* "We set to work at one time to secure from the public fifty or a hundred thousand pounds with which we proposed to revolutionize the trade in novels. It deserves a chapter to itself, that scheme. It shall have it one day." It seems to have been one of the many abortive Anglo-American attempts to publish new fiction in paper covers, as the French do, but was not, Mr. Richards writes.

Herbert Stone had already started on May 15, 1898, an independent experiment with paper covers, but the works included were chiefly copyright novels which his present firm or Stone & Kimball had previously published and for which he was seeking a secondary sale. Indeed, as Frederick A. Stokes, dean of American book publishers recalls, the reprinting of popular novels in cheap paper editions was done for many American publishers in the nineties, "In an effort to replace the fat sales of paper books slaughtered by international copyright in 1891."[10] Distribution of these editions was usually handled by the American News Company until

---

[10]Frederick A. Stokes, "A Publisher's Random Notes, 1890-1935," *Bulletin of the New York Public Library,* November, 1935, Vol. XXXIX, p. 853.

the advent of Grosset & Dunlap, who established the reprint business between cloth covers. Stone was among the first publishers to realize the advantage of having his cheaper editions handled by a specialist firm. In 1898, however, Grosset & Dunlap had not developed their technique of renting plates from the original publishers of popular works and "Stone's Paper Library" was established, leading off with *The Damnation of Theron Ware*. Thirty-six titles, were offered at fifty cents a copy, six dollars a year.

An interesting point in the history of Herbert S. Stone & Company, concerning which the records are incomplete, is how they became successors to Way & Williams in 1898, and why they did not keep on their lists the titles which were transferred to them when this partnership of W. Irving Way and Chauncey Williams closed its doors in 1898, after four years of publishing fine books in Chicago. Twenty-six handsome volumes designed by Will Bradley, Bruce Rogers and others, were advertised in *Publishers' Weekly* September 24, 1898 as "Transfer of Messrs. Way & Williams' Books to Herbert S. Stone & Co.," who had "pleasure in announcing that they have purchased the entire stock and good-will of Messrs. Way & Williams, of Chicago." These same books and others of Way & Williams were included in the catalogue of Stone publications (twenty pages, 192 titles indexed) inserted in *Publishers' Trade List Annual* of 1899. Stone assumed no obligation to complete Way & Williams' contracts for future publications, and is said to have refused to issue Edgar Lee Masters' first *Book of Verses* which, already printed and bound, was scheduled to be published on the very day that Way & Williams went out of business.[11]

In the case of the St. Louis writer, Mrs. Kate Chopin, however, Stone established relations which led to the publication of her best novel, *The Awakening,* in 1900, although they returned a collection of short stories originally sub-

[11] Edgar Lee Masters, *Across Spoon River* (New York: Farrar & Rinehart, 1936), p. 251.

mitted to Way & Williams. Daniel S. Rankin, in *Kate Chopin and Her Creole Stories,* reproduces an entry from her work book:

<blockquote>
A Vocation and a Voice
Collection
To Way and Williams '98
Accepted
Transferred to H. S. Stone Nov. '98
R[eturned]   Feb. 1900
</blockquote>

A full account of Stone's publication of *The Awakening,* and of Mrs. Chopin's troubles with censors, is given in the Bibliography.

No assignments of copyrights were ever made to Herbert S. Stone & Company by Way & Williams, who legally transferred their entire list, with but a few exceptions, to Doubleday & McClure Company on January 26, 1900. Neither W. Irving Way nor Chauncey Williams is living; there is no information in the biographical material on these two men concerning the final disposal of the books they published together; and the letters of Herbert Stone are silent in this matter.

Six months before the close of the century Herbert Copeland and Fred Holland Day retired from the publishing business which they had founded so close to Stone & Kimball in 1893. Two of their Boston friends, who had founded Small, Maynard & Company in 1897, bought the list (excepting Alice Brown's books, which went to Houghton), for a sum reported by *Publishers' Weekly* to have been nine thousand dollars. The letter files and a complete run of Copeland & Day publications were only recently sold by Goodspeed's Book Shop in Boston after Day's death, late in the year 1932, while an appreciation of his work as a follower of William Morris was written by William Dana Orcutt, for the first number of the 1933 volume of *Publishers' Weekly.*

Besides helping to liquidate the stock of Way & Williams in 1899, the Stone firm published in this year its largest list of new titles—fifty. These are too many to discuss in the detail permitted by the smaller totals of earlier years of Herbert S. Stone & Company and Stone & Kimball. Fiction, twenty-one American and eleven foreign works, accounted for thirty-two of the total; juveniles for five; biography for four; with one each in nine other fields. In the attempt to maintain a "balanced list," and in the number of annual issues, Stone could now be counted among the big trade publishers of the day.

Stone's trade total of 60 (including new editions as well as new titles) gave them a tie with Crowell for fourteenth place among American book producers of the year, and first place by a long margin among publishers outside of New York, Boston, or Philadelphia. Their closest Western competitors publishing for the general book trade were in Chicago: Rand, McNally & Company with 18 publications, Laird & Lee with 13, A. C. McClurg & Company with 12. Bowen-Merrill Company of Indianapolis, after the turn of the century, as Bobbs-Merrill, to eclipse all these in sales, published only 12 books in 1899. In New York, the firm of Doubleday & McClure Company, formed as recently as 1897 and dissolved at the end of 1899, published 74, for tenth place among individual publishers of trade books in that year. Among the older houses, Harper's, undergoing financial reorganization in 1899, first under S. S. McClure and associates, later under Colonel George B. M. Harvey, published 82 editions. Scribner's issued 445, and Macmillan, only four years old as an independent concern under George Brett Sr., was high with 615. The totals of these last two firms, however, were swelled by their large numbers of importations.

Herbert Stone never expected to found a regional publishing house, specializing in local authors and works of information on a specific region, such as Frederick J. Schulte had attempted between 1891 and 1893 in Chicago, or William Doxey maintained in San Francisco. His work, like himself, was essentially cosmopolitan. He used that very term when interviewed in 1904 by Herbert Fleming, who was studying the literary interests of Chicago as shown by periodical publications: "[Mr. Stone] was firm in the belief that an essentially cosmopolitan magazine could be published in Chicago and the West." But like every publisher, what he printed depended on whom he met and who were his editorial advisers. As a publisher of the present generation puts it: "Essentially the standards of the imprint are the standards of the publisher and his editorial colleagues. The fields covered by the books of a particular house cannot significantly, except by accident, go much beyond the intellectual interests and standards of the publishing personnel."[12]

Whether because Herbert Stone was now a Chicagoan by choice as well as by birth, or because Lucy Monroe, who was born and lived in Chicago (until she settled in Peking as wife of the American Ambassador to China in 1909), replaced Cleveland-bred, Harvard-educated Harrison Rhodes as chief reader and literary editor; or more plausibly because Way & Williams, who had invested heavily in local writers, had given up—in 1899 there was a noticeable increase in the proportion of Chicago to other American writers.

In fiction, there were *The Fair Brigand,* by George Horton, then literary editor of the *Times-Herald; The Seekers* and *The Wolf's Long Howl,* by Stanley Waterloo, at various times editor of newspapers in St. Louis, Chicago and St. Paul, but always a pillar of Chicago's Press Club; *Doc' Horne* and *Fables in Slang* by George Ade of the *Record.* Mrs. Mary Hartwell Catherwood in 1899 published through Stone, *Spanish Peggy: A Story of Young Illinois.* Lincoln is introduced into the cast of characters, but the illustrations, which included photographs of scenes at New Salem as well

---

[12]Alfred Harcourt, "Publishing Since 1900," *Bulletin of the New York Public Library,* XLI (December 1937), p. 904.

as imaginative drawings by J. C. Lyendecker, are perhaps more authentic Lincolniana. Among several juveniles was *Ickery Ann and Other Girls and Boys,* by Elia W. Peattie of the *Tribune.* "Amy Leslie," dramatic critic of the *News,* was represented by *Some Players,* a miscellany of the greenroom. Dr. Frank Crane, active as a minister and contributor to Chicago newspapers, placed his first book, *The Religion of Tomorrow,* on Stone's list in 1899.

Though the present study is bibliographical rather than literary history, it is pleasant to record that the book of 1899 most interesting to the collector and bibliographer happens also to be the most important literary text. George Moore's *Esther Waters* had been published before in the United States, in pirated editions of 1894 and 1895 after. First let us remember that George Moore's prefaces, though shorter than those of George Bernard Shaw, were as often a highlight of his books. The preface to his play *The Bending of the Bough,* published by Stone in 1900 as the ninth volume of "The Green Tree Library," nominally concerned with "The Intentions of the Irish Literary Theatre," is in reality, an extended essay on the economic basis of cycles in art history. The author's preface to Stone's "Authorized Edition" of *Esther Waters* 1899, states that "The proofs of the first edition of 'Esther Waters' were sent to three leading American publishers. The book was declined by all three, and it was published without the American copyright having been secured." George Moore believed that to a writer "revision is the only morality." When a cheap edition of *Esther Waters* which had been refused circulation by the libraries of W. H. Smith & Son on its original appearance because it included scenes in a lying-in-hospital, was called for in England in 1899, Moore rewrote large sections of his own favorite novel. "... my best book. Now *that* is perfect English." (Conversation with his secretary in 1933, recorded in Joseph Hone, *The Life of George Moore* [London: Victor Gollancz, Ltd., 1936], p.

451.) The revisions made it possible to secure copyright in a new American printing. But in sending proofs of the new English edition (published in May 1896 by Walter Scott) to America, Moore rewrote again, so that publication was delayed from April 10th, when 192 pages were deposited for copyright by Stone at the Library of Congress, until December 9, 1899, when the complete work was entered in the "Weekly Record of New Publications" of *Publishers' Weekly*.

The expansion in business during 1899 and 1900 shot gross receipts up rapidly, as we know from letters written by Herbert Stone to his mother, sister, and grandfather, then travelling in Europe:

February 8, 1899

We have already in Jan. and so much of Feb. this year done more business than we did in the whole of 1897 or the first six months of '98.

February 16, 1899

Ned is still in New York—running things there. So far his trip has been very satisfactory: he has sold a good many books and the expense has not been heavy... The business is doing pretty well—January was as much better than '98 as '98 was better than '97. So—you see we are growing steadily. The McClurg fire has stirred everyone up. We may buy their publishing business and perhaps the old book department. I think Marshall Field will buy the retail books. Effie is still reading proof for us and today I have John Jameson some work collecting accounts.

October 19, 1899

We are head over heels and going beautifully. Ned is slaving until seven or eight every night in N. Y. and things are nearly as bad here. But the prospects were never so good and the sales are booming. I suppose Nov. will be far and away the biggest month we ever have had but this month is not going slow by any means. We have up to today done $12,000 more this year than in the whole of last year—which is not bad... It now looks as if Ned would be in N. Y. until Christmas. Nearly all of our new books are out now or at least merely waiting for the binder to finish his work. And then I shall be freer.

November 2, 1899

Ned is still in N. Y. and working wonders. October was the biggest month we ever had—even bigger than May when we published "Dross." Up to Nov. 1 we have so far this year sold $58,067.26 as against 44 thousand for *all* last year. This shows the increase. I suppose in Nov. we shall do at least $20,000 which will again break records. As a result Ned is happy I think and so am I. I only wish we weren't all so separated. I saw Father the other day for a moment. He helped me to borrow some money from the bank. We have paid the last of the Stone & Kimball notes and the stuff is ours—at last. Ned and I both figure that we shall be able to pay all our debts by Jan. 15, and have money in the bank as well, which will be a new and novel sensation.

November 9, 1899

Ned is getting a man in N. Y. John Hunt who was in his class, to help on the manufacturing here and if he succeeds I shall probably be able to get away. The old business is booming: it never did so well and we are all more than cheerful over it. So the work has not been in vain.

March 29, 1900

I have taken over the whole financial end of the work which Ned has heretofore looked after. This gives him more time to devote to book *selling* on which everything else depends. Besides, now that we are cutting down our manufacturing—so as to reduce expenses—I have time enough to manage this. To tell the truth it is not the work I would do if I had my choice—for it is no simple task to pull the business into really good shape. I think now however—we've got things started right and they ought to work out in time. Incidentally we are closing the N. Y. office (thereby saving $4,000 a year) selling the House Beautiful (for $3,700 cash) and increasing our sales at a big rate. The business for the first three months is just three times what it was last year. All of which is very agreeable.

In addition to the temporary employees mentioned above, there was the buying office in London, now in charge of Harrison Rhodes, and a full staff at Eldridge Court. Besides Lucy Monroe, who has given this list from memory: W. J. F. Dailey, advertising and production manager, Virginia Robie, assistant editor of *The House Beautiful*, W. J. Kirk, bookkeeper, Mr. Muller, clerk, Miss Kass, secretary, an additional stenographer and "other clerks and advertising men who came and went."

Doubtless there was sufficient reason in 1900 for cutting expenses, but one of the distinguishing characteristics of the booklist, the individual typographic treatment of each book, was destroyed when the house of Stone published just ordinary-looking books. The effects of this change in policy were unfortunate for Herbert Stone himself, for, as Lucy Monroe Calhoun says: "Paper, print, spacing and lettering were his delight. He was extravagant in that as in everything. It was this quality that was his undoing. When he had to cut down expenses and could not make the beautiful books he loved, he lost interest. He was the kind of artist who should have had unlimited resources. He would have used them well."

In the early months of 1900, the Way & Williams books went to Doubleday, and old reliable *Theron Ware* was again turned into some ready cash. The Stones approached Grosset & Dunlap with a plan which was immediately accepted and quickly developed further. At this time, wrote George Dunlap, his firm was buying paper editions of popular works from jobbers, and converting them into cloth-bound books for retail distribution. No change was made in the title-page and there was no distinguishing imprint on the binding. Stokes was the first publisher from whom they bought a reprint edition directly, Stone the second and, important in the development of Grosset & Dunlap as second-run publishers in their own right, the twenty-five thousand copies of Harold Frederic's *The Damnation of Theron Ware* sold in paper was "the first reprint edition ever to bear the name of Grosset & Dunlap, and marks a definite stage of progress. From that time on the 'rebind' began to fade; the day of the reprint was dawning."[13] A less important reprint house with which Her-

---

[13]George T. Dunlap, "Genesis of a Publishing Business," *Publishers' Weekly*, August 10, 1936, Vol. CXXVIII, p. 360.

bert S. Stone & Company were doing business was The Monarch Book Company of Chicago, who issued late in 1900 editions with their imprint and in their own bindings of *The Wolf's Long Howl* by Stanley Waterloo and *A Child of the Sun*, by Charles Eugene Banks.

These incidents have been mentioned as evidence that Herbert S. Stone & Company, doubtless because of the special capabilities of M. E. Stone Jr., responded to the strictly commercial problems of distribution, as Herbert S. Stone and Ingalls Kimball had responded to the opportunities afforded them to produce beautiful books.

While these transactions were going on, Stone published thirty new books in 1900: nineteen works of fiction, of which only one of the ten American novels, Herman Knickerbocker Vielé's *Inn of the Silver Moon*, and Bernard Shaw's *Love Among the Artists* of the nine foreign novels, are worth recalling here. The three volumes of plays were all important: Shaw's *Three Plays for Puritans*, Moore's *Bending of the Bough* and Ibsen's *When We Dead Awaken* (tenth and last issue in "The Green Tree Library," begun by Stone & Kimball in 1894). There were two books of travel, a collection of epigrams, and a biography of Edward Fitzgerald by John Glyde. Of two sociological works, George Bird Grinnell's *Indians of Today* was a substantial and well illustrated quarto. The volumes in science and in mechanics were each interesting: Alfred H. Fison's *Recent Advances in Astronomy*, imported in "The Victorian Era Series," and Clinton Edgar Woods' *The Electric Automobile*.

George Ade collected *More Fables in Slang* in 1900 as his last publication with his friend Herbert Stone, for the first book of *Fables* had made his newspaper work in demand nationally. Robert Howard Russell, who then arranged for Mr. Ade's newspaper syndication, had at the time his own book publishing house in New York. He issued *Forty Modern Fables* in 1901, almost extravagantly well printed by D. B.

Updike, who also manufactured several of the Ade books published in succeeding years by various houses. The transfer of Mr. Ade's work to New York publishers was accomplished without hard feeling, but it must have brought home to Stone the typical structural flaw in all attempts to build a general publishing house outside of America's intellectual trading post. American authors, like American artists and inventors, wherever they are born or do their first important work, sooner or later gravitate to New York, if not in person, at least in their business dealings. This is the reason why A. C. McClurg & Company, after sporadic attempts to add a trade book business to their book-selling, now confine themselves in publishing to works of reference for the library trade.[14] This is the reason why Chicago has never sustained a book publisher of general literature exclusively for a longer period than Stone's thirteen years. Indeed, one wonders if it would have been possible for Stone & Kimball and Herbert S. Stone & Company to exist at all in Chicago, if they had depended solely on books. The periodicals were more profitable.

True, Chicago has today firms which make occasional experiments with contemporary literary works, but each has its profitable specialty.[15] Chicago even anticipated New York, in the seventies and eighties of the last century, producing through the activity of such houses as the Lakeside Printing and Publishing Company, Donohue & Henneberry, G. W. Borland, and Belford & Clarke great quantities of paper books in cheap series, and reprint editions in more substantial formats.[16] But the circumstances that no publisher of contemporary, copyrighted books intended to be sold nationally in bookstores has survived in Chicago, with its population of 1,700,000 in 1900 and almost 4,000,000 now, and its geograph-

---

[14]Interview June 20, 1936 with Mr. Joseph E. Bray, at that time Chairman of the Board of Directors of A. C. McClurg & Company.
[15]Rand, McNally & Company, maps; Willett, Clark & Company, textbooks; Reilley & Lee, reprints and juvenile literature.
[16]See Raymond Howard Shove, *Cheap Book Production in the United States, 1870 to 1891* (Urbana: University of Illinois Library, 1937), pp. 4-5, 52, 82-87 and *passim*.

ical position so well suited to the work of distribution, in Mid-America[17] is not accidental, but ineluctable.[18]

1901-1905: BEST SELLERS AND THE HOUSE BEAUTIFUL

Only thirty-seven new books were published in the years 1901-1905, in steadily declining totals of fifteen, eleven, eight, four, and one, the last publication being issued with the imprint of "Herbert S. Stone: The House Beautiful." The income from the business, however, did not decline at as regular a rate as the number of new titles. Indeed the years 1901 and 1902 were probably more profitable than any others of Herbert S. Stone & Company, for in the first year *Graustark* happened, and in the second came *The Story of Mary MacLane*. But George Barr McCutcheon, after the notable successes of his first book and of the second and third, *Castle Craneycrow* (1902), *Brewster's Millions* (1903), in 1904 moved to New York with his books. And the publicity attending Mary MacLane's book ruined her as a person and a writer. *The House Beautiful* was the firm's lifeline between 1903 and 1905, and continues as a profitable enterprise, until 1913 under the direction of Herbert Stuart Stone.

In 1901, of the fifteen books newly published (the total was exactly half that of the previous year, itself forty per

---

[17] Today the largest trade publishers with home offices in the West, Bobbs-Merrill Company of Indianapolis have a law-book business which goes back to 1855. Their first trade book was James Whitcomb Riley's *The Old Swimmin' Hole*, 1883, and their list came into national prominence with the further additions of the historical romances of Charles Major (*When Knighthood Was in Flower*, 1898) and of Maurice Thompson (*Alice of Old Vincennes*, 1900). Since 1906 the manufacturing, advertising and selling offices have been in New York.

[18] The number of firms in Chicago, publishing more than five volumes annually of any type of book, remained substantially unchanged from 1900 to 1935, according to the annual directories of American publishers compiled by *Publishers' Weekly*. In 1900, 1053 organizations published at least one book and 284 of these, publishing five or more, may be called "active" rather than "occasional" publishers. New York had 96 of the active publishers, Boston and Philadelphia each 21, Chicago 15, and 50 other active publishers were distributed in thirty cities and towns (including the university presses of Johns Hopkins, Baltimore, and the University of Wisconsin at Madison). In 1935, there were 669 organizations publishing at least one book, 215 were active, 112 in New York, 18 in Boston, 16 in Philadelphia and 15 in Chicago, with 50 other publishers of more than five books in 1935, in forty cities and towns (including 12 university presses).

cent below the fifty new books of 1899), eight were fiction, three were picture books, one a children's book built around colored photographs of animals, and one each were books of reference, biography, and history. There were several new American authors; Joseph W. Sharts, Harvard classmate of M. E. Stone Jr., and back in Ohio from the Spanish-American War, is represented by his first novel, *Ezra Caine*. *Chapters from Illinois History* was a posthumous publication of the local antiquarian Edward G. Mason, who in 1890 had edited an important collection of papers on early Chicago and Illinois, as Volume IV of the "Collections of the Chicago Historical Society." There were several carry-overs of authors from earlier years: Mrs. Reginald De Koven appears again after a lapse of six years, with *By the Waters of Babylon;* and Herman Knickerbocker Vielé followed his successful novel of the previous year with *The Last of the Knickerbockers.*

Cashel Byron's Profession, with the play made from it, *The Admirable Bashville,* two prefaces and a note on modern prizefighting, make up the last of five volumes Shaw published through Stone. The occasion for this *olla-podrida* was the performance in America of unauthorized dramatizations, and the recent "pirated" edition published in Chicago by Brentano's. (It had appeared in two American cheap series soon after its London book publication in 1886.)

Shaw now (1901) urged his own American publisher, H. S. Stone and Company of Chicago...to go ahead and exploit the "new field of derelict fiction"—a hint which was immediately taken in the publication of *Cashel Byron's Profession,* with the same text as that of the Grant Richards edition. "I had intended to make no further revision in the text (than that of the Walter Scott edition)," writes Shaw in 1901; "but in reading the proofs my pen positively jumped to humanize a few passages in which the literary professionalism with which my heroine expresses herself (this professionalism is usually called 'style' in England) went past all bearing. I have also indulged myself by varying a few sentences, and inserting one or two new ones, so as to enable the American publisher to secure copyright in this edition. But I have made no attempt to turn an 1882 novel into a twentieth century one; and the few alterations are, except for legal purposes, quite negligeable [sic]![9]

Stone made a determined effort in 1901 to develop a business of their own in cheap reprint editions. They had tried a paper-bound series in 1898, with little apparent success, but now that their experience and that of other publishers, with Grosset & Dunlap, had shown that reprint editions could be sold most profitably between cloth covers, they offered the trade "The Eldridge Series" and "The Court Series." *Publishers' Weekly* of September 28, 1901 had a full page of advertisements by Stone, given over to the series offered, at the wholesale price of twenty cents a volume, in cloth. To use the terms of the advertisement, "The Eldridge Series" consisted of: "Cloth bound copyright novels (12mo) by great authors. To the trade 20 cts. net. To supply the demand for low-priced, cloth, copyright novels, by great authors, we have collected a number of splendid titles which we offer to the trade at a remarkably low price. The books are bound as well as when they were first issued, at $1.25, $1.50, and $1.75. It is the only line of the kind on the market." Seventy-two titles—practically all of their fiction books a year or more old—were offered in this series and its companion "The Court Series" (16mo editions). Doubtless these were remainders rather than editions manufactured from stored plates, but at least they served to move the stock, as we know from the large number of Stone fiction titles which have survived in the secondary bindings of these cheap series. Since twelve of the titles thus sold were Stone & Kimball publications, dating back as far as 1894, and fifteen others belonged to the first two years of Herbert S. Stone & Company, the liquidation was healthy. Too many books, especially light fic-

[9] Archibald Henderson, *Bernard Shaw: Playboy and Prophet* (New York: D. Appleton and Company, 1932), pp. 105-6.

tion, were overprinted—Duffield & Company when they succeeded to the business of Herbert S. Stone & Company in 1906, again judging from the number of relics, remaindered many thousands of copies of books originally printed for Stone & Kimball and Herbert S. Stone & Company.

Stone's greatest advertising campaign was made for *Graustark,* in *Publishers' Weekly,* in literary journals, in newspapers. Posters and other publicity devices were used to make the best of a runaway success. The advertising barrage began early in March 1901; the book, the first novel of George Barr McCutcheon, still working on a newspaper in his native Indiana, sold one hundred fifty thousand copies before the end of the year. The story itself, a graceful fairy tale, was written by McCutcheon in 287 days, as one of the ingeniously devised advertisements states,[20] and as another notice informed the trade, was unsolicited and found in the mail. 'Ned' Stone, who wrote the advertisements, says 'Billy' Dailey, picked the manuscript from a group discarded by Herbert, and insisted that it was the work of a great storyteller. Herbert Stone took the manuscript with misgivings, although Lucy Monroe Calhoun found it "gay and charming." A recent letter adds: "I was very disappointed because Herbert did not read it with the same enthusiasm. It was the fastidious side of his nature that was affronted by it. I remember he laughed at the fact that the hero wore detachable cuffs and took them off when he had to fight. It was really because of defects like this that he bought the manuscript outright, so that he would have the right to have it revised. He sent it to a writer in New York state for that purpose, and this held it back for several months." Before *Graustark* went East for polishing, Herbert Stone, Lucy Monroe and Wallace Rice had tried their hands at revising the manuscript. They reduced the bulk by half, reworded the early chapters, and

---

[20]*Publishers' Weekly,* November 9, 1901, Vol. LX, p. 1011. McCutcheon later stated the period of composition to have been December 1898—March 1899, in spare moments at his editorial desk in the offices of the Lafayette *Courier.*

changed the name of the hero from John Noble to Grenfell Lorry. At one point in the book the original name was allowed to stand; this explains, as we discuss further in the Bibliography, the 'point' distinguishing the first issue of *Graustark* from later editions. McCutcheon himself freely admitted that the novel was sold outright for the sum of five hundred dollars, but that Herbert S. Stone & Company and later publishers voluntarily paid him royalties on reprint editions.

Once George Barr McCutcheon was settled in Chicago, where his younger brother John had been writing and drawing for the *Record* since 1889, he quickly finished two other novels, which also received special promotion by Melville E. Stone Jr. *Castle Craneycrow*, a story of European adventure, was published in the summer of 1902, and also serialized in *The House Beautiful*. It had an advance sale of 35,000 copies but did not maintain a place among the best-sellers. In writing *Brewster's Millions*, McCutcheon worked closely with Melville Stone, Lucy Monroe Calhoun and other friends. It is "the tale of a young man who is forced to spend a million dollars, without any resulting gain, by a certain date. 'I didn't know how to spend a million dollars,' says the author, 'so my publisher and other friends and I put our heads together and figured it out. I had to have help on the Italian episode because I'd never been to Italy. Then the final climax of the yacht was a rather labored device; but it worked; and there the story was. The publisher sent it out to various great millionaires of the period with a letter asking if they thought it was possible to spend a million in any way. As I remember it, most of them answered in the negative; but the letters were used in what was a very clever campaign of promotion.'"[21] Another advertising dodge was worked with *Brewster's Millions* in several Western cities. A local bookstore would run a display advertisement that at a specific

---

[21] Arnold Patrick, "Getting into Six Figures: George Barr McCutcheon," *Bookman*, May 1925, Vol. LXI, p. 334.

time and place in the city (Thursday August 27, 1903, on Spring Street between Franklin and Market, in Los Angeles) a hundred dollar bill would be given the first person to ask the question "Are You the Man with the $100.00 Bill?" of the bookseller's representative, who would be in the crowd. There was only one condition in this guess-the-man-contest, that the winner must have in plain sight a copy of *Brewster's Millions.*

Brewster's Millions was published in April 1903 as the work of "Richard P. Greaves," the author and publisher wishing to test the sales of what they knew to be a good story, against the drawing power of George Barr McCutcheon's name, which appeared on the title of *The Sherrods*. This, McCutcheon's most ambitious attempt in 'serious' fiction was published the following September by Dodd, Mead & Company. *Brewster* not only outstripped the other work, but eventually sold more copies than any of the forty-one other novels McCutcheon composed before his death in 1928. It was as popular on the stage as *Graustark,* and like it, has continued to be produced in stock and in the movies. But Herbert S. Stone & Company had lost another Chicago author to an Eastern house. The advance royalty offered for *The Sherrods* is reported by Mr. Dailey to have been $22,000 —a sum the Stones did not try to match.

The Story of Mary MacLane made news in 1902. A manuscript came into the Chicago office of Fleming N. Revell Company, publishers of evangelical literature, and George H. Doran, its young vice-president, attracted by its "meticulous preparation and arresting title," took it home for reading. "I thought no more about it until I sat down to read. The dedication was far from pious or prophetic. As I recall it ran, 'To that devil with the steel-grey eyes who some day, who knows, will come to this weary wooden broken heart of mine, I dedicate this my book.' I turned again to the title-page; it read simply: *I Await the Devil's Coming* by Mary

MacLane. I read on into the book—done in most perfect and painstaking handwriting. I discovered the most astounding and revealing piece of realism I had ever read. Clearly we could not publish it, but Mary must have a publisher. The next day I sent it to dear old Ned Stone, of Stone & Kimball, publishers, and son of Melville. He arranged for its immediate publication but under the simple title *Mary MacLane.* Its success was so great that Ned invited Mary to come from the dunes of Butte, Montana, to visit Chicago. She came."[22]

Mary MacLane for her own sake might better never have left Butte. Only two years out of high school, she was a perplexing problem to the Monroe sisters, with whom she stayed for a time, and to her publishers. Alarmed at her youth and erratic temperament, but interested in her evident capabilities, Melville E. Stone Jr. suggested that Mary MacLane enter Radcliffe.[23] In Cambridge during July 1902, her announced intention to go to college to study chemistry was upset by rejection of her application on the understandable grounds that she was not prepared. Everywhere followed by reporters for the sensational press, since the publication of her book early in June had aroused a storm of comment, mostly denunciatory, Mary MacLane decided to capitalize on her news value and see New York. She accepted an offer from the New York *World* to write four Sunday feature articles for the sum of six hundred dollars and expenses. The arrangement was made against the advice of her publishers, who at length assented, but prevailed on their editor to go with Mary MacLane to New York, in August 1902. In a letter of October 21, 1937, Mrs. Calhoun writes: "It was probably the most difficult month I ever spent, but it held unforgettable moments. She had an affection for me, and at times she

[22]George H. Doran, *Chronicles of Barrabas, 1894-1934* (New York: Harcourt, Brace and Company [1937]), p. 30.
[23]Most of the information which follows is from a series of letters between Mary MacLane and Melville E. Stone Jr., 1902-1911.

was adorable. At other times elusive, evasive, and puzzling. She often gave me the most unpleasant feeling of uncertainty, and from moment to moment I did not know what she would be like."

Mary MacLane was on her own as a journalist in New York and Boston until 1909, when her step-father, a mine operator of Butte, came East to take her home. *The Story of Mary MacLane* had only a *succès de scandale* and *My Friend Annabel Lee* (1903) not even that. In her second book published by Stone she made a deliberate effort to cater to that part of the public which had condemned her frankness. No wonder that in a letter written while *Annabel Lee* was in progress, she says "I do not seem to write so easily in this as in the other book." Mary MacLane was never happy as a writer except when she was her own subject. Comparisons were made by her few favorable critics to Marie Bashkirtseff, whose *Journal* Mary MacLane read as a girl in Butte.[24] Her later books were only rehashings in 1911 and 1917 of *The Story* while her newspaper writings were done only under compulsion. Mary MacLane gambled away her early earnings and was always in debt, dying in poverty and obscurity, Chicago, August 1, 1929. She talked brilliantly, "in a mixture of slang and prose of almost classical purity," Gertrude Atherton wrote of a conversation with her in Butte about 1913. Her letters to Lucy Monroe Calhoun had "a rare and marvellous beauty"; those to M. E. Stone Jr. for ten years after their meeting in 1902, are touching in their mixture of play-acting and pure personal tragedy. In 1908 Mr. Stone assumed personally obligations to her, amounting to a little more than a thousand dollars, and discharged it during the next three years. In addition he ordered articles (delivered with difficulty) for magazines with which he was associated, and solicited work for her among his acquaintances.

[24] H. L. Mencken, who thought Mary MacLane a gifted stylist, labelled her "The Butte Bashkirtseff"; in *Prejudices—First Series* (New York: Alfred A. Knopf, 1919), pp. 123-28.

But most editors came to feel as Arthur Brisbane did when he wrote from the New York *Journal* office, on January 14, 1909: "I haven't given the young woman up as yet, for I want to oblige both you and her if I can. But I'm afraid that she has lost the knack of thinking and writing about it, and has taken to whining, which isn't at all the Mary MacLane idea."

The booklist of 1901 was the last analyzed in detail; the books of George Barr McCutcheon and Mary MacLane have interposed in a way as upsetting to routinized discussion as these quick alternates of optimism and despair, visiting Eldridge Court in 1902 and 1903, upset the customary procedures of Herbert and Melville Stone. For instance, Stone, previously careful in their circularization of the trade, omitted to have a catalogue of their publications made for insertion in *Publishers' Trade List Annual* of 1902. Stone & Kimball, under the influence of their English collaborators had been in 1894, one of the first American publishers to set net prices on individual books. After the example of the British Publishers' Association, the American Publishers' Association was established in 1900, to enforce, with the cooperation of the organized booksellers, uniform net price regulations for subscribing members. Yet Herbert S. Stone & Company were not included in the membership lists periodically printed in *Publishers' Weekly,* until October 18, 1902, and were never active in the organization. Stone's first and second firms had been regular advertisers in the trade journals, but the announcements of Herbert S. Stone & Company in *Publishers' Weekly* cease with the Christmas number of 1901. Advertising of the Stone list in Chicago newspapers and in the nationally read critical journals was sporadic after 1901, even for best-sellers.

The books published in 1902 and 1903 make quick work. Of eleven new titles in 1902, only four were by authors new to Stone lists. The most interesting (out of four) non-fiction works was compiled from the magazine—*The Book of a Hundred Houses*. Volume I, Number I, December 1896, of *The House Beautiful*, had been issued by Klapp & Company from 221 Fifth Avenue, Chicago. Herbert S. Stone & Company were named the publishers beginning with the issue of September 1897. Eugene Klapp remained as editor (part of the time with Henry Blodgett Harvey), until he went, as an engineer, to Cuba during the Spanish-American War. Herbert Stone, relieved of *Chap-Book* duties at the same time, then became editor. Klapp retained part ownership until July 4, 1902, when his quarter-share was purchased for a thousand dollars, and remained an important Eastern contributor for years. Although Ned Stone was titular editor of *The House Beautiful* for a time, he usually worked with the booklist after 1900, while Herbert spent most of his time on *The House Beautiful*.

Herbert Stone was both happy and successful in his work as editor of *The House Beautiful*. As a boy, before he settled on publishing as a career, he had thought of becoming an architect. Now his work brought him into the closest touch with American and foreign architects and decorators, and he was able to turn to business ends the traveling of which he was so fond.[25] Herbert Stone did not lose touch with the arts of book decoration, supervising the design of the magazine, choosing the illustrations and overseeing their reproduction. He commissioned illustrations and cover designs from old friends of *The Chap-Book* and newer artists: Claude Bragdon, Frank Brangwyn, W. A. Dwiggins, Frank Hazenplug, Frederic W. Goudy, B. B. Long, Edward Penfield, Mary Prindiville, Fred Richardson, Fred Stearns and Ivan Swift, among others.

Important articles came from Mary Abbott, C. R. Ashbee, Ida D. Bennett, Claude Bragdon, "Oliver Coleman" *i.e.*

---

[25]Even on his wedding trip of 1901, Herbert Stone found time to collect material on American country homes and Italian palaces.

Eugene Klapp, R. A. Cram, Alice Morse Earle, Sadakichi Hartmann, Frederick Keppel, Harriet Monroe, Anna Morgan, Vernon Louis Parrington, J. W. Pattison, Virginia Robie, Clarence Moores Weed, Carolyn Wells and Madeleine Yale Wynne. In early volumes, there was considerable material, by Harrison Rhodes and W. Irving Way, on title-pages, book bindings and other aspects of book craft.

One of the lessons Herbert Stone learned from the career of his first magazine was that advertising is built by guaranteed circulation and circulation by subscription rather than by newsstand sales. Using prize competitions, question and answer columns, and a varied content of illustrated articles on the history and practice of the applied arts, Stone in the years between 1900 and 1906 moved the monthly circulation of 7,000 (more than half over the counter), up to 40,000 copies, sold almost entirely by mail. On the way (1904) the size was enlarged from 9-1/4 x 6-1/4 to 12 x 9 inches, and the subscription price raised from one to two dollars a year. Advertising came easily from Eastern and foreign dealers in art and household goods, for this was the first American magazine devoted to interior decoration. The editorial alter ego from 1900 on was Virginia Robie, originally from New England, where she had studied at the Boston Museum of Fine Arts. After a period at the Art Institute of Chicago, Miss Robie joined *The House Beautiful,* first as staff contributor, then department editor, assistant editor, associate editor and, for two years after Herbert Stone left it, editor of *The House Beautiful.* Miss Robie, now Professor of Decorative Arts at Rollins College, has been generous with suggestions during the last two years of this work's preparation. Her help has been invaluable, for she was associated in business for a longer time than any person now alive with Herbert Stone. Miss Robie states that she has not regretted the time spent in correspondence, for she looks back on the 'Stone Age' as the most stimulating of her professional years.

Between 1903 and 1905 the magazine was increasingly profitable, and afforded as well an outlet for Herbert Stone's feeling for typography. In 1903, only eight books were issued, two being anthologies of American humorous verse and prose, edited respectively by Wallace Rice and M. E. Stone Jr. Five of the six novels were by native writers, two of which (*Brewster's Millions* and *Annabel Lee*) have already been fully discussed. Only one more is worth mentioning: *The Strange Adventures of Mr. Middleton,* by Wardon Allen Curtis, in 1903 on the editorial staff of the Chicago *Daily News,* and since the war editor of the Manchester, New Hampshire, *Union-Leader.* This gay tale of Arabian nights in Chicago, Mr. Curtis' only work of fiction, should be reprinted. In 1904, when Herbert Stone spent eight months in St. Louis as Commercial Representative of the Philippine Islands, Herbert S. Stone & Company published two books for John U. Higinbotham, one of travel and the other of fiction; one printing of J. W. Pattison's, of the Art Institute, *Painters Since Leonardo;* and issued with moderate success *Roland of Altenburg,* modelled by Edward Mott Woolley, literary editor of the Chicago *Journal,* on *Graustark,* itself a derivative of the school of Anthony Hope's *Prisoner of Zenda.*

The sole publication of 1905, and the last book Herbert Stone ever published, was by his *House Beautiful* associate: Virginia Robie's *Historic Styles of Furniture,* a classic in the field of decoration. This book in its 1905 edition omits in its imprint the "& Company" and adds to the name, "Herbert S. Stone," that of "The House Beautiful." The transition of Herbert Stone from the publisher of general books into the publisher of one specialist periodical was complete.

The separation of the brothers Stone in 1906 and the sale of their booklist was anticipated as early as September 1903, when Herbert hinted in a letter to his mother of "some radical step" which would be necessary because "Ned has been having the everlasting hard time and there seems no great chance of a let-up, as we've got nothing of importance coming out. Mary MacLane's book is a frost—although Brewster keeps on steadily. It may develop into a big success—one can't tell yet. I want Ned to fire the whole staff—cut expenses down to nothing—do what selling he can himself and let the rest go. It would be a very slow way of pulling out but would at least be the most promising—our expenses are too heavy for the amount of business we are doing."

In 1905 they found the firm newly established by Rector K. Fox and Pitts Duffield, both Harvard men of the nineties and both trained in New York publishing houses, willing to discuss an outright purchase. The completed transaction was announced in *Publishers' Weekly* for March 10, 1906, as a purchase of "the entire goodwill, assets, plants, sheets and publishing plant of the Stone Company whose publications will henceforth be catalogued in Fox, Duffield & Co.'s list." The lists of Duffield & Company were purchased in 1934 by Dodd, Mead & Company—also the heirs through their purchase of Small, Maynard & Company of Boston, of Copeland & Day, rivals of Stone & Kimball in their Cambridge days. Dodd, Mead & Company now also publish Bernard Shaw, the only author who complained about the Stone-Duffield merger. Basing his objections on the five-year clause he had inserted in the contract for Grant Richards' 1898 edition of *Plays Pleasant and Unpleasant* (of which the American edition was published by Stone) Shaw sued H. S. and M. E. Stone in the New York Supreme Court, during April 1906, for an accounting of royalties and damages of $25,000 "for alleged wrongful detention of the copyrights" of his plays and other books. The suit came to naught, but Duffield transferred the books to Brentano's in December 1906.

Melville Edwin Stone Jr. won ample distinction as a periodical publisher in New York, especially during the period of his service as editor of *The Metropolitan Magazine*. Attacked by tuberculosis in 1911, when he was thirty-seven

FIG. 7. *George Ade and John T. McCutcheon, 1900*

"The Murders in the Rue Morgue"

"The Masque of the Red Death"

FIG. 8. *Beardsley's illustrations to Poe*

years old, he retired to Italy, Switzerland, the Adirondacks and Arizona in efforts to recover his health, at last succumbing in California on January 4, 1918.

Herbert Stuart Stone edited and published *The House Beautiful* from Chicago until 1910, and from New York until January 1913, when it was sold to "a stock company in which Ellery Sedgwick and MacGregor Jenkins, of the *Atlantic Monthly,* are now the controlling figures," he wrote for his last Harvard Class Book; adding, "Since then I have spent a year as a stock broker—which is quite long enough." When Herbert Stone left New York in 1915, bound for England and the continent via the *Lusitania,* he was gathering material for a new magazine. Virginia Robie "saw Mr. Stone in New York the day before he sailed on the Lusitania. Like all old magazine men he wanted to get back in the old fascinating troublesome game. He told me of his plan to publish a new magazine in the fall of 1915. He felt that there was a place for a publication that would meet changing conditions yet maintain the old traditions and ideals of *The House Beautiful*...He was last seen, so I was told by someone, on the starboard deck helping a mother and child..." The New York *Times* of May 16, 1915, gives an account of the heroic death just off the coast of Ireland of Herbert Stuart Stone in the forty-fourth year of his age. Let his father speak here:

I learned from survivors that my son went to his death as I should have expected him to do. Before he sailed I had given him a note of introduction to Madame Depage, the wife of the eminent Belgian surgeon, who was to be a fellow-passenger. When the torpedo struck the boat Herbert put on a life belt and hunted out Madame Depage. She was a frail little woman and asked if my son would permit her to be attached to him when they went into the water. Before it could be done a certain Doctor Houghton, who knew them both, said he was strong and a good swimmer and had better look after the poor lady. And so it was agreed. Then Herbert saw an unfortunate woman, obviously from the steerage, with no life belt. He took off his own, put it on her, and went to his death unprotected and without a tremor.

CHAPTER V

Notes for Students and Collectors

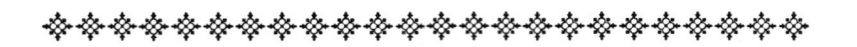

PLACE IN PUBLISHING HISTORY

THE ABIDING INTEREST in the career of Stone & Kimball and Herbert S. Stone & Company, apart from the insight it affords into a past time in book history, is that it is a good story. There remains about it an aura of the optimism which was a characteristic of the circumstances in which Herbert Stone and Ingalls Kimball began their work, and which attends youthful enterprise in any time. It is amazing that two youths, one in his 'teens, and the other barely out of them, should have become nationally prominent as publishers even before they were out of college. Herbert Stone's independent ten-year effort to distribute nationally from Chicago original editions of the best domestic and foreign work in letters is still without parallel. It is a matter of wonder that a publishing house (considering the two a continuous effort) should have lost its identity, after producing important books by such Americans as Hamlin Garland, George Santayana, Harold Frederic and Henry James; which anticipated the tastes of their tomorrow by making available here the work of George Bernard Shaw, George Moore, William Butler Yeats, Maurice Maeterlinck,

Paul Verlaine and Henrik Ibsen; and which also, sold the books of such vastly popular authors as Robert Louis Stevenson, George Ade, Horace Fletcher and George Barr McCutcheon.

A large majority of their three hundred and six book publications are classified as belles-lettres, and their three periodicals are concerned exclusively with literature and the arts. Stone & Kimball and Herbert S. Stone & Company are identified with strictly belletristic tendencies, perhaps more than any other American publishing concern except Ticknor & Fields in New England's "Golden Day." The importance of the editor and the publisher in the production of significant literature is, by its nature, not permanent. Their attitudes and interests are only part of the limiting conditions of the specific time in which important things are written and made public. But the policy of a publishing house, a composite of the astuteness of its editorial staff, the manner of its book production, and the efficiency with which its wares are distributed, can be a consistent expression of individuality and a permanent influence in its craft. There is evidence that the name of Stone & Kimball[1] still holds magic among publishers. For example, two recent addresses given in the "Bowker Memorial Lectures" on publishing history, single out their work. Frederick Stokes comments on their achievement in bringing Chicago forward as a publishing center, and Alfred Harcourt acknowledges the typographic excellence of their books. George H. Doran, another veteran of the trade, states a belief that although they produced "books of beauty and quality," they did not make the public conscious of their standards.[2] That Stone & Kimball and Herbert S. Stone &

---

[1]The first form of the firm name is the one generally recalled, whether reference is actually made to the partnership of Ingalls Kimball and Herbert Stone, formed in Cambridge in 1893, removed to Chicago 1894, to New York 1896, when Ingalls Kimball became sole proprietor; or to Herbert S. Stone & Company, established 1896 in Chicago; in 1897 successor to most of the books of Stone & Kimball when this firm was liquidated. The Stone company in 1906 was sold to Fox, Duffield & Co., absorbed by Dodd, Mead & Co.
[2]George H. Doran, *Chronicles of Barrabas* 1894-1934 (New York: Harcourt, Brace and Company, 1935), p. 83.

Company succeeded in dramatizing the value of their imprint to booksellers and the buying public, even in a measure, was an anticipation by two decades of publishers' publicity methods.

Perhaps the Stone firms receive such disproportionate emphasis (considering their short life and lists) in discussion of the book trade in the nineties because they were among the first to put to use economic and esthetic conditions first operative in that decade. The most important event in American book publishing in the decade of the nineties was the passage of the International Copyright Act in 1891. The same period saw a revitalization of American book design, parallel to the English "Revival of Printing." These influences were more quickly manifested by the appearance of a new group of publishing houses than by changes in practice of larger, longer established concerns. Copeland & Day; Lamson, Wolfe & Company; and Small, Maynard & Company of Boston; R. H. Russell of New York and Way & Williams of Chicago were important contemporaries of Stone & Kimball. As we have seen, the beginnings and endings of these firms are commingled; their books show physical resemblance, and there was considerable interchange of authors. The most important single characteristic which they held in common with Stone & Kimball (formed earlier than the others mentioned), was that they represented the appearance of the amateur in American publishing. That is, most members of these firms entered the business of publishing without having served an apprenticeship; all began strong on the idealistic side and weak on the practical. The lack of staying power, certainly in the case of Stone & Kimball, is more traceable to amateur beginnings, and to chance, than to lack of individual successes or to unfavorable conditions in the trade.

These young publishers, with a common background of taste and education, were the first to combine specialization in belles-lettres with an avowed intention to issue only handsome books. This is not to say that there had not been well-made American books before, or houses distinguished for the literary excellence of their lists. But the joint emphasis on bookcraft and on polite literature, to the exclusion of the profitable specialties, such as schoolbooks or lawbooks, are more comparable to the contemporary development of the private press, or to the later growth of fine printers and cosmopolitan literary publishers in this country, than to any earlier period in American book history. Concentration on the publishing of native and foreign belles-lettres, in well printed and well bound commercial editions, was economically feasible while the lack of copyright protection for foreign authors permitted the country to be flooded with cheap competitive series of reprints.[3] The second firm lived through other important trade changes which characterized the opening of the new century. Stone was not active in the great attempt to maintain published prices by boycott, organized in 1901 through the American Publishers Association and the American Booksellers Association. He was, however, among the first to exploit the possibilities of the reprint business under copyright restrictions, and to experiment with the direct advertising which accompanied the rise of "best-sellerism."

The work of Stone & Kimball and Herbert S. Stone & Company combines to an unusual degree the three interests of personalities, place and period, and has offered an opportunity to examine with some precision a brand of books of proven significance in American culture of the recent past. The conditions under which Ingalls Kimball and Herbert Stone worked are sufficiently similar to the publishing scene of today, that without straining after generalizations, it is possible to bring their experience to bear on at least two

[3] See Raymond Howard Shove, *Cheap Book Production in the United States, 1870 to 1891* (Urbana: University of Illinois Library, 1937), p. 51, for details of the collapse of the cheap book publishing firms after 1891.

important contemporary problems. For, as O. H. Cheney remarks at the outset of his incomparable study of modern publishing economics, "The real problems of the industry are old—the older, the more real."

Is it possible to maintain a publishing business dealing in works of general literature and national interest, in Chicago or elsewhere in the West, while writing talents, no matter where they originate, continuously gravitate to intellectual trading posts in the East, and especially, New York? What, if any, are the special conditions under which such an enterprise can profitably continue? Second, although the closing of the house of Herbert Stone was a loss to Chicago and the Mid-Western region, it offers an example of an incompleted development from the publishing of an inspired amateur to a rounded professional and businesslike plan. To use Cheney's frame of reference again:

The growth of a house is safest when it is orderly—unless the heads know how to consolidate sudden gains. The older houses, particularly those with special departments, have naturally become stabilized at some point where, under ordinary conditions, they can depend on a certain proportion of income from back-list and special books. The newer houses pass through certain definite growth stages until they reach stability; and the history of a large proportion of publishers presents characteristic life-cycles.[4]

The six stages in the cycle demonstrate that a publishing house of any age must continue to grow in interests and connections if it is to continue successfully. By a combination of incidents already detailed in earlier chapters, Herbert Stone's best authors and chief associates in book publishing had left Chicago by 1905, and his gallant effort could not be continued single-handed.

SOURCES AND METHOD

Book publishing has been essentially the adventures of an entrepeneur among authors and printers, and the personal

[4] O. H. Cheney, *Economic Survey of the Book Industry, 1930-31* (New York: National Association of Book Publishers, 1931), p. 4.

account, now almost the sole source, will always be the first fount for the study of publishing history. Unfortunately, none of the principals of the House under consideration left a memoir. Advice from persons employed in important capacities, from authors and manufacturers, plus contemporary information from the trade press, has supplied only a part of the inner view. The letters written by Herbert Stone to his family between 1892 and 1906 make frequent reference to his business interests. Similar personal correspondence of Ingalls Kimball and of Melville E. Stone Jr., his brother's junior partner between 1897 and 1905, has not been preserved in as complete a form and I hope this has not led me to any injustice to their contributions. We should also know more of the editors—the late Harrison Rhodes and Lucy Monroe Calhoun.

The double task of compiling the Bibliography and writing the History has had its own rewards. First, it determined the form and arrangement of the bibliographies, and permitted the cross fertilization of these records from the sources used for the history; providing, for instance, details for the determination of the sequence of publication, and material of human interest for the notes. Second, it brought the realization that for the period in which American book printing, book publishing, and bookselling are separate trades—from about 1850 onwards, and corresponding roughly with the growing dominance of metropolitan over rural civilization in the United States—we have no concrete studies of individual traders in ideas comparable to the monographs on colonial printers or on imprints of various regions during their progress to statehood. We do have studies and bibliographies of fine modern printers and of private presses, but such work, in general, is not concerned with current thought. Periodic trade lists, cumulated catalogues, statistics of copyright, and census reports of manufactures give rough approximations of the content in bulk of books published in the United States since about 1875, but such records do not easily separate out into the streams which have come from the individual publishers of any specific area or limited time.

The existing state of the records does not permit one legitimate sort of inquisitiveness to be satisfied. Many persons have exhibited a desire, well expressed by one publisher, that I should "go over the account books of the firm and put down the partnership arrangement between Mr. Stone and Mr. Kimball, the cost of manufacture in proportion to the selling price, number of copies given away for review or other complimentary distribution, royalties paid to authors, profit or loss on individual titles, and all that sort of thing."[5] But the complete office records, ledgers and letter-files necessary for such "a miniature survey of the publishing business" have not been located in six years of search and I fear they have gone to limbo. The changes in place of publication and in the ownership of the firms' books and magazines, together with the lapse of thirty-four years since Herbert S. Stone & Company went out of business, have obscured the trail.

When Ingalls Kimball bought the book business of Stone & Kimball in 1896, the records were presumably taken to New York. At the public sale of Stone & Kimball in 1897 much autograph material was purchased by collectors and dealers. The William Sharp letters found their way into the Henry E. Huntington Library; the Stevenson file to Everts Wendell and from him to the Widener Library of Harvard College. Walter R. Benjamin, now dean of American autograph dealers, was a large purchaser and kindly permitted me, in 1936 and 1938, to examine such material as remained in his stock. There were other buyers who have held Stone & Kimball autograph material for a long time. Only in the summer of 1939 a group of fifty-one pieces of Stone & Kimball correspondence was sold at a New York auction house. Collectors, librarians and dealers (on the whole) have been most cooperative in allowing letters to be read, and the

[5]Mr. David T. Pottinger of Harvard University Press, in a letter of June 12, 1935.

authors involved have been uniformly courteous in granting permission for their use.

Herbert S. Stone & Company were the largest buyer of copyrights at Stone & Kimball's liquidation sale, and must have taken possession of accounts relating to the books. In 1898, *The Chap-Book* was merged into the Chicago *Dial*. Only fragments of correspondence relating to Stone & Kimball were found in the files, now privately owned, of this periodical. During the years the Stone Company published books from Chicago, offices were also maintained in London and in New York, and perhaps the branch records were never completely collected at the home office. The transfer of the Herbert S. Stone & Company booklist to Fox, Duffield & Company in 1906, "was a straight purchase for plates and merchandise only," writes Mr. Arthur B. Haaser, then Duffield's office manager. "Files, ledgers, and other business records were not included." The only business records of Stone & Kimball and Herbert S. Stone books which went to Dodd, Mead & Company when in 1934 they absorbed the Duffield company, were certain contracts with authors. During the years that Herbert Stone continued to publish *The House Beautiful,* he disposed of part of his autograph collection. Several important manuscripts were included in that portion (the greater) of his library, sold at auction in New York in 1918.[6]

Thus essential business records, such as ledgers, were not available for study. Some of the business correspondence with authors has been quoted in the History; other references will be found in the Bibliography. But an intimate study of the business history of Stone & Kimball or Herbert S. Stone & Company is not practicable unless the ledgers and office files can be recovered now.

[6]*Library of the Late Herbert Stuart Stone:* One of the Founders of the Great American Publishing House, Stone and Kimball, and Editor of The Chap-Book. Sold by Order of the Executors. (New York: The Anderson Galleries, December 16 and 17, 1918; Sale No. 1382.) The catalogue has a fine biographical note by Bliss Carman.

Sources which have been fruitful are, approximately in the order of their use: (1) A transcript of copyright entries filed at the Library of Congress under the names of Stone & Kimball and Herbert S. Stone & Company. (2) Advertisements of the firm in separate leaflets, in their own magazines, *The Chap-Book* and *The House Beautiful;* in the trade press, especially *Publishers' Weekly* and *Publishers' Trade List Annual.* (3) The books themselves, examined in private collections, especially of Mr. Herbert Stuart Stone Jr., Miss Dorothy Colman and Mr. Walter Walden of Chicago; Mr. Raleigh Morgan of Oak Park; Mrs. Kathryn Kimball Cohû of New York and Mr. Hartley Sanders of Washington; and in public institutions, especially Columbia University Library, the Library of Congress, and the Newberry Library. (4) Notices and reviews in literary journals, book trade and printing periodicals, and the Chicago newspapers. (5) The customary book and magazine literature of the printing and publishing trades, of literary biography and history. (6) Personal sources: conversations and correspondence with authors, artists, printers and bookbinders.

There follows this historical introduction, a bibliographical study, recording the sequence, title, contents, appearance, price, reprints and transfers of all publications bearing the imprint of Stone & Kimball and of Herbert S. Stone & Company. This study has been made not only for the sake of the record, but to bring together information on the history of these firms, which is lacking in the personal, manuscript and printed sources. The books are occasionally enigmatic, but by and large, they tell the story as nothing else could; for they are indeed the endproduct of the thought and dealings for which contemporary records are imperfect. It has been possible for the compiler to examine practically all publications. Five editions which were not found are marked with an asterisk; two others, with double asterisk, the compiler suspects will never be found.

Arrangement of the entries is chronological, by year, month and day of publication. All titles of books and magazines are in one series, although Nos. 95-106 and 107-125 were produced within the same period, from May 1896 to August 1897. The first group is included in the "Publications of Stone & Kimball; Cambridge, Chicago and New York, 1893-1897"; the second forms the first entries in the "Publications of Herbert S. Stone & Company; Chicago and New York, 1896-1905." Three checklists are added: "Publications of Way & Williams Reissued by Herbert S. Stone & Company"; "Printings Made for Copyright Purposes Only by Stone & Kimball and Herbert S. Stone & Company"; "Privately Printed Books Produced Under the Supervision of Stone & Kimball and Herbert S. Stone & Company."

The bibliographical entries of publications are divided: (1) *Heading* of serial number and transcript of title-page of the first edition regularly published. This transcript is reasonably exact, but does not reproduce the punctuation of hand-lettered title-pages. Large-paper and other limited issues are given a separate and briefer entry, as in Nos. 8, 8a and 8b. (2) *Production* facts, of size (in inches to sixteenths), pagination, presence of signatures (not set forth in detail), printer, types (text type first, display types second), paper, binding, illustrations, decoration and rubrication. The paginations include all printed leaves and blank pages cognate with them. In describing bindings the publications of John Carter have been helpful; his and Michael Sadleir's preference for general descriptive terms as against exact trade terminology has been followed. I have not attempted, however, to classify the American book cloths used. (3) *Publication,* covering date and circumstances of publication, and price. I have accepted the definitions formulated by Muir, of *edition* as "all copies of a book printed from one setting of type," and of *impression* as "... a new printing from the same setting of type..." with the derived *new impression, revised impression, new edition,* and *revised edition.* "*Publication* means the date on which books are issued to the public, or circulated by the author, and the *first edition* is the first to be so issued or circulated."[6]

Dates of publication have been derived chiefly from the records of deposit of copies in the Copyright Office of the Library of Congress. This is referred to as "Copyright"; "Entered for Copyright" is used where the title was registered and copies were intended to follow later. The "Weekly Record of New Publications" in each number of *Publishers' Weekly;* the *American Catalogue of Books;* the *English Catalogue of Books; Publishers' Circular;* the publishers' prospectuses, announcements, and advertisements have also been used. Some evidence on dating has been taken from correspondence, and inscriptions in office copies and authors' presentation copies. Where month and day of publication are not certain, the volume is entered at the end of the year which appears in its imprint; where month but not day is known, it is inserted at the end of the month. Those volumes copyrighted at the end of one year and dated for the next, are entered by date of copyright, and not of imprint.

(4) *Notes* on matters of typographic and literary interest, references to authorities on the biography and bibliography of authors, and occasionally, location of copies of books known to be rare. Locations have not been given for all titles published as practically all were copyrighted in England or the United States or both, and issued in editions of five hundred and upwards. The Union Catalogue of the national library records by author and edition the holdings of Stone items in libraries throughout the country; and the best collections are still in private hands. Under these circumstances, symbols for locations would be largely useless.

[6]Percy H. Muir, *Points, Second Series, 1866-1934* ("Bibliographia," viii; London: Constable & Co. Ltd; New York: R. R. Bowker Co., 1934), pp. 10, 15, 18.

"The Stone & Kimball imprint," remarks the editor of *Publishers' Weekly,* "remains a mark of editorial distinction and tasteful production, one of the few imprints which holds collectors' interest, even to the most minor issues." Such an interest, maintained over two generations, is a fit commemoration of the early work of Herbert Stone and Ingalls Kimball, who were both true bibliophiles. The books attract the attention of collectors first by their typography—only later, usually, does there come a realization that literary intelligence of a high order went into the choice of titles. It is evident in the books of Stone & Kimball and Herbert S. Stone & Company that there was a unifying artistic imagination behind

FIG. A

all of them. It is therefore difficult to separate the typographic contributions of the two partners. Stone was the more articulate artistically; he did, it will be remembered, illustrations as well as the text of his guidebook to the World's Fair. The vignettes are too small to be reproduced as adequate illustration of his amateur talent, but the book plate used in his college days will serve as an example.

Ingalls Kimball, if not a draughtsman, was inventive in the field of design, as in business. Thus after only a few years experience as a book publisher and designer, he conceived the new principles which went into Cheltenham Type, but had Bertram Grosvenor Goodhue make the actual drawings. Stone, older and more advanced in the study of books, had more to give at the beginning of their publishing days, while Kimball, as Mr. Bradley writes, later carried the Stone & Kimball book tradition into commercial typography.

It would be useless to try to separate minutely the typographic work of the two friends, but in the group of illustrations which follow this chapter, it has been possible in a few cases to attribute designs to one or the other of the partners, and in others to the designers who were commissioned. Mr. Melcher has described the identifying feature of the Stone books better than anyone else: "Whatever designers contributed, the publishers themselves moulded the books as a whole into such a common mood that a Stone & Kimball book is instantly recognized and prized by collectors. They loved the small 12mos, of which we see so few today, the size that Pickering had favored. They liked, too, semi-flat books, gold design on the cover or plain panel." *Grip* of 1896 is inconsequential as literature but charming as an *objet d'art* (Fig. 26). The binding is a shimmering salmon-pink cloth, with bold letter-stamping across spine and both sides; the circular monogram added in the outside corners of the sides, all within a simple rule border and all in gold. The title, set in an amusing display type, is rubricated, as is the conical device. The text type is a familiar old-timer; "Franklin Old Style," cut by Alexander C. Phemister in 1863. The setting was, as customary in the nineties, rather open—there are "rivers." The printer was the then wellknown firm of Fleming, Schiller & Carnrick of New York. The paper was machine-made, but with the Stone & Kimball watermark: laid, pliable, light-weight and pleasantly toned. There is something in the book which baffles description, and it is just that which creates the appeal of the Stone & Kimball books—it might be called warmth or intimacy, or pleasing tactile quality. *Grip,* like so many other Stone books, appeals and satisfies by its very bookishness.

There is nothing revolutionary in the design of the Stone books, where only materials and elements of design available to their contemporaries in publishing appear. There are two things about their design, besides the indefinable aura of charm, which should be mentioned. First, they exhibit as consistent care in commercial book production as has been maintained in this country. Second, there can be seen, between 1893 and 1896, a progression from a deluxe, ornamental style to one graceful but simple and functional. This evolution is one which repeats itself in many careers: in the case of Stone & Kimball, it is likely that the advice of their printers was helpful. Their first printer was the University Press of John Wilson & Son, where Eugene Field had done the limited editions which his Chicago friends sponsored. William Dana Orcutt, then serving his apprenticeship with John Wilson, remembers well the Field manuscripts of the early nineties, and Stone & Kimball and Copeland & Day books which followed. Herbert Stone and Ingalls Kimball had all to learn about practical book production when they began; the staff of the University Press, learned and interested, went out of the way to share their knowledge. Three books only were printed by the house of DeVinne for Stone & Kimball, but Theodore Low DeVinne continued to be interested in their productions to judge from his comments on the Stone & Kimball edition of *Ebb-Tide.* His copy, which came into Mr. Melcher's ownership at the sale of the DeVinne library, is marked throughout with corrections similar to those on the title-page (Fig. B), and was shown in the DeVinne establishment as "A Terrible Example." One wonders if the original publishers ever saw the volume, or heard these corrections

Don't like cond. type.

THE EBB TIDE

A TRIO & QUARTETTE

BY
ROBERT LOUIS STEVENSON
&
LLOYD OSBOURNE

"THERE IS A TIDE
IN THE AFFAIRS OF MEN."

CHICAGO
STONE & KIMBALL
M DCCCXC V

Short 8 on title page!

FIG. B

from Mr. DeVinne; at any rate, the mistakes are not repeated. The chief printer for Stone & Kimball and Herbert S. Stone & Company in Chicago was the Lakeside Press of R. R. Donnelley & Sons Company. The books and the magazines produced for Stone there have an honored place in the Donnelley Memorial Library; and many of the present-day executives of the firm, such as Mr. T. E. Donnelley, remember with appreciation the feeling for design which Herbert Stone felt and transmitted.

If one were asked what was the most beautiful book on the Stone lists, I should suggest that the handsomest book is one they did not publish, but produced privately for the author. This was the quarto edition of 250 copies, of Samuel Eberly Gross's play, *The Merchant Prince of Cornville*, printed at the University Press in 1896. For easy grandeur of style, simple excellence of typography, and careful use of fine materials, I commend this rare book, which has an importance in American literary and legal history, as well as in typography.

This is the first edition of the play, which was the basis for the famous plagiarism suit against Edmond Rostand's *Cyrano de Bergerac*. Gross, a successful real estate dealer, had completed this blank verse romance in 1878 in Chicago, when it was submitted to A. M. Palmer for production. Rejected, it was laid aside until 1889, when Gross left the manuscript with Coquelin at the Porte Saint Martin Theatre in Paris. There was no response here, and *The Merchant Prince of Cornville* was not produced until the eleventh of November, 1896, in London. A single performance was financed by the author, who also commissioned at this time the edition printed under the direction of Stone & Kimball. All the copies were distributed to his friends by Gross.

Cyrano de Bergerac was presented first on the twenty-eighth of December, 1897—at the Théâtre de la Porte Saint Martin, by Coquelin. It was an immediate success on the boards and in printed form, in France and abroad. Early in

1899 Richard Mansfield was playing an English version in New York, when first a friend, and later Gross, became convinced that at least one part of *The Merchant Prince of Cornville*—the dual wooing scene—had been plagiarized by Rostand. Mansfield and his producer, A. M. Palmer, were sued by Gross, who promised to pay costs if Mansfield would not defend. The hearings began in the federal courts of Illinois in June 1899, and the decision came in 1902, from Judge C. C. Kohlsaat. It was in favor of Gross, but rather on circumstantial than literary grounds. The ruling was ridiculed in journalistic, dramatic and academic circles, but the injunction granted in 1902 was maintained until 1920. Edward Vroom was then successful, in spite of the efforts of Gross's widow, in producing an English *Cyrano*. The decision vacating the injunction (by Judge Augustus N. Hand), as well as all the other relevant documents, are given in a careful monograph by Hobart Ryland, *The Sources of the Play Cyrano de Bergerac* (New York: Institute of French Studies, 1936).

Not all the books printed or published by Stone have as amusing histories, as beautiful typography, or as small editions as *The Merchant Prince of Cornville*. Those interested in acquiring a few Stone imprints as examples will probably have no trouble in purchasing them from the nearest antiquarian bookseller. Where condition and completeness are desired, it may be another matter. Not only the natural losses with time have been operative, but several libraries and dozens of collectors have been active. It is fortunate, however, that the books most important to complete a collection are not always the most attractive titles. A few rarities may be mentioned—hardest to get are the reprints of *Pilgrim's Progress, Uncle Tom's Cabin* and *The Wide, Wide World*—difficult also is the *Christmas Garland* of 1901, which has not been seen by the compiler. Juveniles are, as always, difficult to get in original condition; the most pleasing, perhaps, are the three Crane pamphlets; the two Canton volumes; *Noll and the*

Fairies; The Wonderful Stories of Jane and John; and *Just About a Boy*. The vellum-bound set of Poe on hand-made paper is an auction rarity, while the ten copies printed on japan vellum paper were *hors de commerce,* and remain so. Nor are the Beardsley *Illustrations to Poe* common. Four were published in 1901 in an edition of 250 copies, the size of the prints being enlarged from the original drawings received in 1895. We have reproduced (Fig. 8) two of the proof pulls in the original size.

It is customary, as well in closing a piece of historical research as in introducing a bibliography, to explain the weaknesses in methods and results. The present writer has no apologies for the weaknesses which will be obvious to the careful reader, but does beg off from criticism of the list of privately printed books, which he knows is incomplete. Those present in the list as printed were found only through chance, as books of this sort are not entered for copyright under the name of a publisher, nor advertised in the customary sources. Additions and corrections to this list (and of course to the others), will be heartily welcome.

Illustrations

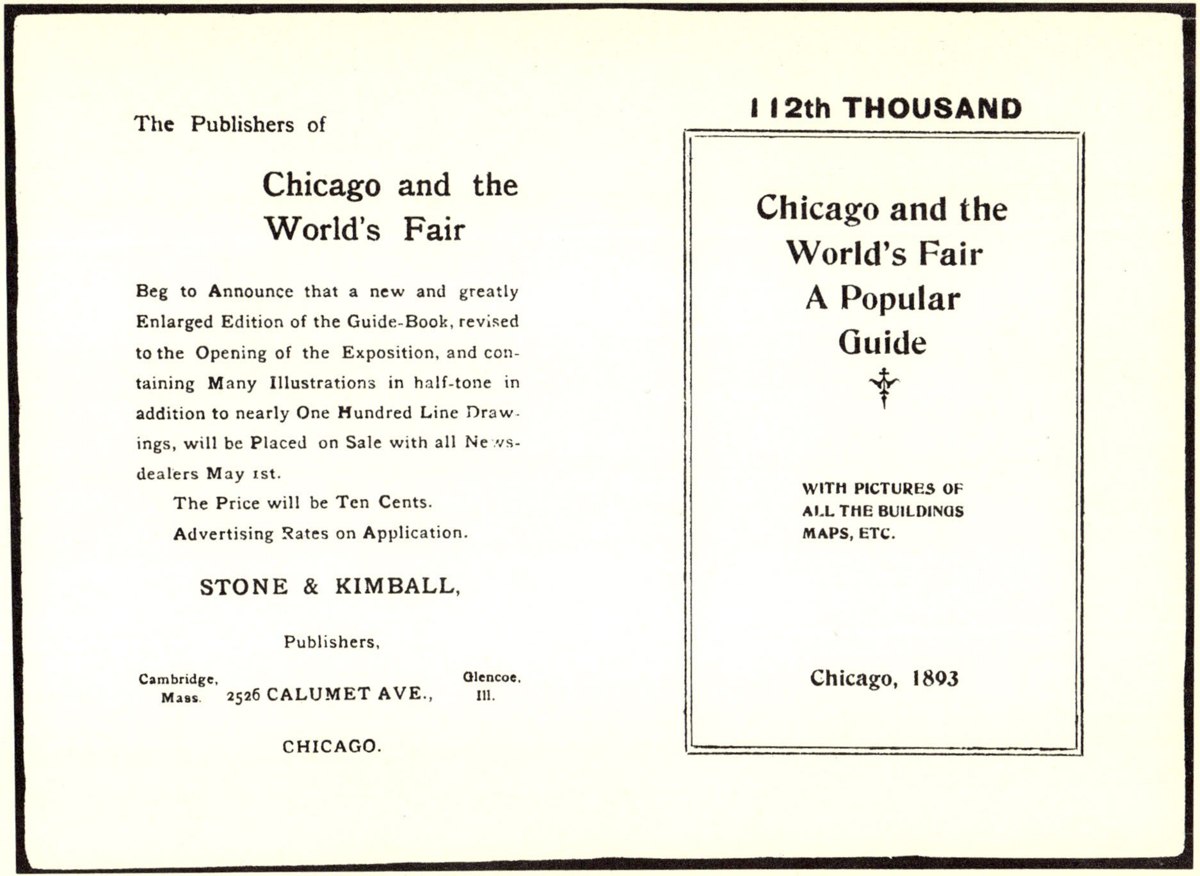

The Publishers of

Chicago and the World's Fair

Beg to Announce that a new and greatly Enlarged Edition of the Guide-Book, revised to the Opening of the Exposition, and containing Many Illustrations in half-tone in addition to nearly One Hundred Line Drawings, will be Placed on Sale with all Newsdealers May 1st.

The Price will be Ten Cents.

Advertising Rates on Application.

STONE & KIMBALL,

Publishers,

Cambridge, Mass. 2526 CALUMET AVE., Glencoe, Ill.

CHICAGO.

112th THOUSAND

Chicago and the World's Fair A Popular Guide

WITH PICTURES OF ALL THE BUILDINGS MAPS, ETC.

Chicago, 1893

FIG. 9. *Covers of the first publication of Stone & Kimball*

THE BUILDING

OF

THE CITY BEAUTIFUL

By JOAQUIN MILLER

CAMBRIDGE & CHICAGO
PUBLISHED BY STONE & KIMBALL IN THE YEAR
MDCCXCIII

FIG. 10B. *Stone & Kimball's Own Favorite Book*

First Editions of American Authors
A Manual for Book=Lovers com=
piled by Herbert Stuart
Stone with an Intro=
duction by Eugene
Field

CAMBRIDGE IN MASSACHUSETTS
PUBLISHED BY STONE & KIMBALL
IN THE YEAR MDCCCXCIII

FIG. 10A. *Stone & Kimball's First Book*

FIG. 11. *Some early bindings for Stone & Kimball*

MAIN-TRAVELLED ROADS

BEING SIX STORIES OF THE MISSISSIPPI VALLEY BY HAMLIN GARLAND, WITH AN INTRODUCTION BY W. D. HOWELLS AND DECORATIONS BY H. T. CARPENTER

CAMBRIDGE AND CHICAGO
PUBLISHED BY STONE AND
KIMBALL IN THE YEAR
MDCCCXCIII

FIG. 12. *Hamlin Garland's first publication with Stone & Kimball*

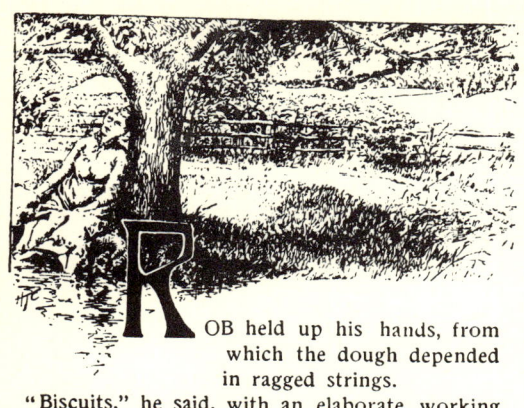

ROB held up his hands, from which the dough depended in ragged strings.

"Biscuits," he said, with an elaborate working of his jaws, intended to convey the idea that they were going to be specially delicious.

Seagraves laughed, but did not enter the shanty door. "How do you like baching it?"

"Oh, don't mention it!" entreated Rob, mauling the dough again. "Come in an' sit down. What in thunder y' standin' out there for?"

"Oh, I'd rather be where I can see the prairie. Great weather!"

"*Im*-mense!"

"How goes breaking?"

"Tip-top! A *leetle* dry now; but the bulls pull the plough through two acres a day. How's things in Boomtown?"

"Oh, same old grind."

"Judge still lyin'?"

139

FIG. 13. *From Main-Travelled Roads. Vignette by H. T. Carpenter. The type is "Elzevir"*

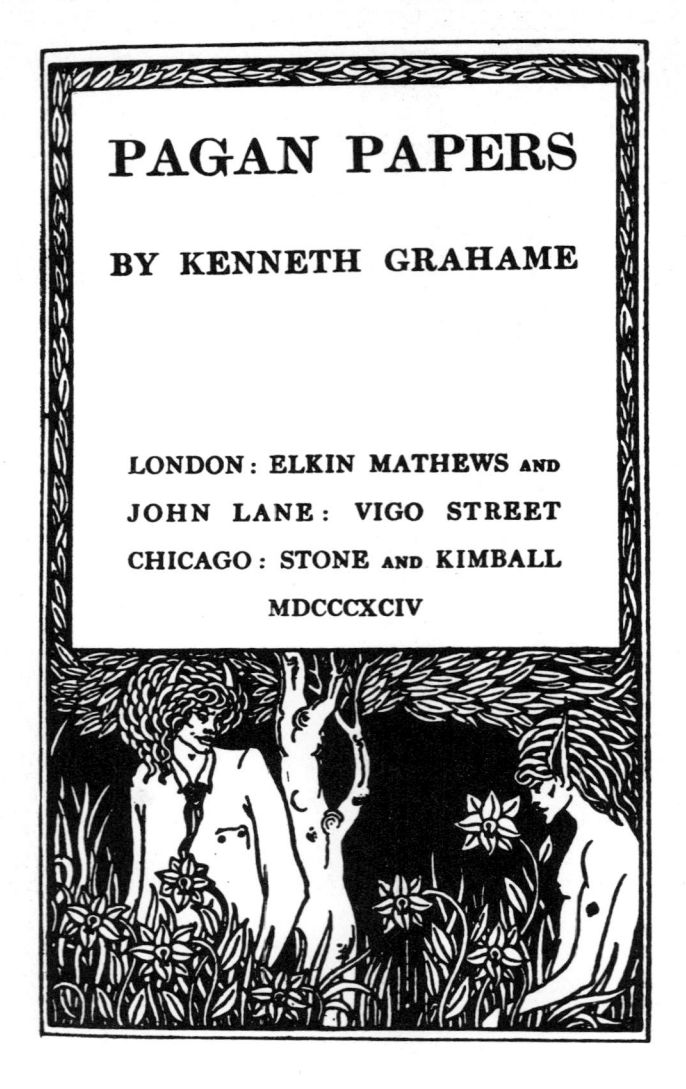

FIG. 14A. *Border by Aubrey Beardsley*

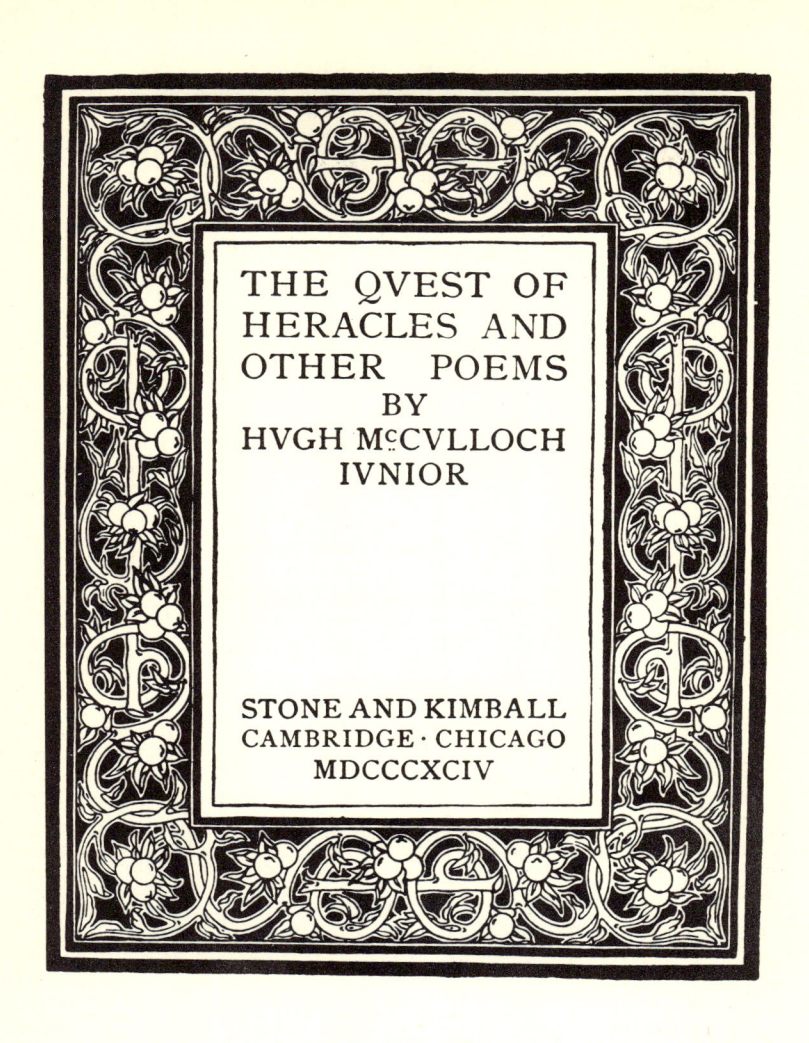

THE QVEST OF
HERACLES AND
OTHER POEMS
BY
HVGH McCVLLOCH
IVNIOR

STONE AND KIMBALL
CAMBRIDGE · CHICAGO
MDCCCXCIV

FIG. 15A. *Border by Pierre la Rose*

FIG. 16B. Border and lettering by the Author

FIG. 16A. Border and lettering by Martin Mower

166

FIG. 17. *Binding by T. B. Meteyard*

THE
Chap-Book
SEMI-MONTHLY

Contents for May 15, 1894

THE UNSLEEPING.   CHARLES G. D. ROBERTS
TITLEPAGE DESIGNED FOR "THE EBB-TIDE."
       T. B. METEYARD
MR. FRANCIS THOMPSON'S POEMS.   BLISS CARMAN
A BITTER COMPLAINT OF THE UNGENTLE READER.
"ME 'N' MAJE."   MARIA LOUISE POOL
THE EGOTIST.
MR. AUBREY BEARDSLEY — AFTER HIMSELF.
ANNOUNCEMENTS.

PRICE 5 CENTS $1.00 A YEAR

Published by
Stone & Kimball
Chicago & Cambridge

FIG. 18. *Volume I, Number 1*

FIG. 19. *Chap-Book cover by Claude Bragdon*

In Russet & Silver

By

Edmund Gosse

Chicago
Stone & Kimball
MDCCCXCIV

Claude Bragdon
FIG. 20. *Typography by H. S. Stone*

FIG. 21. *Binding by Will H. Bradley*

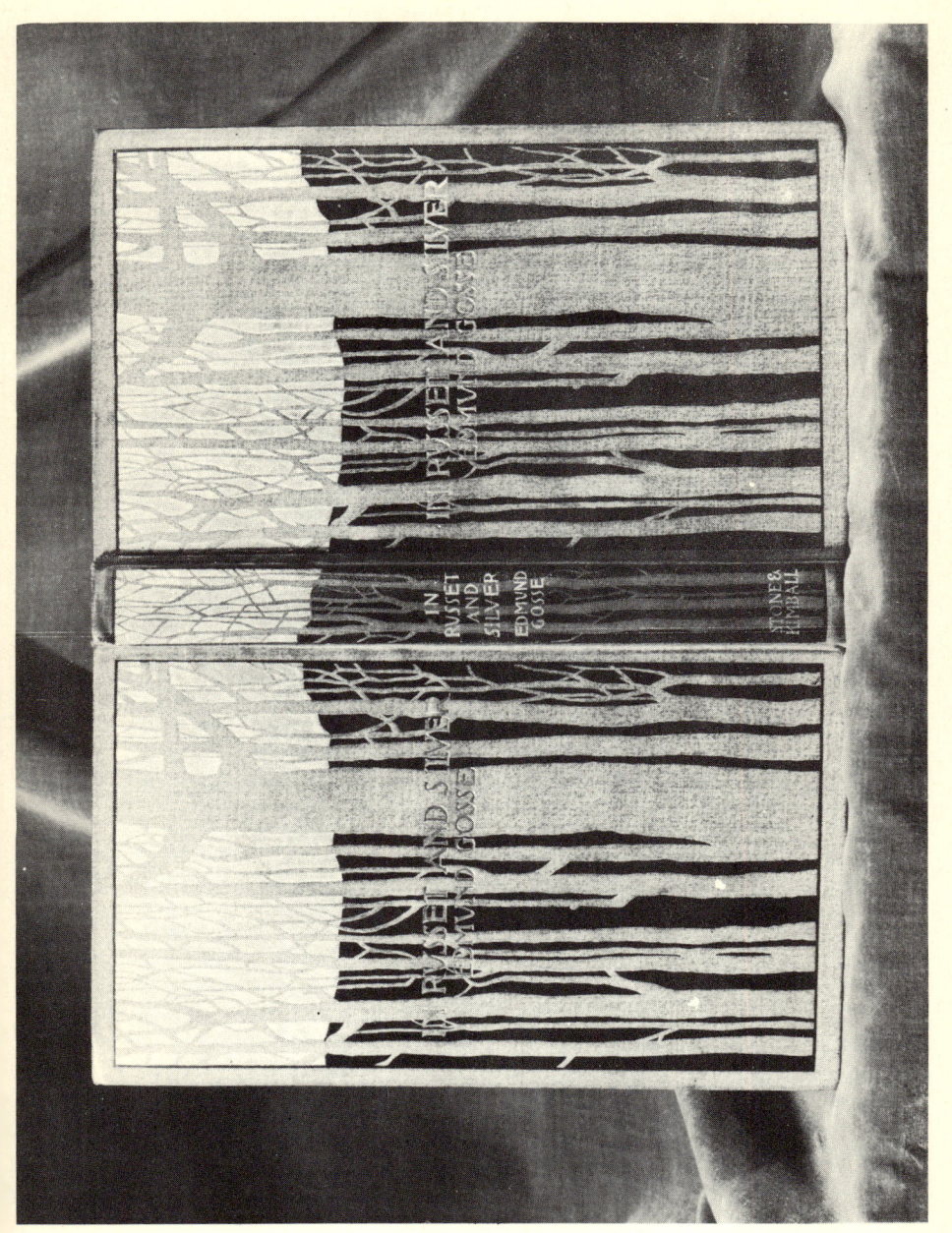

FIG. 22. *Two bindings designed by H. S. Stone*

FIG. 23. *Two bindings designed by Bruce Rogers*

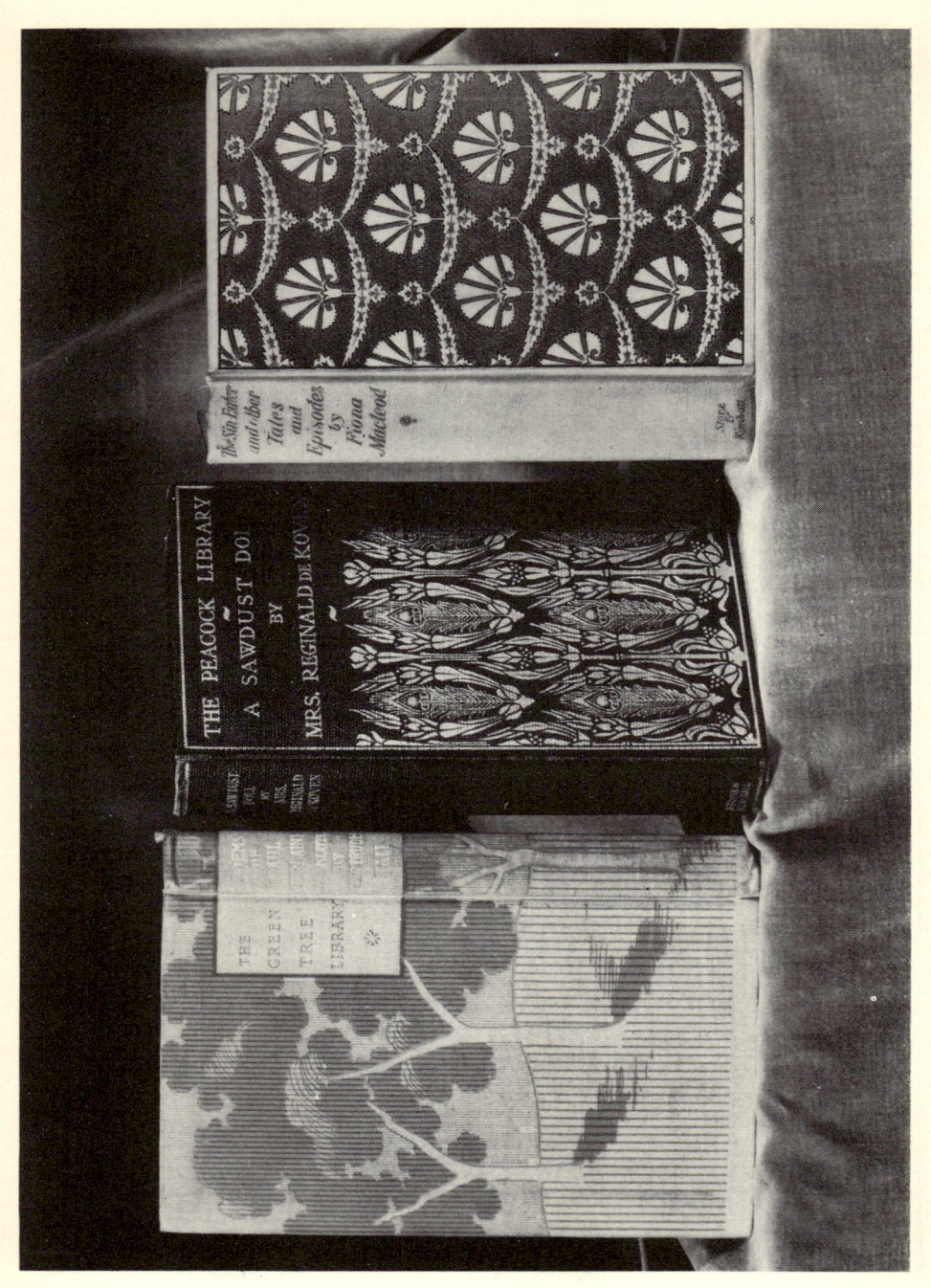

FIG. 24. *Series bindings for Stone & Kimball*

FIG. 25. *Edition bindings for Stone & Kimball*

175

GRIP

BY

JOHN. STRANGE WINTER

NEW YORK
STONE & KIMBALL
M DCCC XCVI

FIG. 26. *Title designed by H. I. Kimball*
The type is "Rimpled"

Face to Face

CHAPTER X.

FACE TO FACE.

WHEN I heard the name of Desmond de Lancy as that of my future comrade of the chain I almost swooned away in the intensity of my excitement. So at last I understood why I had been deprived of my liberty and brought to that hell of torture and despair. After all, Heaven had been very good to me, and mine enemy was delivered into my hand. I could do with him even as I would—I could draw out the pains and penalties of revenge to as fine a nicety as I chose.

These and many other wild and exultant thoughts rang through my head, together with the beating of great drums, the rushing sound of many waters, the ding-dong of huge bells which first rang loud and clear, and then seemed to fade away into the far distance; and when at last the sensation of

121

FIG. 27. *The text type is Modernized Old Style*

EPISCOPO & COMPANY

BY

GABRIELE D'ANNUNZIO

TRANSLATED BY
MYRTA LEONORA JONES

PUBLISHED BY
HERBERT S. STONE
& COMPANY, CHICAGO

MDCCCXCVI

FIG. 28. *Typography by H. S. Stone
Ornament by Frank Hazenplug*

Love's Dilemmas

By ROBERT HERRICK
Author of "The Man Who Wins"
"The Gospel of Freedom," Etc.

H. S. STONE & COMPANY
CHICAGO MDCCCXCVIII

FIG. 29. *Typography and ornaments by Will H. Bradley*

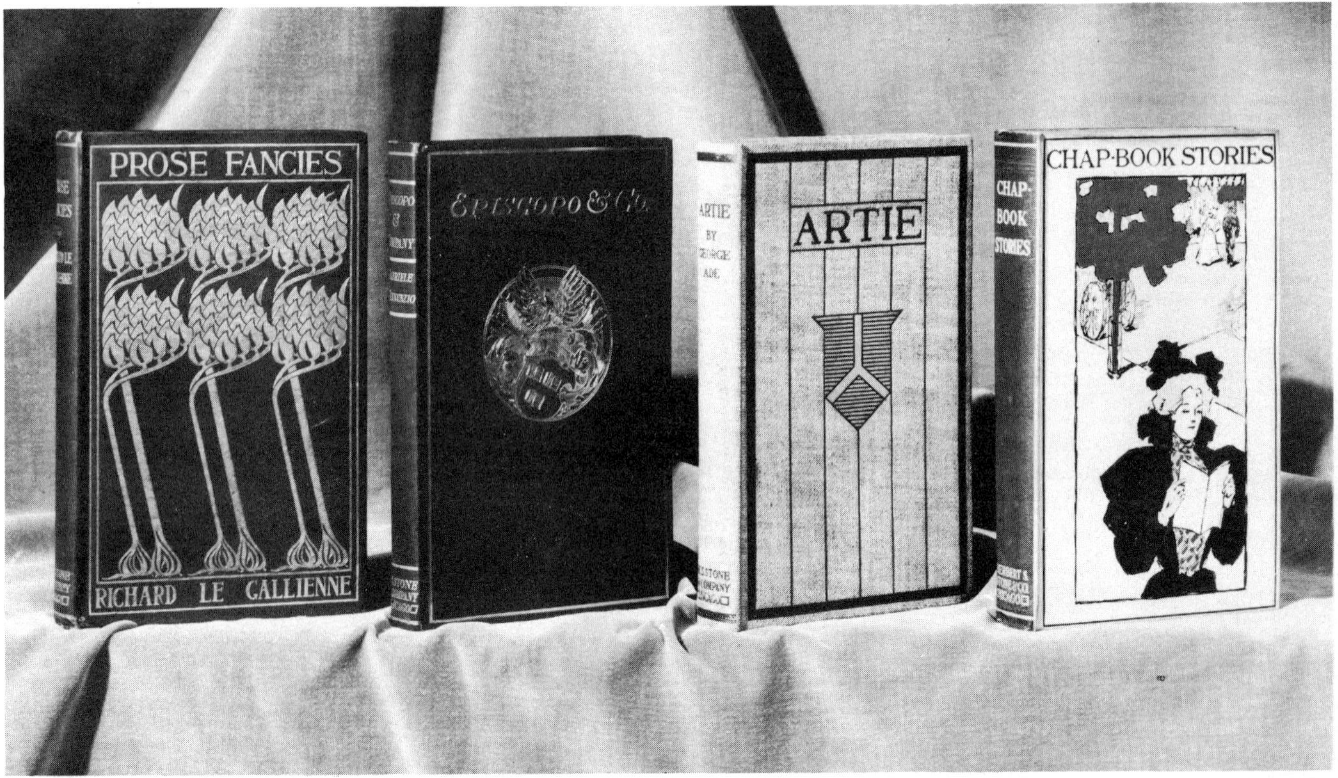

FIG. 30. *Some early bindings for Herbert S. Stone & Company*

FIG. 31. *Some later bindings for Herbert S. Stone & Company*

FIG. 32. *Binding design by Blanche McManus*

FIG. 33. *Stone editions of Shaw*

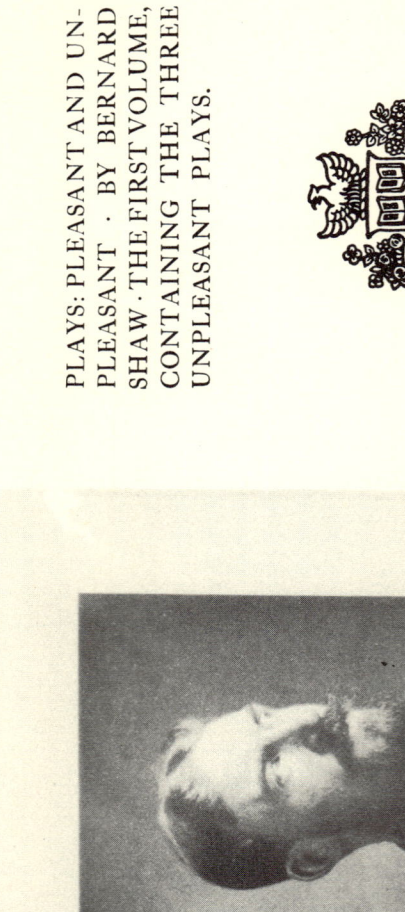

PLAYS: PLEASANT AND UNPLEASANT · BY BERNARD SHAW · THE FIRST VOLUME, CONTAINING THE THREE UNPLEASANT PLAYS.

CHICAGO AND NEW YORK: HERBERT S. STONE AND COMPANY, MDCCCXCVIII

FIG. 34. *Shaw's Portrait and Plays*

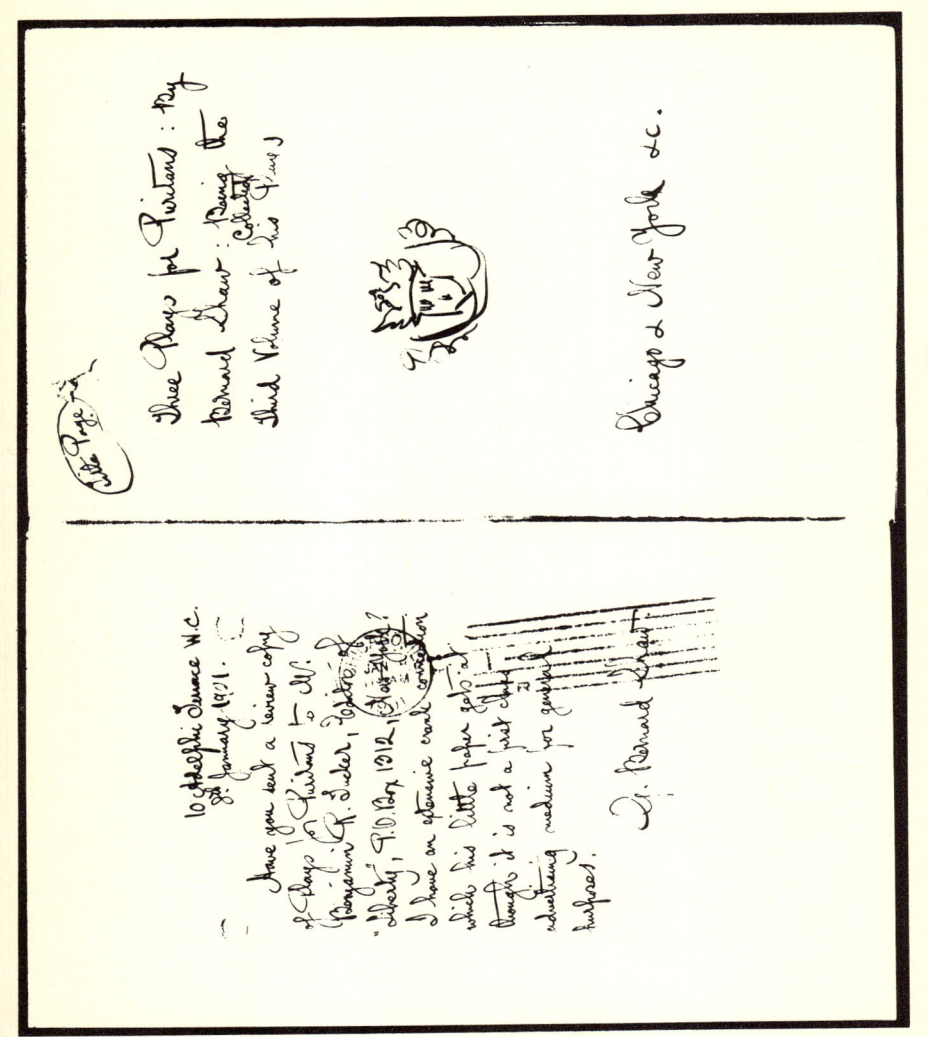

FIG. 35. "G. B. S. Recommends"

GRAUSTARK

THE STORY OF A LOVE BEHIND A THRONE

BY

George Barr McCutcheon

Herbert S. Stone and Company
Eldridge Court, Chicago
MDCCCCI

FIG. 36. *Stone's Best Seller*

FIG. 37. *A First Novel by Wardon Allan Curtis*

FIG. 38. *Poster by John T. McCutcheon for George Ade's Pink Marsh*

FIG. 39. *Poster by J. C. Lyendecker for The Chap-Book*

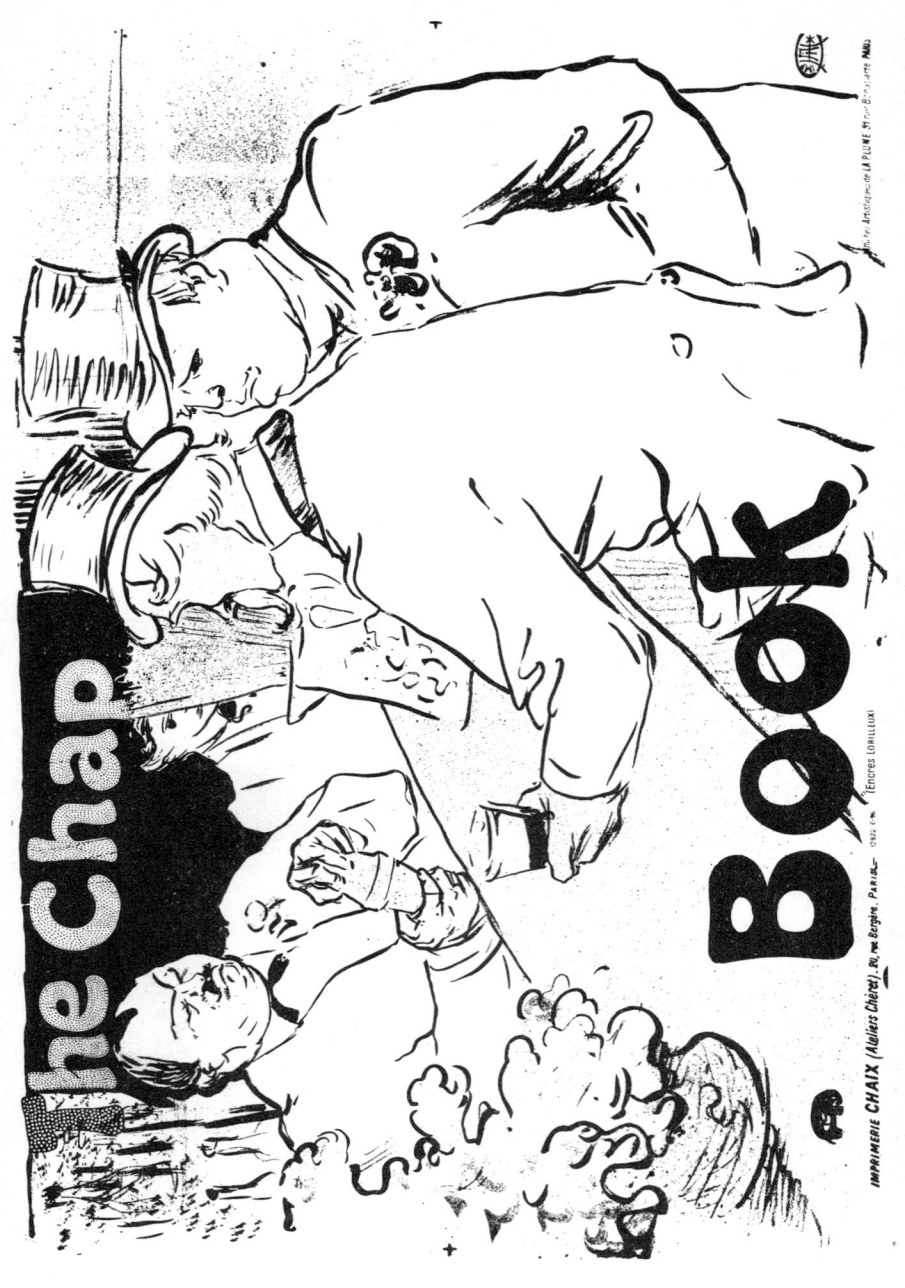

FIG. 40. "Irish-American Bar" by Toulouse-Lautrec: Poster for The Chap-Book

Bibliography

PUBLISHER'S DEVICES

1. Designed by H. S. Stone in 1893. Used first in *First Editions of American Authors* (No. 2).

2. Designed by H. S. Stone in 1893. Used first in *Main-Travelled Roads* (No. 5). Usually printed within blind impression, giving appearance of engraving.

3. Designed by H. S. Stone in 1896. Used first in *Prose Fancies* (No. 107). Usually printed within blind impression.

4. Designed by Frank Hazenplug in 1896. Used first in *Episcopo & Company* (No. 108). Usually printed within blind impression.

5. Probably designed by Claude Bragdon in 1896. Used first in *A Child of the Jago* (No. 113). Usually printed within blind impression.

6. Designed by Claude Bragdon in 1896. Used first in *Essays from The Chap-Book* (No. 119).

7. Probably designed by Claude Bragdon in 1897. Used first in *The Jessamy Bride* (No. 126).

8. Designed by Claude Bragdon in 1898. Used first for a title-page in *A Golden Sorrow* (No. 158). Appears enlarged, with Bragdon's emblem, in advertisements, etc.

9. Bragdon's Device Eight, with extra "sprouts" by Will Bradley. Used first in *Love's Dilemmas* (No. 180).

10. Designed by H. S. Stone in 1899. Used first in *My Father & I* (No. 218).

BINDING MONOGRAMS

Publisher's Devices

TABLE III

1

2

3

4

5

6

7

H.S. STONE AND CO. CHICAGO

8

FAIRE ET TAIRE

10

FAIRE ET TAIRE

9

FAIRE ET TAIRE

I

Publications of
Stone & Kimball
Cambridge, Chicago and New York, 1893-1897

[1]

Chicago | and | The World's Fair | [*rule*] | A Popular Guide | [*rule*] | Illustrated | [*circular vignette*] | Chicago | 1893

5-5/8 x 4-1/4; pp. [4], iv, 64. Printer not given but probably Donohue & Henneberry, Chicago; Modern-face type; newsprint paper. Stapled into paper wrappers of terra-cotta color, sides printed in black; edges cut. Illustrations include four maps, frontispiece and forty drawings in text by Herbert Stuart Stone, seven drawings by John T. McCutcheon.

Published April 1893. 2000 copies at 5 cents.

Written by Herbert Stuart Stone; previously printed for the author and Melville E. Stone Jr. by Donohue & Henneberry, and copyright September 26, 1892 as *Popular Guide to Chicago and the World's Fair*. This impression with changed title and announcement of Stone & Kimball as publishers on back cover, made when 100,000 copies were printed for the Plymouth Rock Pants Company, with their and other advertisements.

See below, pp. 3-4, 8-11 and Fig. 9. The original edition of *Popular Guide* and the separate issues under present title for the publishers and for advertisers, each known at present in unique copies, in Library of Congress, collection of H. Stuart Stone Jr. and Henry E. Huntington library respectively.

[1a] *Advertising Issue*

Size, pagination, type, paper and illustrations as above. Stapled into paper wrappers of blue color, sides printed in black; edges cut.

Printed April 1893. 100,000 copies for free distribution by Plymouth Rock Pants Company.

Advertisements on front and back wrappers of Plymouth Rock Pants

Company; of Quaker Oats on recto of frontispiece; slogans of the distributors and of Yale Pipe Mixture as footlines in text.

[2]
First Editions of American Authors | A Manual for Book Lovers com- | piled by Herbert Stuart | Stone with an Intro- | duction by Eugene Field | [*floret*] | [*device one in red*] | Cambridge in Massachusetts | Published by Stone & Kimball | In the year MDCCCXCIII

6-1/2 x 4-1/4; pp. xxiv, 223, [5]; with signatures. Printed by University Press, Cambridge, in Modernized Old Style type on laid paper. Bound in smooth green cloth over bevel-edged boards; printed in gold on spine and front cover. Title, printed partly in black letter, rubricated. Woodcut ornament at head of p. 1.

Copyright June 26, 1893; colophon dated May 1893. Prospectus issued February 1893. 450 copies at $1.25.

Called "Stone & Kimball's First Book," this is literally the first bound volume published by Stone & Kimball and the first work with that imprint on its title-page. However, the name of Stone & Kimball as publishers appears on the back cover of the pamphlet *Chicago and the World's Fair,* issued in April 1893. See No. 1, pp. 12-16, Fig. 10a. § Device one, square publisher's mark designed by H. S. Stone, with motto "Faire et Taire," used only in this book.

[2a] *Large Paper Issue*
8-1/2 x 6-3/8; pagination, signatures, printer, type and paper as above. Bound in lavender cloth; paper label on spine; edges uncut.

50 copies, numbered and signed by the publishers, at $3.50. Those out of series, reserved for H. S. Stone, H. I. Kimball and Eugene Field, labelled "Editor's Copy."

[3]
The | Terra Cotta Guide | Chicago and the | World's Fair. | [*rule*] | With pictures of all the build- | ings, maps, diagrams, etc. | [*rule*] | Chicago: Stone & Kimball. | 1893

5-5/8 x 4-1/4; pp. 105, [3]; folded frontispiece inserted. Printer not given; Modern-face type; newsprint paper. Stapled into paper wrappers of terra-cotta color; front cover printed in black; edges cut. Illustrations include two maps, one a double-page chart of fair grounds as frontispiece; the drawings by H. S. Stone and John T. McCutcheon made in 1892; additional sketches by a third hand; and fourteen half-tones.

Copyright August 22, 1893. 5000 copies. Probable price 10 cents. Poster issued June 1893.

Revised and enlarged edition of the guidebook written by H. S. Stone in 1892. Described from an unique copy, in the Library of Congress, which now lacks back cover. The front cover here has at head "117th Thousand," an aggregate of all printings.

[4]
Main-Travelled Roads | being six stories of the | Mississippi Valley by | Hamlin Garland, with an | Introduction by W. D. | Howells and Decora- | tions by H. T. Carpenter | [*device two in red*] | Cambridge and Chicago | Published by Stone and | Kimball in the year | MDCCCXCIII

6-1/2 x 4-1/4; pp. [viii], 251, [3]; frontispiece inserted. Printed by University Press, Cambridge, in "Elzevir" type on English wove paper. Bound in green buckram; stamped in gold on sides and spine with cornstalk design and lettering. Binding, frontispiece, six illustrative headpieces and a tailpiece designed by H. T. Carpenter. Title rubricated. Title-page reproduced in Fig. 12, page of text with illustration in Fig. 13, binding in Fig. 11.

Copyright December 4, 1893; listed in *Publishers' Weekly* December 2. Prospectus issued October 1893. Price $1.25. First issued in book form 1891 by Arena Publishing Company, Boston; published in England May 1893 by T. Fisher Unwin. Setting of type and illustrations new in the Stone & Kimball edition; introduction reprinted from *Harper's Magazine*, September 1891. New impressions dated 1894 and 1898; included in Stone's "Court Series," 1900. Republished 1899 by Macmillan with three additional stories; 1909 and since by Harper, 1922 edition having eleven stories and new preface by Garland, 1930 edition twelve stories, and illustrations by Constance Garland. § Hamlin Garland published four other books with Stone & Kimball before the end of 1895; *Prairie Songs*, No. 5, *Crumbling Idols*, No. 19, *Rose of Dutcher's Coolly*, No. 62, *Prairie Folks*, No. 63. Device two, conical publisher's mark with motto "Faire et Taire," probably designed by H. S. Stone, used here for the first time; see Table III.

[4a] *Large Paper Issue*
7-5/8 x 5-7/8; pp. [x], 251, [3]. Printer, type and illustrations as above; handmade wove paper. Bound in cream buckram, stamped in gold on sides and spine with cornstalk design and lettering.

110 copies, numbered and signed by the publishers; 100 for sale at $5.00 net. Some copies also signed by author.

[5]
Prairie Songs | being chants rhymed and | unrhymed of the level lands of the Great West | by Hamlin Garland with | Drawings by H. T. Carpenter | [*device two in red*] | Cambridge and Chicago | Published by Stone and | Kimball in the year | MDCCCXCIII

6-1/2 x 4-1/4; pp. [vi], 1-8, 17-164, [2]. Printed by University Press, Cambridge, in "Elzevir" type on English wove paper. Bound in green buckram; stamped in gold on sides and spine with cornstalk design and lettering. Binding, six full-page illustrations, forty-two headpieces and seven tailpieces designed by H. T. Carpenter. Title rubricated.

Copyright December 4, 1893; listed in *Publishers' Weekly* December 2. Prospectus issued October 1893. Price $1.25. Secondary binding of dark green cloth with same stamping, probably made in 1894.

On verso of title-page in all copies, ". . . this is of the first edition." The volume has not been republished.

[5a] *Large Paper Issue*
7-5/8 x 5-7/8; pagination, printer, type and illustrations as above; handmade wove paper. Bound in cream buckram; stamped in gold on sides and spine with cornstalk design and lettering.

110 copies, numbered and signed by the publishers; 100 for sale at $5.00 net. Most copies also signed by the author.

[6]
The Building | of |The City Beautiful | [*rule*] | by Joaquin Miller | [*rule*] | [*device two in red*] | [*rule*] | Cambridge & Chicago | Published by Stone & | Kimball in the year | MDCCCXCIII

6-1/2 x 4-1/4; pp. [4], iv, 196, [4]; with signatures. Printed by University Press, Cambridge, in Modernized Old Style type on laid paper. Bound in dark grey cloth over bevel-edged boards, stamped in gold on sides and spine with floral ornament and lettering. Trade binding designed by George H. Hallowell. Title in a bold-face type and rubricated.

Copyright December 9. First edition (500 copies at $1.50) issued December 10, 1893, according to copyright page of second and third impressions, May 15 and November 24, 1894. Third edition sold in calf at $3.50. Published in England October 1894 by John Lane. Revised and enlarged edition published 1905 by Albert Brandt, Trenton, N. J.

An Utopian prose romance, with epigraphs in verse for each of its twenty-four chapters. Its unfinished character, remarked by Joaquin Miller in his preface to the 1905 edition, is indicated by the lack of titles for chapters xvi and xxi.

[6a] *Large Paper Issue*

7-7/8 x 5-7/8; pagination, signatures, printer and type as above; handmade wove paper. Bound in grey boards; paper label on spine; edges uncut.

50 copies, numbered and signed by the publishers, at $3.50 net.

Pages 46 and 47 were transposed in arranging the forms for the large paper issue; copies are found either with these pages misplaced, or corrected with pp. 45-48, the seventh and eighth leaves of signature 3, as cancels.

[7]

His Broken Sword by | Winnie Louise Taylor | With an Introduction | by Edward Everett Hale | [*device two in brown*] | Cambridge and Chicago | Published by Stone and Kimball | MDCCCXCIII

7-7/8 x 5-3/8; pp. [4], viii, [9], 354, [4]; with signatures. Printed by University Press, Cambridge, in Modernized Old Style and "Elzevir" types on laid paper. Bound in blue cloth, stamped in gold; on front cover with decorative panel and lettering, on spine with lettering and floret, on back cover with panel. Decorative initial letters begin each chapter.

Copyright December 16, 1893; colophon dated November 28. Price $1.25. First published 1888 by A. C. McClurg & Co.; introduction new in Stone & Kimball printing, identified on copyright page as "Third Edition."

Novel of prison life, by the reformer who later wrote a sociological study of *The Man Behind the Bars*.

[8]

The Holy- | Cross | and other | tales | by Eugene Field | [*ornament*] | Stone & Kimball | Cambridge & Chicago ÷ | MDCCCXCIII [*lettered in red and black within triple rules within floral border*]

6-1/4 x 4-1/4; pp. [viii], [13]-191, [5]; with signatures. Printed by University Press, Cambridge, in Modernized Old Style type on wove paper; blue endpapers. Bound in blue ribbed cloth; decorated on sides with all-over floral design in gold, lettering and crosses in silver, within silver and gold rules; spine lettered in gold and decorated in silver. Binding, title-page, and eleven decorative initial letters designed by Louis J. Rhead.

Copyright December 9. First edition issued December 20, 1893, according to copyright page of second, third and fourth impressions, January 19 and December 1, 1894, January 25, 1896. Prospectus issued, probably October 1893. Price $1.25. Transferred to Scribner 1896.

Eugene Field furnished the introduction to Herbert Stone's *First Editions of American Authors,* and his *A Sentimental Life of Horace* was announced as "In Preparation" for Stone & Kimball. This he never wrote, but before his death on December 12, 1895, Field's poem "Boccacio" was printed in *The Chap-Book* for December 15, 1894. A self-caricature appeared in the issue of February 1, 1895, and a short poem was printed as an advertisement for The Morris Bookshop, October 1, 1894.

[8a] *Holland Paper Issue*

7-3/4 x 5-5/8; vi, [ii], [13]-191, [5]. Printer and type as above; Van Gelder Zonen laid paper. Bound in blue ribbed silk cloth; paper label on spine; edges uncut. Two leaves of Japan vellum paper inserted at front, forming pp. [i-iv], and including title, which is printed in red and green.

110 copies, numbered and signed by the publishers; 100 for sale at $5.00 net.

Dedicatory poem "To Roswell Martin Field," on pp. [v]-vi, does not appear in trade edition. Also added to "Contents," p. [vii], is a line beneath the title of each of the eleven Tales, naming the dedicatee.

[8b] *Japan Paper Issue*

7-3/4 x 5-5/8; vi, [ii], [13]-191, [5]. Printer and type as above; Japan vellum paper. Bound in vellum; stamped in gold and silver on sides and spine from dies used on binding of trade edition; top edge gilt, others uncut.

20 copies, signed by the publishers, 5 for sale, according to the edition notice. This issue was mentioned in the prospectus but price not given; not advertised.

This includes the same material as the Holland paper issue. The description given is of Mr. Frederick Coykendall's copy, which has an autograph poem by Field on a front fly-leaf, not present in other copies recorded. One other copy, described by Mr. J. S. Van E. Kohn, is in a binding of plain vellum, with paper label on spine and top edge stained rose instead of gilt.

[9]

Pagan Papers | by Kenneth Grahame | London: Elkin Mathews and | John Lane: Vigo Street | Chicago: Stone and Kimball | MDCCCXCIV [*within illustrative border*]

6-3/4 x 4-1/4; pp. viii. 165, [3]; with signatures. Catalogue of Mathews & Lane, 16 pp. and dated September 1893, inserted. Printed by T. & A. Constable, Edinburgh, in Scotch Modern-face type on laid paper. Bound in green ribbed cloth, printed in gold on spine. Title-page border by Aubrey Beardsley; see Fig. 14a.

Published in England December 1893 and probably available here at the same time. A note on Stone & Kimball publications in *The Critic* of New York, November 11, 1893, states that the volume "will appear early in December." American issue not advertised nor listed in *Publishers' Weekly*, but is included in Stone & Kimball's first trade catalogue in *Publishers' Trade List Annual,* August 1894. Price $1.50 net.

First importation of Stone & Kimball, followed in April 1894 by three more books from The Bodley Head; all bound as well as printed abroad. § Grahame's first book, incorporating with articles reprinted from English periodicals, the first six of the "Golden Age" essays, which grew to a volume of their own in 1895. See No. 43, and Patrick R. Chalmers, *Kenneth Grahame* (London: Methuen & Co. Ltd. [1933]), pp. 55, 84.

[10]

Lincoln's Grave | by | Maurice Thompson | 18 [*device two*] 94 | Cambridge | and Chicago | Stone | and | Kimball [*within decorative frame and border*]

6-3/4 x 4-3/8; pp. [50] unnumbered. Printed by University Press, Cambridge, in Modernized Old Style type on laid paper. Bound in vellum, printed in gold on spine; silk ties. Title in a bold-face type and rubricated; border by George H. Hallowell.

Copyright February 19; colophon dated January 1894. 450 copies at $1.25. Not reprinted, but appears in secondary bindings of orange buckram and grey boards.

The Phi Beta Kappa poem at Harvard in 1893.

[10a] *Large Paper Issue*

8-1/4 x 5; pagination, printer and type as above; Ruisdael handmade laid paper. Bound in vellum, printed in gold on spine. Issued in marbled paper slipcase.

50 numbered copies, at $3.50. Also appears in secondary binding of grey boards with white paper spine, leather label; edges uncut.

A distinction is made in Merle Johnson's *American First Editions* (3d ed.), between the trade edition of 450 copies with imprint "Cambridge and Chicago" and "50 large paper copies with Cambridge imprint only." Three large paper copies examined have, like the trade edition, the "Cambridge and Chicago" imprint. The title in both issues is on a single leaf, pasted in.

[11]
Sonnets | And Other Verses By | George Santayana | Stone and Kimball | Cambridge and Chicago | MDCCCXCIV [*within decorative frame and border*]

6-3/4 x 4-1/4; pp. [viii], 90. Printer not given here, but identified in colophon of large paper issue as University Press, Cambridge; Modernized Old Style type; laid paper. Bound in rose or blue-black buckram over bevel-edged boards; printed in gold on spine; edges uncut. Border and lettering in title by the author (Fig. 16b).

Copyright March 10, 1894; listed in *Publishers' Weekly* April 21. 450 copies at $1.25. "Second Edition" advertised September 1894; "Revised and Enlarged Edition" published June 1896; see Nos. 79 and 201.

Santayana's first book, printed dissertation of 1889 excepted; see bibliography by Justus Buchler and Benjamin Schwartz in his *Obiter Scripta* (New York: Charles Scribner's Sons, 1936), pp. 301-3. Many of the twenty sonnets had already been printed in the *Harvard Monthly;* the "Other Poems" (reading of half-title and binding) include "Odes," "Various Poems," and the first version of "Lucifer." § Printing at head and foot of spine, as well as color of cloth, varies in binding of first edition, but priority has not been established.

STATE A. Sonnets | And | Other | Poems   in space 11/16"
          Stone | and | Kimball   in space 5/16"
          Blue-black buckram

STATE B. Sonnets | And | Other | Poems   in space 11/16"
          Stone & | Kimball   in space 3/16"
          Rose buckram

STATE C. Sonnets | And | Other | Poems   in space 1/2 "
          Stone | & | Kimball   in space 5/16"
          Blue-black and rose buckram

The copy noted in Merle Johnson's *American First Editions,* with "John Dickinson & Co. Ltd New York" stamped on front cover is presumably one of the regular trade edition, from the files of the firm which supplied Stone & Kimball with paper, and has no general significance.

[11a] *Large Paper Issue*

8 x 5-1/8; pp. [vi], 90, [2]. Printed by University Press, Cambridge, in Modernized Old Style type on Ruisdael handmade laid paper; endpapers of Japan vellum. Bound in vellum, printed in gold on spine. Issued in marbled paper slipcase.

60 numbered copies, 50 for sale at $3.50.

[12]

Low Tide On | Grand Pré | A Book of Lyrics | By Bliss Carman | [*ornament*] | Cambridge & Chicago | Stone and Kimball | [*ornament*] MDCCCXCIV [*ornament; all lettered within ornamental border*]

6-3/4 x 4-1/4; pp. 132, [2]. Printed by University Press, Cambridge, in Modernized Old Style type on laid paper. Bound in green cloth, stamped in gold; on sides with design and lettering by George H. Hallowell, on spine with lettering within rule frame. Title (Fig. 16a) designed by Martin Mower.

First issued in book form November 25, 1893 by Charles L. Webster & Co., New York; this "Second Edition," enlarged by three poems, published March 15, 1894. Price $1.00. "Third Edition," Stone & Kimball, December 1895; later published by Lamson, Wolffe & Co. and Small, Maynard & Co.

Bliss Carman was a founder of *The Chap-Book* in May 1894, and its associate editor until the firm moved to Chicago in August.

[12a] *Large Paper Issue*

7-7/8 x 5-3/4; pagination, printer and type as above; Dickinson handmade laid paper. Bound in blue-grey boards; lettered in green on spine, in blind on sides; edges uncut.

50 numbered copies, signed by the author and the publishers, at $3.50.

[13]

When Hearts | are Trumps | by | Tom Hall | MDCCCXCIV | Stone & Kimball | Cambridge • Chicago [*lettered and illustrated*]

6-3/4 x 4-1/4; pp. xiii, [iii], 128, [4]. Printed by University Press, Cambridge, in Modernized Old Style and black-letter types on laid paper;

endpapers plain or patterned in blue. Bound in blue-white cloth, stamped in gold; on spine and front cover, decorations and lettering; on back cover, decoration. Each page of text within blue decorative border. Title-page, borders, binding and decorative endpapers designed by Will H. Bradley.

Published March 15, 1894, according to copyright page of second and third impressions, July 25 and December 12, 1894. Price $1.25. Prospectus and poster issued, both designed by Bradley. "Third Edition" advertised in half crushed levant at $3.50.

Thomas Winthrop Hall was a graduate of Harvard in 1893 and later a member of its English Department. His verses appeared chiefly in *Life* and were collected by Stokes, who took over this title in 1897. § First work done by Will H. Bradley for Stone & Kimball; other commissions were the cover design for *In Russet and Silver*, No. 29, and seven posters for *The Chap-Book*. Mr. Bradley designed *Love's Dilemmas*, No. 180, for Herbert S. Stone & Company.

*[13a] *Large Paper Issue*

An issue of fifty copies on large paper at $3.50 was mentioned in the prospectus, advertised in *Publishers' Weekly* March 31, 1894, and listed there as published, May 12. It was neither advertised later nor included in the trade lists. No copy has been located.

[14]

The Quest of | Heracles and | Other Poems | by | Hugh McCulloch | Junior | Stone and Kimball | Cambridge • Chicago | MDCCCXCIV [*within decorative border*]

6-7/8 x 4-3/8; pp. 95, [5]; with signatures. Printed by De Vinne Press, New York, in Modernized Old Style type on Van Gelder Zonen handmade laid paper; green decorated endpapers. Bound in olive green cloth, stamped in gold; on spine with lettering and decoration, on sides with lettering and rule borders. Title and binding (Figs. 15a, 11) designed by Pierre la Rose; decorative initial letters.

Copyright March 19, 1894; advertised in *Publishers' Weekly* March 31. 500 copies, 450 for sale at $1.25.

Hugh McCulloch was class poet of 1891 Harvard and assistant in the English department until 1894. A disciple of Verlaine, he wrote for the *Harvard Monthly* in 1890, one of the first American studies of the poet; see René Taupin, *L'Influence du Symbolisme Français sur la Poésie Américaine* (Paris: Honoré Champion, 1929), p. 26. First of three books printed for Stone & Kimball by DeVinne; see pp. 151-3.

[14a] *Large Paper Issue*

8-1/16 x 5-3/16; pagination, signatures, printer and type as above; Ruisdael handmade laid paper; Japan vellum endpapers. Bound in vellum, printed in gold on spine. Issued in marbled paper slipcase.

60 copies, 50 for sale at $3.50.

[15]

A Lover's Diary | Songs in Sequence | By Gilbert Parker | [*type ornament*] | Cambridge and Chicago | Stone & Kimball | M.D.CCC.XCIV | London: Methuen & Company [*within rule border*]

6-3/4 x 4-3/4; pp. 147, [1]; frontispiece inserted. Printed by De Vinne Press, New York, in "Cadmus" type on laid paper; gold decorated endpapers. Bound in pale blue cloth; wreath ornaments in green and gold on sides, lettering in gold; ornament and lettering in gold on spine. Frontispiece and cover designed by Will H. Low; woodcut head- and tailpieces on each page of text. Title rubricated.

Copyright April 9, 1984. 450 copies for sale in America at $1.25 in cloth, $3.50 in calf. Prospectus issued, probably in January 1894. English publication by Methuen (listed in *Publishers' Circular* May 12) from American sheets. Reprinted by University Press, from same plates, for Stone & Kimball in 1894 and 1896; for Macmillan in 1898 and 1904. Reset, less twenty-five sonnets, in 1913, and included with Parker's *Embers* in Vol. XVII of Scribner's "Imperial Edition" of Parker's works.

First published edition; had been printed in Edinburgh for the author before October 1892; in a private edition. § First book published by Stone & Kimball which had an export edition.

[15a] *Large Paper Issue*

8 x 5-1/4; pagination, printer, type and decorations as above; Ruisdael handmade laid paper; Japan vellum endpapers. Bound in blue-grey boards, stamped in blind on sides from dies used on binding of trade edition; paper label on spine; edges uncut.

60 copies, 50 for sale at $3.50.

[16]

The Lower Slopes | Reminiscences of | Excursions Round the | Base of Helicon, under- | -taken for the most part | in early manhood: by | Grant Allen. | London: Elkin Mathews | & John Lane at the sign of | The Bodley Head. 1894. | Chicago: Stone & Kimball [*lettered within illustrative border*]

7-1/2 x 4-3/4; pp. viii, 79, [1]; with signatures. Catalogue of Mathews & Lane, 16 pp. and dated September 1893, inserted. Printed by T. and A. Constable, Edinburgh, in Caslon type on laid paper. Bound in brown ribbed cloth, stamped in gold; on spine with lettering, on front cover with lettering and illustration; edges uncut. Title, half-title and binding designed by J. Illingworth Kay. Title-leaf a cancel.

Listed in *Publishers' Weekly* April 21, 1894; published in England February 1894. Price $1.50 net.

[17]

Plays by John Davidson | Being: An Unhistorical Pasto- | ral: A Romantic Farce: Bruce | A Chronicle Play: Smith A | Tragic Farce: And Scara | mouch in Naxos A | Pantomime | [*harlequin vignette*] | London: Elkin Mathews and John Lane | Chicago: Stone and Kimball 1894.

8-1/4 x 5-7/8; pp. [xii], 294; with signatures. Catalogue of Mathews and Lane, 16 pp. and dated 1894, inserted. Printed by Ballantyne, Hanson and Co., London & Edinburgh, in Modernized Old Style type on laid paper. Bound in lavender cloth over bevel-edged boards; lettered in gold on spine, vignette in gold on front cover; edges uncut. Frontispiece and vignette for title and cover by Aubrey Beardsley. Title rubricated.

Listed in *Publishers' Weekly* April 21, 1894; published in England February 1894. Price $2.00 net.

These were originally printed separately in Scotland. A collection of Davidson's short stories, *Miss Armstrong's and Other Circumstances* was published by Stone & Kimball in May 1896, No. 72. § His poems appeared consistently in *The Chap-Book* and many were separately printed for copyright purposes.

[18]

The Poems of | Thomas Gordon Hake | Selected | With a Prefatory Note by | Alice Meynell | And a Portrait by | Dante Gabriel | Rossetti | London: Elkin Mathews and | John Lane | Chicago: Stone and Kimball | 1894

7-5/8 x 5; pp. viii, 155, [1]; with signatures. Frontispiece and 16 page catalogue of Mathews and Lane, dated January 1894, inserted. Printed by T. & A. Constable, Edinburgh, in Scotch Modern-face type on laid paper. Bound in maroon or tan linen buckram; stamped in gold on spine and front cover with lettering and decoration by Gleeson White; edges uncut.

Listed in *Publishers' Weekly* April 21, 1894; published in England March 1894. Price $1.50 net.

[19]

Crumbling Idols | Twelve Essays on Art | Dealing chiefly with | Literature, Painting and the | Drama by Hamlin Garland | [*device two in red*] | Chicago and Cambridge | Published by Stone and | Kimball in the year | MDCCCXCIV

6-3/4 x 4-1/4; pp [4], ix, [iii], 192, [4]; with signatures. Printed by University Press, Cambridge, in Modernized Old Style type on laid paper. Bound in green cloth; stamped in gold on sides and spine with cornstalk design and lettering. Title in Elzevir type and rubricated.

Copyright April 26, 1894; listed in *Publishers' Weekly* May 19. Hamlin Garland's copy inscribed "First copy at hand May 1st 1894." Later binding distinguished by endpapers with watermark "Stone & Kimball." Not reprinted.

In their original periodical appearance, these critical essays attracted wide attention; see Hamlin Garland, *A Daughter of the Middle Border* (New York: The Macmillan Company, 1921), p. 25. V. L. Parrington described Garland's leading theory of "Veritism" as "realism modified by the local-color school, by French impressionism, and by Whitman—intensely individualistic, ardently social, and militantly democratic."—*The Beginnings of Critical Realism in America* (New York: Harcourt Brace and Company [1930]), p. 293.

[20]

The | Robb's Island Wreck | And Other Stories | by | Lynn R. Meekins | [*device two in red*] | Chicago and Cambridge | Stone and Kimball | MDCCCXCIV [*within rule border*]

6-3/4 x 4-1/4; pp. [viii], 192, [2]; with signatures. Printed by University Press, Cambridge, in Modernized Old Style type on laid paper. Bound in red cloth over bevel-edged boards; lettered in gold on front cover and spine, which is decorated with straight and waved rules. Title rubricated.

Copyright April 26, 1894; colophon dated March; listed in *Publishers' Weekly* May 12. Price $1.00.

Stories of New England, reprinted in part from *Harper's Weekly*.

[21]

Arthur O'Shaughnessy | His Life and His Work | With Selections from | His Poems | [*rule*] | by | Louise Chandler |

Moulton | [*device two in red*] | MDCCCXCIV | [*rule*] Cambridge and Chicago | Published by Stone & Kimball | London: Elkin Mathews & John Lane [*within red rule border*]

6-3/4 x 4-1/4; pp. [ii], 120, [2]; with signatures. Frontispiece inserted. Printed by De Vinne Press, New York, in Caslon type on laid paper. Bound in silver or pale green cloth, stamped in gold; on sides with all-over floral pattern enclosing lettering; on spine with lettering. Frontispiece portrait "drawn by Mr. A. F. Jaccaci from a photograph," printed in red on Japan vellum paper. Decorative typographic headband and initial on first page of text.

Probably published early in May 1894. Entered for copyright March 10, but not deposited until June 15, and not listed in *Publishers' Weekly* until February 23, 1895. Colophon dated "February, March, April, M.DCCC.XC.IV." Advertised in the first number of *The Chap-Book*, for May 15, 1894. 500 copies for America, 450 for sale at $1.25. English edition, from American sheets and in American binding, originally by Mathews & Lane, transferred in October 1894 to John Lane, after the dissolution of their partnership.

Four English editions (Nos. 9, 16, 17, 18) had been imported from Elkin Mathews & John Lane, but this is the first edition exported to them. An earlier exportation (Parker's *A Lover's Diary*, No. 15) was made to Methuen & Company.

[21a] *Holland Paper Issue*

6-7/8 x 4-1/4; pagination, signatures, printer, type and decorations as above; Van Gelder Zonen handmade laid paper. Bound in pale green boards, paper label on spine; edges uncut.

60 numbered copies, 50 for sale at $3.50.

[22]

The |Chap-Book | Semi-Monthly | [*rule*] | Contents for May 15, 1894 | [*rule*] | [*list of contents*] | [*rule*] | Price 5 Cents $1.00 A Year | [*rule*] | Published by | Stone & Kimball | Chicago & Cambridge [*within rule border*]

Periodical continued through July 1, 1898, Vol. IX, No. 4, then absorbed by *The Dial* of Chicago. Imprint became "Chicago" alone September 1, 1894, Vol. I, No. 8. Price changed to 10 cents and $2.00 a year, February 15, 1896, Vol. IV, No. 7. Publisher became H. (later Herbert) S. Stone & Company, May 1, 1896, Vol. IV, No. 12. Size changed from 7-1/2 x 4-1/2 to 12 x 8-1/2 inches, January 15, 1897, Vol. VI, No. 5, at which time subtitle "A Miscellany & Review of Belles Lettres" was added, device six of Herbert S. Stone & Company substituted for contents on cover, etc. Other variations in titling occur, in the small size especially when decorative covers were used, in the large, to permit advertising on cover.

Printers: "Press of Graves & Henry, Cambridge" at foot of back cover of Nos. 3-5, 7-12, of Vol. I. "The Camelot Press, Chicago" (Frederic W. Goudy and C. Lauron Hooper) appears on back cover of Nos. 1-4 of Vol. II. The Lakeside Press, Chicago, was the printer from the middle of the second volume on, although their imprint does not appear until March 15, 1898, Vol. VIII, No. 9. They had advertised in large size issues before this date as "Printers of The Chap-Book." Mr. T. E. Donnelley of the Lakeside Press believes that his firm also printed the magazine in its small size. The connection can be traced back to February 15, 1895, Vol. II, No. 7, when the typography was altered by the addition of heading rules and of decorative initial letters which were used by The Lakeside Press in books printed for Stone & Kimball during 1895. There is a copy in the Chicago Public Library, of the issue for December 15, 1894, Vol. II, No. 3, with "The Lakeside Press, Chicago" at foot of back cover. Otherwise identical with normal copies bearing imprint "The Camelot Press, Chicago," and presumably part of a second run, this copy further identifies the Lakeside Press with the printing of *The Chap-Book* in its second volume. Further, the Camelot Press, according to Mr. Hooper, did only the typesetting for the first four numbers of Vol. II, the presswork being done elsewhere, presumably at Lakeside.

Types: Modernized Old style in Vol. I; Caslon beginning with Vol. II, No. 1 (9 point to Vol. V, No. 1; after, 10 point); Modern-face beginning with Vol. VIII, No. 7. Mr. C. P. Rollins has clarified these matters, in correspondence with the compiler and in his corrections to the Calkins article, in *The Colophon Crier,* No. 2, issued with Part XI of *The Colophon,* September 1932.

Paper: Laid, issued uncut, through Vol. VIII, No. 6. The watermark of "Stone & Kimball | Chicago" and conical device, appears first September 1, 1894, Vol. I, No. 8—the first number in which the imprint was "Chicago" alone. Beginning with August 1, 1896, Vol V, No. 7, the watermark is "H. S. Stone & Company | Chicago." With the beginning of publication in enlarged size (January 15, 1897, Vol. VI, No. 5) "The Chap Book" also appears in watermark. With adoption of Modern-face type (February 15, 1898, Vol. VIII, No. 7) a smooth wove paper, without watermark and issued with edges cut, was used.

Covers: Title as given above was printed in red and black on same paper as text, except June 15 and October 1, 1894, Nos. 3 and 10 of Vol. I, when green cover papers were used. Decorative cover designs were used occasionally beginning October 1, 1895, Vol. III, No. 10, and frequently between May 15, 1896, Vol. V, No. 1, and January 1, 1897, Vol. VI, No. 4, the last issue in the small size. For reproductions see Figs. 18 and 19 and article by Earnest Elmo Calkins, "The Chap-Book," *The Colophon,* Part X, April-March 1932.

Binding: Ten publishers' bindings of blue or red buckram, gold stamped on sides and spine were supplied for the nine half-yearly volumes of twelve numbers; Vol. VI being in two sizes and IX ending with No. 4.

Circulation: 12,206 average reported May 1, 1895, at end of first year and second volume. 14,000-16,500, largely news-stand sales, in 1895-96, according to trade circular issued during course of fifth volume. 14,500 for 1897, reported to Ayer's *American Newspaper Annual,* 1898. Circulation unknown on July 15, 1898, when *The Chap-Book* was merged into *The Dial* of Chicago, but subscription list inconsequential, according to Mr. Herbert S. Browne, then of *The Dial.*

Editors: Herbert Stuart Stone, assisted for the first two months by Bliss Carman, and from September 1, 1894, by Harrison Garfield Rhodes. Names of the editors are given in the masthead of the periodical only between February 15 and December 1, 1896.

Contents: Not indexed in Poole's. Indices to each of the eight completed volumes were supplied by the publishers. A consolidated list of contributors, with pseudonyms identified where possible, follows:

Thomas Bailey Aldrich
John Ashton
"B" *i.e.* Bliss Carman
Irving Bacheller
Mary Baldwin
Ethel Balton
John Kendrick Bangs
Christopher Bannister
"Slim Barcans" *i.e.* Bliss Carman
William Francis Barnard
Gertrude Bartlett
Herbert Bates
Katherine Bates
Max Beerbohm
Lilian Bell
H. H. Bennett
John Bennett
Joel Benton
Elizabeth Bisland
John H. Boner
H. Geraldine Bonner
Neith Boyce
H. H. Boyesen
Virginia Frazer Boyle
Claude Fayette Bragdon
Anna Hempstead Branch

Layton Brewer
Jennie Brooks
Alice Brown
Anna Robeson Brown
Helen Madder Browne
Shan F. Bullock
Gelett Burgess
John Burroughs
Augustus Burton
Richard Burton
George W. Cable
Eleanor B. Caldwell
William Canton
Elizabeth C. Cardozo
Emma Carleton
Bliss Carman
Edith Carruth
Madison Cawein
Frank Chaffee
Joseph Edgar Chamberlin
Robert W. Chambers
Grace Ellery Channing
Coates Chapman
J. J. Chapman
William Marc Chauvenet
John Vance Cheney
Rheta Louise Childe

W. Douglas Colyar
Florence G. Connor
Charles Townsend Copeland
Ralph Adams Cram
Stephen Crane
John Maxwell Crowe
Edward Cummings
William Eleroy Curtis
John Davidson
"A Degenerate," *i.e.* Alice Morse Earle
Reginald de Koven
Mrs. Reginald de Koven
Stanislas De Guaita
Ann Devoore
Nathan Haskell Dole
Anna Vernon Dorsey
Pitts Duffield
Kathleen Hoy Du Freen
Paul Lawrence Dunbar
Alice Morse Earle
Barrett Eastman
James H. Eckels
Louise Betts Edwards
Charles Fleming Embree

"F"
H. B. F. *i.e.* Henry B. Fuller
Alice Katherine Fallows
Mary McNeil Fenollosa
Etta Dexter Field
Eugene Field
Clyde Fitch
John Fox Jr.
Anatole France
Lettice Galbraith
Norman Gale
Hamlin Garland
Lewis E. Gates
Ellen Glasgow
Philip Becker Goetz
Bertram Grosvenor Goodhue
Edmund Gosse
Kenneth Grahame
William Lucius Graves
Arnoul Greban
C. E. Greene
Arthur Grissom
B. C. Guest
Louise Imogen Guiney
Edward Everett Hale Jr.
Gertrude Hall
Ruth Hall
Norman Hapgood
Thomas Hardy
Joel Chandler Harris
Julian Hawthorne
Myles Hemenway
W. J. Henderson
W. E. Henley
L. Hereward
T. W. Higginson
J. N. Hilliard
Katharine Tynan Hinkson
Frank Hird
William Holloway Jr.
Nora Hopper
Richard Hovey
B. H. Howe
Rupert Hughes
George M. Hyde
R. P. Jacobus
Henry James
Kathryn Jarboe
Tudor Jenks

Laurence Jerrold
Hilda Johnson
Ralph Johnson
Hannah Parker Kimball
Gustav Kobbé
Archibald Lampman
Andrew Lang
Pierre la Rose
Wilbur Larremore
Clara E. Laughlin
Agnes Lee
Gerald Stanley Lee
Edwin Lefevre
Anthony Leland
Elizabeth Dike Lewis
W. R. Lighton
Beatrix Demarest Lloyd
William J. Locke
Charles F. Lummis
Harry B. Lummis
Phoebe Lyde
Gertrude F. Lynch
"H. M." *i.e.* Hamilton Wright Mabie
Justin McCarthy
Hugh McCulloch Jr.
John T. McIntyre
Arthur Macy
John Albert Macy
Stéphané Mallarmé
Brander Matthews
Gertrude B. Millard
Rose Edith Mills
William Vaughn Moody
Dorothea Lummis Moore
F. Frankfort Moore
Gouverneur Morris
Harrison S. Morris
Arthur Morrison
Louise Chandler Moulton
E. H. Mullin
George Frederick Munn
Yone Noguchi
Henry Newbolt
Meredith Nicholson
Evelyn Hunter Nordhoff
Frank W. Noxon
Duffield Osborne
Winthrop Packard
Albert Bigelow Paine
John Williamson Palmer

Josephine Preston Peabody
Elia W. Peattie
Joseph Pennell
Lynwode Pereira
Jeannette Barbour Perry
Roland Edward Phillips
John James Piatt
"Picaroon"
Theodosia Pickering
"Periwinkle Podmore"
Percival Pollard
Maria Louise Pool
William Potts
Charles Stuart Pratt
Helen Choate Prince
Edwin Pugh
"Q" *i.e.* Arthur Quiller-Couch
Lulah Ragsdale
Helen Leah Reed
John Regnault
Harrison Garfield Rhodes
Ernest Rhys
Wallace de Groot Rice
R. V. Risley
Charles G. D. Roberts
Theodore Roberts
William Carman Roberts
Clarence Rook
Viola Roseboro'
Beatrice Rosenthal
Clinton Ross
"E. S."
Edwin L. Sabin
Alvan F. Sanborn
P. H. Savage
"Scandal Club," *i.e.* The Editors
Clinton Scollard
Mary McNeil Scott
Evelyn Sharp
William Sharp
A. D. Sheffield
Francis Sherman
Frank Dempster Sherman
M. E. W. Sherwood
Dora Sigerson
Eve Blantyre Simpson
Herbert Small

211

Edmund Clarence Stedman	J. S. Thomson	Anne Hollingsworth Wharton
J. L[incoln] Steffens	O. L. Triggs	Eugene R. White
Charlotte Perkins Stetson	G. K. Turner	Stewart E. White
Nathaniel Stevenson	Paul Verlaine	Kate Douglas Wiggin
Robert Louis Stevenson	Elizabeth Wallace	Ella Wheeler Wilcox
Richard Henry Stoddard	Thomas Walsh	H. M. Williams
Herbert Stuart Stone	Donald Warren	Beatrice Witte
Ruth McEnery Stuart	Jennie Bullard Waterbury	George Edward Woodberry
John B. Tabb	H. B. Marriott Watson	Jean Wright
J. Russell Taylor	William Watson	Theodore Wratislaw
Octave Thanet *i.e.* Alice French	Arthur Waugh	Edith F. Wyatt
	W. Irving Way	S. Levett Yeats
Charles Miner Thompson	Clarence Wellford	William Butler Yeats
John Stuart Thompson	Carolyn Wells	Israel Zangwill
Maurice Thompson	H. G. Wells	
Vance Thompson	Hembert G. Westley	
	Ethelwyn Wetherald	

Illustrations: Woodcuts, drawings and decorations were used consistently during publication in the original format. Decorative cover designs were used in Vol. III and after. Colored plates, photogravures and half-tones were supplied as inserted "Supplements." Illustration was abandoned shortly after change to large size, January 15, 1897, Vol. VI, No. 5, but a few photographs were used after February 15, 1898, Vol. VIII, No. 7. Contributing artists were:

Aubrey Beardsley	Bertram Grosvenor Goodhue	Mary L. Prindiville
Max Beerbohm		J. F. Raffaelli
Paul Berthon	Eugène Grasset	Fred Richardson
A. E. Borie	G. H. Hallowell	Charles S. Ricketts
Will H. Bradley	Tom Harris	Alexandre Seon
Claude Fayette Bragdon	Frank Hazenplug	John Sloan
Horace T. Carpenter	E. S. Holloway	J. E. Southall
F. A. Cazals	Janey Johnson	Albert E. Sterner
Cecil Clark	Joliquet	Robert Louis Stevenson
Raymond M. Crosby	Jossot	Gardner C. Teall
B. Corson Day	T. B. Meteyard	C. W. Traver
G. De Sanctis	Martin Mower	F. Valloton
Andhré dés Gâchons	E. H. New	Rob Wagner
Georges D'Espagnat	William B. Pell	Dawson Watson
Charles Dana Gibson	Edward Penfield	Raphael A. Weed
H. E. Goodhue	Georges Pissaro	L. D. Wildman

Posters: Lithographed or printed in colors, usually measuring about 21 x 14 inches, posters advertised *The Chap-Book* and were in turn advertised therein for sale, usually at a price of 50 cents. Titles of the first fourteen numbers listed below are from the last listing of their own posters, in the issue of December 15, 1896, Vol. VI, No. 3. Numbers 15 and 16 were not advertised; there may be others not discovered. Dates of issue were not given in the advertisements nor on the posters; these have been supplied from contemporary annotations on copies of the posters examined, or from date of first advertisement. Posters not done for *The Chap-Book,* but advertised there for sale, included the several Stone & Kimball book posters; "Living Posters," by Frank Hazenplug, sold for the benefit of the Chicago Visiting Nurse Association; and 156 posters by French artists, listed October 1, 1895, Vol. III, No. 11. *The Chap-Book* Posters were:

1. The Twins, by Will H. Bradley. May 1894.
2. The Blue Lady, by Will H. Bradley. August 1894.
3. The Poet and His Lady, by Will H. Bradley. January 1895.
4. May, by Will H. Bradley. May 1895.
5. The Pipes, by Will H. Bradley. June 1895.
6. Pegasus, by Will H. Bradley. September 1895.
7. The Red Lady, by Frank Hazenplug. November 1895. 16 x 11 inches. Used as cover-design November 1, 1895, Vol. III, No. 12.
8. Thanksgiving Number, by Will H. Bradley. November 15, 1895.
9. The Sandwich Man, by Claude F. Bragdon. December 1895. 42 x 28 inches. Used later with price of *The Chap-Book* corrected to 10 cents, and also reproduced as cover-design for the volume of *Chap-Book Stories, Second Series.*
10. The Carriage, by Claude F. Bragdon. January 15, 1896.
11. The Clowns, by E. B. Bird. March 1896.
12. The Black Lady, by Frank Hazenplug. April 1896.
13. The Green Lady, by Frank Hazenplug. May 1896.
14. The Juggler Sun, by Claude F. Bragdon. June 1896.
15. Irish and American Bar, by Henri de Toulouse-Lautrec. June 1896. 16 x 23-1/2 inches. Commissioned through the office of *La Plume* of Paris, and lithographed there by Imprimerie Chaix. No. 362 in the Toulouse-Lautrec catalogue by Loys Delteil. See Fig. 40.
16. "Woman with Cat," by J. C. Lyendecker. October 1897. See Fig. 39.

[23]
A June Romance | by | Norman Gale |
{ [at left] Stone | & | Kimball | Chicago } [lettered against
    & Cambridge   design, within
  [at right] G. E. Over | Rugby. | England. } rule border]

7 x 4; pp. [viii], 107, [1]; with signatures (sixes). Printed by G. E. Over, The Rugby Press, in Modernized Old Style type on laid paper. Bound in green cloth; lettered and ornamented in gold on spine. Title, headpiece and tailpiece drawn by Basil Johnson.

First advertised in *The Chap-Book* June 1, 1894, as "Second Edition."

Price $1.00. Originally published 1892 by G. E. Over; this edition issued in England June 1894. "Third Edition" advertised in 1895; new edition published in 1899 by Stone in "Blue Cloth Books" series; later included in "Court Series."

"In the early days of its history it [The Rugby Press] was noted for the fanciful manner of its production of volumes of minor verse, which were published, as well as printed by Mr. Over. These, mainly the work of Mr. Norman Gale and his friends, bear the imprint of 'The Rugby Press,' and are of interest to the collector for their typographical style, which, though sometimes imitated, was personal to the Press. Its distinctive features are wide margins and the use of small sizes of type, and gold, red, green and violet inks for printing on unusually white paper."— G. S. Tomkinson, *A Select Bibliography of the Principal Modern Presses* (London: First Edition Club, 1928), p. 223. §Tomkinson indicates that there was a large paper issue in boards of this title. No copies were advertised for sale in the United States, but there is a copy of the regular issue in the collection of Mr. H. I. Sanders of Washington, in decorated boards and with title page tinted. Other Gale volumes published in the United States by Stone & Kimball were *A Country Muse*, No. 30, and *All Expenses Paid*, No. 85.

[24]

The Ebb Tide | A Trio & Quartette | by | Robert Louis Stevenson | & | Lloyd Osbourne | "There is a tide | in the affairs of men." | [*device two in red*] | Stone & Kimball | Chicago & Cambridge | MDCCCXCIV [*within rule border*]

6-5/8 x 4-1/4; pp. 204, [4]; with signatures. Printed by University Press, Cambridge, in Modernized Old Style type on laid paper. Bound in dark green or light green cloth; lettered in gold on spine, pictorial design (by T. B. Meteyard) in green on front cover with lettering below. Title rubricated.

Copyright July 7, 1894; first edition issued July 15, according to copyright page of later impressions. Price $1.25 in cloth, $3.50 in morocco. Poster by T. B. Meteyard issued. Transferred to Scribner May 1896.

First edition in book form; see W. F. Prideaux, *A Bibliography of the Works of Robert Louis Stevenson,* Edited by Mrs. Luther S. Livingston (London: Frank Hollings, 1917), No. 40, pp. 90-92. Appeared in the English periodical *Today,* November 11, 1893—February 3, 1894; London publication by Heinemann was announced in *Publishers' Circular* September 22, 1894. Stone & Kimball's edition was printed in May, according to the colophon, but was not released until the novel's American periodical appearance (*McClure's Magazine,* February—July 1894) was completed. § First of four Stevenson books published by Stone and Kimball; others were *The Amateur Emigrant,* No. 36, *Macaire,* No. 45, and *Vailima Letters,* No. 49. A fifth title, *Weir of Hermiston,* was printed for and copyrighted by Stone & Kimball, but transferred to Scribner before publication; see pp. 82-84.

[25]

The | Land of Heart's Desire | by | W. B. Yeats | [*device two in red*] | Chicago | Stone & Kimball | Caxton Building | MDCCCXIV [*i.e. 1894*]

6-3/4 x 4-1/4; pp. [iv], 43, [5]; with signatures. Printed by University Press, Cambridge, in Modernized Old Style type on laid paper with watermark one. Bound in grey boards; paper label on spine; edges uncut. Frontispiece by Aubrey Beardsley.

Not copyrighted; colophon dated August 1894; first advertised in *Publishers' Weekly* September 29. 450 copies at $1.00; later sold by Stone. Published in England May 1894 by T. Fisher Unwin.

The frontispiece is a reproduction of Aubrey Beardsley's poster advertising the performance of the play at the Avenue Theatre, London, March 1894. Anna Fuller gave the first American presentation in 1898 at a matinée in Chicago's Great Northern Theatre, then just completed; see her *My Chicago* (Chicago: Ralph Fletcher Seymour [1918]), p. 49. § First title published after removal to Chicago and the first volume printed for Stone & Kimball on a specially watermarked paper; conical torch design between initials "S" and "K."

[26]

Sonnets | of | The Wingless Hours. | by | Eugene Lee-Hamilton, | Author of | 'The New Medusa,' 'Imaginary Sonnets,' 'The Fountain | of Youth,' etc. | [*floret*] | Stone & Kimball, | Chicago and Cambridge. | M.D.CCC.XC.IV.

6-3/8 x 5; pp. xii, 115, [1]; with signatures. Printed by Elliott Stock, London, in Modernized Old Style type on Abbey Mills laid paper. Bound in blue-grey boards, white spine with paper label; edges uncut. Title-leaf a cancel.

First advertised in *The Chap-Book* September 15, 1894; in *Publishers' Weekly* September 29. Price $1.00. Published in England by Elliott Stock May 1894.

215

[27]
Rob Roy | or | The Thistle and the Rose | An Opera in Three Acts |
{ [*at left*] Libretto by | Harry B. Smith |} [*circular vig-*
{ [*at right*] Music by | Reginald de Koven | } *nette in red*]
Printed | for Stone and Kimball | MDCCCXCIV

4-3/8 x 6-3/4; pp. [iv], 197, [3]; with signatures. Title and six plates inserted. Printed by Lakeside Press, Chicago, in Modernized Old Style type on laid paper with watermark two. Bound in tan paper wrappers; spine and front cover lettered and decorated in red and black; edges uncut. Illustrations, by Charles Howard Johnson, printed in red.

Not included in trade catalogues or advertisements, and probably issued for theatre sale only, early in October 1894. The play opened in Detroit October 1, before its New York run at the Herald Square theatre. Colophon dated "Autumn 1894." Libretto entered for copyright by Harry B. Smith May 31, 1894, but copies not deposited until January 14, 1895.

Despite the promise of the title, only the libretto is printed. The vocal score was published by G. Schirmer in the same year. § First volume printed on paper with Stone & Kimball's watermark two; the conical torch design between initials "S" and "K" plus "Stone & Kimball | Chicago."

[28]
Pierre and His People | Tales of the Far North | By Gilbert Parker | [*device two*] | Chicago | Stone & Kimball | Caxton Building | MDCCCXCIV

6-3/4 x 4-1/4; pp. [2], vii, [iii], 318, [2]; with signatures. Printed by University Press, Cambridge, in Modernized Old Style type on laid paper with watermark two. Bound in blue-green cloth; stamped in gold on sides and spine; edges uncut.

Copyright October 12, 1894; advertised in *Publishers' Weekly* September 29. Price $1.25 net. Identified on copyright page as "Second Edition"; had been published in New York 1893 by James Clarence Harvey; in London 1892 by Methuen. American edition transferred to Macmillan 1898.

[29]
In Russet & Silver | by | Edmund Gosse | [*floret*] Chicago | Stone & Kimball | MDCCCXCIV

6-3/4 x 4-1/4; pp. xiii, [i], 159, [1]; with signatures. Printed by University Press, Cambridge, in Caslon type on laid paper. Bound in Khaki buckram or tan cloth; stamped on sides and spine with design of trees in maroon and silver, lettering in silver. Binding (Fig. 21) designed by Will Bradley. Title (Fig. 20) rubricated.

Copyright October 23, 1894. Price $1.25 net in cloth, $3.50 in morocco. Published in England by Heinemann October 1894. Two later impressions for Stone & Kimball; "Third Edition" advertised in half crushed levant at $3.50.

[29a] *Large Paper Issue*

7-3/4 x 5-3/4; pp. [2], xiii, [i], 159, [1]; with signatures. Printer and type as above; Japan vellum or Dickinson handmade laid paper; blue endpapers. Bound in tan buckram; decorated on sides with silver fleurons; paper label on spine; edges uncut.

75 copies; numbered from one to ten on Japan vellum, for sale at $6.00; numbered from eleven to seventy-five on Dickinson, at $3.50.

[30]
A Country Muse | by | Norman Gale | First | [*floret*] | Series | Chicago | Stone and Kimball | MDCCCXCIV

7-1/2 x 5; pp. ix, [iii], 145, [3]; with signatures. Printed by T. & A. Constable, Edinburgh, in Scotch Modern-face type on laid paper; title and endpapers on laid paper with Stone & Kimball watermark two. Bound in green cloth; lettered and ornamented in gold on spine. Title-leaf a cancel; title rubricated.

First advertised in *The Chap-Book* December 1, 1894, as "New and Revised Edition." Price $1.25. First published 1892 by David Nutt, London; this edition issued in England November 1894.

[31]
Vistas | by | William Sharp | Chicago | Stone & Kimball | MDCCCXCIV [*against design of green tree*]

6-3/4 x 4-1/4; pp. [viii], 182, [6]; with signatures. Printed by University Press, Cambridge, in Modernized Old Style type on laid paper. Bound in light green, vertical lines in purple and lettering in gold. Binding and title designed by Henry McCarter.

Copyright December 10, 1894; colophon dated October. Series poster by Henry McCarter issued December 1894. First edition 600 copies at $1.25 net. Reissued in 1897 by Herbert S. Stone & Co. Contains "The Whisperer" and a preface not in the English edition, published at Derby by Frank Murray earlier in 1894.

First title issued in "The Green Tree Library," advertised as "A series of books representing what may be called the new movement in literature. The intention is to publish uniformly the best of the decadent writings of various countries done into English and consistently brought together for the first time." Nine other titles, including works of Maeterlinck, Ibsen, Sharp, Verlaine and Moore, were issued in this series before 1900; see Nos. 32, 33, 37, 55, 67, 70, 104, 243 and 247. § Sharp had two other books on the Stone & Kimball list under his own name and three as Fiona Macleod; see Nos. 50, 53, 67, 75, 84, and pp. 76-80.

[32]
The Plays | of | Maurice Maeterlinck | Princess Maleine • The Intruder | The Blind • The Seven | Princesses | Translated by | Richard Hovey | Chicago | Stone & Kimball | MDCCCXCIV [against design of green tree]

6-3/4 x 4-1/4; pp. [viii], 369, [3]; with signatures. Printed by University Press, Cambridge, in Modernized Old Style type on laid paper with watermark two. "Green Tree" binding; see No. 31 and Fig. 24.

Copyright December 10, 1894; colophon dated September. First edition, 600 copies at $1.25 net; reprinted both by Stone & Kimball and Herbert S. Stone & Company; reissued 1906 by Duffield & Company; now published by Dodd, Mead & Company.

Second title issued in "The Green Tree Library," according to advertisements, but printed and copyrighted a little earlier than *Vistas*. § This volume has an introduction by the translator on "Modern Symbolism and Maurice Maeterlinck"; the second series of translations, No. 75, has a preface by the author himself.

[33]
Little Eyolf | by | Henrik Ibsen | Translated by | William Archer | Chicago | Stone & Kimball | MDCCCXCIV [against design of green tree]

6-3/4 x 4-1/4; pp. [ii], 164, [2]; with signatures. Printed by University Press, Cambridge, in Modernized Old Style type on laid paper with watermark two. "Green Tree" binding; see No. 31 and Fig. 24.

Copyright December 14, 1894; colophon dated December. First edition 500 copies at $1.50 net; reprinted January 1895 and later, by Stone & Kimball and by Stone.

Third title issued in "The Green Tree Library," and the first of three Ibsen plays in this series.

[34]
Old Pictures of Life | by | David Swing | With an Introduction | by Franklin H. Head | In Two Volumes | Volume | [*floret*] First | Chicago | Stone and Kimball | MDCCCXCIV

6-3/4 x 4-1/4; 2 Vols., with signatures. I: pp. xxvi, 220, [2]. II: [vi], 191, [3]. Printed by Lakeside Press, Chicago, in Modernized Old Style type on laid paper with watermark two. Bound in green cloth; lettered and ornamented on sides and spine in gold. Titles rubricated.

Copyright December 26, 1894. Price $1.00 a volume in cloth; later made available in half crushed levant at $5.00 a set. Cloth edition sold by Stone after 1897.

Essays, posthumously collected, of the eminent clergyman and founder of the Chicago Literary Club.

[35]
The Works | of | Edgar Allan Poe | [*rule*] | Newly Collected and Edited, with a | Memoir, Critical Introductions, and | Notes, by Edmund Clarence Stedman | and George Edward Woodberry | [*rule*] | The Illustrations by | [*rule*] | Albert Edward Sterner | [*rule*] | In Ten Volumes | Volume I | [*device two in red*] | [*rule*] | Chicago | Stone & Kimball | MDCCCXCIV [*within double rule border*]

7-3/8 x 4-3/4; 10 Vols., with signatures. I: pp. xi, [v], 343, [5]. II: pp. [iv], 334, [2]. III: pp. [viii], 325, [3]. IV: pp. [iv], 297, [3]. V: pp. [viii], 361, [3]. VI: pp. [4], xxxvi, 331, [5]. VII: pp. [viii], 355, [5]. VIII: pp. viii, [iv], 352, [4]. IX: pp. [viii], 317, [3]. X: pp. xxv, [i], 313, [7]. Illustrated with twelve portraits of Poe and his family, chiefly as frontispieces; twenty plates by Sterner; three engravings of Poe's homes; and one reproduction of his manuscript. Printed by University Press, Cambridge, in Modernized Old Style type on laid paper with watermark two. Bound in green cloth, stamped on spine with floral decoration and lettering. Titles rubricated.

First three volumes copyright and dated 1894, but not issued until January 1895; others dated 1895 and issued at intervals between April 1895 and March 1896. Price $1.50 a volume and $15.00 for set in cloth; $40.00 for set in half crushed levant. Many sets remaindered after sale of Stone & Kimball in 1897; see pp. 89-90. Later issued by Herbert S. Stone & Company and by Fox, Duffield & Co.; now published by Scribner's.

The most ambitious publishing project of Stone & Kimball, conceived in enthusiasm and carried out with care, this has remained the standard edition of Poe.

[35a] *Large Paper Issue*

8 x 5; 10 Vols. Pagination, signatures, printer and type as above. Handmade laid paper with watermark one. Illustrations as above, plus proofs on India paper of Sterner's plates and a signed etching by him. Bound in vellum; stamped in gold on spine with floral decoration and lettering.

250 sets at $50.00 net.

This issue was originally advertised as containing eight, later four illustrations by Aubrey Beardsley. Either through the artist's delay in delivery or through the publishers' reluctance to print them at this time, they did not appear in the large paper set. One of the illustrations, "The Masque of the Red Death," appeared in *The Chap-Book* August 15, 1894 and again April 1, 1898. Four Beardsley drawings were separately published by Herbert S. Stone & Co. in 1901; see No. 287 and Fig. 8.

[35b] *Japan Paper Issue*

8 x 5; 10 Vols. Pagination, signatures, printer and type as above. Japan vellum paper. Illustrations as above, plus proofs on India paper of Sterner's plates and a signed etching by him. Bound in vellum; stamped in gold on sides with floral decoration, on spine with decoration and lettering, all in gold. See Fig. 25.

10 sets, none for sale.

This issue was not advertised for sale, and the only copy examined by the compiler is in the collection of Mr. W. J. Kirk, then an office employee of Stone & Kimball. § Supplied with the ten volumes of this issue, and also advertised separately for sale at $5.00 net, was a collection of French etchings illustrating Poe, laid into a folding case of vellum stamped on sides like the binding of the Japan paper issue. This collection described fully below.

[35c] *Extra Etchings Issued for Poe*

[Eighteen Etchings for the Works of Edgar Allan Poe. Drawn and Engraved by Various French Artists. Chicago: Stone & Kimball, 1895]

8 x 5; 18 plates on Whatman paper; enclosed in vellum folder, stamped on sides with floral design, in gold.

First advertised in *The Chap-Book* for January 15, 1896. Price $5.00 net.

No title-page or explanatory printed text, but the legends are in English, the plates having been made originally for an edition of Poe published in London, 1884, by J. C. Nimmo. There are ten plates drawn and engraved by Eugene Wögel; two engraved by T. B. Abot after Wögel; one engraved by Abot after Daniel Vierge; two plates drawn and engraved by F. Férat; one by F. L. Méaulle; one unsigned etching illustrative of "The Tale of Arthur Gordon Pym"; and an etched portrait of Poe by Ben Damman. § This set is perhaps more elusive than any of the books printed for Stone & Kimball, for there is nothing to identify it with the set of Poe except the vellum folder, which is stamped identically with the privately issued Japan vellum set. The only copies of the plates which the compiler has seen, are in the collection of Mr. W. J. Kirk of Oak Park. The pictures are worth hunting for, being highly atmospheric as illustrations, and of high quality as etchings.

[36]
The | Amateur Emigrant | From the Clyde to | Sandy Hook | by | Robert Louis Stevenson | [*floret*] | Chicago | Stone and Kimball | MDCCCXCV [*within rule border*]

6-5/8 x 4-1/4; pp. [viii], 180, [6]; with signatures. Printed by Lakeside Press, Chicago, in Modernized Old Style type on laid paper with watermark two. Bound in green polished buckram; lettered in gold on spine. Title rubricated.

Copyright January 18, 1895; same date given for publication of first edition on copyright page of later impressions. Price $1.25. Transferred to Scribner 1896.

First separate, and first American edition; see Prideaux-Livingston, No. 41, pp. 92 and 247-49. § The first of Stevenson's books published after his death, and autobiographical in character, *The Amateur Emigrant* had a quick success. *The Chap-Book* of February 1, 1895 announced that the entire first edition had been sold on the day of publication; there were four impressions by April 15, 1895.

[37]
Poems | of | Paul Verlaine | Translated by | Gertrude Hall | Pictured by | Henry McCarter | Chicago | Stone & Kimball | MDCCCXCV [*against design of green tree*]

6-5/8 x 4-1/8; pp. x, [ii], 110, [2]. Eight plates, including frontispiece, inserted. Printed by University Press, Cambridge, in Caslon type on laid paper with watermark two. "Green Tree" binding; see No. 31 and Fig. 24.

Portrait frontispiece and drawings by Henry McCarter reproduced in half-tone on Japan vellum paper.

Copyright notice on verso of title-page, but there is no record of original entry or deposit of copies in the Copyright Office. First advertised in *The Chap-Book* March 1, 1895; colophon dated January. 500 copies of the first edition at $1.50 net; reprinted October 1895; later sold by Stone. Fourth title issued in "The Green Tree Library" and the first volume of translations from Verlaine published in English; see G. A. Tournoux, *Bibliographie Verlainienne* (Leipzig: E. Rowohlt, 1912), No. 709, p. 98.

[37a] *Japan Paper Issue*

7-9/16 x 5-3/4; pp. [ix], [iii], 110, [2]. Printer, type and illustrations as above; all on Japan vellum paper. Bound in light green linen buckram, stamped in gold; on spine with lettering, on sides with tree design and "PV" in each outer corner; edges uncut.

100 numbered copies at $10.00 net. Nos. 1-15, with a proof set of illustrations on India paper, $15.00 net.

[38]
A | Sawdust Doll | by | Mrs. Reginald de Koven | [*floret*] | Chicago | Stone and Kimball | MDCCCXCV [*within rule frame within blue decorative border*]

6-3/4 x 4-1/4; pp. [iv], 237, [3]; with signatures. Printed by Lakeside Press, Chicago, in Modernized Old Style type on laid paper with watermark two. Bound in blue buckram; stamped in gold on sides and spine with peacock design and lettering. Binding (Fig. 24) and title-border designed by Frank Hazenplug. Title rubricated; decorative initial letters begin each chapter.

Copyright March 31, 1894. First edition published March 23, according to copyright page of later impressions. 5,000 copies sold at $1.25. Reissued by Stone in 1897; included in the "Court Series" and "Stone's Paper Library," 1900.

First of two titles issued in "The Peacock Library"; the other, Alice Wolf's *A House of Cards*, No. 68, was also a novel of society, and also had a brief life on the best-seller lists.

[39]
The Life | and Opinions of | Tristram | Shandy | Gentleman | by Laurence Sterne | In Two Volumes | Vol. 1. | Chicago | Stone and Kimball | 1895 | London: Methuen & Company

7-5/8 x 5; 2 Vols., with signatures. I: pp. xxx, [ii], 262, [2]; frontispiece inserted. II: [iv], 257, [3]. Printed by T. & A. Constable, Edinburgh, in Scotch Modern-face type on laid paper. Bound in yellow buckram; stamped in gold on sides with rules, lettering and ornament, on spine with lettering. Frontispiece to Vol. I is a reproduction in photogravure of the Reynolds portrait engraved by E. Fisher. Titles rubricated.

First advertised in *The Chap-Book* April 1, 1895; listed in *Publishers' Weekly* April 27. Price $2.50 net.

First title issued in the "English Classics" series, edited by W. E. Henley and published in England by Methuen. Four more editions were imported in 1895, and one in 1896; see Nos. 47, 64, 65, 71. The series was advertised in America in these terms: "The ordinary 'cheap edition' appears to have served its purpose. The public has found out the artist-printers, and is now ready for something better fashioned. This then, is the moment for the issue of such a series as, while well within the reach of the average buyer, shall be at once an ornament to the shelf of him that owns, and a delight to the eye of him that reads." § Introduction to this title by Charles Whibley.

[40]

The | Comedies | of | William Congreve | In Two Volumes | Vol. I | Chicago | Stone and Kimball | 1895 | London: Methuen & Company

7-5/8 x 5; 2 Vols., with signatures. I: pp. xxxi, [i], 192, [2]; frontispiece inserted. II: pp. 217, [3]. Printed by T. & A. Constable, Edinburgh, in Scotch Modern-face type on laid paper. "English Classics" binding; see No. 39. Frontispiece to Vol. I is a reproduction in photogravure of the Kneller portrait engraved by Smith. Titles rubricated.

First advertised in *The Chap-Book* April 1, 1895; listed in *Publishers' Weekly* April 27. Price $2.50 net.

Second title issued in the "English Classics" series. § Introduction by G. S. Street.

[41]

Two Women & A Fool | by | H. C. Chatfield-Taylor | With Pictures by C. D. Gibson | [*device two in red*] | Chicago | Stone & Kimball | MDCCCXCV [*within rule border*]

6-11/16 x 4-3/16; pp. [vi], 232, [4]; with signatures. Eight plates, including frontispiece, inserted. Printed by Lakeside Press, Chicago, in Modernized Old Style type on laid paper with watermark two. Bound in red buckram; lettered in gold on sides and spine within rules. Title rubricated. Decorative initial letters begin each chapter.

Copyrighted April 3, 1895. Two posters by Gibson issued during March and April. 8,000 copies sold at $1.50. Issued 1897 in reduced size, with frontispiece only, at 75 cents; later sold by Herbert S. Stone & Co.

These Gibson illustrations are not noted in Fairfax Downey, *Portrait of an Era As Drawn by C. D. Gibson* (New York: Charles Scribner's Sons [1936]), or in Theodore Bolton, *American Book Illustrators* (New York: R. R. Bowker Company, 1938). § The best-selling novel of any published by Stone & Kimball before *The Damnation of Theron Ware*.

[42]
A Little Sister to the | Wilderness | by | Lilian Bell | [*device two*] | Chicago | Stone & Kimball | MDCCCXCV

6-5/8 x 4-1/8; pp. [viii], 267, [5]; with signatures. Printed by Lakeside Press, Chicago, in Modernized Old Style type on laid paper with watermark two. Bound in grey cloth; stamped in gold on sides and spine with lettering and design by Bruce Rogers (Fig. 23). Decorative initial letters begin each chapter. Title rubricated.

Copyright April 6, 1895; same date given for publication of first edition on copyright page of later impressions. Price $1.25.

First issue of first edition, as described above, has no colophon. Second issue has colophon on recto of leaf following close of text, and beneath author's name on title, "Author of 'The Love Affairs | of an Old Maid.'" Cover design is the first of two done for Stone & Kimball by Bruce Rogers; see Fig. 23.

[43]
The Golden Age | by | Kenneth Grahame | [*floret*] | Chicago | Stone & Kimball | MDCCCXCV

6-5/8 x 4-1/4; pp. [viii], 242, [2]. Printed by University Press, Cambridge, in Caslon type on laid paper with watermark two. Bound in yellow buckram, stamped in gold on sides and spine. Title rubricated.

Copyright May 27, 1895. Price $1.25. Reprinted three times in 1896; American edition transferred to John Lane 1897. Appeared originally in various periodicals, including "the little *Chap-Book* of big Chicago."

The first American edition is given priority over Lane's English edition by I. R. Brussel, who states in *Anglo-American First Editions 1826-1900: East to West* (London: Constable & Co., Ltd.; New York: R. R. Bowker Co., 1935), p. 93: "It was published in Chicago in May, and the London edition was not issued until the following month. The American date of publication is so stated in the publishers' colophon. *The English Catalogue* gives June as the London publication date of this book." The "May" of the colophon, however, is the printer's date of completion rather than evidence of publication, and the Library of Congress copy, received for copyright May 27, 1895, is in a trial binding of yellow buckram with plain sides and top edge stained instead of gilt. Stone & Kimball's edition was not advertised as "Now Ready" in *The Chap-Book* until June 15, 1895, nor listed in the "Weekly Record of New Publications" in *Publishers' Weekly* until June 22. The English edition was listed in *Publishers' Circular* for June 1. These additional facts suggest that English and American publication were simultaneous, if indeed the English edition was not earlier.

[44]
When Valmond Came | To Pontiac | The Story of a Lost Napoleon | by Gilbert Parker | [*floret*] | Chicago | Stone & Kimball | MDCCCXCV

6-5/8 x 4-1/8; pp. 222, [2]; with signatures. Printer not given but probably Lakeside Press, Chicago; Modernized Old Style type; laid paper with watermark two. Bound in green cloth, stamped in gold; on spine with lettering and floret; on sides with design by Bruce Rogers (Fig. 23). Title rubricated.

Copyright June 20, 1895. Price $1.50. Reissued by Herbert S. Stone & Co. in 1897. Published in England by Methuen; listed in *Publishers' Circular* June 8, 1895.

This was always Sir Gilbert's own favorite novel. He placed it first in the collected edition of his works, where he revealed that this "historical fantasy" was "written, printed, revised, and ready for press in five weeks." He had expected, as his letters to Stone & Kimball show, that it would be his most popular book, but its American sale of about 5,000 copies was not comparable to that of *The Seats of the Mighty* published in 1896 by Appleton. § This has the second of two covers designed for Stone & Kimball by Bruce Rogers; see Fig. 23.

[45]
Macaire | A Melodramatic Farce | by | Robert Louis Stevenson | and | William Ernest Henley | [*floret*] | Chicago | Stone and Kimball | MDCCCXCV

6-5/8 x 4-1/4; pp. [viii], 108, [4]; with signatures. Printed by Norwood Press, Norwood, Massachusetts, in Modernized Old Style type on laid

225

paper with watermark two. Bound in green polished buckram, lettered in gold on spine. Title rubricated.

Originally copyright May 27, 1895, from proofs of the play's printing for appearance in *The Chap-Book;* see p. 360. Separately published from a new setting of type, probably late in June. Price $1.00.

[46]
The Love-Letters of | Mr. H. & Miss R. | 1775-1779 | [*rule*] | Edited by | Gilbert Burgess | [*rule*] | [*device two in red*] | [*rule*] | Chicago | Stone & Kimball | MDCCCXCV [*within double rule border*]

7-1/2 x 5; pp. xvii, [i], 19-239, [1]; with signatures. Printed by Ballantyne, Hanson & Co., London & Edinburgh, in Modernized Old Style type on laid paper; title and end papers on Stone & Kimball watermarked paper. American binding of green cloth, lettered in green on sides and spine. Title-leaf a cancel; title rubricated.

Listed in *Publishers' Weekly* August 17, 1895; first advertised in *The Chap-Book* August 1, 1895, Price $1.50. Published in England May 1895 by Heinemann.

[47]
The Adventures of | Hajji Baba | of Ispahan | by | James Morier | In Two Volumes | Vol. I. | Chicago | Stone and Kimball | 1895 | London: Methuen & Company

7-1/2 x 5; 2 Vols., with signatures. I: pp. xxxiii, [i], 242, [2]; frontispiece inserted. II: pp. viii, 266, [2]. Printed by T. & A. Constable, Edinburgh, in Scotch Modern-face type on laid paper. "English Classics" binding; see No. 39. Frontispiece a reproduction in photogravure of the portrait by D. Maclise. Titles rubricated.

Listed in *Publishers' Weekly* August 17, 1895; first advertised in *The Chap-Book* September 15. Price $2.50 net.

Third title issued in the "English Classics" series. §Introduction by E. G. Browne.

[48]
The Marriage of Guenevere | A Tragedy by Richard Hovey | [*device two*] | Chicago | Stone & Kimball | MDCCCXCV

7-1/2 x 4-3/4; pp. 179, [5]; with signatures. Printed by University

Press, Cambridge, in Modernized Old Style type on laid paper with watermark two. Bound in green cloth; stamped in blue on sides and spine with lettering and design by Tom B. Meteyard.

Copyright September 5, 1895. Price $1.50. First published 1891 with *The Quest of Merlin* by United States Book Company, New York; sheets of Stone & Kimball edition reissued by Stone in 1897; with new title-page by Small, Maynard & Co. in 1898.

Part II of "Launcelot and Guenevere, A Poem in Dramas."

[49]

Vailima Letters | being correspondence | addressed by | Robert Louis Stevenson | to | Sidney Colvin | November, 1890-October, 1894 | In Two Volumes | Vol. I | [*device two in red*] | Chicago | Stone & Kimball | MDCCCXCV [*within rule border*]

6-5/8 x 4-1/4; 2 Vols., with signatures. I: pp. [viii], 11-281, [7]; frontispiece portrait (by W. Strang) inserted. II: pp. [2], iv, [ii], [7]-275, [5]; frontispiece (photograph of R. L. S. with Samoan chief) inserted. Printed by University Press, Cambridge, in Modernized Old Style type on laid paper with watermark two. Bound in green polished buckram, stamped in gold on sides and spine. Titles rubricated.

Copyright October 23, 1895; advertised as "Now Ready" in *The Chap-Book* November 1. Price $2.25 net. Reprinted in January 1896; 2,846 copies sold before transfer to Scribner in May 1896.

The first American edition perhaps precedes English publication. Prideaux-Livingston No. 42, pp. 92-94, describes Methuen's edition with the note "Published November 2, 1895," and the Stone & Kimball edition without an exact date of publication. The volumes were printed in October, according to the colophon; and complete copies were received for copyright October 23. G. Hills advises, English edition reprinted by October 29.

[49a] *Dickinson Paper Issue*

8 x 5; 2 Vols., with signatures. I: pp. [x], 11-281, [3]. II: pp. [4], iv, [ii], 7-275, [5]. Frontispieces, printer and type as above. Dickinson handmade laid paper. Bound in green paper boards with paper labels on spines; edges uncut.

100 numbered copies. Not advertised and price not known, but 52 copies were sold before transfer to Scribner's in 1896.

Not listed in Prideaux-Livingston or other Stevenson bibliographies.

[49b] *Japan Paper Issue*

8 x 5; 2 Vols., with signatures. I: pp. [xiv], [11]-281, [7]. II: pp. [8], iv, [ii], 7-275, [7]. Frontispieces, printer and type as above. Japan vellum paper. Bound in red morocco, tooled in gold on sides and spine.

10 numbered copies, presumably not for sale.

Not listed in Prideaux-Livingston or other Stevenson bibliographies.

[50]

Carnation [*ornament*] Series | The Gypsy Christ | And Other Tales | by William Sharp | [*ornament*] | Chicago | Stone & Kimball | MDCCCXCV [*within rule border*]

6-1/8 x 3-3/4; pp. [viii], 282, [6]; with signatures. Printed by Lakeside Press, Chicago, in Caslon type on laid paper with watermark two. Bound in tan cloth; stamped on sides with all-over pattern of carnations against green background (Fig. 24); lettered in green on spine. Series title rubricated.

Advertised as "Now Ready" in *The Chap-Book* November 1, 1895; copyright November 15. Price $1.00. English edition published by Constable January 1896, as *Madge o' the Pool,* contains less material.

First title issued in the "Carnation Series," according to advertisements. Four others, all collections of short stories and all published in 1895, listed directly below.

[51]

Carnation [*ornament*] Series | The Sister of a Saint | And Other Stories | by | Grace Ellery Channing | [*ornament*] | Chicago | Stone & Kimball | MDCCCXCV [*within rule border*]

6-1/8 x 3-7/8; pp. viii, 261, [3]; with signatures. Printer, type, paper, binding and rubrication of the "Carnation Series"; see No. 50 and Fig. 24. Advertised as "Now Ready" in *The Chap-Book* November 1, 1895; copyright November 14. Price $1.00.

Second title issued in the "Carnation Series."

[52]

Carnation [*ornament*] Series | Black Spirits & White | A Book of Ghost Stories | by | Ralph Adams Cram [*ornament*] |Chicago| Stone & Kimball | MDCCCXCV [*within rule border*]

6-1/4 x 3-7/8; pp. [xii], 150, [4]. 16 page catalogue "Concerning the

Books of Stone & Kimball, 1895-1896," inserted. Printer, type, paper, binding and rubrication of the "Carnation Series"; see No. 50 and Fig. 24. This volume issued with green patterned endpapers.

Advertised as "Now Ready" in *The Chap-Book* November 1, 1895; copyright November 29. Price $1.00. Published in England March 1896 by Chatto & Windus.

Third title issued in the "Carnation Series." § Mr. Cram's second book; his first, *The Decadent,* was issued anonymously in 1893 in an edition decorated by Bertram Grosvenor Goodhue and printed under the direction of Copeland & Day.

[53]
Carnation [*ornament*] Series | The Sin-Eater | And Other Tales and Episodes | by | Fiona Macleod | [*ornament*] | Chicago | Stone & Kimball | MDCCCXCV [*within rule border*]

6-1/4 x 3-3/4; pp. [viii], 289, [5]; last three pages advertisements for *Pharais*. Printer, type, paper, binding and rubrication of the "Carnation Series"; see No. 50 and Fig. 24.

Advertised as "Now Ready" in *The Chap-Book* November 1, 1895; copyright October 28 (in trial binding of tan cloth lettered in gold on spine). Price $1.00. Publication by Patrick Geddes & Colleagues, Edinburgh, was scheduled for October 15, but delayed until November 1 at Stone & Kimball's request.

Fourth title issued in the "Carnation Series." § William Sharp's third publication with Stone & Kimball; his first as "Fiona Macleod."

[54]
Carnation [*ornament*] Series | The Gods Give My | Donkey Wings | by | Angus Evan Abbott | [*ornament*] | Chicago | Stone & Kimball | MDCCCXCV [*within rule border*]

6-1/4 x 3-3/4; pp. 135, [5]. 16 page catalogue "Concerning the Books of Stone & Kimball, 1895-1896" inserted. Printer, type, paper, binding and rubrication of "Carnation Series"; see No. 50 and Fig. 24.

Advertised as "Now Ready" in *The Chap-Book* November 1, 1895; copyright November 17. Price $1.00. English edition published November 1895 by Methuen.

Fifth and last title issued in the "Carnation Series." § "Angus Evan Abbott" was a pseudonym of James Barr, Canadian-born journalist, who, like his older brother Robert, settled in London during the eighties to edit the weekly London edition of the *Detroit Free Press*.

[55]
The Massacre of the | Innocents and | Other Tales | by | Belgian Writers | Translated by | Edith Wingate Rinder | Chicago | Stone & Kimball | MDCCCXCV [*against design of green tree*]

6-3/4 x 4-1/4; pp. xii, 292, [2]; with signatures. Printed by Lakeside Press, Chicago, in Modernized Old Style type on laid paper with watermark two. "Green Tree" binding; see No. 31 and Fig. 24.

Copyright November 11, 1895; first advertised in *The Chap-Book* November 15; colophon dated September. Price $1.25 net.

Fifth title issued in "The Green Tree Library." § Short stories by Maeterlinck, Eekhoud, Lemonnier, Jenart, Delattre, Richelle, Ganir, Demolder and Krains.

[56]
Miracle Plays: | Our | Lord's Coming And | Childhood | [*pictorial decoration and two-line motto*] | by Katherine Tynan Hinkson | [*rule*] Chicago: Stone and Kimball [*box*] | [*box*] Caxton Building [*box*] | London: John Lane The Bodley Head | [*box*] MDCCCXCV [*box*] | [*lettered in red and sepia within decorative frame*]

8 x 5; pp. [ii], 86, [8]; title and six illustrations on inserted leaves of Japan vellum paper. Printed by Lakeside Press, Chicago, in "Jensen" and black-letter types on Dickinson handmade laid paper. Bound in green boards, printed in black on front cover; paper label on spine; edges uncut. Title-page and illustrations by Patten Wilson.

Copyright November 11, 1895; advertised in *The Chap-Book* November 15. Price $2.00. English edition listed in *Publishers' Circular* for November 16.

"Jensen" of the American Type Founders Company was copied from William Morris' "Golden" roman type. This is the only book in which it was used for Stone & Kimball, but not to any advantage. The volume is the least attractive of all their publications.

[57]
The Father of the Forest | And Other Poems | by | William Watson | [*device two in red*] | Chicago: Stone & Kimball | London: John Lane | MDCCCXCV

6-3/4 x 4-1/4; pp. [viii], 59, [3]; frontispiece portrait inserted. Printed by Lakeside Press, Chicago, in Modernized Old Style type on laid paper with watermark two. Bound in blue boards stamped in purple on sides and spine with rules, lettering and circular monogram; or grey boards stamped in brown; both issued with edges uncut; or green cloth stamped in gold; with top edge gilt and others uncut. Title rubricated.

Copyright November 11, 1895. Price $1.25. English edition listed in *Publishers' Circular* for November 16.

[57a] *Large Paper Issue*

7-1/2 x 4-1/2; pagination, printer, type and portrait as above; Japan vellum or Dickinson handmade laid paper. Bound in blue boards stamped in blind on sides and spine; edges uncut.

60 copies on large paper, numbered from 1 to 10 on Japan vellum and 11 to 60 on English handmade. Not advertised for sale.

[58]

This Little Pig | His Picture Book | [*illustrations*] | Containing: | This Little Pig | The Fairy Ship | King Luckieboy | With the original | coloured pictures by | Walter Crane | Engraved & Printed by Ed- | mund Evans. | Chicago: Stone & Kimball | London: John Lane Vigo St. [*lettered in red and black*]

10-1/2 x 9-1/2; three pamphlets bound together in blue linen, lettered and illustrated in blue on sides and spine; illustrated endpapers; edges trimmed. Title and preface, [4] pp.; each pamphlet with stiff illustrated wrappers, decorative endpapers and eight wood engravings, printed on one side of the leaf only.

Advertised in *The Chap-Book* November 15, 1895. Price $1.00 or 25 cents for the pamphlets individually. This series of reprints was continued by Lane from London and New York.

"By Way of Preface: THIS LITTLE PIG having gone to market about a quarter of a century ago [with his two present companions] and finding demand so far exceed supply that he has become "out of print" and "scarce," he has been induced to come forward again in the Nursery interest, and now begs to offer himself as a candidate for the suffrages of a new generation. For his policy this little Pig must refer enquirers to his well known family history as pictured in this book, but he can safely promise [all candidates promise] that when "THE FAIRY SHIP" comes in she will be found as full of "good things" for "LUCKIEBOYS" and girls as of old, and fit to be navigated round the world by Captain Duck—or even

231

Drake, or Columbus, and she is already chartered from London to Chicago.

In regard to his new and enterprising publishers, this little Pig would like to add that his travels to market have convinced him of the time honoured truth—"It is a long LANE that hath no turning"—especially when no STONE has been left unturned by the way.

signed:
This little Pig his mark
witness:
Walter Crane"

[59]
A Song of the Sea | My Lady of Dreams | And Other Poems | by | Eric Mackay | Author of "Love Letters of a Violinist" | Chicago | Stone & Kimball | 1895

6-5/8 x 4-3/16; pp. vi, 7-162, [2]; with signatures. Printed by Turnbull & Spears, Edinburgh, in Modernized Old Style type on laid paper. Bound in green cloth over bevel-edged boards; lettered in gold on spine and front cover. Title-leaf a cancel.

First advertised in *The Chap-Book* November 15, 1895. Price $1.25. English edition published June 1895 by Methuen.

[60]
The Story of Blue-Beard | from Perrault illustrated | with pictures and orna- | -ments by Joseph | E. Southall. | [*floral decoration*] | London Lawrence | and Bullen | Chicago Stone | & Kimball | 1895 | [*lettered in red between head- and tailpiece in black*]

7-1/4 x 5-1/4; pp. 61, [3]; with signatures. Printed by Richard Clay & Sons, London & Bungay, in Caslon type on laid paper. Bound in green boards; lettered and decorated in black on spine and front cover; edges uncut. Eight full-page illustrations, vignettes, and decorative borders for each page of text, by Joseph E. Southall.

First advertised in *The Chap-Book* November 15, 1895. Price $1.25.

[61]
Galloping Dick | Being Chapters from the Life and | Fortunes of Richard Ryder, | otherwise Galloping Dick, | sometime Gentleman | of the Road | by | H. B. Marriott Watson | [*floret*] | Chicago | Stone & Kimball | MDCCCXCVI

6-3/4 x 4-1/4; pp. [iv], 270, [2]. Printed by University Press, Cambridge, in Caslon type on laid paper with watermark two. Bound in blue cloth, stamped in white; on spine with lettering; on sides with rules, lettering and medallion head. Title rubricated.

Entered for copyright November 29, 1895, when copies of pp. [iv], 33-223 were deposited.

Price $1.25. Poster by Frank Hazenplug issued. Appears in secondary binding of blue cloth, stamped in red on spine and front cover. Published in England by John Lane during December 1895. The medallion head in that binding, similar to the American, is by Patten Wilson. Appeared serially in *The New Review* and *The Chap-Book*.

[62]
Rose of Dutcher's Coolly | by | Hamlin Garland | [*device two in red*] | Chicago | Stone & Kimball | MDCCCXCV

7-1/2 x 4-3/4; pp. [ii], 403, [3]. Printed by Lakeside Press, Chicago, in Modernized Old Style type on laid paper with watermark two. Bound in green cloth, stamped in gold; on spine with lettering, on sides with cornstalk design. Title rubricated.

Copyright December 10, 1895. Price $1.50.

The last of Hamlin Garland's books issued by Stone & Kimball and the last of the realistic writings of his early period. Its sales were small and its contemporary critical reception mixed. Many of the reviews made comparison with Hardy's *Jude the Obscure*, issued in America at about the same time. Some, like that of W. P. Trent in *The Bookman*, indicated that Garland was reaching the artistic stature of the British author; others like that in *The Critic*, attempted to incite the censorship and suppression which Thomas Hardy was experiencing. (See M. L. Ernst and William Seagle, *To The Pure . . . A Study of Obscenity and the Censor* [New York: The Viking Press, 1928], p. 42.) The intimations are clear in Hamlin Garland's autobiographies that the critical obtuseness and malignancy with which this novel was greeted, especially in the Midwest of which he was writing, helped him to change from the realistic studies of farm life which he had been making since 1887, to the romantic novels of his next period. This study of the intellectual and social development of a country girl was an important novel, not least, as Carl Van Doren has remarked, because it is the first work in American fiction in which a woman's choice between domestic duties and a professional career is squarely faced.

[63]
Prairie Folks | by | Hamlin Garland | [*device two in red*] | Chicago | Stone & Kimball | MDCCCXCV

7-9/16 x 4-3/4; pp. 254, [6]; with signatures. Printed by University Press, Cambridge, in Modern-face, "Elzevir," and Caslon types, on laid paper with watermark two. Bound uniformly with No. 63.

Issued simultaneously with *Rose of Dutcher's Coolly*, but not copyrighted, as it is a revised reprint of the first edition issued by F. J. Schulte, Chicago, in 1893. Price $1.25. Reissued by Herbert S. Stone & Co. in 1897; later included in all three of their reprint series.

An edition of this volume, with frontispiece by H. T. Carpenter, uniform in binding with *Main Travelled Roads*, was advertised by Stone & Kimball in their Spring Announcement for 1894, but was probably never published. No copy has been located, and the present edition was advertised as having been "out of print for two years or more."

[64]
The Lives of | Doctor John Donne | Sir Henry Wotton | Mr. Richard Hooker | Mr. George Herbert | and Doctor Robert | Sanderson, by | Izaak Walton | In One Volume | Chicago | Stone and Kimball | 1895 | London: Methuen & Company

7-1/2 x 5; pp. xxxi, [i], 295, [1]; with signatures. Printed by T. & A. Constable, Edinburgh, in Scotch Modern-face type on laid paper. "English Classics" binding; see No. 39. Title rubricated.

Listed in *Publishers' Weekly* December 21, 1895. Price $1.25 net. Reissued by Herbert S. Stone & Co. in 1897.

Fourth title issued in the "English Classics" series. §Introduction by Vernon Blackburn.

[65]
English Seamen | Howard, Clifford, Hawkins, Drake | Cavendish | by | Robert Southey | Edited, with an Introduction | by | David Hannay | Chicago | Stone and Kimball | 1895 | London: Methuen & Company.

7-1/2 x 5; pp. xvi, 403, [1]; with signatures. Printer not given; Scotch Modern-face and Caslon types; laid paper. "English Classics" binding; see No. 39. Title-leaf a cancel; title rubricated.

Listed in *Publishers' Weekly* December 21, 1895. Price $1.25 net. Reissued by Herbert S. Stone & Co. in 1897.

Fifth title issued in the "English Classics" series and the only one without imprint of T. & A. Constable. It was done in a pale imitation of their style, possibly in the United States, but the difference in composition, imposition and presswork is so marked that a contemporary writer on printing (C. F. Richardson, "Kelmscott Press Work and other Recent Printing,' *Bookman,* November 1896), while praising the series as a whole, truly called this volume "an easy object lesson in bookmaking," when compared with the others.

[66]

Poems { of the day and year } | [*illustration*] | by Frederick Tennyson | London: John Lane, The Bodley Head | Chicago: Stone and Kimball, MDCCCXCV [*lettered within illustrative frame*]

7-5/8 x 5; pp. [viii], 163, [1]; with signatures. Frontispiece and 16 page catalogue of John Lane inserted. Printed by J. Miller and Son, Edinburgh, in Modernized Old Style type on laid paper. Bound in orange buckram, stamped in gold on spine with lettering and decorative bands. The title-page is by Patten Wilson; the frontispiece a photograph of the author.

Published in England November 1895 and probably available here the next month. American publication never advertised by Stone & Kimball, but included in their list of November 1896, at $1.50 net.

Last poems of the laureate's elder brother, incorporating some of the material from his *Days and Hours* of 1854.

[67]

Pharais | A Romance of the Isles | by | Fiona Macleod | Chicago | Stone & Kimball | MDCCCXCV [*against deisgn of green tree*]

6-3/4 x 4-3/8; pp. [4], xi, [i], 144, [2]; with signatures. 16 page catalogue "Concerning the Books of Stone & Kimball, 1895-1896," inserted. Printed by University Press, Cambridge, in Modernized Old Style type on laid paper with watermark two. "Green Tree" binding; see No. 31 and Fig. 24.

Entered for copyright October 28, 1895, but copies not deposited until February 15, 1896; colophon dated December 1895. Price $1.25 net.

Published in England May 1895 by Frank Murray.

Sixth title issued in "The Green Tree Library."

[68]

A House of Cards | by | Alice S. Wolf | [*device two in red*]| Chicago | Stone & Kimball | MDCCCXCVI

6-5/8 x 4-1/4; pp. 281, [3]; with signatures. Printed by Lakeside Press, Chicago, in Modernized Old Style type on laid paper with watermark two. "Peacock" binding; see No. 38 and Fig. 24. Decorative initial letters begin each chapter.

Copyright March 2, 1896. Price $1.25. Reprinted by University Press for Stone & Kimball; reissued by Stone in blue cloth, stamped in gold. Also in "Court Series" and "Stone's Paper Library."

Second and last title issued in "The Peacock Library." The first was *A Sawdust Doll*, No. 38.

[69]
The | Damnation of Theron Ware | by | Harold Frederic | [*device two in red*] | Chicago | Stone & Kimball | MDCCCXCVI

7-1/2 x 4-3/4; pp. 512, [4]; with signatures. Printed by University Press, Cambridge, in Modernized Old Style type on laid paper. Bound in dark green cloth, stamped in gold on sides and spine (Fig. 25). Title rubricated.

Copyright March 6, 1896. Price $1.50. Poster by J. H. Twachtman issued. Published in England by Heinemann on same day; see I. R. Brussel, *Anglo-American First Editions; Part Two: West to East 1786-1930* (London: Constable & Co. Ltd.; New York: R. R. Bowker Co., 1936), p. 21. § 100,000 copies sold by Stone & Kimball and Herbert S. Stone & Co. before transfer to Duffield in 1906. "Eighth Edition" appeared in paper covers May 15, 1898 as No. 1 of "Stone's Monthly Library"; included 1900 in "Stone's Paper Library." 25,000 copies distributed by Grosset & Dunlap about 1900; see pp. 114, 121.

Illumination appears as a subtitle in impressions past the first. Gladstone's praise of Frederic's book under this, its English title, was effectively used in advertising on both sides of the water. §This was the best selling book as well as the most important piece of contemporary literature, published by Stone & Kimball. §It is also in its early printings one of their most competent and compact pieces of bookmaking.

[70]
The Plays | of | Maurice Maeterlinck | Second Series | Alladine and Palomides • Pél- | léas and Mélisande • Home • | The Death of Tintagiles | Translated by Richard Hovey | Chicago | Stone & Kimball | MDCCCXCVI [*against design of green tree*]

6-3/4 x 4-1/4; pp. xv, [i], 235, [5]; with signatures. Printed by University Press, Cambridge, in Modernized Old Style type on laid paper with watermark two. "Green Tree" binding; see No. 31 and Fig. 24.

Advertised as "Now Ready" in *The Chap-Book* March 15, 1896; colophon dated March, but not deposited for copyright until June 17. Price $1.25 net. Like the first series of Maeterlinck plays, reprinted by Stone & Kimball and by Herbert S. Stone & Co.; transferred to Duffield in 1906, and now published by Dodd, Mead & Co.

Seventh title issued in "The Green Tree Library." § Preface by Maeterlinck, in French.

[71]

The Lives of | the Most Eminent | English Poets | by Samuel Johnson | LL.D | In Three Volumes | Vol. I | Chicago | Stone and Kimball | 1896 | London: Methuen & Company

7-1/2 x 5; 3 Vols., with signatures. I: pp. xxxi, [i], 348; frontispiece inserted. II: pp. [viii], 305, [3]. III: pp. [viii], 287, [1]. Printed by T. & A. Constable, Edinburgh, in Scotch Modern-face type on laid paper. "English Classics" binding; see No. 39. Frontispiece to Vol. I is a reproduction in photogravure of the Reynolds portrait engraved by William Dougherty. Titles rubricated.

Advertised in *The Chap-Book* April 15, 1896. Price $1.25 net per volume. Reissued by Herbert S. Stone & Co. in 1897.

Sixth and last title issued in the "English Classics" series. § Introduction by John Hepburn Millar.

[72]

Miss Armstrong's and Other Circumstances | by | John Davidson | [*device two in red*] | New York | Stone & Kimball | MDCCCXCVI

6-3/4 x 4-1/4; pp. [vi], 259, [3]; with signatures. Printed by University Press, Cambridge, in Modernized Old Style type on laid paper with watermark two. Bound in grey or pale green cloth over flexible boards, stamped in gold on sides and spine with rules, lettering and circular monogram. Title rubricated.

Copyright May 8, 1896; colophon dated June. Price $1.25. Methuen's English edition listed in *Publishers' Circular* for May 9. Reissued in 1897 by Stone; later in the "Court Series."

First Stone & Kimball book published from New York, where Ingalls Kimball was now (with Luther C. White) owner of the firm.

[73]
A Woman's Courier | being a tale of the Famous | Forty Conspiracy of 1696 | By William Joseph Yeoman | [*device two in red*] | New York published | by Stone & Kimball | Anno. MDCCCXCVI

7-1/4 x 4-7/8; pp. ix, [i], 340, [2]; with signatures. Printed by University Press, Cambridge, in Modernized Old Style type on laid paper with watermark two. Bound in tan basket-weave cloth; stamped in black on sides and spine, with rules, lettering and circular monogram. Title rubricated.

Copyright May 21, 1896; colophon dated June. Price $1.25. Reissued by Stone in 1897; included in the "Eldridge Series" and "Stone's Paper Library," 1900.

[74]
W. V. Her Book | and Various Verses | by | William Canton | With two Illustrations by C. E. Brock | [*device two in red*] | New York | Stone & Kimball | MDCCCXCVI

6-3/4 x 4-1/4; pp. viii, 150, [2]; with signatures. Two plates, including frontispiece, inserted. Printed by University Press, Cambridge, in Modernized Old Style type on laid paper with watermark two. Bound in white paper boards; pictorial design on sides and lettering on spine, by J. H. Twachtman, lithographed in colors. Title rubricated.

First edition issued June 1896, according to copyright page of "Second Edition," April 1897. Colophon dated June; entered for copyright May 21 but complete copies not deposited. Price $1.25. Poster by F. Berkley Smith issued. English edition by Isbister listed in *Publishers' Circular* for May 16, 1896. Sheets of second printing bound for Stone & Kimball and for Herbert S. Stone & Co. in red cloth; included by Stone in the "Eldridge Series," 1900. Republished 1898 with *The Invisible Playmate* (No. 95) by Dodd, Mead & Co.; the two plus *In Memory of W. V.* appeared 1912 in "Everyman's Library."

[75]
The | Washer of the Ford | Legendary Moralities | and Barbaric Tales | by Fiona MacLeod | [*device two in red*] | New York | Stone & Kimball | MDCCCXCVI

6-3/4 x 4-3/16; pp. [xii], 332, [4]; with signatures. Printed by University Press, Cambridge, in Modernized Old Style type on laid paper with watermark two. Bound in blue cloth, stamped in white on sides and spine; circular design on sides (Fig. 22). Title rubricated.

Copyright June 12, 1896. Price $1.25. Published in Edinburgh May 1896 by Patrick Geddes & Colleagues. Reissued by Herbert S. Stone & Co. in blue cloth, with device in place of design on sides; included in the "Court Series" and "Stone's Paper Library."

"Fiona Macleod's" last publication with Stone & Kimball.

[76]
The | Island of Doctor Moreau | A Possibility | by | H. G. Wells | [*floret*] | New York | Stone & Kimball | MDCCCXCVI

6-3/4 x 4-1/16; pp. [4], vii, [i], 9-249, [3]; with signatures. Printed by University Press, Cambridge, in Caslon type on laid paper with watermark two. Bound in black cloth, stamped in gold on sides and spine with rules, lettering and circular monogram. Title rubricated.

Copyright June 17, 1896. Price $1.25. Methuen's English edition listed in *Publishers' Circular* for April 4. Reissued by Stone in 1897; later in "Stone's Paper Library" and the "Court Series."

"The Red Room," a short story by H. G. Wells, appeared in *The Chap-Book* February 15, 1896, and was also printed separately for copyright purposes.

[77]
Some Correspondence | and | Six Conversations | by | Clyde Fitch | [*floret*] | New York | Stone & Kimball | MDCCCXCVI

6-1/4 x 3-3/4; pp. [vi], 149, [3]. Printed by Lakeside Press, Chicago, in Caslon type on laid paper with watermark two. Bound in white slubbed cloth over red cloth; stamped in black on sides and spine.

Copyright June 26, 1896. Price $1.00. Originally appeared in *The Chap-Book*. Reissued in 1900 by H. S. Stone & Co., in green cloth.

"Slubbed" cloth, in which the irregularities of weaving are preserved, was apparently used for bindings only by Stone & Kimball in the present volume and Nos. 86, 87 and 89. All were executed by the Boston Bookbinding Company.

[78]
The Thlinkets | of | Southeastern Alaska | by | Frances Knapp | and | Rheta Louise Childe | [*floret*] | Chicago | Stone and Kimball | 1896

6-3/4 x 4-1/4; pp. vi, [7]-197, [3]; with signatures. Frontispiece and seventeen plates (photographs) inserted. Printed by University Press, Cambridge, in Modernized Old Style type on laid paper with watermark two. Bound in red basket-weave cloth, paper label on spine. Title rubricated.

Copyright June 26, 1896. Price $1.50.

[79]
Sonnets | And Other Verses By | George Santayana | New York | Stone and Kimball | MDCCCXCVI [*within decorative frame and border*]

6-3/4 x 4-1/4; pp. [iv], 122, [2]. Printed by University Press, Cambridge, in Modernized Old Style type on laid paper with watermark two. Bound in green cloth, printed in gold on spine. Border and lettering in title by the author.

Copyright June 26, 1896. Price $1.25 net. New impression, with additions, of No. 11. Acquired 1897 by Herbert S. Stone & Co. and bound for them without change in title-page. Reissued 1906 by Fox, Duffield & Co., without "Lucifer," here pp. [99]-122. *Lucifer* also separately published in expanded form by Stone in 1899. New edition of the *Sonnets*, revised and with preface by the author, published by Scribner's in 1922.

[80]
An Adventurer of the North | being a continuation of the histories of | "Pierre and His People," and the | latest existing records of | Pretty Pierre | by | Gilbert Parker | [*floret*] | New York | Stone & Kimball | MDCCCXCVI

7-1/2 x 4-3/4; pp. [viii], 218, [2]. Printed by University Press, Cambridge, in Modernized Old Style type on laid paper with watermark two. Bound in light green cloth, stamped in gold on sides and spine with rules, lettering and circular monogram.

Copyright November 18, 1895, in one volume, not for sale, including the stories later issued in *A Romany of the Snows;* see Number 97. Advertised as "In Preparation" late 1895 and early 1896; separately published June 1896. Price $1.25. Reissued by Herbert S. Stone & Co. in 1897; transferred to Macmillan 1898. Methuen's English edition, in one volume, with title *An Adventurer of the North*, listed in *Publishers' Circular* for November 23, 1895.

The first stories in the "Pierre" cycle were published in the United States by J. C. Harvey in 1893, as *Pierre and His People,* and reissued in 1894 by Stone & Kimball (No. 28). A second collection of twenty-one stories, titled by the author *A Romany of the Snows,* was made in the autumn of 1895. Methuen issued them complete, but chose the title *An Adventurer of the North.* "In America," wrote Sir Gilbert Parker in a preface to the collected edition of his works, "the *Adventurer of the North* was broken up into two volumes at the urgent request of my then publishers, Messrs. Stone & Kimball, who had the gift of producing beautiful books, but perhaps had not the same gift of business." Publication of the first volume was delayed seven months; the second half appeared as *A Romany of the Snows,* almost a year later (No. 97).

[8½]
The Purple East | A Series of Sonnets on England's | Desertion of Armenia | by | William Watson | [*device two in red*] | Chicago: Stone & Kimball | London: John Lane | MDCCCXCVI

6-11/16 x 4-1/8; pp. 49, [3]. Printed by Lakeside Press, Chicago, in Modernized Old Style type on laid paper with watermark two. Bound in blue paper boards, stamped in purple on sides and spine. Title rubricated.

Copyright claimed by John Lane, but entry not recorded. Advertised in *The Chap-Book* July 1, listed in *Publishers' Weekly* July 4. Price 75 cents.

Second of two titles by Watson published jointly by Stone & Kimball and John Lane. This volume, first printed in the United States and copyrighted here by John Lane, was reprinted repeatedly abroad, where the poems, concerned with the religious civil war of 1895, had greater topical interest.

[82]
The Yankees of the | East | Sketches of Modern Japan | by | William Eleroy Curtis | Volume I [*floret*] | New York | Stone & Kimball | MDCCCXCVI

7-1/2 x 4-5/8; 2 Vols., with signatures. I: pp. [xiv], 328, [4]. II: pp. [vi], 329-644, [4]. Forty-four photographic illustrations inserted; diagrams in text. Printed by University Press, Cambridge, in Modernized Old Style type on laid paper with watermark two. Bound in salmon buckram or red basket-weave cloth, paper label on spines.

Copyright July 7, 1896. Price $4.00. Reissued by Herbert S. Stone & Co. in 1897.

Reprinted from the Chicago *Record,* for which Curtis was long travelling correspondent and contributor on foreign affairs. He had been the first director of the Bureau of the American Republics, now The Pan-American Union. A book of his on Spanish America was published by Herbert S. Stone & Co. in 1900.

[83]
In a Dike Shanty | by | Maria Louise Pool | [*floret*] | Chicago | Stone & Kimball | MDCCCXCVI

6-3/4 x 4-1/4; pp. [ii], 231, [3]; with signatures. Printed by the University Press, Cambridge, in Caslon type on laid paper with watermark two. Bound in light green linen; illustration by Frank Hazenplug and lettering on front cover in brown; lettered in gold on spine. Title rubricated.

Released for publication September 1896 (listed in *Publishers' Weekly* September 5), but printed in the spring of 1896, before Kimball's purchase and removal of the firm to New York, and copyrighted May 25, 1896. Price $1.25. Reprinted by Herbert S. Stone & Co. in 1898 and later included in their "Eldridge Series."

[84]
Wives in Exile | A Comedy in Romance | by | William Sharp | [*device two in red*] | New York | Stone & Kimball | MDCCCXCVI

6-3/4 x 4-1/4; pp. [viii], 329, [1]; with signatures. Printed by University Press, Cambridge, in Modernized Old Style type on laid paper with watermark two. Bound in paper boards, printed in gold on spine; edges uncut. Title rubricated.

Entered for copyright June 20, 1896; copies (in boards) deposited September 11. Included in *A New List of the Books of Stone & Kimball*, November 1896. Price $1.25. Copyright assigned shortly after publication to Lamson, Wolffe & Co. of Boston; who issued the same sheets, with cancel title and binding of blue buckram, before the end of the year. English edition not published until July 1898, by Grant Richards.

[85]
All | Expenses | Paid | Chicago | Stone and Kimball | and New York | 1896

6-7/8 x 4-3/16; pp. vi, 112, [4]. Printed by T. & A. Constable, Edinburgh, in Scotch Modern-face type on laid paper. Bound in half green cloth, printed in gold on spine; sides of green paper boards. Title-leaf a cancel. Not listed in *Publishers' Weekly*, not advertised, and not included in trade lists. Reviewed in *Bookman* October 1896. Price $1.00. Published in London August 1895 by Constable.

An anonymous satire on the poets of the Bodley Head, since revealed as the work of Norman Gale.

[86]

Lady Bramber's Ghost | by | Charles Charrington | [*floret*] | New York | Stone & Kimball | MDCCCXCVI

6-13/16 x 4-1/4; pp. 141, [3]; with signatures. Printed by University Press, Cambridge, in Caslon type on laid paper with watermark two. Bound in white slubbed cloth over red cloth; stamped in black on sides and spine. Title rubricated.

Copyright October 12, 1896. Price $1.25. Issued October 1896 by Constable, London, in one volume with *A Sturdy Beggar*. Issued in remainder binding of cheap green cloth by Herbert S. Stone & Co. after 1897; also included in the "Court Series."

Charles Charrington was the English actor-manager, known best in this country for his production of Ibsen.

[87]

A Sturdy Beggar | by | Charles Charrington | [*floret*] | New York | Stone & Kimball | MDCCCXCVI

6-13/16 x 4-1/4; pp. 163, [5]; with signatures. Printed by University Press, Cambridge, in Caslon type on laid paper with watermark two. Bound in white slubbed cloth over red cloth; stamped in black on sides and spine. Title rubricated.

Copyright October 12, 1896. Price $1.25. Issued October 1896 by Constable, London, in one volume with *Lady Bramber's Ghost*. Issued in remainder binding of cheap green cloth by Herbert S. Stone & Co. after 1897.

[88]

Grip | by | John Strange Winter | [*device two in red*] | New York | Stone & Kimball | MDCCCXCVI [*within rule border*]

6-11/16 x 4-1/4; pp. 245, [3]; with signatures. Printed by Fleming, Schiller and Carnrick, New York, in Franklin Old Style and "Rimpled" types on laid paper with watermark two. Bound in salmon-colored cloth, stamped in gold on sides and spine. Title rubricated.

Copyright October 12, 1896. Price $1.25.

"John Strange Winter" was a pseudonym of Mrs. Henrietta E. V. Stannard, English author of popular romances. § This is the first book printed for Stone & Kimball by Fleming, Schiller and Carnrick. Franklin Old Style type used for text (Fig. 27) originally was cut for the Dickinson Type Foundry of Boston in 1863 by Alexander C. Phemister, the originator of the first Modernized Old Style type—Miller & Richards' Old Style. The "Rimpled Series" used for the title page (Fig. 26), from Mackellar, Smiths and Jordan Foundry, is identical with "XV Century," first cut in 1896 by Barnhart Brothers & Spindler, later called "Caslon Antique." In these types the outlines are purposely broken and made uneven, to indicate old age.

[89]
Urban Dialogues | by | Louis Evan Shipman | [*type ornament*] | New York | Stone & Kimball | MDCCCXCVI

6-3/4 x 4-1/8; pp. xi, [i], 115, [5]; with signatures. Frontispiece and five plates inserted. Printed by University Press, Cambridge, in Caslon type on laid paper with watermark two. Bound in white slubbed cloth over tan cloth; stamped in black on sides and spine. Illustrations by Charles Dana Gibson. Title rubricated.

Copyright October 14, 1896. Price $1.25. Reprinted from *Life* and *Leslie's Weekly*. Reissued by Herbert S. Stone & Co. in green cloth, and also included in the "Eldridge Series."

The Gibson drawings were not noted by Fairfax Downey in *Portrait of an Era as Drawn by C. D. Gibson* (New York: Charles Scribner's Sons, 1936), nor in the checklist included in Theodore Bolton, *American Book Illustrators* (New York: R. R. Bowker Company, 1938).

[90]
Friend or Fortune | A Story for Boys | by | Robert Overton | With pictures by | Frederic Yohn | [*device two in red*] | New York | Stone & Kimball | MDCCCXCVI

7-3/8 x 4-3/4; pp. 243, [5]; with signatures. Printed by Fleming, Schiller and Carnrick, New York, in Modernized Old Style, "Ronaldson" and Caslon types on laid paper with watermark two. Bound in red cloth with lettering and decoration (by T. B. Hapgood Jr.) in white on sides and spine.

Copyright October 16, 1896. Price $1.50. Reissued by Herbert S. Stone & Co. in 1897; later in the "Eldridge Series" and "Stone's Paper Library." Hapgood's cover design of ship and trellis is hardly one of the best of Stone & Kimball's bindings, but nevertheless won favor in England, where it was commented on by E. F. Strange and reproduced as an example of American work in the *Studio* "Bookbinding Number" of 1900.

[91]
Captain Jacobus | by | L. Cope Cornford | [*device two in red*] | New York | Stone & Kimball | MDCCCXCVI

6-3/4 x 4-1/4; pp. vi, 7-285. Frontispiece and one plate inserted. Printed by University Press, Cambridge, in Caslon type on thin laid paper with watermark two. Bound in blue cloth, stamped in white; on sides with rule borders, lettering and medallion head, on spine with letters. Illustrations by Charles Sheldon. Title rubricated.

Copyright October 20, 1896. Price $1.25. Reissued after 1897 by Herbert S. Stone & Co. in remainder binding of cheap green cloth, and later included in the "Eldridge Series" and "Stone's Paper Library."

The binding is similar to those reproduced in Fig. 22.

[92]
Mademoiselle Blanche | A Novel | by | John D. Barry | [*device two in red*] | New York | Stone and Kimball | MDCCCXCVI

7-1/2 x 4-3/4; pp. [iv], 330, [6]; with signatures. Printed by University Press, Cambridge, in Modernized Old Style type on laid paper with watermark two. Bound in green cloth, stamped in gold on sides and spine with rules, lettering and circular monogram. Title rubricated.

Copyright October 28, 1896. Price $1.25. Reissued by Herbert S. Stone & Co. in 1897.

The author, now columnist of the San Francisco *News,* was then doing newspaper work in New York, where he was also, for two weeks only, reporter for *The Daily Tatler.*

[93]
Boss and Other Dogs | by | Maria Louise Pool | [*device two in red*] | New York | Stone & Kimball | MDCCCXCVI

6-3/4 x 4-1/4; pp. 134, [2]; with signatures. Printed by Fleming, Schiller and Carnrick, New York, in Modernized Old Style type on laid paper with watermark two. Bound in green linen; illustration by Blanche McManus and printing in brown on front cover (Fig. 32); printing in gold on spine.

Entered for copyright October 28, 1896, but copies not deposited. Colophon dated October; advertised in *The Chap-Book* November 15. Price $1.25. Reprinted from *The Chap-Book* and other periodicals.

[94]
At the | Sign of the Sphinx | A Book of Charades | [*rule*] | by Carolyn Wells | [*rule*] | [*quotation*] | [*rule*] | [*device two in red*] | [*rule*] | New York, Published by | Stone and Kimball | in the year MDCCCXCVI [*within rule border*]

245

6-3/4 x 4-1/4; pp. viii, 103, [5]; with signatures. Printed by University Press, Cambridge, in Caslon type on thick laid paper with watermark two. Binding designed by Claude F. Bragdon; grey paper boards with lettering, Egyptian decorations and medallion head on sides, in black and gold; lettering in gold on spine. Title rubricated.

Entered for copyright October 28, 1896, but copies not deposited. Advertised in *The Chap-Book* November 15. Price $1.25. Reissued by Stone in 1897; by Duffield & Co. in 1906, when a "Second Series" was published.

Miss Well's first book. § Claude Bragdon's only book cover for Stone & Kimball; those for Herbert S. Stone & Co. were perhaps more successful.

[95]
The Daily Tatler | [*rule*] | Vol. I, No. 1. New York 7 November, 1896. Price 2 Cents. | [*rule*]

Newspaper continued daily (Sundays excepted) from Saturday, November 7, through Saturday, November 21, 1896, Vol. I, No. 13. Title as above from first page; given on fourth, editorial page, as: The Tatler | Published Daily By | Stone & Kimball, | 139 Fifth Avenue, New York. Printer not given but probably Fleming, Schiller and Carnrick, New York; Franklin Old Style type; newsprint paper. Some sets afterwards stitched into purple paper wrappers, paper label on sides and spine.

Edited by H. I. Kimball and Carolyn Wells. Staff and contributors included: John D. Barry (dramatic critic and ship news reporter), Fitzroy Carrington, Frank Chaffee, Edwin Emerson Jr. ("Pepys's Ghost"), Florence Brooks Emerson, Sadakichi Hartmann (art critic), James Clarence Harvey, W. B. Harte, Henriette and Richard Hovey (on poets and as poets), William Dean Howells (on Riley), Leigh Hunt (hitherto unpublished poem), George Merriam Hyde, F. Edge Kavanagh, George Parsons Lathrop, Maurice Maeterlinck, Clinton Scollard, Esther Singleton, Charles Wright.

The only daily literary newspaper published commercially in the United States. The mid-nineteenth century saw a number of literary sheets produced daily for sale at charity fairs, but *The Daily Tatler* was regularly distributed by news dealers throughout New York City, with such success that it was always sold out before reaching the uptown stands, and several numbers had to be reprinted. On its birth, death and importance, see pp. 85-87, and Thomas Beer, *The Mauve Decade* (New York: Alfred A. Knopf, 1926), pp. 193-96; Carolyn Wells, "A Post-Mortem Statement," *The Chap-Book,* Februray 1, 1897 (Vol. VI, No. 6), pp. 251-52; Carolyn Wells, *The Rest of My Life* (Philadelphia: J. B. Lippincott Company, 1937), pp. 174-75. § There were two trial copies of Vol. I, No. 1, one on lighter and whiter paper than that used, and another on the heavy newsprint paper, with stamping "Sample Copy."

[96]

The Invisible Playmate | A Story of the Unseen | With Appendices | by | William Canton | [*device two in red*] | New York | Stone & Kimball | MDCCCXCVI

6-3/4 x 4-1/4; pp. 95, [1]; with signatures. Printed by Fleming, Schiller and Carnrick, New York, in Modernized Old Style and Caslon types on heavy laid paper with watermark two. Bound in white paper boards; pictorial design on sides and lettering on spine, by J. H. Twachtman, lithographed in colors. Title rubricated.

Copyright notice on verso of title, but there is no record of entry in the copyright office. Colophon dated October; first advertised in *The Chap-Book* November 15, 1896. Price $1.00. First published in book form by Isbister & Co., London in April 1894; issued in paper covers by J. Selwin Tait & Sons, New York, early in 1896. Stone & Kimball sheets appear in red cloth binding dated 1897 and in similar binding for Herbert S. Stone & Co. Reissued 1900 in the "Eldridge Series." Republished 1898 with *W. V. Her Book* (No. 74) by Dodd, Mead & Co.

The bankrupt stock of J. Selwin Tait & Sons of New York was sold during the season 1896-97 by Stone & Kimball, but this is the only title from their list which was reprinted.

[97]

A Romany of the Snows | Second Series of | An Adventurer of the North being | a continuation of Pierre and His | People and the latest existing | records of Pretty Pierre | by | Gilbert Parker | [*floret*] | New York | Stone & Kimball | MDCCCXCVI

7-1/2 x 4-3/4; pp. [viii], 203, [1]. Printed by University Press, Cambridge, in Modernized Old Style type on laid paper with watermark two. Bound in light green cloth, stamped in gold on sides and spine with rules, lettering and circular monogram. Title rubricated.

Copyright notice gives date of 1896, but actually copyrighted on November 18, 1895 in one volume, not for sale, with *An Adventurer of the North*. Separately published November 9, 1896, according to advertisement and review in *The Daily Tatler* of that date; colophon dated October. Price $1.50. Reissued by Herbert S. Stone & Co. in 1897; later in the "Eldridge Series" and "Stone's Paper Library."

The last of Gilbert Parker's books published by Stone & Kimball; see No. 80, and pp. 87-88.

[98]
The Scarlet Coat | by | Clinton Ross | [*device two in red*] | New York | Stone & Kimball | MDCCCXCVI

6-7/8 x 4-1/4; pp. [ii], 309, [3]; with signatures. Printed by University Press, Cambridge, in Caslon type on laid paper with watermark two. Bound in scarlet cloth, printed in gold on sides and spine within rules. Title rubricated.

Copyright notice on verso of title-page, but entry not made and copies not deposited in the Copyright Office. First advertised in *The Chap-Book* November 15, 1896; not listed in *Publishers' Weekly* until December 12, but "Second Thousand" advertised in *The Daily Tatler* November 14. Price $1.25. Reissued after 1897 by Herbert S. Stone & Co. in half red cloth, and included in the "Court Series" about 1900.

[99]
The Puppet | by | Clinton Ross | [*floret*] | New York | Stone & Kimball | MDCCCXCVI

6-7/8 x 4-1/4; pp. [vi], 183, [3]. Printed by Lakeside Press, Chicago, in Caslon type on laid paper with watermark two. Bound in scarlet cloth, printed in gold on sides and spine within rules (Fig. 25). Title rubricated.

Copyright notice on verso of title-page, but entry not made nor copies deposited in the Copyright Office. First advertised in *The Chap-Book* November 15, 1896; "Advance Notice" in *The Daily Tatler* November 12. Price $1.25. Reissued after 1897 by Herbert S. Stone & Co. in half red cloth, and included in the "Court Series" about 1900.

[100]
James | or Virtue Rewarded | [*device two in red*] | New York Stone & Kimball | MDCCCXCVI

7-1/2 x 4-5/8; pp. viii, 285, [3]; with signatures. Printed by Fleming, Schiller and Carnrick in Franklin Old Style and "Rimpled" types on laid paper with watermark two. Bound in green cloth, stamped in gold on sides and spine with rules, lettering and monogram; see Fig. 25. Title rubricated.

Not copyrighted; advertised as "Out Today" in *The Daily Tatler* November 14, 1896; reviewed there November 19. Price $1.50. Reissued by

Herbert S. Stone & Co. in the "Eldridge Series" and "Stone's Paper Library." Published in London May 1896 by Constable.

Probably written by John Charles Tarver, English educator. He is suggested by Halkett & Laing as the author of *Muggleton College,* published by Constable in 1894. The present volume was advertised as "By the Author of Muggleton College."

[101]

Ring o' Rushes | by | Shan F. Bullock | [*device two in red*] | New York | Stone & Kimball | MDCCCXCVI

6-3/4 x 4-1/4; pp. xiii, [v], [3]-230, [2]; with signatures. Printed by Fleming, Schiller and Carnrick, New York, in Modernized Old Style type on laid paper with watermark two. Binding designed by A. P. Rogers; light or dark green cloth; all-over pattern of shamrocks and lettering in green on sides; lettering in green on spine.

Advertised as "Out Today," November 14, 1896 in *The Daily Tatler,* where it was reviewed November 11. Price $1.25. Two of the stories had been separately printed for copyright purposes only, and one of these, "The Splendid Shilling," appeared in *The Chap-Book;* see p. 359.

Volume reissued by Herbert S. Stone & Co. in remainder binding of cheap green cloth; also included in the "Eldridge Series."

[102]

With the Band | by | Robert W. Chambers | [*device two in red*] | New York | Stone & Kimball | MDCCCXCVI

6-3/4 x 4-1/4; pp. xi, [i], 134, [2]; with signatures. Printed by University Press, Cambridge, in Caslon type on laid paper with watermark two. Bound in grey paper boards, stamped in black on sides and spine. Title rubricated.

Deposited for copyright January 21, 1897; listed in *Publishers' Weekly* March 20. Price $1.25.

Kiplingesque verse; the novelist's only book of poetry.

[103]

Ziska | the | Problem of a Wicked Soul | by | Marie Corelli | [*device two in red*] | New York | Stone & Kimball | MDCCCXCVII

7-1/2 x 4-3/4; pp. 315, [5]; with signatures. Printed by University Press, Cambridge, in Modernized Old Style type on laid paper. Bound in dark green patterned cloth printed in gold on sides and spine within band of thick and thin rules. Title rubricated.

Copyright February 17, 1897; listed in *Publishers' Weekly* April 17. Price $1.50. Transferred to Stokes in the same year. Published in England February 1897 by Arrowsmith.

[104]
John Gabriel Borkman | by | Henrik Ibsen | Translated by | William Archer | New York | Stone & Kimball | MDCCCXCVII [*against design of green tree*]

6-3/4 x 4-1/4; pp. [ii], 198, [4]; with signatures. Printed by University Press in Modernized Old Style type on laid paper with watermark two. "Green Tree" binding; see No. 31 and Fig. 24.

Entered for copyright January 5, 1897. Listed in *Publishers' Weekly* March 20. Price $1.50 net.

Eighth title issued in the "Green Tree Library," and the only one with the New York imprint of Stone & Kimball. Later published by Stone from Chicago.

[105]
The | College Year-Book | and | Athletic Record | for the Academic Year | 1896-97 | Compiled and Edited by | Edwin Emerson Jr. | [*device two in red*] | New York | Stone & Kimball | MDCCCXCVII [*within double rule border*]

7-5/8 x 4-3/4; pp. [iii]-vi, 592; with signatures. 24 pages of advertisements at back; endpapers printed with advertising. Printed by University Press, Cambridge, in Modernized Old Style type on laid paper. Bound in blue or orange cloth, printed in black on spine; edges uncut. Title rubricated.

Entered for copyright December 7, 1896, but copies not deposited; listed in *Publishers' Weekly* April 17, 1897. Price $2.00.

Intended to be an American *Minerva Jahrbuch*, with a catalogue of American universities, colleges and schools and a personal index of teachers, as well as an almanac of sports. Not continued by Herbert S. Stone & Co. or any other publisher.

[106]
The Meddling Hussy | Being Fourteen Tales Retold | by | Clinton Ross | [*device two in red*] | New York | Stone and Kimball | MDCCCXCVII

6-11/16 x 4-1/8; pp. xii, 13-400, [4]; with signatures. Frontispiece and two plates inserted. Printed by University Press, Cambridge, in Caslon type on laid paper with watermark three. Bound in scarlet cloth, printed in gold on sides and spine within rules. Title rubricated. The frontispiece and one plate are signed I. W. Taber; the other is by another hand.

Copyright notice on verso of title-page but no entry made and copies not deposited in the Copyright Office. Advertised in *The Chap-Book* May 15, 1897; listed in *Publishers' Weekly* July 3. Price $1.50. Reissued after 1897 by Herbert S. Stone & Co. in half red cloth, and included in the "Court Series" about 1900.

The last publication of Stone & Kimball. §Watermark three has the conical device and the name of Stone & Kimball, with the address "New York."

II
Publications of
Herbert S. Stone & Company
Chicago and New York, 1896-1905

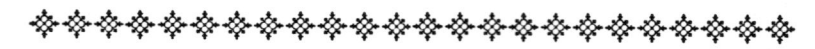

[107]
Prose Fancies | Second Series |by| Richard Le Gallienne | [*device three*] | Herbert S. Stone & Co., Chicago | John Lane, London | MDCCCXCVI [*within rule border*]

6-3/4 x 4-1/4; pp. [viii], 201, [7]. Printed by Lakeside Press, Chicago, in Caslon type on laid paper. Binding (Fig. 30) by Frank Hazenplug; maroon cloth stamped in gold; on sides with floral ornament within rule frame and lettering within rule border, on spine with lettering. Title rubricated.

Copyright June 25, 1896; advertised in *The Chap-Book* June 15; listed in *Publishers' Weekly* July 25. Price $1.25. "Second Edition" advertised 1897; "Third Impression," 1898. Published in London by Lane during 1896; the *English Catalogue* does not give the month of publication.

Device three (Table III), an eagle above a shield bearing three books, presumably designed by Herbert Stone, used here for the first time. § Mr. Le Gallienne's only appearance on the Stone lists; his chief American publisher had been Copeland & Day and was later John Lane.

[108]
[*rule*] | Episcopo | & Company | by | Gabriele D'Annunzio | [*rule*] | Translated by | Myrta Leonora Jones | [*rule*] | [*device four in brown*] | [*rule*] | Published by | Herbert S. Stone | & Company, Chicago | [*rule*] | MDCCCXCVI | [*rule*]

6-11/16 x 4-5/16; pp. [2], xiii, [i], 122, [2]; with signatures. Followed by "Recent Publications of Herbert S. Stone & Co.," 2 pp., and Stone's Catalogue No. 1, 8 pp., inserted. Printed by University Press, Cambridge, in Caslon type on laid paper. Bound in dark green cloth stamped in gold; title and device four within rule border on sides; lettering and rules on spine. See Fig. 30.

Copyright claimed, but entry not made and no copies deposited. Advertised in *The Chap-Book* July 1, 1896; listed in *Publishers' Weekly* August 15. Price $1.25. "Second Edition" advertised in 1897; "Third Impression," 1898.

Device four (Table III), circle enclosing eagle and shield, designed by Frank Hazenplug, used here for the first time. Title-page reproduced in Fig. 28. § This novel, D'Annunzio's first appearance in English, was first offered for publication to Copeland & Day of Boston, according to letters from the translator to that firm, now in the Newberry Library. While they were considering it, Miss Jones received and accepted an offer from Stone. It had been rejected by Dodd Mead & Co., who had reported, Miss Jones wrote on March 22, 1896: "Their readers have not that ready sympathy with realism necessary to make 'Episcopo' a success; that they would be criticized for publishing it and so forth." § The reviews of the Stone edition were decidedly unfavorable. The *Critic* of September 26, 1896, called it "sickly twaddle. . . . Sensuality . . . is caricatured in 'Jude the Obscure' and the work of Signor D'Annunzio." The *Nation* called it "a horrible tale, fortunately short" on December 31, when a second novel of D'Annunzio's, *The Triumph of Death,* had also been translated (by Arthur Hornblow, and published by George H. Richmond & Co. of New York).

[109]
[*rule*] | Checkers | [*rule*] | A Hard-Luck Story by | Henry Blossom Jr. | [*floret*] | Chicago, Herbert S. Stone & Company | MDCCCXCVI [*within double rule border*]

6-11/16 x 4-1/4; pp. [viii], 239, [7]; with signatures. Printed by Lakeside Press, Chicago, in Caslon type on laid paper with watermark two.

Bound in red cloth, stamped in white on sides and spine. Title rubricated. Copyright July 15, 1896; listed in *Publishers' Weekly* July 25. Price $1.25. In "Seventh Edition" by March 1, 1897; "Eighteenth Thousand," during 1898. "Twenty-fifth Thousand," 1899, has frontispiece by John T. McCutcheon. Issued late 1898 in paper wrappers (50 cents), with frontispiece and cover design by McCutcheon. Copyright assigned to Grosset & Dunlap July 24, 1905.

Henry Martyn Blossom was a St. Louisan who had made some reputation with his first book, *The Documents in Evidence* (St. Louis: Buxton & Skinner, 1893). He later turned playwright with a dramatization of *Checkers,* which was concerned with the domestic adventures of a racetrack tout, and later was also the librettist of such popular comic operas as *Mlle Modiste, The Red Mill, The Man from Cook's,* and *Princess Pat.* § Watermark two, as used in most of the Stone & Kimball books between October 1894 and January 1897, is the conical torch design between initials "S" and "K" and also "Stone & Kimball | Chicago."

[110]

Without Sin | a novel | by | Martin J. Pritchard | [*device four*] | Chicago | Herbert S. Stone & Company | MDCCCXCVI [*within rule border*]

7-7/16 x 4-7/16; pp. [x], 298, [6]; with signatures. Printed by Lakeside Press, Chicago, in Modern-face and Caslon types on laid paper with watermark four. Bound in blue buckram stamped in gold; on sides with lettering and strapwork ornament within rule border; on spine with lettering. Title rubricated.

Copyright August 1, 1896; listed in *Publishers' Weekly* August 15. Price $1.25. In "Third Edition," 1898; included that year in "Stone's Monthly Library"; "Fourth Impression" 1899 in cloth and in paper at 50 cents; in 1900 in "Stone's Paper Library." Published in London May 1896 by Heinemann.

"Martin J. Pritchard" was the pseudonym of Mrs. Augustus Moore, English novelist. § Watermark four, "H. S. Stone & Company Chicago | The Chap-Book" appears here for the first time in a book. It was also adopted for *The Chap-Book,* beginning August 1, 1896.

[111]

The | Fearsome Island, | Being a modern rendering | of the narrative | of one Silas Fordred, Master Mari- | ner of Hythe, whose shipwreck and | subsequent adventures are herein set | forth. Also an appendix accounting in a | rational manner for the seeming mar- | vels that Silas Fordred encountered | during his sojourn on the fearsome | is- | land of Don Diego Rodreguez. | [*double rule*] | by Albert Kinross. | [*double rule*] | Chicago: | Printed for Herbert S. Stone & Com- | pany at the Chap-Book offices in the | Caxton Building. 1896 [*within double rule border*]

6-13/16 x 4-1/4; pp. [viii], 142, [2]; 4 pp. of advertisements inserted. Printer not given but probably Lakeside Press, Chicago; Modernized Old Style type; laid paper. Binding designed by Frank Hazenplug; green cloth stamped in green; silhouette design and lettering on sides within rule borders; lettering on spine.

Copyright August 21, 1896; listed in *Publishers' Weekly* October 3. Price $1.25. Published in London by Arrowsmith during August 1896.

[112]

Artie | A Story of the Streets and Town | by | George Ade | Pictures by | John T. McCutcheon | [*device three in red*] | Chicago | Herbert S. Stone & Co. | 1896 [*within double rule border*]

6-5/8 x 4-1/4; pp. [x], 192, [4]. Four pages of advertisements usually inserted. Printed by Lakeside Press, Chicago, in Caslon type on laid paper. Bound in blue-white linen (Fig. 30); stamped in blue on sides and spine with rules and lettering; shield design in blue on tan paper, inserted into front cover, stamped in blue on back. Illustrated with twenty line drawings, including frontispiece. Title rubricated.

Copyright September 24, 1896. Price $1.25. Poster by John T. McCutcheon issued. Reprinted thirteen times before 1901. Seventh printing—twelfth thousand, issued as No. 1 of "Stone's Quarterly," at 50 cents, in paper covers. This has a new McCutcheon drawing of 'Artie Atop a Skyscraper,' on front cover, which is dated August 18, 1897; the edition was actually issued in February 1898. Fifteenth thousand, 1898, was issued in "Stone's Paper Library." Twenty-first thousand, in cheap green cloth, issued 1900; thirtieth thousand, the same year, in blue cloth. Published after 1901 by Grosset & Dunlap and after 1906 by Duffield.

Mr. Ade's first book, collected at the suggestion of Herbert Stone from his "Stories of the Streets and Town" columns in the Chicago *Record*. Mr. Ade had four other titles published by Stone before his books went East in 1900; see Nos. 128, 206, 219, 256 and pp. 96-97, 122-23.

[113]

A Child of the Jago | by | Arthur Morrison | Author of | "Tales of Mean Streets" | [*device five in red*] | Chicago | Herbert S. Stone & Co. | MDCCCXCVI

7-1/2 x 4-3/4; pp. [x], 396, [4]. Frontispiece map and Stone catalogue No. 1, 8 pp., inserted. Printed by Lakeside Press, Chicago, in Caslon type on heavy laid paper with watermark four. Bound in maroon ribbed cloth over bevel-edged boards; stamped in gold on sides and spine with lettering and florets.

Copyright September 28, 1896; advertised in *The Chap-Book* October 15; listed in *Publishers' Weekly* November 7. Price $1.50. "Second Edition" advertised in 1898; included 1900 in both the "Eldridge Series" and "Stone's Paper Library." Methuen's English edition listed in *Publishers' Circular* for October 31, 1896.

Device five (Table III), eagle above a shield and cornucopia below, presumably designed by Herbert Stone, used here for the first time.

[114]
The | Fatal Gift | of Beauty | and Other Stories | by | C. E. Raimond | Author of | "George Mandeville's Husband" | [*device five in red*] | Chicago | Herbert S. Stone & Co. | MDCCCXCVI [*within double rule border*]

6-3/4 x 4-1/4; pp. [x], 248, [6]; Stone catalogue No. 1, 8 pp., inserted. Printed by Lakeside Press, Chicago, in Modernized Old Style and Caslon types on laid paper with watermark four. Bound in tan buckram; stamped in blue on sides and spine; device five in red on sides.

Copyright October 3, 1896; advertised in *The Chap-Book* October 15; listed in *Publishers' Weekly* November 7. Price $1.25. An abridged version of *Below the Salt,* published in London by Heinemann during October 1896.

"C. E. Raimond" was the pen-name of Elizabeth Robins (Mrs. G. R. Parks), the American actress who made her greatest success in England as an interpreter of Ibsen.

[115]
In | Buncombe County | by | Maria Louise Pool | [*device three in red*] | Chicago | Herbert S. Stone & Company | 1896 [*within double rule border*]

6-7/8 x 4-1/4; pp. [iv], 295, [3]; with signatures. Printed by University Press, Cambridge, in Caslon type on laid paper. Binding designed by Frank Hazenplug; lavender board sides with three floral units and lettering, in maroon; maroon cloth spine with lettering in gold; edges uncut. Title in italics and rubricated.

Copyright October 5, 1896; listed in *Publishers' Weekly* November 7. Price $1.25. "Second Edition," October 25, 1896, printed by Lakeside Press from same plates as the first edition. Included in "Stone's Paper Library," 1900.

The first of four books by Miss Pool published by Stone; Stone & Kimball had published two in 1896. § One of the most handsome of Stone publications.

[116]

The Carissima | A Modern Grotesque | by | Lucas Malet | Author of | "The Wages of Sin" | "Colonel Enderby's Wife" | [*device five in red*] | Chicago | Herbert S. Stone & Co. | MDCCCXCVI [*within double rule border*]

7-1/2 x 4-5/8; pp. [ii], 334, [2]; Stone catalogue No. 1, 8 pp., inserted. Printed by Stromberg, Allen & Co., Chicago, in Modernized Old Style and Caslon types on laid paper with watermark four. Bound like No. 113.

Copies deposited in Copyright Office October 22, 1896, but entry not made until March 13, 1902. Listed in *Publishers' Weekly* November 7. Price $1.50. "Second Edition" advertised 1898. English edition published by Methuen October 1896.

"Lucas Malet" is the well-known pen-name of Charles Kingsley's daughter, Mrs. Mary St. Leger Harrison. This is her only appearance on the Stone lists. § The first book printed for Stone by Stromberg, Allen & Co., then their neighbors in Dearborn Street. This firm of printers and lithographers had produced some advertising literature for Stone & Kimball and the "Green Tree Library" poster of 1894.

[117]

The | Land of the Castanet | Spanish Sketches | by | H. C. Chatfield-Taylor | Illustrated | [*device three in red*] | Chicago | Herbert S. Stone & Co. | 1896 [*within double rule border*]

7-1/2 x 4-3/4; pp. [xii], 254, [6]. Frontispiece, twenty-five plates (chiefly photographs) and Stone's catalogue No. 1, 8 pp., inserted. Printed by Lakeside Press, Chicago, in Caslon type on laid paper with watermark four. Bound in red and yellow striped cloth, printed in red on spine. Title rubricated.

Copyright October 23, 1896; listed in *Publishers' Weekly* November 7. Reissued by Duffield in 1906. Price $1.25.

Several of the sketches which make up Mr. Chatfield-Taylor's first travel book had appeared in *The Cosmopolitan*. *Tawny Spain*, published by Houghton Mifflin Co. in 1927, is a revision of the same essays.

257

[118]
Curious Punishments | of | Bygone Days, | by | Alice Morse Earle. | [*double rule*] | [*device five in red*] | [*double rule*] | Chicago: | Printed for Herbert S. Stone & Company | at the Chap-Book offices in the Caxton | Building, 1896. [*within double rule border*]

7-7/16 x 4-3/4; pp. [6], vii, [i], 148, [6]. Twelve illustrations, including frontispiece, and Stone's catalogue No. 1, 8 pp., inserted. Printed by Lakeside Press, Chicago, in Caslon type on laid paper with watermark four. Binding designed by Frank Hazenplug; tan buckram with decorative frame enclosing device five and lettering on sides, in brown and red; lettering on spine in red. The pen drawings by Frank Hazenplug, in old woodcut style, are printed on butchers' brown paper.

Copyright November 11, 1896; listed in *Publishers' Weekly* December 5. Price $1.50. Published in England by Stone during February 1897. New edition published in New York 1922 by Macmillan, with 1896 copyright claimed for Macmillan.

The only book of Mrs. Earle published by Stone; made up from her contributions to *The Chap-Book*. Another collection, on *Old Time Drinks and Drinkers,* announced for publication in 1899, was withdrawn at the author's request. Mrs. Earle's letters to the firm indicate that her reason was the lack of suitable illustrations. She had a good deal to say about the design and illustration of the present volume, comparing the result favorably with her publications through other houses, and in the end expressing satisfaction with Hazenplug's illustrations, although she had thought his work for *The Chap-Book* "meagre and dull" compared with Bragdon's. § The volume was quite successful for a work of its kind; royalties of $443.28 were paid on January 1, 1897, indicating, if the usual 10 per cent royalty maintained, sales of about 3,000 copies within the year.

[119]
Essays | from the | Chap-Book | Being a Miscellany of | Curious and interesting Tales, | Histories, &c; newly com- | posed by Many Cele- | brated Writers | and very delight- | ful to read. | [*device six*] | Chicago. | Printed for Herbert S. Stone & Company, | and are to be sold by them at The | Caxton Building in Dearborn Street | 1896 | [*lettered in red and black within double rule border*]

6-13/16 x 4-1/4; pp. [4], vi, 3-262, [2]; with signatures. Stone catalogue

No. 1, 8 pp., inserted. Printed by Lakeside Press, Chicago, in Caslon type on laid paper with watermark four. Binding designed by A. E. Borie; pink cloth, pictorial design stamped on sides in blue, yellow and green, with lettering in blue, within rule border in black; raised lettering in pink on blue spine. Lettering of title by Claude Bragdon.

Copyright November 13, 1896. Price $1.25.

Device six, a variation of Number five, with eagle above a shield surrounded by baroque ornament, designed by Claude Bragdon, used here for the first time; see Table III. § The publishers' advertisement was not exaggerating when it announced that "the volume is bound in a new and startling fashion." While lithographed designs had been used on paper boards for Stone & Kimball (vide Nos. 74 and 96), this volume, its companion, and No. 129 are the only ones of the period with cloth covers pictorially illustrated by lithography.

[120]

Stories | from the | Chap-Book | Being a Miscellany of | Curious and interesting Tales, | Histories, &c; newly com- | posed by Many Cele- | brated Writers | and very delight- | ful to read. | [*device six*] | Chicago. | Printed for Herbert S. Stone & Company, | and are to be sold by them at The | Caxton Building in Dearborn Street | 1896 [*lettered in red and black within double rule border*]

6-13/16 x 4-3/16; pp. [x], 241, [5]; with signatures. Stone catalogue No. 1, 8 pp., inserted. Printed by Lakeside Press, Chicago, in Caslon type on laid paper with watermark four. Bound like No. 119; reproduced in Fig. 30. Lettering of title by Claude Bragdon.

Copyright November 13, 1896. Price $1.25. "Second Edition," December 1, 1896; included 1900 in the "Court Series" and in "Stone's Paper Library."

[121]

Miss Ayr of Virginia | & Other Stories | by | Julia Magruder | Author of "The Violet" | "The Princess Sonia" | [*device five in red*] | Chicago | Herbert S. Stone & Co. | MDCCCXCVI [*within double rule border*]

6-5/16 x 4-3/16; pp. [xii], 395, [3]; Stone catalogue No. 1, 8 pp., inserted. Printed by Lakeside Press, Chicago, in Caslon type on laid paper with watermark four. Binding designed by F. R. Kimbrough; blue-grey board sides; stamped on sides with tree design in shades of grey; lettered on front in black; green cloth spine with decorative rules and lettering in white; edges uncut.

Copyright December 7, 1896. Price $1.25. Included in 1900 in both the "Court Series" and "Stone's Paper Library."

[122]

Across | the Salt Seas | A Romance of the | War of Succession | by | John Bloundelle-Burton | Author of "In the Way of Adversity," | "The Hispaniola Plate," "A Gen- | tleman Adventurer," etc. | [*device three in red*] | Herbert S. Stone & Co. | Chicago & New York | MDCCCXCVII [*within double rule border*]

7-1/2 x 4-3/4; pp. [iv], 446, [2]. Stone's catalogue dated "March, mdcccxcvii," 16 pp., inserted. Printed by Stromberg, Allen & Co., Chicago, in Ronaldson Old Style type on laid paper with watermark four. Binding designed by Frank Hazenplug; blue cloth; seascape and lettering in blue and gold on sides; lettering in gold on spine. Title rubricated.

Copyright February 17, 1897; listed in *Publishers' Weekly* March 26. Price $1.50. Later included in the "Eldridge Series" and "Stone's Paper Library." English edition published during March 1897 by Methuen.

[123]

Flames | by | Robert Hichens | Author of "The Green Carnation," "An Imagi- | native Man," "The Folly of Eustace," etc. | [*device five in red*] | MDCCCXCVII | Herbert S. Stone & Company | Chicago and New York [*within double rule border*]

7-1/2 x 4-3/4; pp. [viii], 523, [5]; Stone's catalogue dated "March, mdcccxcvii," 16 pp., inserted. Printed by Lakeside Press, Chicago, in Modernized Old Style type on laid paper with watermark four. Binding designed by F. R. Kimbrough; brown or green board sides with rule border, candle decorations and lettering in black and orange; green cloth spine with lettering and decorations in black and yellow.

Copyright March 9, 1897; listed in *Publishers' Weekly* April 17. Price $1.50. "Second Edition" advertised in 1898; "Third Impression" in 1899; later included in the "Eldridge Series" and "Stone's Paper Library." Heinemann's English edition listed in *Publishers' Circular* March 13, 1897:

First Stone publication with imprint "Chicago and New York." The New

York office, in the Constable Building at 111 Fifth Avenue, was maintained until April 1900, after July 1897, under the direction of Melville E. Stone Jr. § First of three Hichens novels published by Stone; see Nos. 146 and 217.

[124]
One Man's View | By Leonard Merrick | Author of "Violet Moses" "The Man | Who was Good" "Cynthia, a | Daughter of the | Philistines" etc | [*device five*] | Herbert S. Stone & Co. | Chicago & New York | MDCCCXCVII

6-11/16 x 4-1/4; pp. [viii], 258, [2]; Stone's catalogue dated "March mdcccxcvii," 16 pp., inserted. Printed by Lakeside Press, Chicago, in Modernized Old Style type on laid paper with watermark four. Bound in black cloth; allover strap-work pattern against gilt background, and gilt lettering on sides; lettering on spine in yellow. Title in blue and black.

Copyright April 8, 1897; advertised in *The Chap-Book* May 15; but not listed in *Publishers' Weekly* until July 17. Price $1.00. Later included in the "Court Series" and "Stone's Paper Library." English edition was published by Grant Richards on May 17, 1897, according to a note from his office to Robert McClure, Stone's London agent.

This novel was the first book commissioned by the London publisher, Grant Richards. The use of blue ink on the title-page was his idea. See Grant Richards, *Author Hunting* (New York: Coward-McCann, Inc., 1934), p. 15.

[125]
The | Impudent Comedian | & Others | by | F. Frankfort Moore | [*rule*] | [*device seven*] | [*rule*] | MDCCCXCVII [*within double rule border*]

7-1/2 x 4-3/4; pp. [x], 274, [4]. Frontispiece, ten plates and Stone's catalogue No. 1, 8 pp., inserted. Printed by Lakeside Press, Chicago, in Caslon type on laid paper with watermark four. Bound in green cloth stamped in white; rules and device four on sides, printing on spine. Illustrations by Robert Sauber. Title rubricated.

Copyright claimed but complete copies not deposited; see below. Advertised in *The Chap-Book* March 15, 1897; listed in *Publishers' Weekly* April 10. Price $1.50. Included in the "Eldridge Series," 1900. English edition published by Pearson during January 1897.

Device seven, eagle above a shield, with streamer enclosing "H. S. STONE AND CO. CHICAGO," used here for the first time. § Several of the stories had originally appeared in *The Chap-Book*. "The Impudent Comedian," then titled "Nell Gwyn," appeared there March 15, 1896, and was also separately copyrighted March 2, 1896; see p. 360.

[126]
The | Jessamy Bride | by | F. Frankfort Moore | [*rule*] | [*device seven*] | [*rule*] | MDCCCXCVII [*within double rule border*]

7-1/2 x 4-3/4; pp. [iv], 416, [4]. Printed by Stromberg, Allen & Co., Chicago, in "Caxton Antique" type on laid paper with watermark four. Bound in green cloth stamped in silver; rules and device four on sides; printing on spine. Title rubricated.

Entered for copyright October 5, 1896. Proofs through p. 144 deposited by October 30, but complete volume not deposited. Published edition advertised in *The Chap-Book* March 15, 1897; listed in *Publishers' Weekly* April 17. Price $1.50. A secondary binding of the sheets of the first edition is in red cloth stamped in white as above, plus printing on sides, and with 16 pp. catalogue dated "March, mdcccxcvii" bound in at back. Hutchinson's English edition listed in *Publishers' Circular* for March 20, 1897.

"The Jessamy Bride" was the name given Mary Horneck by Oliver Goldsmith who, it is said, had been in love with her. This fictional version of the romance had the advantage of being written by an Irish journalist and student of the period, whose *Life of Goldsmith* is well known. *The Jessamy Bride* did not sell well in the beginning, but after three years became a backlog of the business, according to Mr. W. J. F. Dailey, onetime advertising manager of the firm. A *Publishers' Weekly* advertisement of November 25, 1899, states that it took a year to sell the two thousand copies of the first edition, but that it was then in its fifth printing, with sales of a thousand a month. One thousand copies (twelfth thousand, dated 1900) were numbered and signed by the author. It was in its "fifth impression" in August 1899; "Sixty-second thousand" in August, 1900. Cheap editions, with imprints of Grosset & Dunlap, were sold in 1900 and 1902. It was reprinted by Duffield & Co. in 1906, and in 1926 in an "Anniversary Edition," with introduction by Christopher Morley, who said:

> It is one of my private candidates for the world's most sentimental book. It represents Oliver as that curious mixture of Nature's Nobleman and complete simpleton that has become traditional. It would require a more careful scholar than I to offer any opinion as to whether the Goldsmith of Mr. Moore's novel is confirmed by all available testimony. But at any rate Frankfort Moore teaches us to love him, and that is the first step toward understanding.

[127]
Maude: Prose & Verse | By Christina Rossetti; 1850 |

{[*at left*] Chicago | MDCCCXC | VII [*at right*] Herbert S. | Stone & Com- | pany} {[*floral decoration in green, extending through imprint; all within blind impression*]}

6-7/8 x 4-1/4; pp. [viii], 122, [2]; Stone catalogue dated "March, mdcccxcvii," 16 pp., inserted. Printed by Lakeside Press, Chicago, in Caslon type on laid paper. Bound in red paper boards with device five on sides in yellow and paper label on spine; edges uncut. Title-page design by Frank Hazenplug; see No. 160.

Copyright May 21, 1897; advertised in *The Chap-Book* June 1; listed in *Publishers' Weekly* July 3. Price $1.00. Included in the "Court Series," 1900. English edition published by Bowden September 1897.

Juvenilia, published posthumously, with a preface by Christina Rossetti's brother William.

[128]
Pink Marsh | A Story of the Streets and Town | by | George Ade | Author of "Artie" | Pictures by | John T. McCutcheon | [*device three in red*] | Herbert S. Stone & Co. | Chicago & New York | 1897 | [*within double rule border*]

6-5/8 x 4-1/4; pp. [viii], 196, [4]; advertisement for *Artie*, 2 pp., Stone's catalogue dated "March, mdcccxcvii," 16 pp.; frontispiece and thirty-seven plates, inserted. Printed by Lakeside Press, Chicago, in Caslon type on laid paper with watermark four. Bound in green-white linen; stamped in green on sides and spine with rules and lettering; shield design in green on tan paper inserted on front cover, stamped in green on back. Title rubricated.

Copyright May 24, 1897; advertised in *The Chap-Book* June 1; but not listed in *Publishers' Weekly* until the appearance of the "Fifth Edition," December 18, 1897. Price $1.25. Poster by McCutcheon (Fig. 38) issued. Published in London by Stone during August 1897. Included in "Stone's Paper Library," 1900; issued shortly after in cheap cloth by Stone; about 1902 in similar binding with imprint of Grosset & Dunlap. Reissued after 1906 by Duffield.

Pink was even better received by the press than *Artie*. (But the public bought less; only 8,000 by 1900). He was a great favorite of Mark Twain, who wrote, in a letter recently reproduced in a privately printed pamphlet:

July 22/08

Dear Howells—

Thank you once more for introducing me to the incomparable Pink Marsh. I have been reading him again, after this long interval, & my admiration of the book has overflowed all limits, all frontiers. I have personally known each of the characters in the book & can testify that they are all true to the facts, & as exact as if they had been drawn to scale. And how effortless is the limning! it is as if the work did itself, without help of the master's hand.

And for once—just this once—the illustrator is the peer of the writer. The writer flashes a character onto his page in a dozen words, you turn the leaf & there he stands, alive & breathing, with his clothes on and the African ordor oozing out of him! What a picture-gallery it is of instantly recognizable, realizable, unassailable Authentics!

Pink—oh, the shiftless, worthless, lovable black darling! Howells, he deserves to live forever. Mark.

From: George Ade, *One Afternoon with Mark Twain* (Chicago: The Mark Twain Society, 1939).

[129]

For the Love of | Tonita | & | other Tales of the Mesas | by | Charles Fleming Embree | [*floret*] | Herbert S. Stone & Co. | Chicago & New York | MDCCCXCVII [*within double rule border*]

6-3/4 x 4-1/4; pp. [x], 265, [3]; Stone catalogue dated "March, mdcccxcvii," 16 pp., inserted. Printed by Lakeside Press, Chicago, in Caslon type on laid paper with watermark four. Binding designed by Fernand Lungren; mesa scene lithographed on front cover in yellow, brown and blue, within gilt border; spine printed in blue; back cover with border and device five in yellow. Title rubricated.

Copyright August 21, 1897; advertised in *The Chap-Book* September 1; listed in *Publishers' Weekly* October 23. Price $1.25.

[130]

The House Beautiful. | [*double rule*] | Edited by Eugene Klapp | and Henry Blodgett Harvey. | [*double rule*] | Contents for September 15, 1897. | [*double rule*] | [*list of contents*] | [*double rule*] | Copyright, 1897, by Herbert S. Stone

& Co. | [*double rule*] | "Terms of Subscription," etc. [*all within double rule border*]

Periodical still current. Title from first number issued by Herbert S. Stone & Co., September 15, 1897, Vol. II No. 4. Taken over from the founder and publisher, Eugene Klapp, who remained part editor until August 1898, and part owner until May 1902. Continued by Herbert S. Stone & Co. until 1906 and by Herbert S. Stone personally and as "The House Beautiful Company," until 1912. Price changed from 10 cents and $1.00 a year to 20 cents and $2.00 a year in June 1904, Vol. XVI No. 1, when the size was increased from 9-3/4 x 6-7/8 uncut, to 12-3/4 x 9-1/8 inches, cut.

Subtitles: September 1899, Vol. VI No. 4, to May 1901, Vol. IX No. 6, "The House Beautiful; The American Authority on Household Art." June 1901, Vol. X No. 1, "The House Beautiful; A Magazine for All People Who Have a Home." Publisher's address originally Caxton Building, Chicago. Constable Building, New York, added December 1897, Vol. III No. 1. Changed to Eldridge Court, Chicago, June 1898, Vol. IV No. 1; to Republic Building in Chicago, May 1905, Vol. XVII No. 6. Moved to Ashland Building, New York, December 1910.

Printers: Vol. I No. 1, "Printed at the Press of the Ryan and Hart Co., December, MDCCCXCVI." Vol. I No. 5, "Printed at the Press of Stromberg, Allen & Co., April, MDCCCXCVII." Vol. IV No. 6, November, 1898, "R. R. Donnelley & Sons, Printers."

Types: Modern-face; size changes from 12 and 14 point to 10 and 12, February 1898, Vol. III No. 3. With issue of September 1902, Vol. XII No. 4, a lighter variant of the same Modern-face type is used.

Paper: Vol. I-II, laid paper; with Vol. III, wove calendared paper.

Covers: Issues published by Stone began with light green paper cover, lettered in dark green and with device, by Claude Bragdon. Beginning with December 1897, Vol. III No. 1, white covers were used, with printing in red and black and including half-tone illustrations. Issues after June 1898, Vol. IV No. 1, were again on colored paper with lettering in green, with new device, probably by Bragdon. After June 1899, Vol. VI No. 1, covers of white and colored papers with illustrations and lettering by various artists, including Claude Bragdon, W. A. Dwiggins, Frank Hazenplug, F. W. Goudy, Edward Penfield, Fred Richardson, Fred Stearns, and Ivan Swift.

Binding: Green canvas buckram, with paper label on spine.

Circulation: 7,000 average, half newsstand sales, in 1900, according to publisher's advertisement of that year. Reported in Ayer's *American Newspaper Annual* for 1900 as 4,533. Publisher's advertisements of April, September and December 1901 give 9,000, 20,000, and 30,000 respectively.

January 1902 advertisement gives circulation as 40,000; while Ayer's for that year repeats the figure of 4,533. In 1903 Ayer's carried publisher's report of net average circulation as 21,755. In 1905 Ayer's continued figure of 21,755 while the publishers continued to advertise a circulation of 40,000, chiefly newsstand sales.

Editors: Eugene Klapp, December 1896-August 1898; with George Blodgett Harvey as associate, January-August 1898. No editor's name appears again until June 1904, when Herbert Stone is listed as editor. He actually became editor in September 1898. Melville E. Stone Jr. was titular editor during 1900. Virginia Robie, who came to the magazine in 1900 as staff contributor, was successively department editor, assistant editor, associate editor (1903-1913), and editor, 1913-1915.

Contents: Not indexed in *Poole's;* indexed in *Reader's Guide* after 1909. The publishers supplied indexes for each volume except I and IV-VIII. Important contributors to the early volumes were:

Mary Abbott	Sadakichi Hartmann	Harrison Rhodes
C. R. Ashbee	Frederick Keppel	Virginia Robie
Ida D. Bennett	H. Lindeberg	Robert Spencer
Claude Bragdon	George Barr McCutcheon	W. Irving Way
"Oliver Coleman" *i.e.*	Harriet Monroe	Clarence Moores Weed
Eugene Klapp	Anna Morgan	Carolyn Wells
Ralph Adams Cram	Donn Parker	Madeline Yale Wynne
Alice Morse Earle	Vernon Louis Parrington	
Aymar Embury	James William Pattison	

Illustrators: Claude Bragdon, Frank Brangwyn, Frank Hazenplug, Birch Burdette Long, Mary Prindiville, Fred Richardson, Fred Stearns.

[131]
Phyllis in Bohemia | by | L. H. Bickford | & | Richard Stillman Powell | Illustrations by | Orson Lowell | [*floret*] | Herbert S. Stone & Co. | Chicago and New York | 1897 | [*within double rule border*]

6-7/8 x 4-1/4; pp. [2], iv, 5-233, [1]; with signatures. Frontispiece, two plates, and Stone catalogue dated 1897, 24 pp., inserted. Printer not given; Caslon and Modernized Old Style types; laid paper with watermark four. Binding designed by Frank Hazenplug; blue-green cloth with floral decoration, rules and lettering, in red and green, on sides and spine. Orson Lowell's illustrations include three plates reproduced in halftone and twelve vignettes in text, engraved in sepia.

Copyright September 29, 1897. Price $1.25. Poster by Orson Lowell issued in October. "Second Edition" October 1897; included in "Stone's Paper Library," 1900.

"Richard Stillman Powell" was a pseudonym used only for this, his first book, by Ralph Henry Barbour, since well known as the author of boys' books. Luther H. Bickford was then on the staff of the Denver *Times*. This is a satirical comedy of seekers for Bohemia in New York, and as Albert Parry points out in *Garrets and Pretenders, A History of Bohemianism* in America (New York: Covici-Friede Publishers, 1933), the most interesting sections are devoted to the famous Greenwich Village restaurant "Maria's."

[132]
The Vice of Fools | by | H. C. Chatfield-Taylor | Illustrations by | Raymond M. Crosby | [*floret*] | Herbert S. Stone & Co. | Chicago & New York | 1897 [*within double rule border*]

6-5/8 x 4-1/4; pp. [vi], 310, [8]; frontispiece and eight plates inserted. Printed by Lakeside Press, Chicago, in Modernized Old Style and Caslon types on laid paper with watermark four. Bound in tan cloth stamped in blue; peacock design on sides in blue and green. Title rubricated.

Copyright September 29, 1897. Price $1.50. In its fourth thousand before the end of the year; included 1900 in "Stone's Paper Library."

[133]
Eat Not Thy Heart | by | Julien Gordon | [*floret*] | Herbert S. Stone & Co. | Chicago & New York | MDCCCXCVII [*within double rule border*]

6-5/8 x 4-1/4; pp. [viii], 319, [3]. Stone catalogue dated 1897, 24 pp., inserted. Printed by Lakeside Press, Chicago, in Modernized Old Style and Caslon types on laid paper with watermark four. Bound in maroon cloth stamped in gold; floral decorations in each corner of sides. Title rubricated.

Copyright September 29, 1897. Price $1.25. Reprinted in 1898 and in 1899; issued in paper at 50 cents in 1899; included 1900 in "Stone's Paper Library"; 1901 in "Court Series." English edition published December 1897; American sheets and binding with cancel title imprinted: "Herbert S. Stone & Co. | Hastings House | Norfolk Street, Strand | London | 1897."

"Julien Gordon" was the pseudonym of Julie Grinnell (Mrs. Van Rensselaer Cruger), whose earlier novels of society had been published chiefly by Lippincott. She wrote to Herbert Stone on August 14, 1897, while the book was in press:

Before I arrange for "Miss Clyde"—a splendid novel founded on fact—I would wish to see how you scatter & succeed with "Eat Not Thy Heart." If I find it on every book-stand—if I hear it shouted through every train—if I make something out of it—I ask nothing better than to continue with you. *That is what I desire.* Vulgar popularity! I am tired of book shop shelves! I heard a gentleman ask for Julien Gordon's novels on a Hudson River train yesterday. *Of course* there were none. The Lippincotts have managed that there never should be. People wont return to the city, hire a cab, & drive to Brentano's to purchase one of my dollar novels. They take *what is offered to them!* The tastes march with the times. The man bought an old copy of one of Crawford's because it was under his nose. I desire a *screaming* publisher—not a silent one. I want to be advertised —& pushed. The feeder houses are out of date - - - - - You will send me a few copies to place wisely. Kindly do not send my work to the "N Y Sun"—Their great critic Hazeltine admires my work—& he praises it in many periodicals but *Dana* is not friendly to me—& it would go to that silly Saturday reviewer—not to Hazeltine. Your proof correctors are careless. I desire the word *don't* spelled thus. I have corrected it a hundred times—written them on the margin—*no attention* is payed. It returns always as do'nt. It is exasperating—*Please* attend to this for me—if I am not to see the 2nd proofs—How about binding?—What is it to be? I regret the illustrations which enhance the value of stories and help sales & *we have them.* Personally I dislike pictures in novels—but the public is demanding them now. Truly yours

J Grinnell Cruger

Miss Clyde was published by Appleton's, in 1901.

[134]
Menticulture | or | The A-B-C of True | Living | by | Horace Fletcher | [*floret*] | Herbert S. Stone & Co. | Chicago & New York | 1897 [*within rule border*]

7-1/2 x 4-3/4; pp. [ii], 280, [4], including advertisement for *Happiness* and colophon; followed by Stone catalogue dated 1897, 24 pp. Printed by Lakeside Press, Chicago, in Modernized Old Style type on laid paper with watermark four. Bound in green ribbed cloth, stamped in green on sides and spine. Title and shoulder headings rubricated.

Advertised September 1, 1897 in *The Chap-Book* as "Nearly Ready." Price $1.00.

"Enlarged Edition," of a work originally published by McClurg in 1895 and also privately printed in 1897 in a "Vermont Edition" for the friends of W. J. Van Patten of Burlington. The "Twenty-fifth Thousand," was a "Quarantine Edition," with imprint "Distributed through the

Kindergarten Literature Company, Woman's Temple, Chicago, 1898"; and with a printed slip inserted: "Supplied to the Trade by Herbert S. Stone & Co., Chicago and New York." The binding was white and yellow cloth, with halftone pictures inserted in both covers. The first of five of Horace Fletcher's works published by Stone; see pp. 102-3, and Nos. 135, 166, 167, 236.

[135]

Happiness | as found in | Forethought minus Fearthought | by | Horace Fletcher | [*floret*] | Menticulture Series II | [*floret*] Herbert S. Stone & Co. | Chicago & New York | 1897 [*within rule border*]

7-3/8 x 4-3/4; pp. 251, [5], including advertisement for *Menticulture*, and colophon; followed by Stone catalogue dated 1897, 24 pp. Printer, type, paper, binding and rubrication as above.

Copyright October 2, 1897. Price $1.00. "Sixth Thousand" was a "Quarantine Edition," as above.

[136]

The Fourth Napoleon | A Romance | by | Charles Benham | [*floret*] | Herbert S. Stone & Co. | Chicago & New York | 1897

7-1/2 x 4-3/4; pp. [xii], 600, [8]. Printed by Lakeside Press, Chicago, in Modernized Old Style and Caslon types on laid paper with watermark four. Bound in grey-green cloth; stamped in blue on sides and spine with lettering and ornament; tricolor bar beneath crest on front. Title rubricated.

Copyright October 20, 1897. Price $1.50. Included 1900 in the "Eldridge Series" and "Stone's Paper Library." English edition published by Heinemann during March 1898.

Heinemann's edition was printed in England from the American plates, according to extant correspondence between the Stone and Heinemann offices. American sheets had been supplied to English publishers by Stone & Kimball as early as 1894 (vide No. 15) and English editions imported since 1893 (vide No. 9); but this is the first instance observed of printing from the same plates on both sides of the water. *My Father and I* by the Countess Puliga (No. 218) was also published in the same manner. In both cases the authors were British.

269

[137]
Literary Statesmen | And Others | Essays on Men seen from a Distance | by Norman Hapgood | [*device five in red*] | Herbert S. Stone & Co. | Chicago & New York | MDCCCXCVII [*within double rule border*]

7-1/2 x 4-3/4; pp. [viii], 208, [2]; with signatures. Stone's catalogue dated 1897, 24 pp., inserted. Printed by University Press, Cambridge, in Modernized Old Style type on laid paper with watermark four. Bound in green ribbed cloth, printed within rules, in gold, on sides and spine.

Copyright October 27, 1897. Price $1.50. "Second impression" of 1898 also issued in London, with imprint of Duckworth.

The late Norman Hapgood's first book; reprinted from *The Yellow-Book, The Chap-Book, Bachelor of Arts* and other periodicals.

[138]
What Maisie Knew | by | Henry James | [*device five in red*] | Herbert S. Stone & Co. | Chicago & New York | MDCCCXCVII [*within double rule border*]

7-1/2 x 4-3/4; pp. [iv], 470, [2]; with signatures. Printed by University Press, Cambridge, in Modernized Old Style type on laid paper with watermark "Stone & Kimball | New York." Bound in dark grey cloth; stamped on sides with rule border in blind, lettering and florets in gold; on spine with rules, lettering and strapwork ornament in gold (Fig. 31).

Copyright claimed, but no entry made and no copies deposited. Listed in *Publishers' Weekly* November 6, 1897. Price $1.50. "Second Impression," dated 1898, printed at the Lakeside Press, Chicago, from the plates of first edition, but on paper watermarked "H. S. Stone & Company | Chicago | The Chap Book." Heinemann's edition, in its regular issue with an 1898 title-page, but listed in the *English Catalogue* for September 1897, is given priority by I. R. Brussel, *Anglo-American First Editions: West to East, 1786-1930*, pp. 78-79.

Concerning *What Maisie Knew,* an interesting account of Henry James' method of writing and the problems it presented his publishers, was given in 1921 by Gelett Burgess in the Introduction to *My Maiden Effort,* a collection of author's reminiscences similar to the recent *Breaking into Print.* Mr. Burgess wrote:

> Sooth to say, the payment authors receive is funny money. I once told Mr. Henry James that I received from the *Chap Book* twenty dollars for reviewing my first book—and eight dollars more for protesting

against the ignorance and prejudice of my reviewer. And sadly, bitterly, he told me the secret of "What May[!]sie Knew."

Would you believe that for that sublime piece of psychology he received, for serial and book rights, only $150? It shows how the artist regarded his work in ante cinema days. So absorbed was he with the theme that, notwithstanding the fact that he had contracted to write, for that absurd honorarium, merely one short story, he spun it out, chapter after chapter to its logical and fascinating end.

But there was, as usual, another side to the affair. The *Chap Book* eschewed serials at that time, and the last thing it wanted was a serial by so esoteric a writer as Henry James. But on the installments kept coming, on and on, forever. And at last, to get even, Mr. Herbert Stone informed me, he had to publish the book!

At all but two points, this agrees very well with other, contemporary evidence. The length of the book was surely unexpected, for even if a short story had been ordered originally, *What Maisie Knew: A Novelette* was announced for publication in Stone's first catalogue, in the fall of 1896. This entry was repeated in the "Weekly Record of New Publications" in *Publishers' Weekly* for December 12, 1896, with the star indicating that the volume had not been actually seen. This announcement shows that *book* publication was anticipated by Stone even before the work had grown, during *serial* publication, to full novel length. It appeared in *The Chap-Book* between January 15 and August 1, 1897 and in the English *New Review* February-July 1897. That the book was not printed early and held ready for publication, while serial publication was being completed (as with *The Ebb Tide*, No. 24), we know from two minor facts. First, the author's corrected page proofs had reached only to p. 130 on June 10, 1897, when they were forwarded from Stone's London office to Chicago. Second, the first edition, as noted above, was printed at the University Press on paper watermarked "Stone & Kimball | New York." This was the third watermark of Stone & Kimball, adopted just before Kimball went out of business, used only in his last publication, *The Meddling Hussy*, published between May 15 and July 3, 1897, and printed at the University Press. The small stock of paper with this watermark held in Cambridge would hardly have been turned over to his former partner by Kimball before the latter decided between July and October 1897 to abandon publishing. § The purchase price for serial rights in England and America was £75, according to Henry James' signed receipt.

[139]
The Smart Set | Correspondence & Conversations | by | Clyde Fitch | 1897 | [*floret*] | Chicago & New York | Herbert S. Stone & Co. [*within double rule border*]

6 x 4-1/4; pp. [xii], 201, [3]. Printed by Lakeside Press, Chicago, in Caslon type on laid paper with watermark four. Bound in white canvas ruled in blue, with lettering, circular monogram and florets on sides in red, and lettering on spine in blue. Title rubricated.

Copyright November 19, 1897. Price $1.00. Apparently not reprinted, but appears in secondary bindings of white canvas with printing on spine only, edges uncut; and in smooth grey-green cloth ruled and printed in yellow and green, top edge gilt.

Fitch gave a public reading from the dialogues, in the winter of 1897, at a "Chap-Book Tea," judging from an unpublished letter to M. E. Stone Jr. Acknowledging receipt for payment, while enroute to New York, he also sends a clipping concerning his book:

> Please give the enclosed notice to Herbert—*dont lose it!* We might never again get another as good! Tho' one came today, & from Boston too—saying I was a brilliant social philosopher!! They are wrong, what I am is a public *Reader!* (nit.)
>
> As you value yr life let me know when you are coming to New York—& give my best feelings to the 3 of a kind that run the Chap Book.
>
> Yours always—Clyde Fitch

[140]

How to Play Golf | by | H. J. Whigham | [*three florets*] Herbert S. Stone & Company | Chicago & New York | MDCCCXCVII [*within double rule border*]

7-3/4 x 5-1/4; pp. [viii], 313, [3]. Printed by Stromberg, Allen & Co., Chicago, in Ronaldson Old Style type on calendared paper; blue endpapers. Bound in dark blue cloth; stamped in yellow on sides and spine with rules, lettering and thistle decorations; edges uncut. Illustrated throughout with halftones, chiefly from "chronomatographic pictures," *i.e.* action photographs, by E. Burton Holmes.

Entered for copyright in 1897, but copies not deposited until February 16, 1898. Advertised in *The Chap-Book* November 15, 1897; listed in *Publishers' Weekly* March 26. Price $1.25. Reprinted several times; "New Edition-Fourth Thousand" has an additional chapter on the Amateur Tournament of 1898; "Sixth Edition," one on the tournament of 1900, by Caspar Whitney.

This is the best of the early American instruction books on golf; and the first on any topic anywhere to be illustrated with action photographs.

Mr. Whigham, then of the Chicago *Tribune,* was American Amateur Champion in 1896 and 1897. He was one of the contributors to *The Spanish-American War* (No. 179) and was later a collaborator of M. E.

Stone Jr. on the *Metropolitan Magazine,* succeeding to the editorship in 1912.

[141]
A Realized Ideal | by | Julia Magruder | Author of "The Violet" | "The Princess Sonia" | "Miss Ayr of Virginia" | [*device five in red*] | Herbert S. Stone & Company | New York | MDCCCXCVIII [*within double rule border*]

6-5/8 x 4-3/8; pp. [viii], 135, [9], including advertisement for *Menticulture,* and colophon; Stone's catalogue dated 1898, 24 pp., inserted. Printed by Lakeside Press, Chicago, in Modernized Old Style and Caslon types on laid paper with watermark four. Binding designed by Frank Hazenplug; lavender cloth, stamped on sides with rule border, lettering and floral design in yellow and green; spine printed in gold.

Copyright February 23, 1898; listed in *Publishers' Weekly* April 30. Price $1.25. Second impression the same year; included 1900 in the "Court Series."

Advertised as "An unobtrusive protest in favor of sweetness and of sentiment in fiction."

[142]
Priscilla's Love Story | by | Harriet Prescott Spofford | Author of "A Master's Spirit" | "An Inheritance" | "A Scarlet Poppy" | [*floret*] Herbert S. Stone & Company | Chicago & New York | MDCCCXCVIII [*within double rule border*]

6-3/4 x 4-1/4; pp. [viii], 129, [7]. Printed by Lakeside Press, Chicago, in Caslon, Modernized Old Style and Modern-face types on laid paper with watermark four. Bound in grey-green cloth with geometrical border design in blue and white across sides and spine; lettered in blue.

Copyright March 19, 1898; listed in *Publishers' Weekly* April 21. Price $1.00. Reprinted from *Harper's Magazine.*

[143]
Here & There & Everywhere | Reminiscences | by | M. E. W. Sherwood | [*device five within double rule border*] | Herbert S. Stone & Company | Chicago & New York | MDCCCXCVIII [*within thin within thick rule border*]

8-3/4 x 5-1/2; pp. [xiv], 301, [9], including advertisement of *Menti-*

culture, and colophon. Frontispiece, ten plates (all photographs), and Stone catalogue dated 1898, 24 pp., inserted. Printed by Lakeside Press, Chicago, in Caslon and Modernized Old Style types on laid paper. Bound in dark green ribbed cloth, stamped in gold; lettering (within double rule border) on front cover; lettering on spine; each corner of sides tipped with small gold square.

Copyright March 21, 1898; listed in *Publishers' Weekly* April 30. Price $2.50. Published in London by Stone during April 1898.

Mrs. Mary Elizabeth (Wilson) Sherwood was then well known as a speaker and writer on such subjects as social usages and entertaining. Most of these papers had appeared in the New York *Times.* Another volume of recollections of her travels and acquaintanceships with personages, chiefly royal, had been published in 1897 by Harper's, with the title *An Epistle to Posterity.*

[144]

A Bride of Japan | by Carlton Dawe | [*device five in red*] | Herbert S. Stone & Company | Chicago & New York | MDCCCXCVIII [*within double rule border*]

7-1/8 x 4-1/2; pp. [viii], 268, [4]; with signatures. Printed by Lakeside Press, Chicago, in Ronaldson Old Style and Caslon types on wove paper. Bound in yellow cloth stamped in red; on sides with rules, printing and rising sun ornament; on spine with printing and circular monogram; edges trimmed.

Copyright March 26, 1898; listed in *Publishers' Weekly* April 23. Price $1.50. Included 1900 in the "Eldridge Series" and "Stone's Paper Library." Hutchinson's English edition listed in *Publishers' Circular* for April 9.

[145]

Eve's Glossary | { [*at left of design*] By the | Marquise | de | Fontenoy [*at right of design*] Herbert S. Stone & Co. | Chicago & New York

[*all lettered within double rule border within green ornamental border*]

8-1/2 x 6-3/4; pp. viii, 285, [3]; with signatures. Printed by University Press, Cambridge, in Caslon type on laid paper with watermark four. Bound in purple cloth, with lettering and decorations in green and bronze on sides and spine. Each printed page within green ornamental border, designed by Frank Hazenplug, who also did the title and binding.

Copyright March 30, 1898. Prospectus issued early in 1898. Price $3.50. Issued later the same year in "Popular Edition" at $2.00.

The "Marquise de Fontenoy," actually Marguerite Cunliffe-Owen, Comtesse du Planty et de Sourdis, was a syndicated newspaper columnist in the nineties and later the author of *The Martyrdom of an Empress* and *The Tribulations of a Princess*.

[146]

The Londoners | by | Robert Hichens | Author of "The Green Carnation," "An Imagi- | native Man," "The Folly of Eustace," etc. | [*device five in red*] | Herbert S. Stone & Company | Chicago & New York | MDCCCXCVIII [*within double rule border*]

7-1/2 x 4-3/4; pp. [viii], 338, [6], including advertisement for *Flames*, and colophon. Printed by Lakeside Press, Chicago, in Modernized Old Style type on laid paper with watermark four. Binding designed by Claude Bragdon; rules, lettering, pictorial and heraldic design on sides and spine in white, red, yellow and black.

Copyright March 31, 1898; listed in *Publishers' Weekly* April 30. Price $1.50. "Third Impression" advertised in 1899. Heinemann's English edition listed in *Publishers' Circular* for April 2.

[147]

The Rise and Growth of | Democracy | in Great Britain | by | J. Holland Rose, M. A. | Late Scholar of Christ's College, Cambridge; author of | "The Revolutionary and Napoleonic Era" | Herbert S. Stone & Company | Chicago & New York | MDCCCXCVIII

7-1/4 x 4-3/4; pp. viii, [9]-252; with signatures. Printed and bound by the British publishers Blackie & Son, at Glasgow; Modernized Old Style type; laid paper. Bound in red cloth; stamped in gold on spine, in black on front cover; edges cut. Title-leaf a cancel.

First advertised in *Publishers' Weekly* March 12, 1898; listed there December 17. Price $1.25. Published in London by Blackie during 1897.

First volume of eight published by Stone from the "Victorian Era Series," edited by the historian J. Holland Rose, and published by Blackie & Son, Limited, of Glasgow, London and Dublin. The most important texts issued by Stone were the present volume and the last selection, Sir J. Arthur Thomson's famous popularization of *The Science of Life* (No. 239). The series as a whole, however, lived up to the terms of its advertisement, that:

> The series is designed to form a record of the great movements and developments of the age, in politics, economics, religion, industry, literature, science and art, and of the life work of its typical and influential men.
> The individual volumes are contributed by leading specialists in the various branches of knowledge which are to be treated in the series.

[148]

The Anglican | Revival | by | J. H. Overton, D. D. | Rector of Epworth and Canon of Lincoln; author of | "The English Church in the Nineteenth Century (1800-1833)" | "Life of John Wesley," &c. &c. | Herbert S. Stone & Company | Chicago & New York | MDCCCXCVIII

7-1/4 x 4-7/8; pp. vi, [ii], [9]-299, [1]; with signatures. Printed and bound by Blackie in Glasgow; see No. 147. Title-leaf a cancel.

First advertised in *Publishers' Weekly* March 12, 1898; listed there December 17. Price $1.25. Published in London by Blackie during 1897. Second title imported in the "Victorian Era Series."

[149]

John Bright | by | C. A. Vince, M. A. | Formerly of Christ's College, Cambridge | Herbert S. Stone & Company | Chicago & New York | MDCCCXCVIII

7-1/4 x 4-3/4; pp. vi, [7]-246; with signatures. Printed and bound by Blackie in Glasgow; see No. 147. Title-leaf a cancel.

First advertised in *Publishers' Weekly* March 12, 1898; listed there December 17. Price $1.25. Published in London by Blackie during 1897. Third title imported in the "Victorian Era Series."

[150]

Plays: Pleasant and Un- | pleasant • By Bernard | Shaw • The First Volume, | Containing the Three | Unpleasant Plays | [*device five*] | Chicago and New York: | Herbert S. Stone and | Company, MDCCCXCVIII

Plays: Pleasant and Un- | pleasant | • By Bernard | Shaw • The Second Vol- | ume, Containing the | Four Pleasant Plays. | [*device five*] | Chicago and New York: | Herbert S. Stone and | Company, MDCCCXCVIII

7-5/8 x 4-3/4; 2 Vols. I: pp. xxxi, [i], 244, [4]. Frontispiece (photograph of Shaw by F. H. Evans) inserted. II: pp. xix, [i], 338, [6]. Printed by Lakeside Press, Chicago, in Caslon type on thin laid paper with watermark four. Bound in smooth blue cloth, paper labels on spines; edges uncut.

Volume I entered for copyright April 18; one copy deposited April 21, a second May 3. Volume II entered for copyright May 16, but copies deposited April 18. Listed in *Publishers' Weekly* June 4. Price $2.50.

"Second Impression," 1899; reissued by Stone in 1905; later published by Brentano's and now by Dodd, Mead & Co. Grant Richards' English edition listed in *Publishers' Circular* for the week preceding April 23, 1898, and presumably published simultaneously with Stone's edition.

First publication of Shaw's plays in America. The first volume contains a "Preface: Mainly About Myself"; "Widower's Houses" (Shaw's first play and the only one previously printed); "The Philanderer"; and "Mrs. Warren's Profession." The second volume has a "Preface"; "You Never Can Tell"; "Arms and the Man" (the first play of Shaw's produced in this country; by Richard Mansfield, on September 17, 1894, in New York); "Candida"; and "The Man of Destiny." First of five Shaw titles; see Nos. 169, 260, 263, 283, Figs. 33-35, pp. 98-101, 125-26, 136.

[151]
A Champion | In the Seventies | [*rule*] | by | Edith A. Barnett | [*rule*] | [*device five in red*] | [*rule*] | Chicago | Herbert S. Stone & Co. | 1898 [*within double rule border*]

7-5/8 x 4-11/16; pp. [4], viii, 365, [5]. Printer not given but probably Stromberg, Allen & Co., Chicago; Ronaldson Old Style and Caslon types; laid paper with watermark four. Bound in green cloth striped on sides and spine in dark green; edges uncut.

Copyright April 22, 1898; listed in *Publishers' Weekly* June 18. Price $1.50. Included 1900 in the "Eldridge Series" and "Stone's Paper Library." Heinemann's English edition was listed in *Publishers' Circular* for April 30.

An early feminist novel; the English edition has the subtitle: "Being the true record of some passages in a conflict of social faiths."

[152]
A Revolutionary Love-Story | and | The High Steeple of | St. Chrysostom's | by | Ellen Olney Kirk | [*floret*] | Herbert S. Stone & Company | Chicago & New York | MDCCCXCVIII [*within double rule border*]

6-3/4 x 4-1/4; pp. [viii], 255, [1]; with signatures. Printer not given but Lakeside Press or Stromberg, Allen & Co. of Chicago; Ronaldson Old Style type; laid paper with watermark four. Bound in tan cloth, stamped in red and black; similar to No. 142.

Copyright April 29, 1898; listed in *Publishers' Weekly* June 11. Price $1.25.

[153]
The Rainbow's End: | Alaska | by | Alice Palmer Henderson | [*device five in red*] | Herbert S. Stone & Company | Chicago & New York | MDCCCXCVIII [*within double rule border*]

7-1/2 x 4-5/8; pp. [x], 296, [2]. Frontispiece and eighteen plates (photographs), inserted. Printed by Stromberg, Allen & Co., Chicago, in Caslon and Ronaldson Old Style types on laid paper with watermark four. Bound in blue cloth; rainbow design in green and bronze extending across both covers; rules and lettering in bronze.

Copyright July 25, 1898; listed in *Publishers' Weekly* August 20. Price $1.50. "Second Impression," 1899.

[154]
The New Economy | A Peaceable Solution of the Social Problem | by | Laurence Gronlund, M. A. | Author of "The Coöperative Commonwealth," etc. | "The longer I live the more it grieves me to see man taken up with | some false notion and doing just the opposite of what he wants to do." | —Goethe. | [*device five in red*] | Herbert S. Stone & Company | Chicago & New York | MDCCCXCVIII [*within double rule border*]

7-1/2 x 4-5/8; pp. [xii], 364. Printer not given; Ronaldson Old Style type; laid paper with watermark four. Bound in green ribbed cloth, stamped in dark green on sides and spine.

Copyright September 3, 1898; listed in *Publishers' Weekly* October 8. Price $1.25.

Laurence Gronlund, Danish-born Socialist writer and lecturer, was then labor editor of Hearst's New York *Journal.* His most important work, *The Cooperative Commonwealth* (1884) is described in the *Dictionary of American Biography* as "the first comprehensive work in English on socialism; and presented the views of German writers, and especially those of Karl Marx with such modifications as Gronlund felt necessary in order to adapt them to the American environment."

[155]
Etiquette | for | Americans | by | A Woman of Fashion | [*device five in red*] | Herbert S. Stone & Company | Chicago & New York | MDCCCXCVIII [*within double rule border*]

6-11/16 x 4-5/16; pp. [xvi], 273, [3]; followed by 4 pp. of advertisements. Printed by Lakeside Press, Chicago, in Ronaldson Old Style type on laid paper with watermark four. Binding designed by Frank Hazenplug; red cloth lettered in white on sides and spine; scroll and floral ornament in white and green on sides.

Copyright September 26, 1898. Price $1.25. "Second Impression" advertised in 1899. "New and Revised Edition" published by Duffield in 1909.

The authorship of this work was carefully concealed; the publishers advertising that: "It is probable that no woman thoroughly qualified to write upon this subject would be willing to sign her name to this book. It is written by a person who is regarded all over the country as an authority upon this subject. Matters of good form are so constantly changing that there is at present a great need for such a book."

[156]
A | Slave to Duty | & | Other Women | by | Octave Thanet | [*device five*] | Herbert S. Stone & Company | Chicago & New York | MDCCCXCVIII [*within double rule border*]

6-5/8 x 4-1/4; pp. [x], 221, [1]. Frontispiece, by Violet Oakley, inserted. Printed by Stromberg, Allen & Co., Chicago, in Ronaldson Old Style type on laid paper. Bound in white cloth; lettered in green on sides and spine; geometrized floral design in green and red on sides.

Copyright September 26, 1898; listed in *Publishers' Weekly* October 29. Price $1.25. Included 1900 in the "Court Series."

Alice French was a contributor to *The Chap-Book,* but this collection of short stories, from *Harper's* and *Scribner's,* is her only book published by the Stone firms.

[157]
The | Money Captain | by | Will Payne | Author of "Jerry, The Dreamer" | [*device five*] | Herbert S. Stone & Company | Chicago & New York | MDCCCXCVIII [*within double rule border*]

6-5/8 x 4-1/8; pp. [viii], 323, [5]. Printer not given; Caslon and Ronaldson Old Style types; laid paper. Bound in blue or blue-green cloth, stamped in yellow; on sides with rules, lettering and border of dollar signs; on spine with lettering.

Copyright September 26, 1898; listed in *Publishers' Weekly* November 5. Price $1.25. Included 1900 in the "Court Series" and "Stone's Paper Library."

Mr. Payne in 1898 was on the staff of the weekly *Economist* of Chicago; this novel deals with the local utility situation. Its publication is described in the Stone correspondence as the new beginning of an effort to publish more Chicago authors. This plan had an impetus in the month *The Money Captain* was published, when the list of Way & Williams of Chicago was transferred to Herbert S. Stone & Company; see further pp. 114-15, 357-58.

[158]
A | Golden Sorrow | by | Maria Louise Pool | [*device eight in red*] | Herbert S. Stone & Company | Chicago & New York | MDCCCXCVIII [*within double rule border*]

7-1/2 x 4-1/2; pp. [viii], 441, [3]. Printed by Stromberg, Allen & Co., Chicago, in Ronaldson Old Style type on bulked laid paper with watermark four. Bound in olive-green ribbed cloth; rule borders in blind; lettering and medallion in gold on front cover; lettering in gold on spine; device five in blind on back cover.

Copyright October 7, 1898; listed in *Publishers' Weekly* December 3. Price $1.50. Included 1900 in the "Eldridge Series."

Device eight, eagle above a shield with streamer below, bearing motto "Faire et Taire"; and designed by Claude Bragdon, used here for the first time.

[159]
In the Cage | by | Henry James | [*device five in red*] | Herbert S. Stone & Company | Chicago & New York | MDCCCXCVIII [*within double rule border*]

7-1/2 x 4-5/8; pp. [iv], 229, [3]. Printed by Lakeside Press, Chicago, in Caslon and Ronaldson Old Style type on laid paper with watermark four. Bound like No. 138.

Entered and deposited for copyright August 8, 1898; listed in *Publishers' Weekly* October 8. Price $1.25.

I. R. Brussel, in *Anglo-American First Editions: Part Two: West to East 1786-1930*, p. 78, gives priority to the English edition, stating: "According to *The English Catalogue*, this book was published during August 1898. It is first noted as published by *The Publishers' Weekly*, dated October 8, 1898." But according to "Books of the Week" in *Publishers' Circular*, Duckworth's edition was published in the week preceding their issue of August 20. Stone's edition, as noted above, was received at the Library of Congress August 8. Entries of their publications were often delayed two months before listing in the "Weekly Record of New Publications," in *Publishers' Weekly*. However, the facts that the volume was not reviewed until late in the year (the first notice being in the New York *Critic* for December 1898); and not advertised in *Publishers' Weekly* until September 24, 1898, (and then among "List of Books to be Published in September," with a quotation from an English review), lends additional weight to Mr. Brussel's assertion. The LeRoy Phillips bibliography of Henry James lists the American before the English edition, but gives no dates for comparison.

[160]

Some Verses | By Helen Hay | [*double rule*] | [*at left*] Chicago & | New York | MDCCCXCVIII [*at right*] Herbert | S. Stone | & Company

[*floral decoration, in green, extending through imprint; all within blind impression; within double rule*]

6-5/8 x 4-1/4; pp. viii, 72, [4]. Printed by Lakeside Press, Chicago, in Modern-face type on laid paper with watermark four. Bound in grey paper boards; paper labels on sides; edges uncut. Title-page design by Frank Hazenplug; see No. 127.

Copyright October 17, 1898; listed in *Publishers' Weekly* December 17. Price $1.00. "Second Impression" in 1899. Published in London by Duckworth during November 1898.

The first book of John Hay's daughter, since known (as Mrs. Payne Whitney) as an author of children's books. Herbert Stone met Miss Hay in London in the summer of 1898, and through her, Henry James, as letters to his family reveal.

[161]
The | Borderland | of | Society | by | Charles Belmont Davis | [*double rule*] | Frontispiece by | Cecil Clark | [*double rule*] | Herbert S. Stone & Co. | Chicago & New York | MDCCCXCVIII

6-5/8 x 4-1/4; pp. [xiii], 247, [5]; frontispiece inserted. Printer not given, but probably Lakeside Press, Chicago; Modern-face type; laid paper. Bound in light blue ribbed cloth; borders in blind; lettering and decorations on sides in white; lettering in white on spine.

Copyright October 24, 1898; listed in *Publishers' Weekly* December 10. Price $1.25. Included in all three of Stone's reprint series.

The author was Richard Harding Davis' younger brother. These short stories, reprinted from *Century*, *Harper's* and other periodicals, made his first book.

[162]
The | Son of Perdition | by | William A. Hammond, M. D. | Author of "Lal," "Dr. Grattan," "Mr. Oldmixon," "A Strong Minded | Woman," "On the Susquehanna," etc. | [*quotation from John XXI.25.*] | [*device eight*] | Herbert S. Stone & Company | Chicago & New York | MDCCCXCVIII [*within double rule border*]

7-3/8 x 4-7/8; pp. [viii], 494, [4]. Printed by Stromberg, Allen & Co., Chicago, in Caslon and Ronaldson Old Style types on laid paper with watermark four. Bound in black cloth stamped in yellow on sides and spine.

Copyright October 24, 1898; listed in *Publishers' Weekly* December 3. Price $1.50. Included 1900 in the "Eldridge Series" and "Stone's Paper Library." Copyright assigned October 26, 1904, to Mrs. W. A. Hammond.

[163]
The Jew The Gypsy | and El Islam | by the late Captain | Sir Richard F. Burton | K.C.M.G. F.R.G.S. etc. | [*four lines of quotations*] | Edited with a Preface and Brief Notes | by | W. H. Wilkins | Herbert S. Stone & Company | Chicago and New York | MDCCCXCVIII

9-7/8 x 6-1/2; pp. xix, [i], 351, [1]; with signatures. Frontispiece portrait inserted. Printer not given, but undoubtedly British; Modern-face type; laid paper, not watermarked, for text; laid paper, with Stone's watermark four, for endpapers. American binding of metal-blue cloth, paper label on spine; edges uncut. Title rubricated.

Advertised as "Just Published" in *Publishers' Weekly* October 29, 1898. Price $3.50 net. Published in England by Hutchinson during April 1898.

The English edition had already been imported by Charles Scribner's Sons, listed for them in "Recent New Publications" of *Publishers' Weekly*, August 13, 1898; at $10.00 net. The Stone advertisements remarked: "This is the English edition which is catalogued elsewhere at $10.00." N. M. Penzer's famous annotated bibliography of Burton (London: A. M. Philpot Ltd., 1923), lists neither American issue, but gives interesting information about the content of the book, one of the few Burton manuscripts which escaped the holocausts made after his death by Lady Burton and her sister.

[164]
The First Cruiser Out | A Cuban War Story | Visitors at Grampus Island | and | The Tale of an Oar | by | William O. Stoddard | [*device eight*] | Chicago and New York | Herbert S. Stone and Company | Mdcccxcviii

7-1/2 x 4-3/4; pp. [vi], 291, [7], including 4 pp. of advertisements and colophon; eight plates inserted. Printed by Lakeside Press, Chicago, in Caslon, Modernized Old Style and Modern-face type on laid paper with watermark four. Bound in yellow cloth; stamped in black on sides and spine, pictorial design on sides.

Copyright October 31, 1898. First advertised in *Publishers' Weekly* March 12, 1898, to contain only "Visitors at Grampus Island" and "The Tale of an Oar."

[165]
Gloria Mundi | A Novel | by | Harold Frederic | Author of "The Damnation of Theron Ware," "In the | Valley," "The Copperhead," etc. | [*device eight in red*] | Herbert S. Stone & Company | Chicago & New York | MDCCCXCVIII [*within double rule border*]

7-1/8 x 4-1/2; pp. [viii], 580, [12], including colophon and 10 pp. of advertisements. Printed by Lakeside Press, Chicago, in Ronaldson and Caslon types on laid paper with watermark four. Bound in red ribbed cloth, stamped in black; front cover with rules, lettering and floret; spine with rules, lettering; back cover with rules and device four.

Published November 1, 1898, according to advertisements, which also indicate that three printings were sold out before publication. Price $1.50. Date of deposit of complete copies for copyright is not available, as the book was serialized in the *Cosmopolitan*, January-November 1898, and copyright assigned by its owner and editor, John Brisben Walker, to Herbert S. Stone & Co. on November 10, 1898. Reprinted after publication for Stone, and in 1899, for H. B. Claflin Co. as No. 8 of their "International Paper Novels." Heinemann's original English edition listed in *Publishers' Circular* for November 5.

Harold Frederic, despite the success of *The Copperhead* (1893), was better known as a journalist than as a novelist before the publication of *The Damnation of Theron Ware* in 1896 by Stone & Kimball (by Heinemann as *Illumination*). That remained his masterpiece, writes Ernest Sutherland Bates in the *Dictionary of American Biography*, adding: "His last three novels, *March Hares* (1896), *Gloria Mundi* (posthumous, 1898), and *The Market Place* (posthumous, 1899), all dealing with English life, were written in failing health and during domestic trouble; they added little to his reputation." § The considerable commercial success of *Gloria Mundi* was partly due to its periodical publication during the author's last illness, and its book publication coincident with Frederic's death on October 19, 1898, in England, where he had been London correspondent of the New York *Times* since 1884. His illness and death were sensational news in England and America, as Frederic, a Christian Scientist, refused medical aid after a stroke of partial paralysis in August 1898. An inquest was held after his death in which his daughter testified before a coroner's jury to her belief that her father was insane. The jury decided after weeks of deliberation that "the deceased was merely a strong-minded, obstinate and self-opinionated man."

[166]
That Last Waif | or | Social Quarantine | A Brief | by | Horace Fletcher | Advocate for the Waifs | Author of | "Menticulture" and "Happiness" | [*floret*] | Published for the Waifs | and Distributed through the | Kindergarten Literature Com- | pany, Woman's Temple, Chicago [*title within rule border; printed slip inserted:* Supplied to the Trade | by | Herbert S. Stone & Co. | Chicago and New York]

7-3/8 x 5-1/8; pp. 270, [6]; 4 pp. on "Individual Cooperation" inserted. Printed by Lakeside Press, Chicago, in Modernized Old Style type on laid paper. Bound in cloth; front cover white with halftone picture inserted, rules and lettering in blue; spine white with lettering in blue; back cover yellow with halftone picture inserted, lettering in blue.

Copyright December 3, 1898; listed in *Publishers' Weekly* December 17. Price $1.50. American sheets issued in England by B. F. Stevens during September 1898.

[167]
What Sense? | or | Economic Nutrition | by | Horace Fletcher | Author of "The A-B-C of Snap Shooting" (out of print)| "Menticulture," "Happiness," "That Last | Waif; or Social Quarantine" | [*floret*] | Herbert S. Stone & Company | Chicago & New York | MDCCCXCVIII [*within double rule border*]

5-5/8 x 4; pp. [vi], 128, [2]. Printed by Lakeside Press, Chicago, in Modernized Old Style type on laid paper with watermark four. Bindings: Gift edition, as deposited in Library of Congress; yellow paper with sides stamped in red and black. The trade edition was advertised in boards, but no copy has been located.

Copyright December 3, 1898; listed in *Publishers' Weekly* December 17. Price 75 cents.

The fourth of Fletcher's works published by Stone, this is the first devoted to the theories of diet and mastication later known as "Fletcherizing." The present title was later bound up with his pamphlet *Glutton or Epicure,* No. 236.

[168]
New Stories | from the | Chap-Book | Being a Miscellany of | Curious and interesting Tales, | Histories, &c; newly com- | posed by many Cele- | brated Writers | and very delight- | ful to read. | [*device six*] | Chicago. | Printed for Herbert S. Stone & Company, | Eldridge Court and at the Constable | Building New York | 1898 [*lettered and printed in red and black within double rule border*]

6-3/4 x 4-5/16; pp. [x], 260, [6]. Printed by Lakeside Press, Chicago, in Caslon type on laid paper. Bound in pink cloth; Claude Bragdon's *Chap-Book* poster of "The Sandwich Man" reproduced on both sides in red and rule borders in black; raised lettering in pink on red spine. Issued with top edge gilt or stained pink; other edges uncut. Lettering in title by Claude Bragdon.

Copyright claimed, but no entry made and no copies deposited; listed in *Publishers' Weekly* December 3. Price $1.25.

The last of three compilations from contributions to *The Chap-Book;* see Nos. 119 and 120. The first book to feature in its imprint the new Chicago office of the house of Stone on Eldridge Court.

[169]
The Perfect Wagnerite | A Commentary on the | Ring of the Niblungs by | Bernard Shaw | [*device five*] | Chicago and New York: | Herbert S. Stone and | Company, MDCCCXCIX

7-1/2 x 4-3/4; pp. vi, [ii], 170, [2]. Printed by Lakeside Press, Chicago, in Caslon type on laid paper with watermark four. Bound in blue cloth with paper label on spine.

Copyright December 3, 1898. Price $1.25. Reissued by Stone in 1905; in 1909 by Brentano's.

Grant Richards' original English edition, dated 1898, was listed in *Publishers' Circular* for December 17, 1898, two weeks after the deposit of the American edition in the Copyright Office. Stone's edition, however, was not listed in *Publishers' Weekly* until May 6, 1899, when another edition, of 140 pages, and presumably from Grant Richards' sheets, had already been listed as imported for Charles Scribner's Sons, in the issue of March 25, 1899. The inference from the copyright date that Stone's was the first edition published in England or America cannot be supported by the dating of reviews, for *The Perfect Wagnerite* met with surprising critical inattention in the United States. No reviews appeared in Chicago newspapers; none are indexed in *Poole's* or in the *Readers' Guide*, nor in the three important national critical journals, *Critic* and *Bookman* of New York and *Dial* of Chicago. A review appeared in the New York *Daily Tribune* only on May 6, 1899. The importation of the English edition when the work had already been printed and copyrighted here, is faintly inexplicable. § The Wells bibliography states that *The Perfect Wagnerite* was first printed in the New York periodical *Liberty*. Other bibliographies do not support the attribution, and Mr. Gilbert H. Doane, Librarian of the University of Wisconsin, who kindly examined the files preserved at Madison, states that no part of the essay is included in Shaw's contributions to that periodical, during 1895 and 1896.

[170]
The | Penalties of Taste | and | other essays | by | Norman Bridge | [*device eight*] | Herbert S. Stone & Company | Chicago & New York | MDCCCXCVIII [*within double rule border*]

7-1/2 x 4-3/4; pp. [vi], 164, [2]; followed by 4 pp. of advertisements. Printed by Lakeside Press, Chicago, in Caslon and Ronaldson Old Style types on laid paper with watermark four. Bound in green ribbed cloth, stamped in gold on sides and spine.

Entered for copyright on November 28, 1898; no copy deposited. Listed in *Publishers' Weekly* December 17. Price $1.50.

First book of the distinguished Chicago physician and financier, later the benefactor of the California Institute of Technology, the University of California and the University of Chicago.

[171]
Memoir of | Robert, Earl Nugent | With Letters, Poems, and Appendices | by | Claud Nugent | With twelve reproductions from family portraits by | Sir Godfrey Kneller, Sir Joshua Reynolds, | Gainsborough and others | [*device five*] | Herbert S. Stone & Co. | Chicago & New York | MDCCCXCVIII

8-3/4 x 5-3/4; pp. vii, [v], 352; with signatures. Twelve plates, including frontispiece, inserted. Printed by Richard Clay & Sons, Limited, London & Bungay, in Caslon type on wove paper. Bound in green ribbed cloth, paper label on spine; edges uncut.

Listed in *Publishers' Weekly* December 17, 1898. Price $3.50. Published in England by Heinemann during October 1898.

This and the two titles below were bound as well as printed in Great Britain.

[172]
Catherine Sforza | by | Count Pier Desiderio Pasolini | Authorized Edition, Translated and Prepared | With the Assistance of the Author | by | Paul Sylvester | Illustrated with numerous reproductions from | original pictures and documents | [*device five*] | Herbert S. Stone & Co. | Chicago & New York | MDCCCXCVIII

8-3/4 x 5-5/8; pp. xvi, 400; with signatures. Frontispiece inserted. Printed by Richard Clay & Sons, Limited, London & Bungay, in Modernized Old Style type on wove calendared paper. Bound in grey or green cloth, paper label on spine; edges uncut. Frontispiece portrait reproduced in photogravure; thirty-nine illustrations in text printed as half-tones and line-engravings.

Listed in *Publishers' Weekly* December 17, 1898. Price $3.50 net. Published in England by Heinemann during October 1898.

[173]
The Palmy Days of | Nance Oldfield | by | Edward Robins | With Portraits | [*woodcut*] | Chicago | Herbert S. Stone & Co. | 1898

8-7/8 x 5-3/4; pp. [viii], 277, [1]; with signatures. Frontispiece and twelve plates (all portraits) inserted. Printed by Ballantyne, Hanson & Co., London & Edinburgh, in Modernized Old Style type on wove calendared paper. Bound in green cloth, paper label on spine; edges uncut.

Listed in *Publishers' Weekly* December 17, 1898. Price $3.50 net. Published in England by Heinemann during September 1898.

[174]
The |Free-trade Movement | and its Results | by | G. Armitage Smith, M.A. | Principal of the Birkbeck Institution, and | Lecturer on Economics for the London Society for the | Extension of University Teaching | [*device five*] | Herbert S. Stone & Company | Chicago & New York | MDCCCXCVIII

7-1/4 x 4-7/8; pp. viii, [9]-244; with signatures. Printed and bound by Blackie in Glasgow; see No. 147.

Recorded in the *American Catalogue* 1895-1900, but not listed in *Publishers' Weekly*. First advertised there March 11, 1899. Price $1.25. Probably available here during 1898, as it is so dated, and was published by Blackie in London during April 1898.

Fourth title imported in the "Victorian Era Series." Previous issues, Nos. 147-49, had title-leaves inserted as cancels; this and succeeding issues were imprinted for Stone in Glasgow.

[175]
London | In the Reign of Victoria | (1837-1897) | by | G. Laurence Gomme, F. S. A. etc. | [*device five*] | Herbert S. Stone & Company | Chicago & New York | MDCCCXCVIII

7-1/4 x 4-7/8; pp. viii, 248; with signatures. Printed and bound by Blackie in Glasgow; see No. 147.

Recorded in the *American Catalogue,* 1895-1900, but not listed in *Publishers' Weekly*. First advertised there March 11, 1899. Price $1.25. Probably available here during 1898, as it is so dated, and was published by Blackie in London during November 1898.

Fifth title imported in the "Victorian Era Series."

[176]
Successful | Houses | by | Oliver Coleman | "East, west, hame's best." | [*device eight in red*] | Herbert S. Stone & Company | Chicago & New York | MDCCCXCIX [*within double rule border*]

8-1/2 x 6-3/4; pp. [6], vii, [i], 165, [5]. Printed by Lakeside Press, Chicago, in Modern-face type on wove calendared paper. Bound in tan cloth, stamped in red and green; design of country house on sides, signed "H" for Frank Hazenplug. Illustrated with halftones from photographs, and one line engraving.

Copyright December 8, 1898; listed in *Publishers' Weekly* April 1, 1899. Price $1.50. Reissued in 1901 by Stone, in 1906 by Fox, Duffield & Co.

"Oliver Coleman" was the pseudonym used by Eugene Klapp, founder of *The House Beautiful,* for his articles in the magazine. A similar compilation from the periodical, *The Book of One Hundred Houses,* 1902, contained notes by "Oliver Coleman" and Virginia Robie.

[177]
Stories from the | Old Testament | for Children | by | Harriet S. B. Beale | [*device eight in red*] | Herbert S. Stone & Company | Chicago & New York | MDCCCXCIX [*within double rule border*]

8-1/2 x 6; pp. [xii], 409, [7]. Printed by Lakeside Press, Chicago, in Modern-face type on laid paper with watermark four. Bound in red buckram, stamped in blue on sides and spine.

Copyright December 12, 1898. Price $1.50.

Mrs. Beale, as she has recently written in H. Stuart Stone Jr.'s copy of the book, was a friend both of Herbert Stuart Stone Sr. and his father, Melville E. Stone.

[178]
After-Supper Songs | by | Elizabeth Coolidge | [*device five in red*] | Published by Herbert S. Stone and Company | Chicago and New York | MDCCCXCIX

8-3/8 x 12; pp. [viii], 62, [2]. Printed by Lakeside Press, Chicago, in Caslon and Jenson types on wove calendared paper. Bound in smooth red cloth, stamped on sides and spine in yellow; illustration in red, white and green, on yellow paper, inserted into both covers; edges cut. Words and music of twenty songs, each with an illustration in color. Each page of text within double rule border.

Copyright December 22, 1898. Price $2.00. "Second Impression," 1899.

"To the little boy who sings them these songs are dedicated." Albert Sprague Coolidge was also apparently the model for the illustrations. § Elizabeth Sprague Coolidge's first publication; the whole first edition was sold in three days before Christmas, according to the publisher's advertisements.

[179]
The | Spanish-American War | The Events of the War Described | by Eye Witnesses | Illustrated | [*device eight, within rule frame*] | Herbert S. Stone & Company | Chicago and New York | 1899 [*within thin within thick rule border*]

8-1/4 x 6-1/2; pp. 8, 228, [4]. Printed by Lakeside Press, Chicago, in Caslon and Modernized Old Style types on wove calendared paper. Bound in blue cloth, stamped in silver on sides and spine; wheel decoration in red and silver on sides; edges trimmed. Illustrated with photographs, drawings and maps, in halftone and line engraving.

Copyright December 28, 1898. Price $1.50. Secondary binding of light blue cloth, without stamping on back cover.

No editor's name appears, but Mr. Wallace Rice stated in 1939, that Herbert Stone and he made the compilation from news accounts. Among those journalists whose stories were reprinted were: John T. McCutcheon, William Schmedtgen, W. A. M. Goode, H. J. Whigham, Kennett F. Harris, Malcolm McDowell, Howbert Billman, George E. Graham, Henry Barrett Chamberlin.

[180]
Love's | Dilemmas | [*rule*] | [*decoration*] | [*rule*] | By Robert Herrick | Author of "The Man Who Wins" | "The Gospel of Freedom," Etc. | [*rule*] | [*device nine*] | H. S. Stone & Company | Chicago MDCCCXCVIII

7-1/2 x 5; pp. [viii], 193, [3]. Printed by University Press, Cambridge, in Caslon black-letter, roman and italic types on wove paper. Bound in natural linen, stamped on front cover and spine with lettering in red; decorations on sides and spine in chocolate-brown. Binding, typographical design, decorative initial letters and printer's flowers by Will Bradley; title-page reproduced in Fig. 29.

Copyright February 18, 1899; listed in *Publishers' Weekly* May 6, 1899. Price $1.25. Included 1900 in the "Eldridge Series"; reissued 1906 by Fox, Duffield & Company.

The most attractive of Stone's later publications and the only one completely designed by Will Bradley, then working at the University Press in Cambridge. The publisher's device nine, as redrawn by him, is an elaboration of number eight, designed by Claude Bragdon. The Bradley version was used again only in *Euphrosyne and Her Golden Book* of 1901. § Six short stories; the only book Herbert Stone published for Robert Herrick, whom he had known in Cambridge and in Chicago since 1890.

[181]

Sand 'N' Bushes | by | Maria Louise Pool | [*device eight in red*] | Herbert S. Stone & Company | Chicago & New York | MDCCCXCIX [*within double rule border*]

7-1/2 x 4-1/4; pp. vii [i], 364, [2]. Printer not given; but probably Lakeside Press or Stromberg, Allen & Co.; Ronaldson Old Style type on laid (ribbed) paper. Bound in green ribbed cloth; stamped in gold; on front cover with lettering and circular ornament, on spine with lettering; on back cover with device five in blind; blind rules throughout.

Copyright February 23, 1899. Price $1.50. Included 1900 in the "Eldridge Series."

[182]

A | Heaven-Kissing | Hill | by | Julia Magruder | Author of "Miss Ayr of Virginia," "A Realized | Ideal," etc. | [*ornament and series emblem*] | Herbert S. Stone and Company | Chicago and New York | MDCCCXCIX [*within rule border*]

6-1/2 x 3-7/8; pp. [viii], 159, [1]. Frontispiece by Blanche Ostertag, inserted. Printer not given, but Lakeside Press, Chicago; Ronaldson Old Style type on cheap laid paper. Bound in blue cloth, stamped in white on sides and spine with rules and lettering; series emblem in blue on white paper inserted on front cover, stamped in white on back cover; endpapers patterned in blue and green. Binding, endpapers and series emblem designed by Frank Hazenplug.

Copyright March 6, 1899. Price 75 cents.

First title issued in the "Blue Cloth Books" series of romantic fiction. Four other titles were issued in this series during 1899; three, like the above, were new publications; one, Norman Gale's *A June Romance,* was a reprint of an early Stone & Kimball publication, No. 23.

[183]
Ickery Ann | and Other Girls and | Boys | by | Elia W. Peattie | [*device eight*] | Herbert S. Stone & Company | Chicago & New York | MDCCCXCIX [*within double rule border*]

7-3/8 x 4-7/8; pp. [xiv], 286, [6]. Printed by Lakeside Press, Chicago, in Caslon, Modernized Old Style and Modern-face types on laid paper. Bound in tan cloth stamped in brown; sides include illustration of child, in green and black; circular monogram in maroon on spine.

Entered for copyright during 1898, but copies not deposited until March 17, 1899; Lucy Monroe's copy dated March 27, 1899. Listed in *Publishers' Weekly* May 6. Price $1.25. Included 1900 in the "Eldridge Series."

Most of the stories had been previously printed in *The Youth's Companion* and *St. Nicholas*. Two of Mrs. Peattie's books originally published by Way & Williams were reissued by Stone at about this time. These were *Pippins and Cheese* and *A Mountain Woman,* which had a binding by Bruce Rogers.

[184]
The Cougar-Tamer | & Other Stories of | Adventure | by | Frank Welles Calkins | [*device eight*] | Herbert S. Stone & Company | Chicago & New York | MDCCCXCIX [*within double rule border*]

7-1/2 x 4-3/4; pp. [viii], 262, [2]. Frontispiece and seven plates inserted. Printed by Lakeside Press, Chicago, in Caslon, Modernized Old Style (open) and Modern-face types on laid paper. Bound in khaki buckram stamped in black and green; on spine with lettering; on front with rules, lettering, and design of cougar atop shield. The frontispiece is by Gilbert Goul; the other illustrations by various hands.

Copyright March 23, 1899; listed in *Publishers' Weekly* May 6. Price $1.50. Included 1900 in the "Court Series."

Mr. Calkins' *Tales of the West,* originally published as three pamphlets in 1893 by M. A. Donohue & Co., and later combined into one volume for Way & Williams, was reissued by Herbert S. Stone & Company at about this time. *The West* appears first in *Publishers' Trade List Annual* for 1899 and remained listed until 1902.

[185]
A | Little Legacy | & | Other Stories | by | Mrs. L. B. Walford | [*ornament and series emblem*] | Herbert S. Stone and Company | Chicago and New York | MDCCCXCIX [*within rule border*]

6-1/2 x 3-3/4; pp. [vi], 344, [2]. Frontispiece, by Violet Oakley, inserted. Printed by Lakeside Press, Chicago, in Ronaldson Old Style type on cheap laid paper. "Blue Cloth Books" binding; see No. 182.

Copyright April 8, 1899. Price 75 cents. Included 1900 in the "Court Series."

Second title issued in the "Blue Cloth Books" series of romantic fiction.

[186]
The Passion of | Rosamund Keith | by | Martin J. Pritchard | Author of "Without Sin" | "Can Wisdom be put in a Silver Rod, | Or Love in a Golden Bowl?" | —W. Blake | [*device four in red*] | Herbert S. Stone and Company | Chicago and New York | MDCCCXCIX

7-1/2 x 4-3/4; pp. [viii], 477, [3]. Printed by Lakeside Press, Chicago, in Caslon and Modernized Old Style types on laid paper. Bound in blue buckram; stamped in white on sides and spine, ornament by Frank Hazenplug on sides.

Copyright April 10, 1899; listed in *Publishers' Weekly* June 3. Price $1.50. Included in the "Eldridge Series," 1900. Heinemann's English edition published in April 1899.

"Martin J. Pritchard," pseudonym for Mrs. Augustus Moore, was represented in the first list of Herbert S. Stone & Co. with the novel, *Without Sin* (No. 110).

[187]
A | Fair Brigand | by | George Horton | [*device eight*] | Herbert S. Stone and Company | Chicago and New York | MDCCCXCIX

6-5/8 x 4-1/4; pp. [viii], 330, [2]. Frontispiece and ten plates by Morgan, inserted. Printed by Lakeside Press, Chicago, in Modernized Old Style type on laid paper. Bound in green cloth; lettered in white on sides and spine; silhouette design by Frank Hazenplug on sides, within white and green rules.

Copyright April 17, 1899. Price $1.25. Included 1900 in the "Court Series" and "Stone's Paper Library." Reissued about 1902 by Monarch Book Company of Chicago.

The author's second novel, the first, *Constantine,* having been published by Way & Williams in 1897. Mr. Horton was then literary editor of the Chicago *Times-Herald.* While he was still American Consul at Athens, his poem, *In Unknown Seas,* had been privately printed by Stone & Kimball in 1895; see p. 361.

[188]
Dross | [*rule*] | By Henry Seton Merriman | Author of | "With Edged Tools," "The Sowers," etc. | [*device five*] | [*rule*] | Herbert S. Stone & Co. | Chicago and New York | MDCCCXCIX [*within double rule border*]

7-1/2 x 4-5/8; pp. [viii], 330, [6]. Frontispiece and twenty-seven plates, by Robert Sauber, inserted. Printed by Lakeside Press, Chicago, in Modernized Old Style type on cheap laid paper. Bound in red cloth, stamped in white on sides and spine; device four on sides.

Ready April 15, 1899, according to advertisement in *Publishers' Weekly;* listed there June 3. Price $1.75. Copyright notice is dated 1896; entered for copyright September 21, 1896, and copies of pp. 1-54 deposited October 2, 1896.

Printing of this novel of "Henry Seton Merriman" (Hugh Stowell Scott), the popular romanticist, was begun in 1896, as the copyright records indicate. It was delayed through difficulties in settling the contract. Herbert Stone wrote from London to his brother in Chicago on June 11, 1898:

> ... about Dross. I think the thing has been settled as nicely as we could wish and I look on my work on Wednesday as worth a little more than one thousand dollars. We are to have "Dross" and to publish it in the Spring of next year. We pay £100 advance on account of a royalty. The serial rights for which we had contracted are withdrawn and we pay nothing for them. This gives us precisely what we want and a new book by Merriman in the Spring will mean a considerable profit. "In Kedar's Tents" sold 15000 copies in America and Harper will publish "Roden's Corner" this autumn. Then we step in and get all the benefit for which we pay less than half what Harper had to give. I have word from Watt in a day or two making all this a formal proposition ...

The novel was not serialized in this country, nor published in book form in England, according to Thomas Seccombe in the *Dictionary of National*

Biography. There is no entry in the *English Catalogue* for an edition of *Dross,* and the British Museum Catalogue lists only the Canadian copyright edition of W. J. Gage, published in Toronto in 1899. Robert Sauber, the illustrator, was English; presumably his plates had appeared in some British periodical when the novel was serialized there. The American book sales justified Herbert Stone's optimism; 15,000 were sold by August 1899; 40,000 by August 1900.

[189]
Oliver Iverson | His Adventures During Four Days | and Nights in the City of | New York in April of | the Year 1890 | by | Ann Devoore | [*ornament and series emblem*] | Herbert S. Stone and Company | Chicago and New York | MDCCCXCIX [*within rule border*]

6-1/2 x 3-3/4; pp. [xii], 181, [5]. Frontispiece, by Violet Oakley, inserted. Printer not given, but probably Lakeside Press, Chicago; Ronaldson Old Style type on cheap laid paper. "Blue Cloth Books" binding; see No. 182.

Copyright April 17, 1899. Price 75 cents. Included 1900 in the "Court Series."

Third title issued in the "Blue Cloth Books" series of romantic fiction.

[190]
D'Arcy of the Guards | or | The Fortunes of War | by | Louis Evan Shipman | [*device eight in red*] | Herbert S. Stone and Company | Chicago and New York | MDCCCXCIX [*within double rule border*]

6-5/8 x 4-1/4; pp. [viii], 237, [3]. Printed by Lakeside Press, Chicago, in Modern-face type on laid paper. Bound in grey cloth stamped in blue; ornament in grey against green background on sides.

Copyright April 17, 1899. Ready April 15, according to advertisement in *Publishers' Weekly*. Price $1.25.

This novel of the American revolution was originally written in 1898 as a play. Mr. Shipman wrote, in the entertaining *True Adventures of a Play* with "Mr. E. H. Sothern before me as the ideal for my Irish guardsman." Sothern declined it, so did Richard Mansfield and John Drew. While waiting for the decision of the last named,

> I can take the opportunity to tell of the base use to which I put my Irish hero and colonial heroine during the interim. Finding it difficult to get them on the boards, I decided to put them between: in other

words to make a book of them; to subject them to the ignominy of the printed page; then whose heritage, though denied, should have been the glare of the "bunch" and "spots" and the irradiation of glimmering "foots." For ulterior motive I had an idea that perhaps publishers' advertising and some favorable reviews might point out to the wary and lethargic who sat in the high places that a perfectly good play was going a begging.

The novel was declined by Macmillan, but accepted by Stone on February 18, 1899, publication following quickly. The moderate success of the book encouraged the British actor Robert Taber to take an option, but he gave only a copyright performance in England, and that not until 1901. The play was first produced in America by Henry Miller in 1901, and, much revised during its road tour, had considerable success in New York and again on the road in 1901 and 1902. Its first English commercial production was given by Sir George Alexander in 1910, when it was already a standard item of repertory in this country. In 1913 it was made into an early American movie by Augustus Thomas' "All Star Feature Corporation."

[191]
The | Wolf's Long Howl | by | Stanley Waterloo | [*device eight in red*] | Herbert S. Stone & Company | Chicago & New York | MDCCCXCIX [*within double rule border*]

7-7/16 x 4-1/4; pp. [viii], 288, [4]. Printed by Lakeside Press, Chicago, in Caslon and Modern-face types on laid paper. Binding designed by Will Bradley; red cloth, stamped in black on sides and spine; circular design of wolf's head in black on white paper, inserted in sides; see Fig. 31.

Copyright April 22, 1899; published same day, according to advertisement in *Publishers' Weekly*. Price $1.50. Included in the "Eldridge Series," 1900. Reissued about 1905 with imprint of Monarch Book Company, Chicago.

This collection of short stories was the first book of the Chicago journalist and author published by Stone; a second was *The Seekers* of 1900. Stanley Waterloo's books came to their list by way of Way & Williams. Stone reissued in 1899 the well known juvenile, *The Story of Ab,* and his novels, *A Man and A Woman* and *An Odd Situation.*

[192]
The | Awakening | by | Kate Chopin | Author of "A Night in Acadie," | "Bayou Folks," etc. | [*device eight, reduced, in*

red] | Herbert S. Stone & Company, | Chicago & New York | MDCCCXCIX | [*within double rule border*]

7-1/2 x 4-3/4; pp. [viii], 303, [5]. Printed by Lakeside Press, Chicago, in Modernized Old Style type on laid paper with watermark five. Bound in green linen; stamped on sides with floral border in green and red; printed on sides and spine in red.

Copyright April 24, 1899. Ready April 22, according to advertisement in *Publishers' Weekly;* Lucy Monroe's copy dated April 22. Price $1.50. Probably reprinted one or more times by Stone; reissued 1906 by Duffield. Published in England by Stone in July 1899.

The Awakening was the last book published by Mrs. Kate Chopin, of New Orleans and St. Louis; of her second and best novel, concerned with the tragedy of a married woman's emotional life, Daniel S. Rankin writes in his monograph on Kate Chopin, that

> *The Awakening* met with a storm of adverse criticism. Harshness and bitterness were not absent from the reviews that extolled the novel as an artistic achievement. The author's motives were attacked; even her character. The book was taken from circulation by order of the librarian of the St. Louis Mercantile Library. Kate Chopin was denied membership in the Fine Arts Club of the city. She was asked by one of the local newspapers to give an interview justifying her book. This she would not do. Stunned and bewildered by the reception of her story, with a feeling of grim humor she authorized this announcement in the July 1899 number of *Book News,* published in New York:
>
> "Having a group of people at my disposal, I thought it might be entertaining (to myself) to throw them together and see what would happen. I never dreamed of Mrs. Pontellier making such a mess of things and working out her own damnation as she did. If I had had the slightest intimation of such a thing I would have excluded her from the company. But when I found out what she was up to, the play was half over and it was then too late.
>
> St. Louis, Mo., May 28, 1899   *signed:* KATE CHOPIN"
>
> Her sense of humor, evident in this notice, saved the situation in part, but she was hurt. She never spoke of this at any time.

Mrs. Chopin did write of her disappointment to her publishers, on July 7, 1899, singling out the St. Louis *Post-Dispatch* review as the exception which was "able and intelligent." In the fall she gave an interview to the *Post-Dispatch,* which scrupulously avoided mention of her controversial novel. Perhaps some of the moral opprobrium in which the novel was briefly and unjustly held was due to the simultaneous publication, in serial form of Tolstoi's *Awakening,* which we now know as the novel *Resurrection.* This was running in the monthly *Cosmopolitan* until August 1899, when John Brisben Walker discontinued it, after the author and his translator (Louise Aylmer Maude) had refused to accept censorship. (See J. Allen Smith, "Tolstoy's Fiction in England and America, 1862-1938," unpublished Ph.D. dissertation, Department of English, University of Illinois, 1939). It was believed by Mrs. Chopin's children and by literary critics and biographers, that she never wrote again before her death in 1904. Rankin submits bibliographical evidence that Mrs. Chopin wrote and published several short stories between 1900 and 1902. It is certain, however, that her literary development was warped by the public reception of what we now accept as an early masterpiece of clinical realism. Mrs. Chopin's book came to Eldridge Court through Way & Williams, whose edition of *A Night in Acadie* Stone reissued in 1899. A third manuscript originally sent to Way & Williams by the author was returned by Stone in February 1900. This collection of short stories, titled "A Vocation and a Voice," has remained unpublished. Since no reason is given in the author's notebooks for its return, Rankin infers that: "Perhaps the bitter reception given *The Awakening*, although the novel sold well, intimidated the publishers." Herbert Stone had not, in the cases of *Rose of Dutcher's Coolly* and *The Damnation of Theron Ware*, been concerned over threats of censorship. More likely the rejection was necessitated by intentionally smaller lists of books which his company published after 1900, and to the assignment of all the Way & Williams copyrights to Doubleday, McClure Company on January 26, 1900.

[193]
Studies in the | Psychology of Woman | by | Laura Marholm | Translated by | Georgia A. Etchison | [*device eight in red*] | Herbert S. Stone and Company | Chicago and New York | MDCCCXCIX [*within double rule border*]

7-1/2 x 4-3/4; pp. [iv], 348, [8]. Printed by Lakeside Press, Chicago, in Caslon and Ronaldson Old Style types on laid paper with watermark five; brown endpapers. Bound in navy-blue buckram with rules and printing on spine in gold.

Copyright April 24, 1899. Ready April 22, according to advertisement in *Publishers' Weekly*. Price $1.50. Published in England by Grant Richards during October 1899.

"Laura Marholm," Mrs. Laura Mohr Hansson, was a Swedish dramatist and novelist; this translation is from the 1897 German edition of her *Zur Psychologie der Frau*.

[194]
The History | of Gambling | in England | by | John Ashton

| Author of "Social Life in the Reign of Queen Anne" | "A History of English Lotteries," etc. | [*device eight*] | Herbert S. Stone & Company | Chicago and New York | Duckworth & Company | London: MDCCCXCIX

8-1/2 x 5-1/2; pp. viii, 286, [2]; with signatures. Printed by Turnbull & Spears, Edinburgh, in Modernized Old Style type on wove paper. Bound in red buckram, paper label on spine; edges uncut.

Listed in *Publishers' Weekly* May 6, 1899; ready April 22, according to advertisement in that magazine. Price $2.50.

The English antiquarian John Ashton had been a contributor to *The Chap-Book* on the subject of old chap-books.

[195]

Can We Disarm? | by | Joseph McCabe | written in collaboration with | Georges Darien | Author of 'Biribi,' etc. | Herbert S. Stone & Co. | Chicago and New York | 1899

7-1/2 x 5; pp. [viii], 151, [5]; with signatures. Printed by Richard Clay and Sons, London & Bungay, in Caslon and Modern-face types on laid paper. Bound in brown buckram; printed in blue on spine; rules and lettering in blue on sides, with decoration of crown, shield and soldier in brown.

Listed in *Publishers' Weekly* May 6, 1899. Price $1.25. Included in the "Eldridge Series" and "Stone's Paper Library" 1900. Published in England by Heinemann during January 1899.

1,000 copies in quires were supplied by Heinemann on February 16, 1899; the cost to Stone being £25 plus £1/14/4 for casing and consul's fee. This was a larger number of copies than was customarily imported in English non-fiction, but the firm of Stone was hopeful about disarmament and generally anti-imperialistic during the Spanish-American war and its aftermath.

[196]

A Short History | of the | United States | by | Justin Huntly M'Carthy | [*five lines of titles and quotation*] | [*device eight*] | Herbert S. Stone & Company | Chicago & New York | MDCCCXCIX [*within double rule border*]

7-1/2 x 4-3/4; pp. [8], [i]-x, vii-viii, 1-370, [6]. Printed by Lakeside

Press, Chicago, in Modernized Old Style type on laid paper. Bound in blue ribbed cloth, stamped in red and white; eagle ornament on sides.

Entered for copyright August 25, 1898 and pp. 1-28 deposited November 25, 1898. Published edition listed in *Publishers' Weekly* May 6, 1899. Price $1.50. Published in England by Hodder & Stoughton during December 1898.

[197]
The | Maid He Married | by | Harriet Prescott Spofford | [*ornament and series emblem*] | Herbert S. Stone and Company | Chicago and New York | MDCCCXCIX [*within rule border*]

6-1/2 x 3-3/4; pp. [iv], 201, [3]. Frontispiece by Violet Oakley, inserted. Printed by Lakeside Press, Chicago, in Modernized Old Style type on cheap laid paper. "Blue Cloth Books" binding; see No. 182.

Copyright May 8, 1899. Advertised in *Publishers' Weekly* as "Ready May 6." Price 75 cents. Reprinted from *Harper's Magazine*. Included 1900 in the "Court Series."

Fourth title issued in the "Blue Cloth Books" series of romantic fiction. The fifth and last title was a reprint *A June Romance,* originally published in 1894 by Stone & Kimball.

[198]
The Lady of the | Flag-Flowers | by | Florence Wilkinson | [*device eight in red*] | Herbert S. Stone and Company | Chicago and New York | MDCCCXCIX [*within double rule border*]

6-3/4 x 4-1/4; pp. 6, 364, [2]. Printed by Lakeside Press, Chicago, in Ronaldson Old Style type on laid paper with watermark five. Binding designed by Frank Hazenplug; light green linen, lettered in green on sides and spine, floral design in green and violet on sides.

Copyright May 8, 1899; Lucy Monroe's copy dated May 6. "Ready April 22," according to *Publishers' Weekly* advertisement. Price $1.50. Included 1900 in the "Eldridge Series."

The author, daughter of William Cleaver Wilkinson, professor at the University of Chicago, then lived in Hyde Park; this is her first book.

[199]
Esther Waters | A Novel | by | George Moore | Revised and Enlarged Edition | [*device eight in red*] | Herbert S. Stone

and Company | Chicago and New York | MDCCCXCIX [*within double rule border*]

7-1/2 x 4-11/16; pp. [4], ix, [i], 504, [4]. Printed by Lakeside Press, Chicago, in Ronaldson Old Style type on laid paper with watermark five. Bound in blue cloth, stamped in silver on sides and spine; see Fig. 31.

Entered for copyright April 10, 1899; copies of pp. 1-192 deposited same day, but complete copies not deposited until 1904. Actually published sometime in 1899; advertised as "Ready May 17" in *Publishers' Weekly;* listed there December 9. Price $1.50. "New edition," 1901; since reissued by Duffield, Brentano and others. Scott's English edition listed in *English Catalogue* for May 1899, but not entered in the "New Editions of the Week" in *Publishers' Circular.*

This is a revision of Moore's own favorite novel, originally published in England in 1894 and soon pirated here; see further pp. 118-19.

[200]

Vengeance of the | Female | Edited by | Marrion Wilcox | Author of "A Short History of the War | with Spain" | [*device eight*] | Herbert S. Stone & Company | Chicago & New York | MDCCCXCIX [*within double rule border*]

7-1/2 x 4-3/4; pp. vi, 318, [8]. Five plates, including frontispiece, and one facsimile, inserted. Printed by Lakeside Press, Chicago, in Modernized Old Style type on laid paper. Bound in tomato-red cloth, printed in white on sides and spine; illustration by Frank Hazenplug, in violet, on sides.

Copyright May 26, 1899. Advertised in *Publishers' Weekly* as ready May 17. Price $1.50. Included 1900 in the "Eldridge Series."

Observations of life in Italy, Spain, and Spanish-America, mostly reprinted from *Harper's Magazine.*

[201]

Lucifer | A Theological Tragedy | by | George Santayana | [*device eight, reduced, in red*] | Herbert S. Stone and Company | Chicago and New York | MDCCCXCIX [*within double rule border*]

6-5/8 x 4-1/4; pp. [viii], 187, [3]. Printed by Lakeside Press, Chicago, in Modernized Old Style type on laid paper with watermark five. Bound in smooth green cloth, printed in gold on spine.

Copyright May 27, 1899; ready May 17, according to advertisement in

Publishers' Weekly. Reissued by Duffield after 1906; reprinted in 1924 by Dunster House of Cambridge.

"Lucifer, A Prelude," which had appeared in the 1894 and 1896 editions of Santayana's *Sonnets*, is reprinted, with some changes, as Act I. The other acts had not been printed before.

[202]

The | Carcellini Emerald | With Other Tales | by | Mrs. Burton Harrison | [*device eight*] | Herbert S. Stone and Company | Chicago and New York | MDCCCXCIX [*within double rule border*]

7-3/8 x 4-3/4; pp. [viii], 314, [4]. Frontispiece and seven plates inserted. Printer not given; Modernized Old Style type; laid paper with watermark five. Bound in red buckram; stamped on sides and spine with lettering and arabesque designs in green and white. The illustrations are by W. A. Rogers, Violet Oakley and Henry Hutt.

Copyright May 29, 1899; ready May 17 according to advertisement in *Publishers' Weekly*. Price $1.50. Included in the "Eldridge Series" 1900.

This earned $216.67 in royalties by December 9, 1899, according to a letter from publisher to author.

[203]

Scoundrels & Co | by | Coulson Kernahan | Author of "Captain Shannon," "A Book of Strange Sins," | "A Dead Man's Diary, etc. | [*device eight in red*] | Herbert S. Stone and Company | Chicago and New York | MDCCCXCIX [*within double rule border*]

6-11/16 x 4-1/4; pp. [4], x, 320, [2]. Printed by Lakeside Press, Chicago, in Ronaldson Old Style type on laid paper with watermark five. Bound in tan paper boards; rules and lettering on front and spine in green; pattern of heads on front in black and red; circular monogram on back, in red; edges uncut.

Copyright June 15, 1899; listed in *Publishers' Weekly* December 9, 1899. Price $1.25.

This picaresque novel, one of the best of the English author's dozen, was not published in his own country.

[204]

The | Bushwhackers | & | Other Stories | by | Charles Egbert Craddock | Author of "In the Tennessee Mountains," "The

| Story of Old Fort Loudon," etc. | [*device eight, reduced, in red*] | Herbert S. Stone & Company | Chicago & New York | MDCCCXCIX [*within double rule border*]

6-3/4 x 4-1/4; pp. [x], 312, [6]. Printed by Lakeside Press, Chicago, in Caslon and Modernized Old Style types on laid paper with watermark five. Binding designed by Frank Hazenplug; grey boards, with lettering and landscape design in blue, grey and white on front cover, lettering on spine in white, monogram and rule borders in white on back; edges uncut.

Copyright June 26, 1899. Price $1.25. In "Fourth thousand" by August 1899.

Mary Noailles Murfree's only publication with Stone; two other stories of Kentucky besides the title-story are included: "The Panther of Jolton's Ridge," and "The Exploit of Choolak, the Chickasaw."

[205]
In | Castle & Colony | by | Emma Rayner | Author of "Free to Serve" | [*device eight in red*] | Herbert S. Stone and Company, Chicago and New York | MDCCCXCIX [*within double rule border*]

7-7/16 x 4-3/4; pp. [viii], 467, [5]. Printed by Lakeside Press, Chicago, in Modernized Old Style, Ronaldson, and Modern-face types on laid paper with watermark five. Bound in tomato-red cloth; rules and lettering on sides and spine in white, floral pattern in green and white on sides.

Copyright June 26, 1899. Price $1.50. "Second Impression," 1899. Published in London by Stone December 1899.

Free to Serve, Miss Rayner's first historical novel, had been published in 1897 in Boston by Copeland & Day, who abandoned publishing in 1899; see p. 115.

[206]
Doc' Horne | A Story of the Streets and Town | by | George Ade | Author of "Artie," "Pink Marsh," etc. | Pictures by | John T. McCutcheon | [*device eight*] | Herbert S. Stone and Company | Chicago and New York | MDCCCXCIX [*within double rule border*]

6-5/8 x 4-3/8; pp. [viii], 292, [4]. Printed by Lakeside Press, Chicago, in Ronaldson Old Style type on wove calendared paper. Bound in pink-white linen; stamped in red on sides and spine with rules and lettering;

shield design in red on tan paper inserted into front cover, stamped in red on back. Illustrated with frontispiece, one full-page plate and forty-nine line drawings in text.

Copyright June 29, 1899; listed in *Publishers' Weekly* July 22. Price $1.25. Reached eighth thousand by 1900, when it was included in the "Court Series." Published after 1901 by Grosset & Dunlap; after 1906 by Duffield.

Like Mr. Ade's two earlier books, reprinted from the Chicago *Record*. The author has inscribed in a copy presented to his niece:

> This book was never a big seller, probably because it did not appeal to women. However, many men, including William Dean Howells, spoke well of it.

[207]

The Life of | Maximilien Robespierre | with extracts | from his unpublished correspondence | by | George Henry Lewes | [*two lines of quotations*] | Third Edition | with a portrait and an illustration | Herbert S. Stone & Company | Chicago and New York

7-1/2 x 5; pp. xv, [i], 397, [3], including advertisements and colophon; with signatures. Two plates inserted. Printed by Richard Clay & Sons, London & Bungay, in Modern-face type on wove paper. Bound in red cloth, stamped in gold on spine and front cover; edges uncut. Not listed in *Publishers' Weekly;* not advertised there or in *Publishers' Trade List Annual* by Stone. Price not known. Dated from the advertisements at back, of Irving & Terry's production of the play "Robespierre," by Sardou, in London, on April 15, 1899. This "Third Edition" published in England May 1899 by Chapman & Hall.

Another instance of conflict between Herbert S. Stone & Co. and Charles Scribner's Sons, in the matter of importation, was the publication by Scribner's of the same edition of this title in the spring of 1899; Routledge published another edition, in paper, in both New York and London. The popularity of the book in 1899 was doubtless due to the production of the Sardou play in that year by Irving and Terry.

[208]

The | Perils of Josephine | by | Lord Ernest Hamilton | Author of | "The Outlaws of the Marches," "The Mawkin of the Flow" | [*device eight*] | Herbert S. Stone & Company | Chicago & New York | MDCCCXCIX [*within double rule border*]

304

7-7/16 x 4-3/4; pp. vi, 329, [5]. Printer not given; Caslon and Modernized Old Style types; laid paper with watermark five. Bound in red cloth, stamped in yellow; rules, lettering and device four on front cover, lettering on spine, circular monogram on back.

Copyright July 14, 1899. Price $1.50. Included in "Eldridge Series," 1900. Unwin's English edition listed in *English Catalogue* for July 1899.

[209]

To London Town | by | Arthur Morrison | Author of 'A Child of the Jago,' 'Tales of Mean | Streets,' etc. | [*device eight in red*] | Herbert S. Stone & Company | Chicago & New York | MDCCCXCIX [*within double rule border*]

7-3/8 x 4-3/4; pp. [xii], 298, [2]. Printed by Lakeside Press, Chicago, in Caslon and Modernized Old Style types on laid paper with watermark five. Bound in rose cloth; lettering on front cover and spine, circular monogram on back, in white; roadside scene in brown on front (Fig. 31).

Copyright September 8, 1899; listed in *Publishers' Weekly* December 16. Price $1.50. Reissued by Duffield in 1906. Methuen's English edition listed in *Publishers' Circular* for September 16, 1899.

Author's note, p. [xi]: "I designed this story, and indeed began to write it, between the publication of *Tales of Mean Streets* and that of *A Child of the Jago,* to be read together with those books; not that I pretend to figure in all three—much less in any one of them—a complete picture of life in the eastern parts of London, but because they are complementary each to the two others."

[210]

The | Picture Book | [*rule*] | of | Becky Sharp | [*rule*] | a play in four acts | by | Langdon Mitchell | [*rule*] | Founded on Thackeray's "Vanity Fair" | [*rule*] | Produced September 12, 1899 | by Mrs. Fiske | [*rule*] | [*ornament including publishers' device*] | Published by | Herbert S. Stone and Company | Chicago and New York | [*rule*]

11-3/4 x 9-3/8; pp. [32] unnumbered. Printed by Lakeside Press, Chicago, in Caslon and Modernized Old Style types on wove calendared paper. Stapled into grey paper wrappers; printed in red on both covers; edges trimmed. Illustrated with photographs by Byron and Sarony, and with drawings.

Not listed in *Publishers' Weekly* until April 14, 1900, but doubtless available in September 1899. Price 25 cents.

With "An Appreciation" by Edward Fales Coward. The cast included Tyrone Power as Steyne and Maurice Barrymore as Rawdon Crawley.

[211]
Lesser Destinies | by | Samuel Gordon | [*device eight in red*] | Herbert S. Stone and Company | Chicago and New York | John Murray, London | MDCCCXCIX [*within double rule border*]

7-1/2 x 4-3/4; pp. [viii], 310, [10]. Printed by Lakeside Press, Chicago, in Ronaldson Old Style type on cheap laid paper. Binding designed by Frank Hazenplug; tan cloth, stamped on front cover with lettering in white within rule frame, decoration in brown below; spine with lettering in brown; back cover with circular monogram in brown.

Entered for copyright May 17, 1899, when proof copies were deposited. Complete copies deposited September 23. Listed in *Publishers' Weekly* December 9. Price $1.25. Murray's edition, from American sheets, listed in *English Catalogue* for May 1899.

[212]
Was It Right To | Forgive? | A Domestic Romance | by | Amelia E. Barr | [*device eight*] | Herbert S. Stone and Company | Chicago and New York | MDCCCXCIX [*within double rule border*]

7-1/2 x 4-3/4; pp. [viii], 294, [2]. Printed by Lakeside Press, Chicago, in Ronaldson Old Style type on laid paper. Bound in red cloth; floral design and lettering in white on sides; printing on sides in red against white, printing and floral decoration in white on spine.

Copyright September 30, 1899; listed in *Publishers' Weekly* December 9, 1899. Price $1.50. Included 1900 in the "Eldridge Series."

The only one of Mrs. Barr's seventy-five novels published by Stone.

[213]
Love Made Manifest | by | Guy Boothby | Author of | "The Beautiful White Devil," "Dr. Nikola," "Pharos, the Egyptian," &c. | [*device eight*] | Herbert S. Stone and Company | Chicago and New York | MDCCCXCIX [*within double rule border*]

7-1/2 x 4-3/4; pp. [x], 330, [4]. Frontispiece and three plates inserted.

Printer not given; Caslon and Ronaldson Old Style types on laid paper. Bound in blue cloth stamped in bronze; on front cover with rules, lettering and decoration; on spine with rules and lettering; on back cover with circular monogram. Illustrations by Lucy E. Kemp-Welch.

Copyright September 30, 1899. Price $1.25. Included 1900 in the "Eldridge Series." Published in London by Ward and Locke during August 1899.

First of two romances by this English author, published by Stone.

[214]
Resolved to be Rich | A Novel | by | E. H. Cooper | Author of | "The Marchioness Against the County," "Children, Race-horses, | and Ghosts," etc. | [*device eight in red*] | Herbert S. Stone and Company | Chicago and New York | MDCCCXCIX [*within double rule border*]

7-7/16 x 4-1/2; pp. [viii], 354, [6]. Printed by Lakeside Press, Chicago, in Ronaldson and Modernized Old Style types on laid paper. Bound in green diagonally ribbed cloth, stamped in bronze; lettering and moneybag design on front cover; lettering on spine; circular monogram on back.

Copyright October 2, 1899. Price $1.25. Included 1900 in both the "Eldridge Series" and "Stone's Paper Library." Published in England by Duckworth during October 1899.

[215]
The | Human Interest | A Study in Incompatibilities | by | Violet Hunt | Author of | "A Hard Woman," "Unkist Unkind," "The Maiden's Progress." | [*device eight in red*] | Herbert S. Stone and Company | Chicago and New York | MDCCCXCIX [*within double rule border*]

7-1/2 x 4-3/4; pp. [viii], 279, [3]. Printed by Lakeside Press, Chicago, in Modern-face type on laid paper with watermark five. Bound in maroon ribbed cloth; stamped on front cover with lettering in gold and ornamental device in blind; lettering on spine in gold; device five on back cover in gold.

Copyright October 2, 1899; listed in *Publishers' Weekly* November 11, 1899. Price $1.25. Included 1900 in the "Eldridge Series" and "Stone's Paper Library." Published in England by Methuen during October 1899.

[216]
A Widower & | Some Spinsters | Short Stories | by | Maria Louise Pool | [*device eight in red*] | Herbert S. Stone & Company | Chicago & New York | MDCCCXCIX [*within double rule border*]

7-3/8 x 4-3/4; pp. [x], 326, [8]. Four plates, including frontispiece, inserted. Printed by Lakeside Press, Chicago, in Caslon and Ronaldson Old Style types on laid paper. Bound in green ribbed cloth with decoration and lettering on front cover in gold; lettering in gold on spine; rule border and device five in blind on back. Illustrated from photographs; the frontispiece is a portrait of the author.

Copyright October 4, 1899. Price $1.50. Included 1900 in the "Eldridge Series."

The last of Miss Pool's books published by Stone; posthumously edited by "C. M. B.," and with a biographical preface by Dr. Amand M. Hale.

[217]
The Slave | A Romance | by | Robert Hichens | Author of "Flames," "The Londoners," "The Green | Carnation," Etc. | [*device eight in red*] | Herbert S. Stone and Company | Chicago and New York | MDCCCXCIX [*within double rule border*]

7-7/16 x 4-3/4; pp. [viii], 463, [1]. Printer not given but probably Lakeside Press, Chicago; Modern-face type on laid paper with watermark five. Bound in tan cloth, stamped in red on sides and spine, with lettering, rules and decorations.

Entered for copyright October 17, 1899, when pp. 1-348 were deposited. Complete copies deposited February 23, 1900. Listed in *Publishers' Weekly* March 31, 1899. Price $1.50. Included 1900 in "Eldridge Series." Heinemann's English edition listed in *Publishers' Circular* for October 21, 1899.

[218]
My Father & I | A Book for Daughters | by | The Countess Puliga | [*device ten in red*] | Herbert S. Stone & Company | Chicago & New York | MDCCCXCIX [*within double rule border*]

7-1/2 x 4-3/4; pp. [viii], 279, [9]. Frontispiece inserted. Printed by Lakeside Press, Chicago, in Modernized Old Style type on laid paper. Bound in light blue cloth, stamped in white on sides and spine with lettering and decoration.

Copyright October 23, 1899. Price $1.25. Published in England by Heinemann during February 1900.

Device ten (p. 193), a variant of the original conical mark of Stone & Kimball, used here for the first time. § The American plates were shipped to England, but Henrietta Consuelo (Sansom), Contessa di Puliga (whose books were usually issued under the pseudonym "Brada"), rejected them because she had not seen galley proofs, according to a letter of March 27, 1900, from Heinemann to Stone. The Countess' father, Charles Sansom, was a member of the circle of the Countess of Blessington and the Count D'Orsay; the latter's portrait of Sansom is reproduced as the frontispiece.

[219]
Fables | [rule] | in | [rule] | Slang | [rule] | by | George | Ade | Illustrated | by | Clyde J. | Newman | [rule] | Published by | Herbert S. Stone | and Company | Chicago & New York | MDCCCC [within decorative border across two pages]

6 x 4-1/4; pp. [2], [xii], 201, [3]. Printed by Lakeside Press, Chicago, in Caslon type on laid paper. Bound in yellow buckram; rules and lettering in dark blue, and floral decoration in light blue, on front cover; rules and lettering on spine in blue; circular monogram on back in blue. Title-pages lettered in red and black by Frank Hazenplug. Forty-six illustrations in line by Clyde J. Newman. Binding designed by Frederic W. Goudy.

Copyright October 26, 1899; listed in *Publishers' Weekly* December 9. Price $1.00. Poster, "The Fool Killer," by Clyde J. Newman, issued "Nineteenth thousand" numbered and signed by the author. Advertised in 1900 as "Nearing its One-Hundredth Thousand," but actually reached, while published by Stone, only its sixty-ninth thousand, in 1901. Published by Grosset & Dunlap after 1902; by Duffield after 1906. English publication, during October 1900, by C. Arthur Pearson, and Canadian publication, earlier, by McLeod of Toronto; both editions from American sheets.

Mr. Ade's most famous book appeared by accident, at least as regards its time of publication. *The College Widow* was to have been the Ade book of 1899 published by Stone; the last complete number of *The Chap-Book,* for July 1, 1898, listed it for future publication, in these terms:

Up to the present time, Mr. Ade has published two books of short stories, "Artie" and "Pink Marsh," both of which have had a large sale, although they were collections of short stories. The present volume is a novel full of humorous incidents and vivid character pictures, and will surpass in popularity both of his other books.

Mr. Ade has made, on July 23, 1938, the following statement for inclusion here:

> The College Widow was never written as a story *or* novel. In 1898 I discussed the story with Herbert Stone and promised to write it out in book-length but my work on *The Chicago Record* took so much of my time that I never tackled The College Widow until I did it as a play in 1905. Because I had promised a book to Stone and Co. I submitted some Fables in 1899, so the first book of Fables (Fables in Slang) took the place of The College Widow. It was copyrighted as a play only & later published by Samuel French.

[220]

Standard Whist | An Exponent of the Principles and Rules of the Modern Scientific | Game of Whist as adopted by the American Whist League | at the Ninth American Whist Congress Con- | vening at Chicago, July 10, 1899 | by | Annie Blanche Shelby | [*eleven lines of sub-title*] | [*circular monogram*] | Herbert S. Stone & Company | Chicago & New York | MDCCCXCIX [*within double rule border*]

6 x 4-1/4; pp. xxiv, 232, [4]. Printed by Lakeside Press, Chicago, in Modernized Old Style type on laid paper. Bound in blue cloth, stamped on sides and spine in yellow; edges uncut.

Copyright October 27, 1899. Price $1.00.

This book is the only Stone publication where the circular monogram, used frequently on bindings, appears on the title-page.

[221]

San Isidro | by | Mrs. Schyler Crowninshield | [*device ten in red*] | Herbert S. Stone & Company | Chicago & New York | MDCCCC [*within double rule border*]

7-1/2 x 4-3/4; pp. [x], 312, [6]. Printed by Lakeside Press, Chicago, in Caslon, Modernized Old Style and Modern-face types on laid paper. Binding designed by Frank Hazenplug; yellow buckram, stamped in green and yellow on sides and spine, palm design on sides. Title rubricated.

Copyright November 11, 1899. Price $1.50.

[222]
Just About a Boy | by | Walter S. Phillips | (El Comancho) | [*device eight in red*] | Herbert S. Stone & Company | Chicago & New York | MDCCCXCIX [*within double rule border*]

6-7/8 x 4-1/4; pp. [x], 233, [1]. Printer not given; Caslon and Modern-face types on laid paper with watermark five. Bound in green cloth stamped in black; ornamental border enclosing lettering on front cover; lettering on spine and back; edges uncut.

Copyright November 11, 1899. Price $1.25. "Second impression" 1900.

"El Comancho" is the well-known hunter, sportsman, and editor of the Pacific Coast; the lettering and border of the binding were done by him.

[223]
The Life of | William Makepeace | Thackeray | by | Lewis Melville | With Portraits and Illustrations | In Two Volumes | Vol. I | [*device ten in red*] | Herbert S. Stone and Company | Chicago and New York | MDCCCXCIX [*within double rule border*]

8-3/4 x 5-3/4; 2 Vols. I: pp. [4], xi, [i], 301, [7]. II: pp. [xii], 345, [3]. Thirty-eight plates inserted. Printed by Lakeside Press, Chicago, in Caslon, Modernized Old Style and black-letter types on laid paper with watermark five; blue endpapers. Bound in red cloth with leather label on spines; ornament on front covers and circular monogram on backs, in gold. Illustrations include portrait frontispieces, and forty reproductions of original covers, illustrations, unpublished drawings, letters, etc.

Copyright November 13, 1899; advertised in *Publishers' Weekly* as "Ready November 22"; listed there December 9. Price $10.00; soon reduced to $7.50. Later issued in cheap red cloth and in three-quarter morocco. Published in England by Hutchinson during September 1899.

"Lewis Melville's" (Lewis S. Benjamin's), was the first substantial life of Thackeray.

[223a] *Large Paper Issue*
9-1/2 x 6-1/4; 2 Vols. I: pp. [4], xi, [i], 301, [3]. II: pp. [xvi], 345, [3].

Printer and type as above; handmade wove paper. Bound in half blue cloth, spines printed in gold; white paper sides, decorated in blue; edges uncut.

100 numbered copies; not advertised for sale.

[224]

The Religion of | To-morrow | by | Frank Crane | "Lo, I am with you alway" | Matthew, XXII, 20 | [*device ten*] | Herbert S. Stone & Company | Chicago & New York | MDCCCXCIX [*within double rule border*]

7-1/2 x 4-1/2; pp. viii, 367, [9]. Portrait frontispiece inserted. Printed by Lakeside Press, Chicago, in Caslon and Modernized Old Style types on laid paper with watermark five. Bound in green ribbed cloth, printed in gold on spine.

Copyright November 22, 1899. Price $1.50.

Dr. Crane's first book. He was then pastor of the Hyde Park Church in Chicago and had recently been contributing "Pulpit Editorials" to the Chicago daily *Record;* see C. H. Dennis, *Victor Lawson* (Chicago: University of Chicago Press, 1935), pp. 165-66.

[225]

Spanish Peggy | A Story of Young | Illinois | by | Mary Hartwell Catherwood | [*device ten*] | Herbert S. Stone & Co.] | Chicago & New York 1899 [*within triple rule border*]

8-11/16 x 5-11/16; pp. [vi], 85, [3]. Frontispiece and twelve plates inserted. Printed by Lakeside Press, Chicago, in Caslon type on laid paper with watermark five. Bound in smooth red cloth, stamped in yellow on sides and spine; illustration in brown on yellow paper, inserted into front cover; circular monogram stamped on back. Illustrations include frontispiece and five plates by J. C. Lyendecker, and five photographs of the Lincoln country.

Copyright November 13, 1899; advertised in *Publishers' Weekly* as "Ready November 22"; listed there December 9. Price $1.50. "Second Impression" in 1899; reissued by Fox, Duffield & Co. in 1906.

The first edition of this book is now of some rarity, being collected for its Lincoln interest. J. B. Oakleaf's *Lincoln Bibliography* (Cedar Rapids: The Torch Press, 1925), No. 297, lists only the Fox, Duffield & Co. reissue of 1906. § The Lyendecker illustrations are not included in the checklist in Bolton's *American Book Illustrators* (New York: R. R. Bowker Company, 1938).

[226]
The | Wonderful Stories of | Jane and John | by | Gertrude Smith | With Illustration by | Alice Woods | [*device eight within double rule border*] | Herbert S. Stone & Company | Chicago & New York | MDCCCXCIX [*within double rule border*]

8-3/4 x 5-5/8; pp. [2], vii, [i], 74, [4]. Ten color plates, including frontispiece, inserted. Printed by Lakeside Press, Chicago, in Caslon type on laid paper with watermark five. Bound in red cloth, stamped in yellow on sides and spine.

Copyright November 13, 1899; listed in *Publishers' Weekly* December 9. Price $1.50.

The Library of Congress copy of this interesting juvenile was missing in 1939; copies were examined in two private collections.

[227]
Famous Trials | Of the Century | Weare and Thurtell | The Burke and Hare Case | The Queen against Courvoisier | Barber's Case | The Queen against Madeleine Smith | The Road Mystery | The Queen against Pritchard | The Tichborne Case | By | J. B. Atlay, M. A. | Barrister-at-Law | Author of 'The Trial of Lord Cochrane' | Chicago and New York | Herbert S. Stone and Co. | London: Grant Richards | MDCCCXCIX

7-1/2 x 5; pp. [iv], vii-[xii], 393, [1]. Frontispiece and five plates (all portraits) inserted. Printed by T. & A. Constable, Edinburgh, in Modernface type on laid paper. Bound in red buckram with paper label on spine; edges uncut.

Listed in *Publishers' Weekly* December 1, 1899. Price $1.75. Richards' edition issued during November, 1899.

[228]
Sir Arthur Sullivan | Life Story, Letters | and Reminiscences | by | Arthur Lawrence | With Critique by B. W. Findon and Bibliography | by Wilfrid Bendall | [*device eight in red*] | Herbert S. Stone and Company | Chicago and New York | MDCCCC [*within double rule border*]

8-3/4 x 5-3/4; pp. [1]-8, [ix]-xii, 340, [2]. Frontispiece, ten plates (all portraits), and eight facsimiles, inserted. Printed by Lakeside Press, Chicago, in Modernized Old Style type on laid paper with watermark five; brown endpapers. Bound in tan buckram with leather label on spine; device five on front cover and circular monogram on back, in gold.

Copyright December 4, 1899. Price $3.50. Bowden's English edition issued during December 1899.

The manuscript was mailed from England on October 10, 1899, and copies were ready for sale in America December 4; the speed naturally affected the quality of bookmaking. § Sir Arthur Sullivan revised the book in manuscript, supplied the music autographs reproduced, and rewrote Chapter XIII "Anecdotal"; it is stated in a letter dated October 10, 1899, from Arthur Lawrence to Bowden, the English publisher.

[229]

Running the Cuban | Blockade; Captain | Jack; The Boy Wreckers | by | William O. Stoddard | Author of "The First Cruiser Out" | Illustrations by F. A. Carter | [*device eight*] | Herbert S. Stone and Company | Chicago and New York | MDCCCC [*within double rule border*]

7-1/2 x 4-3/4; pp. [viii], 200, [4]. Eight plates inserted. Printed by Lakeside Press, Chicago, in Ronaldson Old Style and Caslon types on laid paper with watermark five. Bound in yellow cloth, stamped in black; on front cover with lettering and illustration, on spine with lettering, on back with device five.

Copyright December 4, 1899. Price $1.50. Included 1900 in the "Eldridge Series."

[230]

A | Modern | Reader and Speaker | Edited by | George Riddle | [*device eight*] | Herbert S. Stone and Company | Chicago and New York | MDCCCC [*within double rule border*]

7-7/16 x 4-3/4; pp. [x], 629, [1]. Printer not given but probably Lakeside Press, Chicago; Ronaldson Old Style type; laid paper with watermark five. Bound in blue buckram, printed in gold on spine.

Copyright December 8, 1899; listed in *Publishers' Weekly* December 9. Price $1.50. Reprinted in 1902.

[231]
Famous Ladies | of the [*two florets*] | English Court | by [*two florets*] | Mrs. Aubrey | Richardson | With Eighty-three | Illustrations [*ornament*] | [*ornament*] | Herbert S. Stone & Company | Chicago and New York | MDCCCXCIX

8-1/2 x 5-3/4; pp. xvi, 467, [1]; with signatures. Printed by J. S. Virtue and Company, London, in black-letter and Modernized Old Style types on wove calendared paper. American binding of blue smooth cloth, stamped in silver on sides and spine. Title rubricated.

Listed in *Publishers' Weekly* December 9, 1899. Price $3.50. Published in England by Hutchinson during April 1899.

Preface signed "Jerusha D. Richardson," as author of the book.

[232]
The Seekers | by | Stanley Waterloo | Author of "The Wolf's Long Howl," "The Story of Ab," | "A Man and a Woman," etc. | [*device eight*] | Herbert S. Stone & Company | Chicago & New York | MDCCCC [*within double rule border*]

7-3/8 x 4-3/4; pp. [viii], 257, [7]. Printed by Lakeside Press, Chicago, in Caslon and Modern-face types on laid paper with watermark five. Bound in red cloth, stamped in black on sides and spine with rules and lettering, circular monogram in black on white paper, inserted on sides.

Copyright December 9, 1899. Price $1.50. Included 1900 in "Eldridge Series."

[233]
Rose Island | The Strange Story of a | Love Adventure at Sea | by | W. Clark Russell | [*device eight in red*] | Herbert S. Stone and Company | Chicago and New York | MDCCCXCIX [*within double rule border*]

7-1/2 x 4-3/4; pp. [x], 359, [7]. Printed by Lakeside Press, Chicago, in Caslon and Ronaldson Old Style types on laid paper. Binding designed by Frank Hazenplug; tan cloth; wave design in white across covers and spine; lettering in black on front cover and spine.

Listed in *Publishers' Weekly* December 16. Price $1.25. Published in England by Edwin Arnold during October 1900.

[234]
Henry Irving. | Ellen Terry. | etc. | by | Gordon Craig. A Book of | Portraits | [*lettered in black against design in tan and green*]

12-1/2 x 9-1/2; pp. [42] unnumbered; including nineteen mounted plates. Printed by Lakeside Press, Chicago, in Caslon type on wove paper; drawings on proof paper. Bound in tan paper boards, lettered and decorated in black, red and green front cover; circular monogram on back; edges cut. The plates are colored woodcuts and tinted drawings reproduced in half-tone.

Copyright December 23, 1899. Price $1.00. Not published in England.

This book had its origin with one drawing of the artist's mother, Ellen Terry, and one of her artistic collaborator, Sir Henry Irving, commissioned of Craig in 1898, for *The Chap-Book*. Remaining unused because the magazine was discontinued on July 15, 1898, they were purchased for £10 in the summer of 1899, to be used for Miss Leslie's book of *Players* (No. 235). They did not appear there, but others were ordered to fill out this slim collection, Craig's first published book. The reproductions were made in Chicago, presumably at the Lakeside Press, which did the letterpress; Craig was very dissatisfied with the quality of reproduction, not having seen proof, and even complained that "2 or 3 of the drawings have been *altered* in certain lines." Letter of January 7, 1900, in the Stone family collection.

*[234a] *Special Paper Issue*
An issue of 100 copies on special paper, royal octavo bound in buckram, at $3.50, was advertised in *Publishers' Weekly*. No copy has been located.

[235]
Some Players | Personal Sketches | By | Amy Leslie | [*device ten in orange*] | Herbert S. Stone & Company | Chicago & New York | MDCCCC [*within double rule border*]

7-1/2 x 5; pp. [xii], 624, [4]. Thirty-five portrait plates inserted. Printed by Lakeside Press, Chicago, in Modernized Old Style type on wove paper. Bound in green cloth stamped in gold, on front with lettering and rule, on spine with lettering, on back with circular monogram.

Copyright December 28, 1899; listed in *Publishers' Weekly* December 9. Price $2.00. Reissued in cheap cloth, 1901.

Biographical sketches of sixty-one prominent American, English and French actors and actresses. Reprinted from the Chicago *Daily News,* for which Miss Leslie (Mrs. Lillie West Brown Buck), was for forty years dramatic critic. Portraits of Ellen Terry and Henry Irving by Gordon Craig were to have been included, but they are not; see No. 234.

[235a] *Large Paper Issue*

9-1/2 x 6-1/4; pp. [x], 624, [2]. Thirty-seven portrait plates, and six facsimiles, inserted. Printer and type as above; Japan vellum or hand-made wove paper; red endpapers. Bound in yellow buckram stamped in gold, as above, plus masque of comedy stamped in color on front cover.

"This edition consists of seventy-five copies on Imperial Japanese vellum, numbered from 1 to 75, and one hundred copies on plate paper, numbered from 76 to 175." $5.00 was the price for copies on plate paper, $10.00 for those on Japan.

This issue has additional illustrations in the form of a portrait frontispiece signed by the author, two extra photographs of Ellen Terry and Emma Eames, and facsimiles of autograph letters.

[236]
Glutton or Epicure | Two Booklets in One | by | Horace Fletcher | Including | Nature's Food Filter, or When and What | To Swallow | and | What Sense? or Economic Nutrition | [*floret*] | Herbert S. Stone & Company | Chicago & New York | MDCCCXCIX [*within double rule border*]

6 x 4-1/4; pp. [x], 61, [1]; [vi], 128, [2]. Printed by Lakeside Press, Chicago, in Modernized Old Style type on laid paper; with watermark five in first pamphlet and watermark four in second. Bound together in tan boards; stamped in grey on sides and spine; edges uncut. Each pamphlet has separate title-page, rubricated.

Deposited for copyright March 26, 1900. Listed in *Publishers' Weekly* June 9, 1899; but not included in *Publishers' Trade List Annual* issued August 1899. Price $1.00. Published in London by Stone during August 1900.

What Sense? had been previously issued separately; see No. 167.

[237]
Recent Advances | in | Astronomy | by | Alfred H. Fison, D. Sc. | [*device five*] | Herbert S. Stone & Company | Chicago & New York | MDCCCXCIX

317

7-1/4 x 4-7/8; pp. vi, [ii], 242; with signatures. Printer not given, but printed and bound by Blackie in Glasgow; see No. 147.

Listed in *Publishers' Weekly* February 17, 1900, but advertised there as published, March 11, 1899. Price $1.25. Blackie's edition issued in London during December 1898.

Sixth title imported in the "Victorian Era Series."

[238]
Charles Kingsley | and | The Christian Social Movement | by | Charles William Stubbs, D. D. | Dean of Ely | Author of "Village Politics," "Christ and Democracy," | "Christ and Economics," &c. &c. | [*five lines of quotations*] | Herbert S. Stone & Company | Chicago & New York | MDCCCXCIX

7-1/4 x 4-7/8; pp. viii, [9]-199, [1]; with signatures. Printer not given but printed and bound by Blackie in Glasgow; see No. 147. Device five is printed on verso of title.

Listed in *Publishers' Weekly* February 17, 1900, but advertised there as published, March 11, 1899. Price $1.25. Blackie's edition published in London during January 1899.

Seventh title imported in the "Victorian Era Series."

[239]
The | Science of Life | An | Outline of the History of Biology | and Its Recent Advances | by | J. Arthur Thomson, M. A. | [*two lines of titles*] | [*device five*] | Herbert S. Stone & Company | Chicago & New York | MDCCCXCIX

7-1/4 x 4-7/8; pp. x, 246, [2]; with signatures. Printer not given, but printed and bound by Blackie in Glasgow; see No. 147.

Listed in *Publishers' Weekly* February 17, 1900, but advertised there as published, March 11, 1899. Price $1.25. Blackie's edition issued in London during February 1899.

Eighth and last title imported in the "Victorian Era Series."

[240]
A Man Adrift | being | Leaves from a Nomad's | Portfolio | by | Bart Kennedy | [*device eight*] | Herbert S. Stone & Company | Chicago & New York | MDCCCC [*within double rule border*]

7-1/2 x 4-3/4; pp. viii, 342, [2]; with signatures. Printer not given, but undoubtedly British; Modernized Old Style and Caslon types; laid paper. Bound in tan cloth; lettering, rules and illustration on front cover, in blue and black; lettering on spine, rules and circular monogram on back, in black. See Fig. 31.

Not listed in *Publishers' Weekly*, but included in *American Catalogue* 1895-1900. Price $1.25. Included 1901 in the "Eldridge Series." English edition published during November 1899 by Greening & Co.

[241]
Answers [*rule*] of the [*rule*] Ages | I. K. L. | L. C. W. | [*device eight in red*] | Herbert S. Stone and Company | Chicago and New York | MDCCCC [*within double rule border*]

5-3/4 x 4-1/4; pp. [x], 135, [3]. Printed by Lakeside Press, Chicago, in Ronaldson Old Style and black-letter types on laid paper. Bound in blue ribbed cloth, printed in gold within rule on front cover and spine. Text printed in red and black.

Copyright January 4, 1900; listed in *Publishers' Weekly* March 24. Price 75 cents.

The compilers were probably one person, Clarence Wellford.

[242]
Two Gentlemen | In Touraine | by | Richard Sudbury | [*device eight*] | Herbert S. Stone and Company | Chicago and New York | MDCCCXCIX [*within green decorative border*]

8-1/2 x 6-3/4; pp. [10], iv, 341, [7]. Frontispiece and sixteen plates (all photographs, six double-page), inserted. Printed by Lakeside Press, Chicago, in Ronaldson Old Style and Caslon types on laid paper with watermark five. Bound in green ribbed cloth stamped in gold; lettering and decoration on front cover; lettering on spine. Circular monogram on back cover in gold. Each page of text within green decorative borders.

Copyright January 19, 1900. Price $3.50.

"Richard Sudbury" was a pseudonym for Charles Hammond Gibson of Boston. The other gentleman was "Comte de Persigny."

[243]
The | Bending of the Bough | A Comedy in Five Acts | by | George Moore | Herbert S. Stone & Company | Chicago and New York | 1900 [*against design of green tree*]

6-3/4 x 4-1/4; pp. [4], xxvi, 192, [4]. Printed by Lakeside Press, Chicago, in Modernized Old Style type on laid paper, with watermark five. "Green Tree" binding; see No. 31 and Fig. 24.

Copyright February 21, 1900; listed in *Publishers' Weekly* April 21. Price $1.25. Unwin's English edition listed in *Publishers' Circular* February 24.

Ninth title issued in "The Green Tree Library," the first of two with imprint "Herbert S. Stone & Company." Perhaps more important than the play is the long preface by Moore on "the intentions of the Irish Literary Theatre," actually an extended essay on trends in art history. Joseph Hone's *Life of George Moore* (London: Victor Gollancz Ltd., 1936), pp. 219-23, points out that Moore's play was only a revision of "The Tale of a Town," by Edward Martyn. It was first produced for the "Irish Literary Theatre," of which Martyn, Moore and Yeats were directors, at the Gaiety Theatre in Dublin (by a company of English actors), on February 19, 1900.

[244]

The | Indians of To-day | by | George Bird Grinnell, Ph.D. | Author of "Pawnee Hero Stories and Folk Tales," "Blackfoot Lodge Tales," "The | Story of the Indian," etc., etc. | Illustrated with Full-page Portraits of Living Indians | [*device eight in red*] | Herbert S. Stone & Company | Chicago & New York | MDCCCC [*within double rule border*]

12 x 8-3/4; pp. [xii], 185, [5]. Fifty-five plates inserted. Printed by Lakeside Press, Chicago, in Caslon type on laid paper with watermark six. Bound in tan canvas; rules, lettering and illustration on front cover, in black, red and yellow; rules, lettering and floret on spine, in black; rules and device eight on back cover in black.

Copyright March 17, 1900; listed in *Publishers' Weekly* April 7. Price $5.00. English edition, from American sheets, published by C. Arthur Pearson during October 1900. Revised edition, in smaller format, published by Duffield in 1915.

**[244a] *Handmade Paper Issue*

A "Special Limited Edition of one hundred copies on hand-made paper," at $10.00 net, was advertised in *Publishers' Trade List Annual* for 1899 and 1900. No copy has been located.

[245]

The Valley of the | Great Shadow | by | Annie E. Holdsworth | (Mrs. Lee-Hamilton) | [*device eight in red*] | Herbert S. Stone & Company | Chicago & New York | MDCCCC [*within double rule border*]

7-1/2 x 4-3/4; pp. v, [i], 254, [8]. Printed by Lakeside Press, Chicago, in Modernized Old Style type on laid paper with watermark five. Bound in blue linen; medallion in blue and white on front cover; lettering on front cover and spine in white; circular monogram on back cover against white ground.

Copyright April 2, 1900; listed in *Publishers' Weekly* April 14. Price $1.25. Heinemann's English edition issued during 1900.

Annie Holdsworth was well-known in England as a novelist, even before she married the distinguished poet Eugene Lee-Hamilton, whose *Sonnets of the Wingless Hours* had been issued in America by Stone & Kimball in 1894. But Herbert S. Stone & Company discovered that the American book buying public knew too little of Annie Holdsworth-Lee-Hamilton, and had to ask Heinemann for publicity material. A photograph of Miss Holdsworth holding a copy of this book was sent, and found its way into many American magazines.

[246]
The | Electric Automobile | Its | Construction, Care | and Operation | by | C. E. Woods, E.E., M.E. | [*device eight*] | Herbert S. Stone & Company | Chicago & New York | MDCCCC [*within double rule border*]

7-1/2 x 4-7/8; pp. [2], viii, 177, [3]. Twenty-one plates inserted. Printed by Lakeside Press, Chicago, in Ronaldson Old Style and Caslon types on laid paper with watermark six. Bound in black cloth, stamped in yellow; rules and lettering on both covers and spine, circular monogram on back cover; top edge stained yellow, others uncut.

Copyright April 7, 1900. Price $1.25.

[247]
When We Dead | Awaken | A Dramatic Epilogue in | Three Acts | by | Henrik Ibsen | Translated by | William Archer | Herbert S. Stone & Company | Chicago & New York | MDCCCC [*against design of green tree*]

6-3/4 x 4-3/16; pp. [x], 157, [3]. Printed by Lakeside Press, Chicago, in Modernized Old Style type on laid paper with watermark four. "Green Tree" binding; see No. 31 and Fig. 24.

Copyright April 20, 1900; listed in *Publishers' Weekly* May 5, 1900. Price $1.25. Heinemann's English edition listed in *Publishers' Circular* March 31, 1900.

Tenth and last title issued in "The Green Tree Library." §Ibsen's last play; written in failing health, it does not rank among his greatest efforts, but is most valuable for its personal revelations. Ibsen chose the very title to indicate awareness of the end; and the protagonist is an aging artist who finds the only solution to personal and aesthetic problems in death. Ibsen himself once said that it was meant to be an epilogue to all his dramas since *A Doll's House*.

[248]
Marshfield | The Observer | & | The Death-Dance | Studies of Character & Action | by | Egerton Castle | Author of "The Pride of Jennico," "Young April," | "Consequences," etc., etc. | [*device eight in red*] | Herbert S. Stone & Company | Chicago & New York | MDCCCC [*within double rule border*]

7-7/16 x 4-3/4; pp. [12], xiii, [i], 270; 8 pp. of advertisements inserted. Printer not given; Caslon and Ronaldson Old Style types; laid paper with watermark five. Binding designed by Frank Hazenplug; spine of blue cloth ruled in blind and lettered in white; sides of blue-grey boards; rules, lettering and floral design in blue and white, on front, rules in blue, circular monogram on blue ground, on back.

Listed in *Publishers' Weekly* May 5, 1900. Price $1.50. Published in England during October 1900.

"Marshfield the Observer," six connected short stories, was separately deposited for copyright by the publisher April 20, 1900; "The Death Dance," a long story had been separately copyrighted in 1898 by the author. Two other short stories by Egerton Castle, English novelist, and authority on fencing and bookplates, were copyrighted by Herbert S. Stone & Company in 1899 and 1900; these were "The Herd-Widdiefon," and "Endymion in the Barracks," included in the section "Marshfield the Observer." Two other stories make up the volume: "The Mills of Passion" and "The Phantasm of Passion."

[249]
Po' White Trash | and other | One-Act Dramas | by | Evelyn Greenleaf Sutherland | Certain of the plays being written in | Collaboration with Emma Sheridan- | Fry and Percy

Wallace Mackaye | [*device eight*] | Chicago | Herbert S. Stone and Company | MDCCCC [*within double rule border*]

7-1/2 x 4-3/4; pp. [viii], 232. Printed by Lakeside Press, Chicago, in Caslon and Modern-face types on laid paper with watermark five. Bound in grey cloth, stamped in yellow; on front cover with rules, lettering and floret, spine with lettering, back cover with circular monogram and rules.

Copyright August 4, 1900; listed in *Publishers' Weekly* Price $1.25.

Of the nine plays, "In Far Bohemia" and "Rohan the Silent" were written by Mrs. Sutherland in collaboration with Mrs. Sheridan-Fry; "A Song at the Castle" with Mr. Mackaye. Six of them had been produced— by Henry Woodruff, William Farnum and Alexander Salvini.

[250]
The Idle Born | A Comedy of Manners | by | H. C. Chatfield-Taylor | Author of "Two Women and a Fool," "The Land of the | Castanet," "The Vice of Fools," "An American Peeress," etc. | In Collaboration with | Reginald De Koven | [*device eight in red*] | Herbert S. Stone and Company | Eldridge Court, Chicago | MDCCCC [*within double rule border*]

6-3/4 x 4-1/4; pp. [8], ix, [i], 248, [6]. Printed by Lakeside Press, Chicago, in Modernized Old Style type on laid paper with watermark five. Bound in tan cloth; lettering and decorations in black and silver on front cover; lettering on spine in black; circular monogram against black background on back.

Copyright August 25, 1900; listed in Publishers' Weekly December 1, 1900. Price $1.25.

This collaboration of brothers-in-law had been published as the leading contribution in the first issue of *The Smart Set,* as the winner of a thousand dollar prize for the best novel of society submitted. The Stone advertisement in *Publishers' Weekly* of September 29, 1900, stated that the magazine sold 150,000 copies of the first issue, and that the first edition in book form would consist of 25,000 copies. If this intention was carried out, *The Idle Born* had the largest first printing of any Stone publication. *The Story of Mary McLane* (No. 295) had a first printing of 20,000.

[251]
Little Lords of | Creation | by | H. A. Keays | [*device eight*]

| Herbert S. Stone & Company | Chicago & New York | MDCCCC [*within double rule border*]

6-3/4 x 4-1/4; pp. [viii], 273, [7]. Printed by Lakeside Press, Chicago, in Caslon and Modernized Old Style types on laid paper with watermark five. Bound in tan linen with rules, lettering and decoration in maroon and black on front cover and spine; circular monogram in maroon ground on back cover.

Copyright September 10, 1900; listed in *Publishers' Weekly* December 1, 1900. Price $1.25. Included 1901 in the "Court Series."

The first book of the late Mrs. Hersilia A. (Mitchell) Keays, concerned with the upbringing of a first child.

[252]

The | Engrafted Rose | A Novel | by | Emma Brooke | Author of | "A Superfluous Woman," "The Confession of Stephen | Whapshare," "Transition," and "Life the Accuser" | [*device eight in red*] | Herbert S. Stone and Company | Chicago and New York | MDCCCC [*within double rule border*]

7-3/8 x 4-3/4; pp. [viii], 357, [3]. Printed by Lakeside Press, Chicago, in Modern-face, Caslon and black-letter types, on laid paper with watermark six. Bound in green ribbed cloth, stamped in gold; on front cover with design and lettering; on spine with lettering, on back with lettering.

Entered for copyright February 23, 1900, when copies of pp. 1-147 were deposited. Complete copies deposited September 13, 1900; listed in *Publishers' Weekly* December 1. Price $1.50. Included in the "Eldridge Series," 1901. Hutchinson's English edition published during February 1900.

[253]

The | Fortune of a Day | by | Grace Ellery | Channing-Stetson | [*device eight*] | Chicago | Herbert S. Stone & Company | MDCCCC [*within double rule border*]

6-11/16 x 4-1/4; pp. [viii], 319, [1]. Printer not given; Caslon and Modernized Old Style types; laid paper with watermark five. Bound in tan linen with lettering and illustration on front cover, and lettering on spine, in green and blue; circular monogram, on green ground, on back cover.

Copyright September 14, 1900; listed in *Publishers' Weekly* December 1, 1900. Price $1.50. Included 1901 in the "Court Series."

Mrs. Channing-Stetson had published *The Sister of a Saint and Other Stories,* with Stone & Kimball in 1895, as the second volume in the "Carnation Series" (No. 51).

[254]
A Soul in Bronze | A Novel of Southern California | by | Constance Goddard Du Bois | Author of "A Modern Pagan," "The | Shield of the Fleur-De-Lis," Etc. | [*device eight*] | Herbert S. Stone and Company | Chicago and New York | 1900 [*within double rule border*]

6-11/16 x 4-1/4; pp. [x], 311, [7]. Printed by Lakeside Press, Chicago, in Modern-face type on laid paper with watermark five. Bound in blue cloth; with lettering, decorative border and illustration (of Indian motifs) on front cover, in red and gold; lettering on spine in red; circular monogram on back cover in red.

Copyright September 17, 1900; listed in *Publishers' Weekly* December 1, 1900. Price. $1.25. Included 1901 in the "Court Series."

This story of Indian life by Miss Du Bois, anthropologist and friend of the American Indian, had originally appeared in a California magazine. Dedicated to the memory of Helen Hunt Jackson, it was compared by a few reviewers to *Ramona.*

[255]
Dartnell | A Bizarre Incident | by | Benjamin Swift | Voglio un amore doloro, lento! | Herbert S. Stone Company | Chicago and New York | 1900

7-1/2 x 4-5/8; pp. [iv], 186, [2]; with signatures. Printed by Ballantyne, Hanson & Co., Edinburgh & London, in Modernized Old Style type on wove paper. American binding of blue cloth spine printed in gold; grey board sides with rule border and device five in white on front cover, rule border and circular monogram in white on back; edges uncut.

Listed in *Publishers' Weekly* March 24, 1900. Price $1.25. Issued in England by Heinemann during November 1899.

The first novel of "Benjamin Swift" (William Romaine Paterson, historian and novelist), published in America by Stone; a second, *Nude Souls,* quickly followed (No. 256). The present work was imported in sheets, Heinemann supplying 520 copies, and billing 500 at 10-1/2 d., for a total of £21/17/6. We gather that the American issue was easily disposed of at a reasonable profit (allowing an additional $100 for binding, $50 for advertising and an average 40 per cent discount), about

$200 must have been cleared, and no copies of *Dartnell* were remaindered. This encouraged Stone to contract through Harrison Rhodes, then his London agent, for the right to print *Nude Souls* in America, paying £50 advance on royalties to Mr. Paterson, through Sydney Pawling of Heinemann, who advised Herbert Stone that he had "not read anything for ten years so amazingly strong and in many ways superb as this new book." The second novel, however, was not sufficiently popular to be reprinted, and a good part of the first printing (probably 1,500 copies) had to be remaindered in 1901.

[256]
Nude Souls | A Novel | by | Benjamin Swift | Author of "The Tormentor," "The Destroyer," | "Dartnell," "Siren City," etc. | Der Leib ist in der Seele, nicht die Seele im Leibe | [*device eight in red*] | Herbert S. Stone and Company | Eldridge Court, Chicago | MDCCC [*within double rule border*]

7-1/2 x 4-3/4; pp. [xii], 406, [6]. Printed by Lakeside Press, Chicago, in Ronaldson and Caslon types on laid paper with watermark six. Bound in tan linen; floral design on front cover in green and gold; lettering on front and spine in green; circular monogram on back cover against green background.

Entered for copyright May 19, 1900, when incomplete copies were deposited. Complete copies were deposited September 17, 1900; listed in *Publishers' Weekly* December 8, 1900. Price $1.50. Included 1901 in the "Eldridge Series." Heinemann's English edition published May 17, 1900.

Sydney Pawling of Heinemann's requested that the American edition be issued on May 17th, simultaneously with the English edition, but as English proofs were forwarded only on the day of his letter, April 2, 1900, Stone had time to print only a few pages for copyright purposes (see note to No. 255), deferring actual publication to the fall season. It did not sell well and no further works of Benjamin Swift (William R. Paterson) were published by Stone.

[257]
A | Child of the Sun | by | Charles Eugene Banks | Illustrations by | Louis Betts | [*device eight*] | Herbert S. Stone & Company | Eldridge Court, Chicago | MDCCCC [*within double rule border*]

8-3/8 x 6-1/8; pp. [x], 166, [8]. Sixteen colored plates inserted. Printed by Lakeside Press, Chicago, in Modernized Old Style and Caslon types on laid paper with watermark six. Bound in tan linen; illustration of Indian against setting sun, in brown, white and yellow, on front cover; printing on front and spine in brown; circular monogram on back against brown background.

Copyright September 21, 1900; listed in *Publishers' Weekly* December 1, 1900. Price $1.50. Reprinted about 1903 by Monarch Book Company; in 1905 by Stone. Published in England by C. Arthur Pearson during November 1900, from American sheets.

The only novel of the late C. E. Banks, author of several works of biography, drama and poetry. Banks was then doing newspaper work in Chicago, as was the illustrator. These were the first book illustrations for Stone made by Louis Betts, since well known as a portraitist. Mr. Betts also assisted in the production of the elusive Stone edition of *Uncle Tom's Cabin* (No. 271).

[258]
More | [rule] | Fables | [rule] | by | George | Ade | author of | Fables in Slang | Illustrated | by | Clyde J. | Newman | [rule] | Published by | Herbert S. Stone | and Company | Chicago & New York | MDCCCC [*within decorative border across two pages*]

6 x 4-1/4; pp. [xii], 218, [2]. Four pages of advertisements inserted. Printed by Lakeside Press, Chicago, in Caslon type on laid paper with watermark six. Bound like *Fables in Slang*, No. 219. Title-pages lettered in red and black by Frank Hazenplug. Forty illustrations in line by Clyde J. Newman.

Copyright October 18, 1900; listed in *Publishers' Weekly* December 1. Price $1.00. English publication during September 1902 by C. Arthur Pearson.

More Fables was the last of the Ade books published by Herbert S. Stone & Company. The reason for Mr. Ade's change of publishers is given in his statement of July 23, 1938:

> Robert H. Russell was the first to manage syndicate releases of Fables. The first were released, I think, in 1900. He was handling Pete Dunne's "Dooley" sketches at the same time. I published Forty Modern Fables with Mr. Russell because he had already promoted the material in the syndicate and put me in the way of collecting some important revenues. It was simply an extension of our friendly relations and did not arise from any dissatisfaction regarding my previous relations with Stone & Co.

[259]
Between the Andes | and the Ocean | An Account of an Interest- | ing Journey Down the West | Coast of South America from | The Isthmus of Panama to | The Straits of Magellan | by | William Eleroy Curtis | [*three lines of titles*] | [*device eight in red*] | Herbert S. Stone and Company | Eldridge Court, Chicago | MDCCCC [*within double rule border*]

8-3/4 x 5-3/4; pp. [xii], 442, [2]. Thirty-two plates, including frontispiece, inserted. Printed by Lakeside Press, Chicago, in Ronaldson Old Style and Caslon types on laid paper with watermark six. The illustrations are photographs reproduced in halftone and drawings reproduced by zinc engravings, by Lavin, Schmedtgen, Newman and Ellingson.

Copyright October 29, 1900; listed in *Publishers' Weekly* December 1, 1900. Price $2.50.

Another travel book of W. E. Curtis, like this reprinted from the Chicago *Record,* was published by Stone & Kimball in 1896 (No. 82).

[260]
Love Among the Artists | by | George Bernard Shaw | Author of "Plays Pleasant and Unpleasant," "The Per- | fect Wagnerite," "Three Plays for Puritans," etc. | [*device eight in red*] | Herbert S. Stone and Company | Eldridge Court, Chicago | MDCCCC [*within double rule border*]

7-1/2 x 4-3/4; pp. [4], viii, 3-443, [3]. Printed by Lakeside Press, Chicago, in Ronaldson Old Style type on laid paper with watermark six. Bound in light green linen stamped in green; on front cover with lettering, rules and floral design, on spine with lettering, on back cover with circular monogram.

Copyright October 29, 1900; listed in *Publishers' Weekly* December 8, 1900. Price $1.50. Reprinted by Stone in 1905, reissued by Brentano's in 1909.

This is a famous "Anglo-American First Edition"; being the first printing in book form of Shaw's third novel, written in the eighties. It was reissued by Brentano's in 1909, but not published in London until Constable issued a cheap edition in 1914. The definitive words on the history of this novel have been spoken by Maurice Holmes in *Some Bibliographical Notes on the Novels of George Bernard Shaw* (London: Dulau & Co.

Ltd. [1930]). Mr. Holmes lays the ghost previously raised in the Shaw bibliography of Geoffrey H. Wells, of an earlier edition "pirated" by Stone or some other American publisher. Holmes proves that Stone's was the first printing since the novel's original appearance in *Our Corner* between November 1887 and December 1888. Holmes, and later Henderson, both with the assistance of G. B. S., make it clear that the American publication of this book was in no sense a "piracy," but was approved and probably suggested in 1900 by Shaw. Herbert S. Stone & Co., authorized American publishers of Shaw's plays and criticism since 1897 (see Nos. 150, 169, and pp. 100-1), found themselves in competition with Brentano's, who were responding to the Shavian boom by publishing new editions of his works not copyrighted in America; issuing *Cashel Byron's Profession* in 1899 and *An Unsocial Socialist* in 1900. Shaw later rewarded Brentano's for their interest by insisting on the transfer of his copyrights to them in 1906, when Fox, Duffield & Co. succeeded to the Stone business. In 1900, however, writes Archibald Henderson, ". . . Shaw saw no reason why his own publisher should not 'exploit the new field of derelict fiction' and made the necessary changes in the text of *Love Among the Artists,* in the serialized form, to enable Stone to secure copyright."— *Bernard Shaw: Playboy and Prophet* (New York, D. Appleton and Company, 1932), p. 109.

[261]
Griselda | by | Basil King | "—Forgiveness, sweet | To be granted, or received." | —Wordsworth. | Herbert S. Stone and Company | Eldridge Court, Chicago | MDCCCC [*within double rule border*]

6-3/4 x 4-1/4; pp. [x], 333, [9]. Printed by Lakeside Press, Chicago, in Ronaldson Old Style and Caslon types on laid paper with watermark six. Binding designed by "G"; red cloth with heraldic and floral border in black and gold on front cover enclosing lettering in gold; lettering on spine in gold; circular monogram on gold ground on back cover.

Copyright November 10, 1900; listed in *Publishers' Weekly* December 8, 1900. Price $1.25. Included 1901 in the "Court Series."

Basil King is best remembered for his religious writings and his novel *The Street Called Straight.*

[262]
The Inn of the | Silver Moon | by | Herman Knickerbocker Viele | [*device ten in red*] | Herbert S. Stone & Company | Eldridge Court, Chicago | MDCCCC [*within double rule border*]

6-1/2 x 4-1/4; pp. [x], 198, [4]. Frontispiece and eight plates inserted. Printed by Lakeside Press, Chicago, in Modernized Old Style and Caslon types on laid paper with watermark six. Binding designed by Mary Prindiville; mauve smooth cloth with illustration and lettering on front cover in black and white; lettering on spine in black; circular monogram on back against black ground. The illustrations are drawings by Edward Cucuel, reproduced in halftone.

Copyright November 23, 1900; listed in *Publishers' Weekly* December 8, 1900. Price $1.25. Published in England by Murray during December 1902.

The author was the oldest (born 1856) son of the Union general Egbert Ludovicus Vielé, and Teresa (Griffin) Vielé, writer on life along the Indian frontier. Herman Knickerbocker Vielé studied civil engineering in his father's office in New York and practiced there and in Washington, where he was responsible for much of the capital's expansion during the eighties. Retiring from business in 1894, he indulged first his taste for painting, and held several exhibitions in New York and elsewhere. In literature he was more successful; *The Inn of the Silver Moon*, his first book, and the second, *The Last of the Knickerbockers* (No. 284) were well received, as were six others published before his death in 1908. § Egbert Ludovicus Vielé Jr., a brother younger by seven years, is well known as the French poet Francis Vielé-Griffin.

[263]
Three Plays | for Puritans | by Bernard Shaw: | Being the Third Volume | of his Collected Plays | [*device five*] | Chicago and New York | Herbert S. Stone and | Company, MDCCCCI

7-5/8 x 4-3/4; pp. [2], xxxviii, [3]-315, [3], including advertisements and colophon. Printed by Lakeside Press, Chicago, in Caslon type on thin laid paper with watermark six. Bound in dark blue-green smooth cloth with paper label on spine; edges uncut. See Fig. 35.

Entered for copyright in 1900; two copies of the prefaces and all but the last page of the first act of "The Devil's Disciple" deposited for copyright November 30, 1900 (pp. xxxviii, 30); but complete copies not deposited until February 23, 1901. Advertised in *Publishers' Weekly* November 24, 1900 as *Four Plays for Puritans;* the same title listed there December 8. Price $1.50. *Three Plays for Puritans* advertised as ready in *Publishers' Weekly* March 16, 1901, quoting from a review in the Chicago *Times Herald* (by George Horton, February 28, 1901). Grant Richards' English edition listed in *Publishers' Circular* for January 19, 1901.

Contains three prefaces: "Why for Puritans?"; "On Diabolonian Ethics";

and the famous "Better than Shakspear?"; three plays: "The Devil's Disciple" (produced by Richard Mansfield in 1897 and Shaw's first 'successful' play); "Caesar and Cleopatra," and "Captain Brassbound's Conversion"; each with its "Notes." The New York *Critic* of August 1900 quotes a contemporary letter of Shaw concerning this volume:

> My next volume of plays will be called 'Three Plays for Puritans,' and will contain 'The Devil's Disciple,' 'Caesar and Cleopatra,' and 'Captain Brassbound's Conversion,' the play I wrote last summer for Ellen Terry. The reason that I call 'Caesar and Cleopatra' 'the play that beat Mr. Mansfield,' is that after his success in 'The Devil's Disciple,' which I class only as a melodrama, I wanted him to try higher and harder, and play Julius Caesar. When he blenched, there were ructions, and I am still in my most boundless attitude toward him and all the others.

Geoffrey H. Wells' bibliography of Shaw lists as No. 25 the Richards edition, with note: "This edition was published in January 1901. The first American issue (Stone, Chicago) bore the date 1900, but Shaw writes that publication 'was simultaneous, whatever date was put on the imprint.'" While the incomplete copyright deposits made by Stone were dated 1900, all copies of the published edition examined are dated 1901.

[264]
The Life of | [*two florets*] Edward Fitz-Gerald | By John Glyde [*two florets*] | With an Introduction by Edward Clodd | Sometimes President of the Omar Khayyam Club | Chicago and New York [*two florets*] | Herbert S. Stone and Company | 1900

7-5/8 x 5; pp. xvi, 358, [2]; with signatures. Frontispiece portrait inserted. Printed by T. & A. Constable, Edinburgh, in Modernized Old Style type on wove paper. American binding of green ribbed cloth with paper label on spine; edges uncut.

Listed in *Publishers' Weekly* December 8, 1900. Price $2.00. English publication by C. Arthur Pearson made during April 1900.

The Appendix includes a "Bibliography of the versions and editions of the *Rubaiyat* of Omar Khayyam, by Edward Fitz-Gerald and others, which have been published in England, the United States, and on the Continent. Arranged according to date of publication," pp. 341-348. This was made with the help of "a list issued by Mr. Mosher, Portland, Maine, who has published a larger number of Fitz-Gerald's translations than any other publisher in the United States." There is also a "Bibliography of articles in Reviews and Magazines relating to Fitz-Gerald and Omar," pp. 349-[359].

[265]

The Monk Wins | by | Edward H. Cooper | [*device eight*] | Herbert S. Stone & Company | Eldridge Court, Chicago | MDCCCC [*within double rule border*]

7-7/16 x 4-3/4; pp. [viii], 351, [1]; with signatures. Printer not given but plates are British; Modernized Old Style type in text, Caslon for title-page (set in United States); laid paper with watermark six. Bound in blue mottled linen with spur and harness decoration in black and white on front cover; rule border and lettering in black on front; lettering in black on spine; circular monogram on black ground on back.

Listed in *Publishers' Weekly* December 8, 1900. Price $1.50. Included 1901 in the "Eldridge Series." English publication by Duckworth made during October 1900.

The second of two novels of English sporting life by E. H. Cooper published by Stone. *Resolved to Be Rich* (No. 214) was even less well appreciated by American bookbuyers than *The Monk Wins*.

[266]

Wooings and Weddings | In Many Climes | by | Louise Jordan Miln | Author of | "When We Were Strolling Players in the East," "Quaint Korea," | "An Actor's Wooing," "Little Folk of Many Lands," etc., etc. | With Many Illustrations | Herbert S. Stone & Company | Chicago & New York | MDCCCC

8-11/16 x 5-5/8; pp. xx, 395, [1]; with signatures. Forty-eight plates, including frontispiece, inserted. Printed by William Brendon & Son, Plymouth [England], in Caslon and Modernized Old Style types on wove paper; endpapers and inserted leaves at front and back on laid paper with Stone's watermark six. American binding of white buckram stamped in gold; lettering on front cover within rococo decorative frame; lettering on spine and device five on back. Illustrations from photographs.

Listed in *Publishers' Weekly* December 8, 1900. Price $7.50. English publication made by C. Arthur Pearson during October 1900.

The binding title, by which this volume was advertised and has since been known, is *Wooings and Weddings in Many Lands*.

[267]

The | Conscience of Coralie | by | F. Frankfort Moore | Author of "The Jessamy Bride," "The Impudent | Comedian," etc. | [*device eight*] | Herbert S. Stone & Company | Chicago & New York | MDCCCC [*within double rule border*]

7-1/2 x 4-7/8; pp. [vi], 465, [7]. Eight plates, by F. H. Townsend, inserted. Printed by Lakeside Press, Chicago, in Caslon type on laid paper with watermark six. Bound in red cloth stamped in white with rules and lettering; device five on sides.

Entered for copyright September 21, 1900; copies deposited January 15, 1901. Listed in *Publishers' Weekly* December 8, 1900. Price $1.50. Published in England by C. Arthur Pearson during September 1900.

The third and last American publication of F. Frankfort Moore with Stone; *The Jessamy Bride* (No. 126) was the only startling success.

[268]
The Love of an | Uncrowned Queen | Sophie Dorothea, Consort | of George I., and her Correspondence | with Philip Christopher Count Königs- | marck (Now first published from the originals) | by | W. H. Wilkins | M. A. Clare College, Cambridge, | Fellow of the Royal Historical Society | Author of "The Romance of Isabel Lady Burton" | With 42 Portraits and Illustrations | Vol. I | Herbert S. Stone & Company | Chicago and New York | MDCCCC

9 x 5-3/4; 2 Vols.; with signatures. I: pp. xv, [i], 341, [3]. Frontispiece and ten other portraits, eight photographs, and two facsimiles, inserted. II: pp. vii, [i], 343-673, [1]. Frontispiece and nine other portraits, nine photographs, and two facsimiles, inserted. Printed by Hazell, Watson, & Viney, Ld., London and Aylesbury, in Caslon and black-letter types on laid paper. Bound in red cloth; stamped on front cover with double rule border in gold, and coronet in gold, blue and white; spine with rules and lettering in gold; back cover with double rule border in gold and circular monogram on gold ground; edges uncut. Titles rubricated; title-leaf for Vol. I a cancel.

Listed in *Publishers' Weekly* December 8, 1900. Price $7.50 net. Published in London by Hutchinson earlier in 1900.

A larger and cheaper edition of these letters was soon called for. The Lakeside Press printed a one-volume edition for publication in April 1901 (No. 274).

*[269]
The Wide, Wide World. By Susan Warner. With Illustrations

by Fred Pegram. Chicago: Herbert S. Stone & Company; London: C. Arthur Pearson, 1901.

8vo, cloth. Price $1.00.

Advertised in *Publishers' Weekly* March 16, 1901, together with Nos. 270 and 271, as "Three Old Books in New Dress. These reprints are from entirely new plates, beautifully illustrated, and attractively bound in cloth. The series is issued in connection with C. Arthur Pearson, of London."

Up to time of going to press, no copy of this edition had been seen by the compiler. He is confident, however, that the book exists. Pearson's English issue is listed in the *English Catalogue* for October 1900. A Grosset & Dunlap edition, not dated but issued about 1903, has been examined, which bore on the verso of the title this legend: "The Copyright of the Illustrations in this volume is the | property of Herbert S. Stone & Company."

*[270]
Pilgrim's Progress. By John Bunyan. With Illustrations by H. M. Brock. Chicago: Herbert S. Stone & Company; London: C. Arthur Pearson, 1901.

8vo, cloth. Price $1.00.

Advertised in *Publishers' Weekly* March 16, 1901, together with Nos. 269 and 271.

No copy of this edition has been seen by the compiler, with Stone imprint. Pearson's English issue, listed in the *English Catalogue* for September 1900, is not dated, and bears on verso of title this legend: "The Copyright of the Illustrations in this volume is the property of C. Arthur Pearson, Ltd."

*[271]
Uncle Tom's Cabin. By Harriet Beecher Stowe. With Illustrations by Louis Betts. Chicago: Herbert S. Stone & Company; London: C. Arthur Pearson, 1901

8vo, cloth. $1.00.

Advertised in *Publishers' Weekly* March 16, 1901, together with Nos. 269 and 270. Pearson's English issue is listed in the English Catalogue for April 1901. No copy has been seen by the compiler, but Mr. Louis Betts, the artist, has in recent correspondence assured him that the American issue was actually published.

[272]

Chapters | from | Illinois History | by | Edward G. Mason | [*device ten in red*] | Herbert S. Stone and Company | Eldridge Court, Chicago | MDCCCCI [*within double rule border*]

9-3/8 x 6-1/4; pp. [x], 322, [8]. Frontispiece portrait inserted. Printed by Lakeside Press, Chicago, in Ronaldson Old Style and Caslon types on laid paper. Bound in grey cloth stamped in black on sides and spine. Title rubricated.

Copyright February 14, 1901. Price $2.00.

Posthumously collected papers of this distinguished Chicago antiquarian. The longest contribution, "The Land of the Illinois," had not been printed before.

[272a] *Plate Paper Issue*

9-3/8 x 6-1/4; pp. [x], 322, [8]. Frontispiece portrait, edition notice, and fourteen plates, all on Japan paper, inserted. Printer and type as above; "Old Stratford" wove plate paper. Bound in thin vellum over stiff boards; rules and lettering in gold on spine; double rule borders on sides.

"This edition is limited to One Hundred copies, of which this is No. ...." Price $10.00 net.

This issue was advertised as "extra-illustrated." The plates are chiefly reproductions of paintings and monuments.

[273]

Graustark | [*rule*] | The Story of a Love | Behind a Throne | [*rule*] | By | George Barr McCutcheon | [*rule*] | [*device ten in red*] | [*rule*] | Herbert S. Stone and Company | Eldridge Court, Chicago | MDCCCCI [*within double rule border*].

7-7/16 x 4-3/4; pp. [viii], 459, [3]. Printer not given, but Lakeside Press, Chicago; Ronaldson Old Style type; laid paper. Bound in grey-blue cloth; stamped in white, front cover including a pictorial design with lettering.

Published March 21, 1901, according to later advertisements; listed in *Publishers' Weekly* March 23; but not deposited for copyright until April 10, and earliest inscribed (to Lucy Monroe) copy observed is dated April 8, 1901. Price $1.50. Over 100,000 copies of original edition sold before reprints were made, beginning late 1902; in paper for American News Company, cloth for Grosset & Dunlap, half leather for Hurst & Company. Transferred in 1905 to Dodd, Mead & Company and has remained in print, in editions from this house and Grosset & Dunlap. English editions published by Grant Richards April 1902; translations include a Norwegian edition issued 1913 at Decorah, Iowa by B. Anundsen Publishing Company.

"Noble's" for "Lorry's" in line 6 of page 150, as distinguishing the first printing from later ones, is an accepted point, but the significance of this slip, not a printer's mistake but an editorial lapse, is not so generally known. In McCutcheon's original draft, the hero's name was John Noble; it was changed by the publishers to Grenfell Lorry. The reduction of the manuscript in size and other changes were begun by Herbert Stone, Lucy Monroe and Wallace Rice, and completed by a fourth editor. § The outright purchase of the manuscript, to permit freedom in revision, also enabled the Stones to give it an advertising budget unusual for their books. With well-managed publicity and on its own merits, *Graustark* became a national best-seller within two months of its publication, and established McCutcheon, with his first book, among the most popular of American romanticists. For this reason and because he was voluntarily paid royalties on reprints, McCutcheon never considered the sale price of $500 a bad bargain, remaining on the friendliest terms with the Stones and bringing them his next two novels. See Nos. 296, 299, pp. 127-29. and articles on McCutcheon in *Bookman,* October 1911, May 1925, January 1929.) § This was first edition bound for Stone by the Lakeside Press, according to Mr. H. P. Zimmerman; there are many variant bindings, especially on the second issue of the first edition.

[274]

The Love of an | Uncrowned Queen | Sophie Dorothea, Consort | of George I., and her Correspondence | with Philip Christopher Count Königs- | marck (Now first published from the originals) | by | W. H. Wilkins | M. A., Clare College, Cambridge, | Fellow of the Royal Historical Society, | Author of "The Romance of Isabel Lady Burton." | [*device ten in red*] | Herbert S. Stone and Company | Chicago and New York | MDCCCCI

8 x 5-3/8; pp. [4], xi, [i], 578, [6]. Frontispiece portrait inserted. Printed by Lakeside Press, Chicago, in Ronaldson Old Style, Caslon and black-letter types on laid paper. Bound in red cloth; stamped on front cover with rule border in gold, and coronet in gold, blue and white; spine with rules and lettering in gold; back cover with rule border and device five in gold.

Copyright April 12, 1901. Price $2.00 net.

New, and first American, impression of No. 268, which had been issued from sheets supplied by the English publisher. Hutchinson also issued a one volume "popular edition" in 1901. A "New and Revised Edition" was issued by Longmans Green & Company in 1903, for both England and America. Stone's sheets were reissued from New York during 1906, by his successor.

[275]
Mexico City | An Idler's Note-Book | [rule] | by | Olive Percival | [rule] | [device ten] | [rule] | Herbert S. Stone and Company | Eldridge Court, Chicago | MDCCCCI [within double rule border]

6-1/4 x 4-1/4; pp. [x], 208, [6]. Seven plates, including frontispiece, inserted. Printer not given; Ronaldson Old Style type; laid paper with watermark six. Bound in tan cloth; illustration and lettering in blue and black on front cover; lettering on spine and circular monogram on back, in black. Binding and five illustrations designed by Frank Hazenplug; two plates are from photographs.

Copyright May 11, 1901; listed in *Publishers' Weekly* March 23, 1901. Price $1.25.

Miss Percival's first book; reprinted in part from the *Times* of Los Angeles, where the author was then an insurance underwriter.

[276]
Mrs. Reginald De Koven | [rule] | By the | Waters of Babylon | [rule] | [device ten in red] | [rule] | Herbert S. Stone and Company | Eldridge Court, Chicago | MDCCCCI [within double rule border]

7-1/2 x 4-3/4; pp. [viii], 348, [4]. Printed by Lakeside Press, Chicago, in Modernized Old Style type on laid paper. Bound in blue ribbed cloth; lettering and decoration in black and white on front cover; lettering on spine in white; circular monogram on back cover, on white ground.

Copyright May 11, 1901; listed in *Publishers' Weekly* June 1. Price $1.50. Anna Farwell De Koven's first book, *A Sawdust Doll*, concerned with contemporary society, had been issued by Stone & Kimball in their "Peacock Library" of 1895. This historical romance was her second novel, and the last book published with Stone.

> *By the Waters of Babylon* was written amid many social occupations during the winter of 1901 in our second 16th Street (Washington)

house, and brought me my first experience in the search for historical atmosphere. I dipped, all unconscious of the extent of the domain, into Assyriology in my efforts to learn something of Babylon and its Persian kings. My earnestness quite terrified Mr. Adler, then the curator of the Smithsonian Institution, who was a very respected authority on this period. "My God! she is serious!" I heard him whisper under his breath as I plied him with questions. With great patience he took several weeks, as he admitted, to prepare answers to some of them. As I reread this book, with its Babylonian cover depicting the towers of the city, I find it satisfactory in description and the evocation of the painted palaces, the rivers and walls and the burning desert, but wholly devoid of any adequate characterization of the persons of the story. The attempt to realize apparently living people in so distant and unfamiliar a period has failed in the hands of many writers, whose names I would not dare to mention. It was indeed far beyond my capacity, but the descriptive parts were praised in the critical reviews, and its dramatic possibilities, as I have related, very nearly attained to public and possibly successful recognition.—Mrs. Reginald DeKoven, *A Musician And His Wife* (New York: Harper and Brothers, 1926), pp. 194-95. On pp. 147-49 Mrs. DeKoven also relates the origin of her interest in Greek and Asiatic history, from a comment made by Oscar Wilde in London.

[277]
Ezra Caine | by | Joseph Sharts | [*device ten*] | Chicago: Published by | Herbert S. Stone & Company | MDCCCCI [*within double rule border*]

7-3/8 x 4-5/8; pp. [viii], 142, [6]. Printed by Lakeside Press, Chicago, in Caslon type on laid paper with watermark six. Bound in green ribbed cloth; lettering and design in grey and turquoise on front cover; lettering on spine in white; circular monogram on back cover on turquoise ground. Title rubricated.

Copyright May 20, 1901; listed in *Publishers' Weekly* June 22. Price $1.25.

Joseph Sharts, Harvard '97, read the long 'ghost story' of *Ezra Caine* as a class exercise in the famous course "English 22" under William Vaughn Moody. Melville E. Stone Jr., hearing it there in 1895, suggested that it be submitted to Stone & Kimball, who a year later, declined it. On May 7, 1900, Mr. Sharts wrote to Herbert S. Stone & Co., offering a new work, *The Romance of a Rogue*. This was accepted and published in 1902 (No. 293). But 'Ned' Stone, then junior partner in the firm remembered *Ezra Caine* and asked for it again. § The copy Mr. Sharts presented to his

Dayton, Ohio, schoolmate and Harvard room-mate, H. M. Lydenberg, Harvard '97, now director of the New York Public Library, is inscribed:

> To *Harry M. Lydenberg*
> Who
> Stood by and Comprehended
> When
> The Machine turned this
> Out
> With the compliments of
> The Machine.

[278]

Sawdust & | Spangles | [*rule*] | Stories & Secrets | of the Circus | [*rule*] | by | W. C. Coup | [*rule*] | [*device ten in red*] | [*rule*] | Herbert S. Stone and Company | Eldridge Court, Chicago | MDCCCCI [*within double rule border*]

7-1/2 x 4-3/4; pp. [4], xv, [i], 262, [6]. Ten plates, including frontispiece, inserted. Printer not given but probably Lakeside Press, Chicago; Ronaldson Old Style and Caslon types; laid paper with watermark six. Bound in red cloth; front cover has picture of clown in black and white, and lettering in red; spine has lettering in black; back cover has circular medallion on black ground.

Copyright May 25, 1901; listed in *Publishers' Weekly* June 22. Price $1.50.

William Cameron Coup, who died in Chicago in 1895, was a well-known figure in the showmen's world. As a circusman, he had brought P. T. Barnum back into the field; he had built the original Aquarium and Hippodrome in New York, and in 1883, the Chicago Museum. The autobiographical manuscript left at his death was published by his son, who contributed an unsigned "Foreword." § Most extant copies bear presentation inscription from W. W. Coup. It is believed that most of the edition was taken up by the Coup family for presentation to friends in the show business. Mr. Walter Scholl of Chicago, owner of an outstanding collection on circus history, believes that the book as printed is largely *not* the work of W. C. Coup. § *Sawdust & Spangles* is rare today in any condition, but a prime copy should have these points: (1) Glassine protective wrapper. This is the only Stone publication absolutely known to have had a dust-jacket. (2) Front fly-leaf present (often torn out), with inscription. (3) Frontispiece a portrait of W. C. Coup. There were only a limited supply of these and before the complete edition was bound a picture of a 'Circus Lady,' signed "G. Verbeek" was substituted. (4) Nine plates in text (there is no list of illustrations), as follows:

1. "Capturing Wild Animals for the Show," signed "Verbeek"; facing p. 24.
2. "When a White Elephant Was Needed," not signed; facing p. 40.
3. "Then the Shout Would Go Down the Line for Romeo," signed "Verbeek"; facing p. 78.
4. "When Rival Showmen Burned a Bridge . . ." not signed; facing p. 114.
5. 'The Herd of Young Elephants,' signed "Gustave Verbeek"; facing p. 126.
6. 'The Early Steps in Training Wild Animals,' signed "Gustave Verbeek"; facing p. 175.
7. "Every Lion Gave a Roar and Made a Wild Leap," signed "Verbeek"; facing p. 182.
8. 'A Bear Loose in Fifth Avenue,' signed "Gustave Verbeek"; facing p. 210.
9. "A Spectator Jumped into the Ring and Tried to Shoot the Clown," signed "Gustave Verbeek"; facing p. 218.

[279]
Euphrosyne | [rule] | and | Her "Golden Book" | [rule] | By Elsworth Lawson | [rule] | [device nine] | [rule] | H. S. Stone & Company | Chicago MDCCCCI [within double rule border]

7-1/2 x 4-3/4; pp. [xii], 141, [7]. Printed by Lakeside Press, Chicago, in Caslon black-letter, roman and italic types on laid paper with watermark six. Bound in light green smooth cloth; front cover and spine stamped with rules, lettering and ornament, in green and gold; back cover has Bradley ornament in green. Title rubricated.

Copyright May 31, 1901; advertised in *Publishers' Weekly* March 16; listed there June 22. Price $1.25.

Elsworth Lawson's first book, followed in 1903 by a second and last, *From the Unvarying Star* (London & New York: The Macmillan Company). *Euphrosyne's* advertisement in *Publishers' Weekly* stated: "One of the largest wholesalers of books advised the publishers not to issue this story, because it was 'too good to be popular.' Notwithstanding the fact, we are issuing the book in order to prove that no book can be too good."
§ The design of *Euphrosyne* is modelled, unsuccessfully, on *Love's Dilemmas* (No. 180), printed by Will Bradley at the University Press in 1899. The choice of types is identical, but the paper and presswork inferior; the specially designed publisher's device is used, but not the baroque orna-

ment which balanced it; the Bradley decorative initials appear at chapter openings; and a floral ornament is reproduced on the back cover.

**[280]
An American Book of Gardening. By Ida D. Bennett. Chicago: Herbert S. Stone & Company, 1901.

8vo, cloth. Price $2.00.

Listed in the "Weekly Record of New Publications" in *Publishers' Weekly* for August 24, 1901, with star indicating that the book had not been seen. It was first advertised by Stone in *Publishers' Weekly* on March 16, 1901, at $1.50. The issue of May 25 was more definite: "With nearly 200 illustrations. 8vo, cloth. $2.00." Another listing of the title appeared in *Publishers' Trade List Annual* for September 1901.

A four-page leaflet of new publications, issued early autumn 1901, also included the *American Book of Gardening*. The copy preserved by Mr. W. J. Kirk of Oak Park has a pencilled note opposite: "Wanted." This may mean that the published book was wanted by a bookseller, or that manuscript was wanted by the publisher. Mr. Kirk, then office manager of Herbert S. Stone & Company, has no copy of the book in his collection of Stone imprints, nor does he remember its publication. No entry was made, and no copy deposited, at the Copyright Office. There is no copy in the Library of Congress, nor in any of the large libraries throughout the country which contribute to the Union Catalog. Application to the Garden Club of America, and reference to horticultural dictionaries, brought no results. § Opinion: The book was never published by Stone; the manuscript perhaps transferred to McClure, Phillips & Company, who issued the late Miss Bennett's first book, *The Flower Garden,* in 1903.

*[281]
The Christmas Garland: A Miscellany of Verses, Stories and Essays. Chicago: Herbert S. Stone & Company, 1901.

Advertised in *Publishers' Weekly* March 16, 1901 and later; listed in the "Weekly Review of New Publications" in Publishers' Weekly for December 28, 1901, with * indicating that the book had not been seen. A copy of the book was apparently seen by the late Frederick Winthrop Faxon, who listed it as No. 105 in his careful bibliography of "Literary Annuals," in *Bulletin of Bibliography* for July 1908. It is listed as having been examined by the compiler, but no copy has been preserved in Mr. Faxon's personal or business library. *The Christmas Garland* of 1901 was not entered for copyright (being reprint material) and no copy is listed in the Union Catalog of the Library of Congress. § Opinion: On the strength of Mr. Faxon's authority and because the title was so often advertised by Stone, the compiler presumes that it exists. There were two issues, according to the Publishers' Weekly advertisement of September 28, 1901, which gives the fullest information about the book:

> THE CHRISTMAS GARLAND: A Miscellany of Verses, Stories, and Essays By Well-Known Authors. Illustrated in colors. Two editions. Limited edition de luxe, bound in white padded silk, gilt edges, in a box, $3.50 net. Popular edition, bound in white vellum cloth, gilt top, in a box, $2.00.
>
> Messrs. Herbert S. Stone & Company have pleasure in announcing a modern revival of the "Gift Book" so popular in this country fifty years or more ago. It is believed the public will welcome a collection of verses and stories by the best known writers, selected with judgment, and printed and bound with taste.
>
> The authors include Octave Thanet, Maurice Thompson (author of "Alice of Old Vincennes"), Maria Louise Pool, George Ade, Louise Chandler Moulton, Clyde Fitch, John Burroughs, I. Zangwill, Ella Wheeler Wilcox, John Kendrick Bangs, Edmund Gosse, Robert Louis Stevenson, and many others. The illustrations are all in color and cover a wide variety of popular subjects. The book is admirably adapted to the holiday season, beautifully printed, bound and boxed.
>
> This is a novelty and is just what your holiday trade wants.

[282]

Animals | [*rule*] | A Popular Natural | History of Wild Beasts | [*rule*] | by Wallace Rice | [*rule*] | [*device eight in red*] | [*rule*] | Herbert S. Stone & Company | Publishers Chicago MDCCCCI [*within double rule border*]

9-1/4 x 7-1/8; pp. xxii, 313, [5]. Forty-nine colored plates, including frontispiece, inserted. Printed by Lakeside Press, Chicago, in Ronaldson Old Style and Caslon types on laid paper. Bound in light green cloth, stamped in green on sides and spine; device four on back; edges trimmed. Copyright October 21, 1901; listed in *Publishers' Weekly* November 9. Price $2.00.

This book was written, the author stated in 1938, to put to use the colored photographs by A. W. Mumford, of the Nature Study Company. These had been separately copyrighted by Mumford in 1900 and soon after were acquired by Herbert S. Stone & Company.

[283]

Cashel Byron's Profession | Newly Revised | With Several

Prefaces and an Essay on Prizefighting | Also | The Admirable Bashville | or, Constancy Unrewarded | Being the Novel of Cashel Byron's Profession | done into a Stage Play in Three | Acts and in Blank Verse | by | George Bernard Shaw | Author of "Plays Pleasant and Unpleasant," "The Perfect | Wagnerite," "Three Plays for Puritans," | "Love Among the Artists," etc. | [*device ten in red*] | Herbert S. Stone and Company | Eldridge Court, Chicago | MDCCCCI [*within double rule border*]

7-1/2 x 4-3/4; pp. xxvi, 376, [2]. Printed by Lakeside Press, Chicago, in Modernized Old Style and Caslon types on laid paper. Bound in chocolate-brown linen; stamped on front cover with figure of a pugilist in white, and lettering including legend "Authorized Edition" in black, all within black rule border; spine lettered in black; device five in black on back cover. *The Admirable Bashville* has separate half-title and title, pp. [305-8].

Copyright October 23, 1901; listed in *Publishers' Weekly* November 9. Price $1.50. Not reprinted by Stone, but appears in a secondary binding of violet-brown cloth as above. Grant Richards' English edition listed in the *English Catalogue* for October 1901; but not in *Publishers' Circular*.

Shaw's fourth novel, which originally appeared in the English periodical *To-Day* between April 1885 and March 1886. H. H. Champion, editor of the magazine, put together an edition of 1,000 copies from the type of its periodical appearance, and issued it from the "Modern Press" in April 1886. The first American publication was as No. 109, December 31, 1886, of "Harper's Handy Series"; it soon after appeared as No. 937 of George Munro's "Seaside Library." In 1899 Brentano's published an edition of *Cashel Byron's Profession,* presumably copied from the "New Edition, Revised," which had been published in London by Walter Scott in 1889. When Shaw heard of the Brentano "piracy" he returned the £10 "honorarium" which Harper's, as was their pleasant custom, had sent him in 1886. Also as a matter of principle, they refused to accept the money, and there ensued an extraordinary, amusing and important correspondence, surely on the highest moral level of any communications between an American publisher and an English author, on the question of "piracy." This was printed complete in *The Critic* for August 1900, pp. 114-16, and has been excerpted by Henderson, but has apparently escaped the attention of students of international copyright. Shaw was much more concerned at this time with the commercial value of his dramatic copyrights, and, as Henderson writes in the revised edition of the biography:

When Shaw heard rumors that there were several American stage versions of *Cashel Byron's Profession,* and that one of these had actually been played in New York, with the boxing scenes under the management (so stated) of James J. Corbett, the famous pugilist, he realized the necessity of protecting himself, as the British law of copyright did not protect him. It was necessary for him to write his own dramatization of the novel, go through the legal farce of hiring a hall licensed for theatrical performances, have a sort of mock performance of the play, and pay two guineas to the King's Reader of Plays. Accordingly Shaw wrote *The Admirable Bashville; or Constancy Unrewarded,* a blank-verse dramatization of *Cashel Byron's Profession* in one week. The copyrighting performance was held on March 13, 1901, at Victoria Hall, Notting Hill, London. To complete the transaction, the novel was brought out the same year in its third and final form by Grant Richards, London; and with it was bound *The Admirable Bashville,* two prefaces and a note on modern prize-fighting.

Henderson goes on to discuss the authorized American publication of this *olla podrida,* again quoting Shaw's phrase about encouraging Stone to exploit the "new field of derelict fiction," first used in connection with *Love Among the Artists* (No. 260). Henderson's words permit the inference that the publication of the novel and play in America was merely a byproduct of Shaw's activities and Richards' publication and intended as a balance to Brentano's unauthorized publication of the novel. On the contrary, the whole point of Shaw's dramatization and performance would have been lost in America if the revised novel had not also been printed here. The Copyright Act of 1891 granted to authors "the exclusive right to dramatize . . . any of the works for which copyright shall have been obtained." Shaw was interested in the dramatic possibilities of his most popular novel—possibilities which were being exploited without his concurrence in America. The publication of a revised and authorized edition of the novel secured to him dramatic rights for America, just as the performance of the play in Great Britain secured him performance rights there. The publication of the play in America, with its separate title-page mentioning its English performance and claiming American copyright, only emphasized these American rights. Actually the play was not separately copyrighted, according to the records in Washington. Stone's publication, to recapitulate, contained prefaces on "Novels of My Nonage" (where Shaw talks of the circumstances of their birth and the revisions in the present issue); "The Morals of Pugilistic Fiction"; and "Stevenson's Eulologium"; the novel of *Cashel Byron's Profession,* revised for a second time since its serial publication; and the play, with a separate half-title quoting Stevenson's delight in Bashville (Henderson believed these to have been omitted in America), and a separate title-page with copyright notice on verso: "This play has been publicly performed within the United Kingdom. It is entered at Stationers' Hall and the

Library of Congress, U. S. A. Copyright, 1901, by Herbert S. Stone and Company. All Rights Reserved."

[284]
One Forty-Two | The Reformed | Messenger Boy | by | Henry M. Hyde | With Illustrations by Ellsworth | Young | [*device ten in red*] | Herbert S. Stone and Company | Eldridge Court, Chicago | MDCCCCI [*within double rule border*]

6-5/8 x 4-1/4; pp. [x], 204, [2]. Thirty-two illustrations in text by F. Young. Printer not given; Modernized Old Style type; laid paper with watermark six. Bound in red cloth; stamped in white with rules and lettering on front cover and spine; circular monogram on white ground on back.

Copyright October 28, 1901; listed in *Publishers' Weekly* October 7. Price $1.25.

Reprinted from the Chicago *Tribune;* Mr. Hyde is now Washington correspondent of the Baltimore *Sun.* He had published an *Animal Alphabet* through George M. Hill of Chicago in 1900. *One Forty-Two* was advertised as "The Greatest Slang Book," and "A Second Checkers." Its sales success was only moderate.

[285]
The Last of the | Knickerbockers | A Comedy Romance | by | Herman Knickerbocker Vielé | Author of The Inn of the | Silver Moon | "Give me faces and streets." | —Walt Whitman | [*device ten in red*] | Herbert S. Stone & Company | Eldridge Court, Chicago | 1901 [*within double rule border*]

7-1/2 x 4-3/4; pp. [xii], 354, [2]. Printed by Lakeside Press, Chicago, in Modernized Old Style type on laid paper. Bound in mauve cloth, illustration on front cover in grey, white, and red, printing in grey and white; printing in white on spine; circular monogram on white ground on back.

Copyright October 30, 1901; listed in *Publishers' Weekly* November 9. Price $1.50. Issued in England by Stone during December 1901.

This was not, like *The Inn of the Silver Moon* (No. 262) a "best seller." It is, however, an even better humorous romance.

[286]
Ruskin's Principles | of Art Criticism | [*rule*] | by | Ida M. Street | Sometime Western Collegiate Alumnae Fellow in

English | Literature at the University of Michigan | [*rule*] | [*device ten*] | [*rule*] | Herbert S. Stone & Company | Publishers Chicago MDCCCCI [*within double rule border*]

7-1/2 x 4-7/8; pp. viii, 457, [3]. Printer not given; Ronaldson Old Style type; laid paper. Bound in dark red ribbed cloth over boards with bevelled edges; printed in gold on spine.

Copyright November 1, 1901. Price $1.60 net.

[287]

Four Illustrations | for the Tales of Edgar | Allen Poe, Drawn by | Aubrey Beardsley | [*portrait inserted on tissue*] | Herbert S. Stone & Company | Eldridge Court, Chicago, 1901

10-7/8 x 7; pp. [16] unnumbered; plus four drawings, 8-1/2 x 5-1/8, each mounted on cardboard. Text and drawing on Japan vellum paper; all enclosed in printed paper folder.

Copyright November 20, 1901; listed in *Publishers' Weekly* December 28. 250 numbered copies at $5.00 net.

"These drawings are now published for the first time," according to the publishers' advertisements. The copyright on them was originally entered by Stone & Kimball, who had commissioned Beardsley to do a set of eight pictures illustrating the "Tales" for the large-paper issue of their set of Poe. Four were received before Beardsley's death, but not included in the published volumes for reasons which remain obscure. One print, "The Masque of the Red Death," was published in *The Chap-Book* for October 15, 1894. The others were "The Murders in the Rue Morgue," "The Black Cat," and "The Fall of the House of Usher."

§ The later history of these drawings is as interesting as the earlier. A "Colonial Publishing Company" of Pittsburgh reissued the present set of four pictures about 1912, apparently without permission. The "Aubrey Beardsley Club" of Indianapolis issued in 1929 a portfolio of seventeen Beardsley drawings for Poe, of which only the four described above had ever been printed before.

[288]

The | Golfer's | Rubaiyat | by | H. W. Boynton | [*ornament including publisher's device*] | Herbert S. Stone | & Company | Chicago 1901 [*lettered in red and black*]

6-3/4 x 4-1/4; pp. [88] unnumbered. Printer not given; Modernized Old

Style type; laid paper with watermark six. Bound in green boards; decoration and lettering on front cover in red; edges uncut. Binding, title, and illustrative borders, framing each page of text, by Frank Hazenplug.

Copyright November 18, 1901; listed in *Publishers' Weekly* December 7. Price $1.00. Grant Richards' English edition (500 copies from American sheets) published during April 1903.

These humorous verses escape by a month being Mr. Henry Walcott Boynton's first book. His life of Washington Irving was issued October 1901 in the "Riverside Biographical Series." Mr. Boynton writes, 24 October 1939, when returning corrected galley proof of this entry, "It was written in Andover. One of the young Stones had been in my English classes while I was teaching at Phillips Academy. It must have been Melville E. Stone, Jr. Having emitted these verses, it occurred to me that he, or H. S. Stone & Co., might be induced to publish them, and they were and did."

[289]
The Book | of a | Hundred Houses | A Collection of Pictures, | Plans and Suggestions for | Householders | [*device ten*] | Herbert S. Stone & Company | Eldridge Court, Chicago, 1902 [*within thin within thick rule border*]

8-1/2 x 6-3/4; pp. vii, [i], 403, [5]. Frontispiece inserted; photographs, plans, and drawings in text. Printed by Lakeside Press, Chicago, in Modernized Old Style type on wove calendared paper. Bound like No. 176.

Copyright January 30, 1902; first advertised in *The Dial*, for November 1, 1901; listed in *Publishers' Weekly* December 14, 1901. Price $1.60 net.

Compiled from *The House Beautiful* by Virginia Robie and "Oliver Coleman" (See No. 176). Other contributors were Joy Wheeler Dow, Claude Bragdon and Harriet Monroe. Some of the plates had already appeared in a pamphlet titled *Illustrations of the House Beautiful*. This was a collection of twenty-one photographs and two drawings by Birch Burdette Long. Deposited for copyright January 6, 1901, but never advertised for sale, it was probably intended to advertise *The House Beautiful* and as a trial issue of *The Book of a Hundred Houses*.

[290]
The Crimson Wing | [*rule*] | by | H. C. Chatfield-Taylor | Author of "Two Women and a Fool," "The Idle Born." | etc., etc. | [*rule*] | [*device ten in red*] | [*rule*] | Herbert S. Stone

& Company | Chicago and New York | MCMII [*within double rule border*]

7-1/2 x 4-3/4; pp. [xviii], 356, [6]. Printed by Lakeside Press, Chicago, in Modernized Old Style and Caslon types on laid paper. Bound in green cloth; illustration and lettering on front cover in red, grey and white; lettering on spine in white; circular monogram on white ground on back cover.

Copyright March 6, 1902. Price $1.50. Issued in England by Stone during September 1902; later by Grant Richards.

A novel of the Franco-Prussian War. Mr. Chatfield-Taylor's last publication with Stone. His correspondence with the firm indicates that 'Ned' and not Herbert Stone, or Lucy Monroe, was the editor in charge of revisions, proofs, etc.

[291]

The | Rewards of Taste | And Other Essays | [*rule*] | by | Norman Bridge, M. D. | [*rule*] | [*device ten*] | Herbert S. Stone & Company | Chicago and New York | MCMII [*within double rule border*]

7-1/2 x 4-3/4; [xii], 270, [6]. Printed by Lakeside Press, Chicago, in Modernized Old Style type on laid paper. Bound in green ribbed cloth, printed in gold on spine and front cover, within rules.

Copyright March 8, 1902. Price $1.50.

Dr. Bridge's second book; the first, *The Penalties of Taste,* also published by Stone (No. 170) is advertised opposite the title-page.

[292]

The | Carpenter Prophet | A Life of Jesus Christ | and a Discussion | of His Ideals | by | Charles William Pearson | [*device ten in red*] | Herbert S. Stone and Company | Chicago and New York | MCMII [*within thin within thick rule border*]

7-1/2 x 4-3/4; pp. [6], ix, [i], 288, [8]. Printed by Lakeside Press, Chicago, in Modernized Old Style and Caslon types on laid paper. Bound in red cloth, stamped in gold on spine with rules, lettering and circular monogram; on front with lettering within frame.

Copyright March 24, 1902; listed in *Publishers' Weekly* April 26, 1902. Price $1.50.

[293]
The | Romance of a | Rogue | by | Joseph Sharts | Chicago | Herbert S. Stone & Company | 1902 [*lettered and decorated*]

7-9/16 x 4-5/8; pp. [iv], 249, [3]. Colored frontispiece inserted. Printed by Lakeside Press, Chicago, in Modernized Old Style type on laid paper. Bound in red smooth or green ribbed cloth; stamped in gold; lettering and design on front cover, lettering on spine. Binding, title, frontispiece, headpieces and decorative initial letters designed by Frank Hazenplug.

Copyright March 24, 1902; listed in *Publishers' Weekly* August 26. Price $1.50.

Mr. Sharts' second book; his first had also been published by Stone, as No. 277. It is not possible to determine priority of the red and green bindings. The copy early presented to Mr. Harry Lydenberg is in green; the copy preserved by Mr. W. J. Kirk of Stone's office, is in red.

[294]
Mazel | by | Richard Fisguill | [*device eight in red*] | Herbert S. Stone & Co. | Eldredge Court, Chicago | MCMII [*within double rule border*]

7-1/2 x 4-3/4; pp. [x], 321, [5]. Printed by Lakeside Press, Chicago, in Modernized Old Style and Caslon types on laid paper. Bound in mauve cloth; illustration, lettering and rules on front cover, in black, white and red; lettering on spine in black; circular device on back cover, on black ground.

Copyright April 7, 1902; listed in *Publishers' Weekly* April 26. Price $1.50.

The copyright of this romantic novel by "Richard Fisguill" was transferred on May 23, 1905 to Richard H. Wilson. Professor Wilson used a pseudonym no doubt because he published in the same year, his doctoral dissertation at Johns Hopkins, on "The Preposition à; The Relation of Its Meanings Studied in Old French."

[295]
The Story | of | Mary MacLane | By Herself | [*device ten in red*] | Chicago | Herbert S. Stone and Company | MCMII [*within thin within thick rule border*]

7-1/16 x 4-1/2; pp. [vi], 322. Portrait frontispiece inserted. Printer not given; Modernized Old Style, Caslon and black-letter types; laid paper. Bound in salmon-red cloth; stamped in white with ornamental rule frame and lettering on front cover, simple rule frame and lettering on spine.

"Published April 26, 1902," on verso of title. Deposited for copyright same day but not listed in *Publishers' Weekly* until June 14. Reprinted twice by Stone; reissued by Duffield in 1911, with an additional chapter. Price $1.50. Published in England by Grant Richards during November 1902.

Concerning the publication of this first and only important book by Mary MacLane, see pp. 129-32. § The first printing was 20,000 copies, according to information received from Mr. Herbert P. Zimmerman of the Lakeside Press. The two later printings were also large runs. The second impression was issued in cheaper dark-red cloth; the third in red cloth and smaller in size, at 75 cents. All have stamping shown in Fig. 31.

[296]
Castle | Craneycrow | [*rule*] | by | George Barr McCutcheon | Author of Graustark | [*rule*] | [*device ten in red*] | [*rule*] | Chicago | Herbert S. Stone and Company | MCMII [*within double rule border*]

7-1/2 x 4-3/4; pp. [viii], 391, [9]. Printed by Lakeside Press, Chicago, in Modernized Old Style and Caslon types on laid paper. Bound in green cloth; illustration and lettering on front cover in green, yellow and white; circular monogram on back cover on green ground. Title rubricated.

"Issued August 15, 1902," on verso of title. Deposited for copyright August 13, 1902; listed in *Publishers' Weekly* August 23. Price $1.50. Reprinted several times by Stone, and serialized in *House Beautiful* September 1902–October 1903. Grant Richards' English edition published during November 1903.

Castle Craneycrow was given its title by John Tinney McCutcheon, the novelist's younger brother, from a rhyme known to them both, "Chickamy, chickamy Craneycrow/Went to the well to wash my toe." § This second romance sold well although it did not receive the tremendous advertising given *Graustark* or the pseudonymous *Brewster's Millions*. George Barr McCutcheon was approached by Dodd, Mead & Company after the success of *Castle Craneycrow* had given assurance that *Graustark* was not a flash-in-the-pan, and offered a substantial sum on advance of royalties for his next novel. (An author friend of the late George Barr McCutcheon mentions the sum of $20,000; the former bookkeeper of Herbert S. Stone and Company thinks of $26,000.) Herbert S. Stone and Company could not meet such an offer, but were glad to get *Brewster's Millions* by "Richard P. Greaves." This book was published in Chicago during April 1903 while George Barr McCutcheon's new novel, *The Sherrods*, was issued in New York during September 1903.

[297]
The | Life of a Woman | by | R. V. Risley | Author of "Men's Tragedies," etc. | [*device ten in red*] | Chicago | Herbert S. Stone & Company | MCMII

7-1/2 x 4-3/4; pp. [xii], 325, [7]. Printed by Lakeside Press, Chicago, in Modernized Old Style type on laid paper. Bound in orange cloth, stamped in green with rules, lettering and decoration on front cover and spine, circular monogram on green ground on back cover. Title rubricated.

"Issued September 25, 1902," on verso of title; deposited for copyright October 20. Price $1.50. Issued in London by Stone during December 1902.

The last book published by Richard Voorhees Risley, one of the few American contributors to *The Yellow Book*. John Lane had published in 1897, his first and best-remembered novel, *The Sentimental Vikings*.

[298]
Noll and the Fairies | by | Hervey White | Illustrated by | Elizabeth Krysher | [*vignette*] | Herbert S. Stone and Company | Eldridge Court, Chicago | MCMIII [*within double rule border*]

6 x 4-1/4; pp. [vi], 221, [5]. Frontispiece (tinted) and two plates inserted. Printed by Lakeside Press, Chicago, in Modernized Old Style type on laid paper with watermark six. Bound in smooth green cloth; rules, illustration and lettering in blue and white on front cover; blue rules and white lettering on spine; circular monogram on white on back cover. In addition to the frontispiece and two plates, Elizabeth Krysher contributed vignettes as head- and tail-pieces in text.

"Published October 25, 1902," on verso of title. Deposited for copyright November 14, 1902; listed in *Publishers' Weekly* November 22. Price $1.00.

Hervey White, a classmate of Herbert Stone and Ingalls Kimball at Harvard, was then a resident of Hull House. He had been a reference librarian at the John Crerar Library between 1896 and 1899. He prefers to be known not for his writings (twenty-three volumes), "but as the founder and owner of the Maverick Colony of Artists and Craftsmen; the Sunday Afternoon Chamber Music Concerts (1915); the Maverick Press (1910); the Maverick Theatre (1925); and of a series of pageants known as The Maverick Festivals (1914-1931)."

[299]
Brewster's Millions | [*rule*] | by | Richard Greaves | [*rule*] | [*device ten in red*] | [*rule*] | Chicago | Herbert S. Stone & Co. | MCMIII [*within double rule border*]

7-1/2 x 4-3/4; pp. [viii], 325, [5]. Printed by Lakeside Press, Chicago, in Modernized Old Style and Caslon types on laid paper. Bound in rough light red, or smooth dark red, cloth; stamped in gold with lettering on spine, and circular monogram on back cover; decorative medallion inserted into front cover with author given as "Richard P. Greaves," in gold on black.

"Issued April 20, 1903," on verso of title. Deposited for copyright same day; entered in *Publishers' Weekly* May 9. Price $1.50. Reprinted during 1903 and 1904 for Stone; reissued by Grosset & Dunlap after 1904.

George Barr McCutcheon's third and last book published in Chicago, and the most successful of his writings. Issued under the pseudonym of "Richard Greaves," it far outsold *The Sherrods,* published under his proper and already well-known name, by Dodd, Mead & Company (See Note to No. 296). § *Brewster's Millions,* as the author was always ready to admit, was a composite of his and his friends' inventions. George Barr McCutcheon always paid part of the royalties to his brother Ben, who had helped him develop the original idea. The publishers and their editor also participated, although less heavily than in *Graustark.* The "First Copy," dated April 17, 1903, has the inscription:

Dear Miss Monroe,
   With many happy returns from the book, Richard P. Greaves. In April 1903.

   To Miss Lucy Monroe, the author, with the kindest regards of an interested reader.
                      M. E. Stone Jr.
Not Guilty!
          Herbert Stuart Stone
And me!
          [Lucy Monroe]

[300]
Truth and a Woman | by | Anna Robeson Brown | [*device ten in red*] | Herbert S. Stone & Company | Chicago :: :: :: MDCCCCIII [*within double rule border*]

6-3/4 x 4-3/8; pp. [viii], 206, [2]. Printed by Lakeside Press, Chicago, in Ronaldson Old Style and Caslon types on laid paper with watermark six.

Bound in pale green linen; lettered in gold on spine and front cover; design in green and blue on front cover; circular monogram on blue ground on back.

"Copyright May 23, 1903," on verso of title. Deposited for copyright same day; listed in *Publishers' Weekly* June 6. Price $1.25.

The first book of Anna Robeson Brown, now as Mrs. Charles A. Burr, known as the biographer of Weir Mitchell and Alice James.

[301]
My Friend | Annabel Lee | [*rule*] | by | Mary MacLane | [*rule*] | [*device ten in red*] | [*rule*] | Chicago | Herbert S. Stone and Company | MCMIII [*within double rule border*]

7-1/2 x 4-3/4; pp. [xii], 262, [6]. Portrait frontispiece inserted. Printed by Lakeside Press, Chicago, in Modernized Old Style, Caslon, and blackletter types on laid paper. Bound in maroon cloth, stamped in white; ornamental rule frame and lettering on front cover; simple rule frame and lettering on spine; circular monogram on back.

"Issued September 1, 1903," on verso of title. Deposited for copyright August 27, 1903; listed in *Publishers' Weekly* September 13. Price $1.50.

This did not meet with even the popular success of *The Story of Mary MacLane*, and was the last new book the author published for thirteen years; see p. 131.

[302]
The | Strange Adventures | of Mr. Middleton | by | Wardon Allan Curtis | [*illustration in green, within rules*] | Chicago | Herbert S. Stone & Company | MCMIII [*within double rule border*]

7-1/4 x 4-13/16; pp. [vi], 311, [3]. Printer not given; Caslon and Modernized Old Style types; wove paper. Bound in grey cloth, stamped in white on front cover and spine; illustration on front cover in black, white and tan; circular monogram on white ground on back. Chapter headings printed in six point on recto of each page below the running title. Copyright October 16, 1903. Price $1.50.

[303]
A Book of | American | Prose Humor | Being a Collection of Humorous | and Witty Tales, Sketches, Etc.; | Composed by

the Best Known | American Writers | [*device eight in red*] | Chicago | Herbert S. Stone & Company | 1904 [*within double rule border*]

6-3/4 x 4-1/4; pp. [4], x, 249, [1]. Printed by Lakeside Press, Chicago, in Caslon type on laid paper with watermark six. Bound in green gabardine cloth, stamped in gold; lettering, rules, and ornament on front cover and spine.

Copyright December 2, 1903; listed in *Publishers' Weekly* December 19, 1903. Price $1.25.

Edited by Melville E. Stone Jr.

[304]

A Book of | American | Humorous Verse | Being a Collection of Humor- | ous | and Witty Verses composed | by the Best Known | American Writers | [*device eight in red*] | Chicago | Herbert S. Stone & Company | 1904 [*within double rule border*]

6-3/4 x 4-1/4; pp. [4], xxv, [i], 251, [5]. Printed by Lakeside Press, Chicago, in Caslon type on laid paper with watermark six. Bound in green gabardine cloth, stamped in gold with rules, lettering and ornament on front cover and spine.

Copyright December 5, 1903; listed in *Publishers' Weekly* December 19. Price $1.25. Appears in secondary binding of grey cloth stamped in blue.

Edited by Wallace Rice.

[305]

The | Highroad | Being | The Autobiography | of an Ambitious | Mother | [*device ten in red*] | Chicago | Herbert S. Stone & Company | MCMIV [*within double rule border*]

7-1/2 x 4-3/4; pp. [iv], 289, [3]. Printed by Stromberg, Allen & Co., Chicago, in Modernized Old Style and Caslon types on laid paper. Bound in olive-green cloth, lettering and landscape in green and white on front cover; lettering in white on spine; circular monogram on white ground on back.

Copyright May 7, 1904. Price $1.50.

The authorship of this interesting work has not been revealed.

[306]
Painters | Since | Leonardo | Being a History of Painting from | The Renaissance to the | Present Day | by | James William Pattison | [*floret*] | Published by | Herbert S. Stone & Company | 1904

9-1/4 x 6-3/4; pp. viii, [6], ix-xi, [i], 288, [2]. Ninety-eight illustrations, including frontispiece, inserted. Printer not given; Modernized Old Style and Caslon types; wove calendared paper. Bound in green ribbed cloth stamped in gold; rules and lettering on sides and spine. Title-leaf a cancel.

Copyright May 16, 1904. Price $4.00 net.

This book was made up from the popular lectures which J. W. Pattison was then giving at the Art Institute of Chicago, and which were published serially in *The House Beautiful.*

[307]
Roland | of Altenburg | by | Edward Mott Woolley | [*device ten in red*] | Chicago | Herbert S. Stone & Company | MCMIV [*within double rule border*]

7-7/16 x 4-3/4; pp. [iv], 350, [2]. Printer not given; Modernized Old Style and Caslon types; laid paper. Bound in olive-green cloth; illustration on front cover in white, orange and green; lettering in orange and black; lettering on spine in white; circular monogram on white ground on back.

Copyright September 29, 1904. Price $1.50.

On September 24, 1905, Herbert S. Stone & Company assigned to Mr. Woolley the copyright of *Alias Mr. Short.* This was the original title of *Roland of Altenburg,* writes the author in *Free-Lancing for Forty Magazines* (Passaic Park, N. J.: Edward Mott Woolley Associates, 1927). It was run serially in the Chicago *Journal,* where Mr. Woolley was then working, and:

> Before *Alias Mr. Short* was finished serially, four publishers offered to put it in book form, on a royalty plan, with small advance payments.
> I entered into a contract with a Chicago publisher, the same house that had put out George Barr McCutcheon's *Graustark,* with an advance to me of two hundred and fifty dollars, and in due season my book appeared under the new title, *Roland of Altenburg.* Much of it had been rewritten or revised, and the publisher's editorial department had taken liberties with it that did not please me.
> I have always believed the original title to be better than the other, and that the story in its first form had more merit in many respects

355

than the revision, though it lacked polish. It is difficult to incorporate in a book the opinions of half a dozen persons.

[308]

Three Weeks | in | Europe | The Vacation of a Busy Man | by | John U. Higinbotham | [*device ten in red*] | Chicago | Herbert S. Stone & Company | MCMV [*within double rule border*]

7-3/8 x 4-3/4; pp. x, 274, [4]. Fifty-one photographs, including frontispiece, inserted. Printed by Lakeside Press, Chicago, in Modernized Old Style and Caslon types on laid paper. Bound in brown cloth; lettering and seascape in black, blue and white on front cover; lettering in white on spine; circular monogram on white ground on back.

Copyright October 27, 1904. Price $1.25.

The first of several travel books by J. U. Higinbotham, then cashier of the newly organized National Biscuit Company in Chicago.

[309]

Historic Styles | in | Furniture | by | Virginia Robie | [*floret in red*] | Published by | Herbert S. Stone | The House Beautiful | Chicago, 1905 [*within double rule border*]

8-1/2 x 6-3/4; pp. [xii], 196, including illustrations. Printed by Lakeside Press, Chicago, in Modern-face type on wove calendared paper. Bound in grey boards (paper label on front cover), with tan cloth spine; top edge cut.

Copyright November 20, 1905. Price $1.60 net. Reprinted in revised form, by Houghton Mifflin Company.

Between 1905 and 1913, Herbert Stuart Stone devoted all his time to the periodical, *The House Beautiful*. This is the last book he published.

III
PUBLICATIONS OF WAY & WILLIAMS REISSUED BY HERBERT S. STONE IN 1899
(Dates of Original Issue Given)

Adams, Mary M. *The Choir Visible: Verses.* 1897.

Amory, Esmerie. *The Epistolary Flirt: A Story in Dramatic Form.* 1896.

Armstrong, Eliza. *The Teacup Club: A Satire.* 1897.

Bain, R. Nisbet. *Russian Fairy Tales.* Illustrated by C. M. Gere. 1895.

Baring-Gould, Sabine. *Old English Fairy Tales.* Illustrated by F. D. Bedford. 1895.

Baum, L. Frank. *Mother Goose in Prose.* Illustrated by Maxfield Parrish. 1897.

Bridges, Robert. *Purcell Ode.* Designed by Bruce Rogers. 1896.

Browne, Francis Fisher. *Volunteer Grain: Verses.* 1895.

Calkins, Frank Welles. *[Tales of] The West.* 1895.

Cheney, John Vance. *Queen Helen, and Other Poems.* 1895.

Chopin, Kate. *A Night in Acadie: A Novel.* 1897.

Cleary, Kate M. *Like a Gallant Lady: A Novel of Nebraska Life.* Cover by Will Bradley. 1897.

Clover, Sam T. *Paul Traver's Adventures: The Story of a Boy's Tour of the World.* Illustrated by Bert Cassidy. 1897.

Coonley Ward, Lydia A. *Under the Pines, and Other Verses.* 1895.

Drachmann, Holger. *Paul and Virginia of a Northern Zone.* 1895.

Field, H. D. and R. M. *The Muses Up-to-Date: A Book of Plays for Children.* 1897.

Forman, H. Buxton. *The Books of William Morris: A Biography and Bibliography.* 1897.

Gissing, George. *The Emancipated: A Novel.* 1895.

Hemingway, Percy. *The Happy Wanderer, and Other Poems.* 1896.

Henry, Stuart. *Hours with Famous Parisians.* 1897.

Horton, George. *Constantine: A Novel of Greece under King Otho.* 1897.

Johnston, Richard Malcolm. *Pearce Amberson's Will: A Novel.* 1898.

Judah, Mary Jameson. *Down Our Way: Short Stories.* 1897.

Lang, Andrew. *The Miracles of Mme. Ste. Katherine of Fierbois.* 1897.

Lang, Andrew, translator. *Aucassin and Nicolete.* 1895.

Lummis, Charles F. *The Enchanted Burro: Stories and Sketches.* 1897.

McChesney, Dora Greenwell. *Miriam Cromwell, Royalist: A Romance of the Great Rebellion.* 1898.

Munkittrick, R. K. *The Acrobatic Muse: Verses.* 1897.

Noel, Roden. *My Sea, and other Posthumous Poems.* 1895.

Payne, William Morton. *Little Leaders: Essays reprinted mostly from the Dial.* 1895.

Peattie, Elia W. *A Mountain Woman: Short Stories.* Cover by Bruce Rogers. 1896.

Peattie, Elia W. *Pippins and Cheese: Connected Stories and Conversations.* 1897.

Pollard, Percival. *Dreams of To-Day: Sketches.* 1897.

Read, Opie. *Bolanyo: A Novel.* 1897.

Snow, Florence L. *The Lamp of Gold: Verses.* 1896.

Thanet, Octave [i.e. Alice French]. *A Book of True Lovers.* 1897.

Thwaites, Reuben Gold. *Afloat on the Ohio.* 1897.

Waterloo, Stanley. *A Man and a Woman: A Novel.* Cover by Will Bradley. 1897.

Waterloo, Stanley. *An Odd Situation.* 1896.

Waterloo, Stanley. *The Story of Ab: A Tale of the Time of the Cave Men.* Cover by Will Bradley. 1897.

White, William Allen. *The Real Issue: Kansas Stories.* 1896.

Wynne, Madeleine Yale. *The Little Room, and Other Stories.* 1895.

Yale, Catherine Brooks. *Nim and Cum, and the Wonderhead Stories.* Designed by Bruce Rogers. 1897.

IV
PRINTINGS MADE FOR COPYRIGHT PURPOSES ONLY BY STONE & KIMBALL AND HERBERT S. STONE & COMPANY

[*Customarily only 12 copies printed; * indicates those not examined.*]

*Benson, Edward Frederic. *The Taming of Dodo.* From *The Chap-Book,* May 15, 1897, Vol. VII, No. 1.

Bullock, Shan F. *Rogue Bartley.* Deposited for copyright April 4, 1896.

Bullock, Shan F. *The Splendid Shilling.* From *The Chap-Book,* April 15, 1896, Vol. IV, No. 11. Deposited for copyright March 28, 1896.

*Chambers, Robert W. *The God of Battles.* Deposited for copyright May 27, 1897.

Davidson, John. *A Ballad of a Workman.* Deposited for copyright January 13, 1896.

*Davidson, John. *The Last Rose.* Deposited for copyright during 1895.

*Davidson, John. *A New Ballad of Tannhaeuser: A Poem.* From *The Chap-Book,* July 1, 1896, Vol. V, No. 4.

*Davidson, John. *The Pioneer.* From *The Chap-Book,* February 15, 1898, Vol. VIII, No. 7.

Davidson, John. *Spring Song: A Poem.* From *The Chap-Book,* May 1, 1896, Vol. IV, No. 12. Deposited for copyright between April 4 and 11, 1896.

*Davidson, John. *Waiting: a Song of the Submerged Tenth.* From *The Chap-Book,* January 15, 1897, Vol. VI, No. 5.

Hardy, Thomas. *The Duke's Reappearance: A Tradition.* From *The Chap-Book,* December 15, 1896, Vol. VI, No. 3.

Hopper, Nora. *The Miller's Song.* Deposited for copyright July 6, 1896.

[Macfall, Haldane]. *The Wooings of Jezebel Pettyfer*...by Hal Dane. Deposited for copyright June 4, 1898.

Moore, Frank Frankfort. *Nell Gwyn*. From *The Chap-Book*, March 15, 1896, Vol. IV, No. 9. Deposited for copyright March 2, 1896. Included in *The Impudent Comedian*, 1897.

*Morrison, Arthur. *A Vision of Toyokuni*. From *The Chap-Book*, August 1, 1896, Vol. V, No. 6.

*Newbolt, Henry. *The Last Word: A Poem*. From *The Chap-Book*, March 15, 1898, Vol. VIII, No. 9.

*Pugh, Edwin. *The Poor Idealist*. From *The Chap-Book*, April 15, 1897, Vol. VI, No. 11. Entered for copyright March 29, 1897.

*Sharp, Evelyn. *Little Elizabeth*. From *The Chap-Book*, April 1, 1896, Vol. IV, No. 10.

Stevenson, Robert Louis. *Macaire*. By R. L. S. and W. E. Henley. From *The Chap-Book*, June 1 & 15, 1895, Vol. III, Nos. 2 & 3. Separately printed and deposited for copyright May 27, 1895. Afterwards reprinted in book form.

Stevenson, Robert Louis. *Weir of Hermiston*. Part I, deposited for copyright January 4, 1896; part II, February 6; part III, March 5; *part IV, April 4; *parts V and VI, April 7, 1896.

Watson, William. *The Captive's Dream: A Poem*. From *The Chap-Book*, July 15, 1897, Vol. VII, No. 6. Deposited for copyright July 6, 1897.

*Watson, William. *A Fly Leaf Poem*. Deposited for copyright during 1895.

Watson, William. *The Wider Optimism*. Deposited for copyright July 6, 1897.

Wells, Herbert George. *The Red Room*. From *The Chap-Book*, February 15, 1896, Vol. IV, No. 7. Deposited for copyright February 7, 1896.

*Yeats, William Butler. *S. Patrick and the Pedants*. From *The Chap-Book*, June 1, 1896, Vol. V, No. 2.

V
PRIVATELY PRINTED BOOKS PRODUCED BY STONE & KIMBALL AND HERBERT S. STONE & COMPANY

Blair, Edward T. *A History of the Chicago Club*. Printed at the Lakeside Press, 1898.

Bulkeley, Benjamin Reynolds. *The Shifting Wind*. Printed at the Lakeside Press, 1895.

Burleigh, B. W. and Wenzloff, G. G., editors. *A Book of Dakota Rhymes*. Printed at the Lakeside Press, 1898.

Emerson, Adaline Talcott. *Love-Bound, and Other Poems*. Printed at the University Press, 1894. "Second Edition," 1895.

Gross, Samuel Eberly. *The Merchant Prince of Cornville; a Comedy*. Printed at the University Press, 1896.

Horton, George. *In Unknown Seas: A Poem*. Printed at the University Press, Cambridge, 1896.

Rule, Lucien V. *The Shrine of Love and Other Poems*. Printed at the Lakeside Press, 1898.

Sons of the Revolution. *Yearbook of the Illinois Society*. Printed at the Lakeside Press, 1895.

Index

References in arabic numerals are to pages in the History; those in roman numerals are to the illustrations, by figure number; those in italics are to the Bibliography, by entry number and not by page.

Abbott, Angus Evan, 54
Abbott, Mary, quoted, 54-55
"Across the Salt Seas," 122
Adams, Franklin Pierce, 10
Adams, Mary M., *357*
Ade, George, 96-97, 122-23; vii, xxxviii; *112, 128, 206, 219, 258, 281*
"The Admirable Bashville," *283*
"An Adventurer of the North," *80, 97*
"The Adventures of Hajji Baba of Ispahan," *47*
Advertising, 81, 127-28, 132, 134, 146
"After-Supper Songs," *178*
Aldrich, Thomas Bailey, 22
Alexander, Sir George, *190*
"All Expenses Paid," *85*
Allen, Grant, 78, *16*
"The Amateur Emigrant," 61; *24, 36*
"An American Book of Gardening," *280*
American Booksellers Association, 141
"The American Indians of To-day," *244*
American Library Association, 92
American News Company, *273*
American Publishers Association, 141
Amory, Esmerie, *357*
Anderson, James A., quoted, 91-92
"The Anglican Revival," *148*
"Animals," *282*
"Answers of the Ages," *241*
Anundsen Publishing Co., *273*
Appleton, D., & Co., 87; *44, 133*
Archer, William, *104, 247*
Arena Publishing Co., *4*
Armstrong, Eliza, *357*
Arnold, Edwin, *233*
Arrowsmith, publishers, *103, 111*
Art Institute of Chicago, *306*
"Artie," *112, 128, 219*
Ashbee, C. R., *130*
Ashton, John, 48; *22, 194*
"At the Sign of the Sphinx," *94*

Atlantic Monthly, 137
Atlay, J. B., *227*
Atwater, L. D., agent, 9
Auction Sales, 88-89, 145
Authors
 advances, 77; *188, 255, 307*
 contracts, 60-61, 100-101, 145
 relations with, 76 ff.
 royalties, 81 ff.
 sales, 144
 trading in, 87
"The Awakening," 114-15; *192*

Bacheller, Irving, *22*
Baldwin, Mary, *22*
Bain, R. Nislet, *357*
Ballantyne, Hanson and Co., printers, *17, 46, 173, 255*
Balton, Ethel, *22*
Bangs, John Kenrick, *22, 281*
Banks, Charles Eugene, *257*
Bannister, Christopher, *22*
Barbour, Ralph Henry, 103; *131*
Balfour, Graham, 82-83
Baring-Gould, *357*
Barnard, William Francis, *22*
Barnett, Edith A., *151*
Barnhart Brothers & Spindler, *88*
Barnum, P. T., *278*
Barr, Amelia E., *212*
Barr, James, *54*
Barry, John D., 78, 84; *92, 95*
Barrymore, Maurice, *210*
Bartlett, Gertrude, *22*
Bates, Ernest Sutherland, *165*
Bates, Herbert, *22*
Bates, Katherine, *22*
Baum, L. Frank, *357*
Baxter, Charles, 58-62, 82-84
Beale, Harriet S. B., *177*
Beardsley, Aubrey, 20, 31, 51, 57, 87; viii, xiv; *9, 17, 22, 25, 35, 287*

363

Beer, Thomas, 87
Beerbohm, Max, 52-53, 70; *22*
Bell, Lilian, *22, 42*
Bendall, Wilfrid, *228*
"The Bending of the Bough," 118, 122; *243*
Benham, Charles, *136*
Benjamin, Lewis S., *223*
Benjamin, Walter R., *144*
Bennett, H. H., *22*
Bennett, Ida D., *130, 280*
Bennett, John, *22*
Benson, E. F., *359*
Benton, Joel, *22*
Berthon, Paul, *22*
Best-sellers, 72, 126-28, 141; xxxvi; *41, 273, 299*
Betts, Louis, *257, 271*
Bibliographical arrangement, 147-48
Bickford, L. H., 103; *131*
Bierce, Ambrose, 46
Bindings, 147, 150, 151; xi, xxi-v, xxx-ii
Bird, E. B., 36; *22*
Bisland, Elizabeth, *22*
"Black Spirits & White," *52*
Blackburn, Vernon, *64*
Blackie & Son
  See Victorian Era Series
Blair, Edward J., 36
Blessington, Countess of, *218*
Blossom, Henry Martyn, Jr., 96; *109*
Bloundelle-Burton, John, *122*
Blue Cloth Books Series, *23, 182, 185, 189, 197*
Bobbs Merrill Company, 116
Bodley Head
  See Lane, John; Mathews, Elkin & John Lane
Boner, John H., *22*
Bonner, H. Geraldine, *22*
"A Book of American Humorous Verse," *304*
"A Book of American Prose Humor," *303*
"The Book of A Hundred Houses," 133; *176, 289*
"A Book of Dakota Rhymes," 361
Booklists
  Stone & Kimball
    1893, 12-19

    1894, 21-22, 71-72
    1895, 72-73, 75n
    1896, Chicago, 73
    1896-97, New York, 76ff., 84-85
  H. S. Stone & Co.
    1896, 95-96
    1897, 102-3
    1898, 112-13
    1899, 116-17
    1900, 122-23
    1901, 124-25
    1902, 132-33
    1903-5, 135
The Bookman, 48-49; *62, 65, 85, 169, 273*
Boothby, Guy, 213
"The Borderland of Society," *161*
Borie, A. E., 95; *22, 119*
"Boss and Other Dogs," xxxii; *93*
Boston Bookbinding Company, 87; *77*
Bourget, Paul, 2
Bowden, publishers, *127, 228*
Bowles, J. M., 26, 28
Boyce, Neith, *22*
Boyesen, H. H., *22*
Boyle, Virginia Frazer, *22*
Boynton, Percy Holmes, 45n
Boynton, Henry Walcott, *288*
"Brada," *218*
Bradley, Will H., 36, 41, quoted 40, 67, 95; xix, xxix; *22, 94, 118, 119, 120, 130, 146, 158, 168, 180, 289*
Branch, Anna Hempstead, *22*
Brandt, Albert, publisher, *6*
Brangwyn, Frank, *130*
Brendon, William, and Son, printers, *266*
Brentano's, 125; *150, 169, 199, 260, 283*
Brewer, Layton, *22*
Brewer's Block, 27
"Brewster's Millions," 105, 128ff., 136; *299*
"A Bride of Japan," *144*
Bridges, Robert, *357*
Bridge, Norman, *170, 291*
Brisbane, Arthur, quoted, 132
Brock, C. E., *74*
Brock, H. M., *270*
Brooke, Emma, *252*

Brooks, Jennie, *22*
Brown, Alice, *22*
Brown, Anna Robeson, *22, 300*
Browne, E. G., *47*
Browne, Francis Fisher, *357*
Browne, Helen Madder, *22*
Brussel, I. R., *159*
"The Building of the City Beautiful," x; *6*
Bulkeley, B. R., *316*
Bullock, Shan F., *359; 22, 101*
Bunyan, John, *270*
Burgess, Gelett, quoted 37-38; *22, 138*
Burgess, Gilbert, *46*
Burleigh, B. W., *361*
Burroughs, John, *22, 281*
Burton, Augustus, *22*
Burton, Richard, *48; 22*
Burton, Sir Richard F., *163*
"The Bushwackers," *204*
Business Records, 145
Butler, Mrs. Ruth Lapham, *244*
The Butterfly, 30-31
"By the Waters of Babylon," *276*

Calhoun, Lucy Monroe (Mrs. W. J. Calhoun)
  See Monroe, Lucy
Calkins, Earnest Elmo, 68; *22*
Calkins, Frank Welles, *357; 184*
The Camelot Press, 26, 68; *22*
"Can We Disarm?" *195*
Canton, William, *22, 74, 96*
Cantwell, Robert, quoted 44
"Captain Jacobus," *91*
"The Carcellini Emerald," *202*
Cardozo, Elizabeth C., *22*
"The Carissima," *116*
Carleton, Emma, *22*
Carman, Bliss, 20-21, 26-28, 46; ii; *12, 22*
Carnation Series, 73; *50-54*
Carpenter, H. T., 18; xiii; *4, 5, 22, 63*
Carpenter, John Alden, 104
"The Carpenter Prophet," *292*
Carrington, Fitzroy, *95*
Carruth, Edith, *22*
Carter, John, *147*
"Cashel Byron's Profession," 125-26; *260, 283*
Caslon antique type, *88*

Castle, Egerton, *248*
"Castle Craneycrow," 128; *296*
"Catherine Sforza," *172*
Catherwood, Mary Hartwell, 11, 117; *225*
Cawein, Madison, 48; *22*
Caxton Club, 65
Cazals, F. A., 34; *22*
Chaffee, Frank, *22, 95*
Chamberlin, Joseph Edgar, *22*
Chambers, Robert W., *359; 22, 102*
"A Champion in the Seventies," *151*
Channing-Stetson, Mrs. Grace Ellery, *22, 51, 253*
The Chap-Book, 25-54, 145; *8, 12, 13, 17, 21, 22, 61, 76, 110, 118, 125, 138, 156, 194, 219, 234*
Chap-Book
  Covers xviii-xix
  Music Hall, 63-64
  Posters, 36-37; xxxix-xl
  Readings, *139*
  Teas, 49n, 54, 63-64
Chapman, Coates, *22*
Chapman, J. J., *22*
Chapman & Hall, publishers, *207*
"Chapters from Illinois History," *272*
Charrington, Charles, *86, 87*
Chatfield-Taylor, H. C., 49n, 66, 72, 95; *41, 117, 132, 250, 290*
Chatto & Windus, publishers, *52*
Chauvenet, William Marc, *22*
"Checkers," 96; *109*
Cheltenham Press, 70, 90-93
Cheltenham type, 90-92, 150
Cheney, John Vance, 47, 65, 357; *22*
Cheney, O. H., quoted, 142
Cheret, Jules, 35
Chicago
  as a literary centre, 66-67, 75, 116-18, 123-24, 138, 142
  Club, 65, 361
  Daily News, 10, 75; *235*
  Record, 117; *82, 112, 206, 219, 224, 259*
  Times-Herald, 117; *187, 263*
  Tribune, 118
  World's Fair, 3-4, 9-12
"Chicago and the World's Fair," 10; ix; *1*
"A Child of the Jago," *113, 209*

365

"A Child of the Sun," *257*
Childe, Rheta Louise, *22, 78*
Chopin, Kate, 114-15, 357; *192*
"The Christmas Garland," *281*
Claflin, H. B. Co., *165*
Clark, Cecil, *22*
Clarkson, Ralph, 64-65
Clay, Richard & Sons, *60, 171, 172, 195, 207*
Cleary, Kate M., 357
Cliff-Dwellers, 65
Clodd, Edward, 264
Clover, Samuel Travers, 9, 357
Coleman, Oliver, 112; *130, 176, 289*
Collations, 147
Collector interest, 149
"The College Widow," *219*
"The College Yearbook," 105
Columbia University Library, 146
Colvin, Sir Sidney, 62; *49*
Colyar, W. Douglas, *22*
Congreve, William, *40*
Connor, Florence G., *22*
"The Conscience of Coralie," *267*
Constable, T. and A., printers, *9, 16, 18, 30, 39, 40, 47, 50, 64, 71, 85, 86, 87, 100, 227, 260, 264*
"Constantine," *187*
Coolidge, Albert Sprague, *178*
Coolidge, Elizabeth Sprague, 178
Coonley-Ward, Lydia A., 357
Cooper, Edward H., *214, 265*
"The Coöperative Commonwealth," *154*
Copeland, Charles Townsend, *22*
Copeland & Day, 20-21, 28-29, 115, 136; *52, 107, 108, 205*
Copyright, 119, 140, 141, 146; *283*
  assignments, 87-88, 114-15, 121, 136
  conflicts after sale, 88, 136
  defined, 148
  printings, 84, 359-60
Corelli, Marie, 85; *103*
Cortissoz, Royal, quoted 93-94
Cornford, L. Cope, *91*
Cosmopolis, 82-83
Cosmopolitan Magazine, *117, 165*
Costs, 144; *195, 255, 273*
"The Cougar-Tamer," *184*
"A Country Muse," *23, 30*
Coup, William Cameron, *278*

Court Series, 126; *23, 38, 63, 68, 72, 75, 76, 86, 98, 99, 106, 120, 121, 124, 127, 133, 141, 157, 161, 184, 185, 187, 197, 206, 251, 253, 254, 261*
Covell, Laura Kimball, quoted 7-8, 92
Coward, Edward Fales, *210*
Craddock, Charles Egbert, *204*
Craig, Gordon, *234*
Craig Press, Chicago, 18
Cram, Ralph Adams, 20, 27-29; *22, 52, 130*
Crane, Frank, 118; *224*
Crane, Stephen, 21, 46; *22*
Crane, Walter, *58*
"The Crimson Wing," *290*
The Critic, 9, 62, 108, 169, 263, 283
Crosby, Raymond M., *22, 132*
Crowe, John Maxwell, *22*
Crowninshield, Mrs. Schyler, *221*
Cruger, Mrs. Julie Grinnell, *133*
"Crumbling Idols," *4, 19*
Cucuel, Edward, *262*
Cummings, Edward, *22*
Cunliffe-Owen, Marguerite, *145*
"Curious Punishments of Bygone Days," 48; *118*
Curtis, Wardon Allan, 135; xxvii; *302*
Curtis, William Eleroy, *22, 82, 259*
"Cyrano de Bergerac," 153

Dailey, W. J. F., 14, 57, 74, 120, 127; *126*
The Daily Tatler, 85-87; *92, 95*
"The Damnation of Theron Ware," 73-74, 87; *69, 165, 192*
D'Annunzio, Gabriele, 21, 95-96; *108*
"D'Arcy of the Guards," *190*
"Dartnell," *255*
Davidson, John, 20, 52, 359; *17, 22, 72*
Davis, Charles Belmont, *161*
Davis, Richard Harding, 96; *161*
Dawe, Carlton, *144*
Day, B. Corson, *22*
"Days and Hours," *66*
"The Decadent," *52*
"A Degenerate," *22*
"Degeneration," 50
De Guaita, Stanislas, *22*
De Koven, Reginald, *22, 27, 250*

366

De Koven, Mrs. Reginald, 49n, 66, 125; *22, 38, 276*
Dennis, Charles Henry, 11-12; *224*
De Sanctis, G., 22
D'Espagnat, Georges, 22
Detroit Free Press, 54
Devices, Table III; *2, 4, 107, 108, 113, 119, 126, 158, 180, 218*
DeVinne Press, 151-53; *14, 15, 21*
Devoore, Ann, *189*
The Dial, 145; *22, 169*
Dickinson, John & Co., *11*
Dickinson Type Foundry, *88*
Distribution, 122
"Doc' Horne," *206*
"The Documents in Evidence," *109*
Dodd, Mead & Company, 48-49, 136; *32, 70, 74, 96, 108, 150, 273, 296, 299*
Donnelley, R. R. & Sons
  See Lakeside Press
Donnelley, T. E., 65, 153
Donohue, M. A. & Co., publishers, *184*
Donohue & Henneberry, printers, 5; *1*
Doran, George H., 129, quoted 139
D'Orsay, Count, *218*
Doubleday, McClure Company, 115, 116; *192*
Dow, Joy Wheeler, *289*
Doxey, William, publisher, 117
Drackman, Holger, 357
Drew, John, *190*
"Dross," *188*
Du Bois, Constance Goddard, *254*
Duckworth, publishers, *137, 159, 160, 214, 265*
Duffield, Pitts, 22
Duffield & Company, 127; *32, 69, 70, 94, 112, 117, 126, 128, 155, 192, 199, 201, 206, 244, 295*
  See also Fox, Duffield & Company
Du Freen, Kathleen Hoy, 22
Dunbar, Paul Lawrence, 22
Dunne, Finley Peter, 31-32, 62-63; *258*
Dunster House, *201*
Duodecimos, 65-66
Dwiggins, W. A., *130*

Eames, Emma, *235a*

Earle, Alice Morse, 48; *22, 118, 130*
Eastman, Barrett, 22
"Eat Not Thy Heart," *133*
"The Ebb-Tide," 59-67, 69, 151-53; xvii; *24, 138*
Eckels, James H., 22
Editions
  defined, 147
  exported, *15, 21, 118, 128, 133, 136, 143, 166*
  imported, 20; *9, 163 195, 255*
  limited, 58
  paper, 113-14
  remainders, 76-89
  reprints, 74, 121, 126, 141
  size, 148; *250, 295*
  subscription, 57
Editorial policy, 45 ff., 51, 56-57, 95-97, 117, 139, 141
  See also Booklists
Edwards, Louise Betts, 22
El Comancho, *222*
Eldridge Court
  See Offices
Eldridge Series, 126; *63, 73, 74, 83, 89, 90, 91, 96, 97, 100, 101, 113, 122, 123, 125, 136, 144, 151, 158, 161, 162, 180, 181, 183, 186, 191, 195, 198, 200, 202, 208, 212, 213, 214, 215, 216, 217, 229, 232, 240, 252, 256, 265*
"The Electric Automobile," *246*
"Embers," *15*
Embree, Charles Fleming, *22, 129*
Embury, Aymar, *130*
Emerson, Adaline Talcott, 361
Emerson, Edwin, Jr., *95, 105*
Emerson, Florence Brooks, *95*
English authors, 52, 76, 97
English Classics Series, 72-73; *39, 40, 47, 64, 65, 71*
"English Seamen," 65
"The Engrafted Rose," *252*
"Episcopo & Company," xxviii; *108*
"Essays from the Chap-Book," *119*
"Esther Waters," 118-19; *199*
Etchison, Georgia A., *193*
"Etiquette for Americans," *155*
"Euphrosyne and Her Golden Book," *180, 279*
Evans, Edmund, *58*

Evans, F. H., *150*
"Eve's Glossary," *145*
Expenses, 136
"Ezra Caine," 125; *277*

"Fables in Slang," 97; *219*
"A Fair Brigand," *187*
Fallows, Alice Katherine, 22
"Famous Ladies of the English Court," *231*
"Famous Trials of the Century," *227*
Farnum, William, *249*
"The Fatal Gift of Beauty," *114*
"The Father of the Forest," *57*
Faxon, Frederick Winthrop, 37, 41; *281*
"The Fearsom Island," *111*
Fenollosa, Mary McNeil, 22
Field, Etta Dexter, *357*; 22
Field, Eugene, 10-17, 32n, 62-63, 151; *2, 8, 22*
Field, Roswell Martin, *357*
Finances, 56, 63, 74, 85, 88-89, 110-111, 119-120
  See also Magazine circulation; Sales of books
Financial records, 144
Findon, B. W., *228*
"The First Cruiser Out," *164*
First edition, definition, 148
"First Editions of American Authors," 5, 13-16; x; *2, 8*
Fisguill, Richard, *294*
Fiske, Mrs. Minnie Maddern, *210*
Fison, Alfred H., *237*
Fitch, Clyde, 22, 77, *139, 281*
Fitz-Gerald, Edward, *264*
"Flames," *123*
Fleming, H. E., 53, 117
Fleming, Schiller and Carnrick, printers, 150; *88, 90, 93, 95, 96, 100, 101*
Fletcher, Horace, 102-3; *134, 135, 166, 167, 236*
"The Flying Dutchman," 104
Fontenoy, Marquise de, *145*
"For the Love of Tonita," *129*
Forman, H. Buxton, *357*
"The Fortune of a Day," *51, 253*
"The Fourth Napoleon," *136*
Fox, John Jr., 22
Fox, Duffield & Company, 136, 145; 35, 79, *176, 180, 225, 260, 275*
  See also Duffield & Company
France, Anatole, 31; *22*
Franklin Old Style type, 150; *88*
Frederic, Harold, 73-74; v; *69, 165*
"Free to Serve," *205*
"The Free-Trade Movement and Its Results," *174*
French, Alice, *358*; *22, 156, 281*
French, Samuel, *219*
French artists and authors, 31-34, 76, 97
"Friend or Fortune," *90*
Fuller, Henry B., 64; *22*

Gâchons, Andhré des, 34; *22*
Galbraith, Lettice, 22
Gale, Norman, *22, 23, 30, 85*
"Galloping Dick," *61*
Gamble, Alan H., quoted 90-91
Garland, Hamlin, 11, 17-18, 46, quoted 66, 71-72, 88-89; xi-xiii; *4, 5, 19, 22, 62, 63*
Gates, Lewis E., 22
Geddes, Patrick & Colleagues, 79; *53, 75*
Gere, C. M., *357*
Gibson, Charles Dana, *22, 41, 89*
Gibson, Charles Hammond, *242*
Gilliss, Walter, 91-92
Gissing, George, *357*
Glasgow, Ellen, 22
"Gloria Mundi," *165*
"Glutton or Epicure," *167, 236*
Glyde, John, *264*
"The Gods Give My Donkey Wings," *54*
Goetz, Philip Becker, 22
"The Golden Age," 88; iii; *9, 43*
"A Golden Sorrow," *158*
Goldsmith, Oliver, *126*
"The Golfer's Rubáiyát," *288*
Gomme, G. Laurence, *175*
Goodhue, Bertram Grosvenor, 20, 27-29, 91-93, 150; *22, 52*
Goodhue, H. E., 22
Goodridge, Elizabeth Stone, 13
Goodspeed, Charles E., 23, 115
Gordon, Julien, *133*
Gordon, Samuel, *211*
Gosse, Edmund, *22, 29, 281*

Goudy, Frederic W., 12, 26, quoted 68-69; *22, 130*
Goul, Gilbert, *184*
Grahame, Kenneth, 20, 88; iii; *9, 22, 43*
Grasset, Eugène, 34, 35; *22*
"Graustark," 105, 124, 126-28; xxxvi; *273, 307*
Graves, William Lucius, *22*
Graves & Henry, printers, 26, 29; *22*
Greaves, Richard P., *299*
Greban, Arnoul, *22*
The Green Tree Library, 32, 71, 98, 122; *31, 33, 37, 67, 70, 104, 243, 247*
Greene, C. E., *22*
Greening & Co., publishers, *240*
Grinnell, George Bird, 122; *244*
"Grip," 150, 151; xxvi-vii; *88*
"Griselda," *261*
Grissom, Arthur, *22*
Gronlund, Laurence, 112; *154*
Gross, Samuel Eberly, 153, 361
Grosset & Dunlap, 114; *69, 109, 112, 126, 128, 206, 219, 269, 273, 299*
Guest, B. C., *22*
Guiney, Louise Imogen, 28, 47; *22*
"The Gypsy Christ," *50*

Haaser, Arthur B., quoted 145
Hake, Thomas Gordon, *18*
Hale, Edward Everett, *7*
Hale, Edward Everett Jr., *22*
Hall, Gertrude, *22, 37*
Hall, Ruth, *22*
Hall, Thomas Winthrop, *13*
Hallowell, George H., *6, 10, 12, 22*
Hamilton, Lord Ernest, *208*
Hammond, William A., *162*
Hannay, David, *65*
Hapgood, Norman, *22, 137*
Hapgood, T. B. Jr., *90*
"Happiness," 102-3; *134, 135*
Harcourt, Alfred, 117, 139
Hardy, Thomas, 359; *22, 62*
Harlow, Arthur, 76
Harper and Brothers, 116; *4, 143, 188, 283*
Harper's Magazine, 142, 156, *161*
Harper's Weekly, *197*
Harris, Joel Chandler, *22*
Harris, Tom, *22*

Harrison, Mrs. Burton, *202*
Harrison, Mrs. Mary St. Leger, *116*
Harte, Bret, *95*
Harte, Walter Blackburn, 48
Hartman, Sadakichi, *95, 130*
Harvard
 Advocate, 5, 29, 104
 College, 1-4, 23-24, 104-6; *10, 13, 14*
 Crimson, 1, 3-5, 104
 Library, 5, 15, 59, 144
 Monthly, 5, 21, 47; *11, 14*
Harvey, Henry Blodgett, 133; *130*
Harvey, James Clarence, 28, 80, 95
Hasty Pudding Club, 104
Hawthorne, Julian, *22*
Hay, Helen, *160*
Hazell, Watson & Viney, Ld. printers, 268
Hazenplug, Frank, 36, 73, 95, 103, 111; xxviii; *22, 38, 61, 83, 107, 108, 111, 115, 118, 122, 127, 130, 131, 141, 145, 155, 160, 176, 182, 186, 187, 198, 200, 204, 211, 219, 221, 233, 248, 258, 275, 288, 293*
Head, Franklin H., *34*
"A Heaven-Kissing Hill," *182*
Heinemann, William, 24, 29, 46, 69, *110, 123, 136, 146, 151, 165, 171, 172, 173, 186, 195, 217, 218, 245, 247, 255, 256*
Hemenway, Myles, *22*
Hemingway, Percy, *357*
Henderson, Alice Palmer, *153*
Henderson, Archibald, quoted 98-99; *260, 283*
Henderson, W. J., *22*
Henley, William Ernest, 62, 360; *22, 39, 45*
Henry, Stuart, *357*
"Here & There & Everywhere," *143*
Hereward, L., *22*
Herrick, Robert, *180*
Hichens, Robert, 103; *123, 146, 217*
Higginson, T. W., 14; *22*
"The Highroad," *305*
Higinbotham, John U., *308*
Hilliard, J. N., *22*
Hinkson, Katharine Tynan, *22, 56*
Hird, Frank, *22*
"His Broken Sword," *7*

369

"Historic Styles in Furniture," 135; *309*
"The History of Gambling in England," *194*
Hodder & Stoughton, publishers, *196*
Holdsworth, Annie E., *245*
Holloway, E. S., *22*
Holloway, William Jr., *22*
Holly Tree Tavern, 27
Holmes, E. Burton, *140*
Holmes, Clarence H., quoted 27, 63
Holmes, Maurice, *260*
"The Holy Cross," xi; *8*
Hope, Anthony, 32
Hopper, Nora, 359; *22*
Horneck, Mary, *126*
Horton, George, 357, 367; *187, 263*
Houghton Mifflin Company, 115; *117*
The House Beautiful, 112, 128, 133-35, 137; *130, 176, 306*
"A House of Cards," *38, 68*
Hovey, Carl, quoted 105-110
Hovey, Henriette, *95*
Hovey, Richard, 27, 28, 46-47, 86, 97; *22, 32, 48, 70, 95*
"How to Play Golf," *140*
Howe, B. H., *22*
Howells, William Dean, 11; *4, 95, 206*
Hubbard, Elbert, 40-41
Hughes, Rupert, *22*
"The Human Interest," *215*
Hunt, Leigh, *95*
Hunt, Violet, *215*
Huntington Library, 76n, 144
Hurst & Company, publishers, *273*
Hutchinson, publishers, *126, 144, 163, 223, 231, 252, 268, 275*
Hutt, Henry, *202*
Hyde, George Merriam, *22, 95*
Hyde, Henry M., *96; 284*
I. K. L., *241*
"I Await the Devil's Coming"
 See "The Story of Mary MacLane"
Ibsen, Henrik, 122; *33, 104, 247*
"Ickery Ann and Other Girls and Boys," *183*
"Indians of Today," *122*
"The Idle Born," *250*
"Illumination"
 See "The Damnation of Theron Ware"

"Illustrations of the House Beautiful," *289*
Impression, defined, 147
Imprint value, 140
"The Impudent Comedian," *125*
"In a Dike Shanty," *83*
"In Buncombe County," *115*
"In Castle & Colony," *205*
"In Memory of W. V.," *74*
"In Russet and Silver," 69-70; xx, xxi; *13, 29*
"In the Cage," *159*
"In Unknown Seas," *187*
Inland Printer, 16, 36, 42
"The Inn of the Silver Moon," *262*
"The Invisible Playmate," *74, 96*
Irving, Sir Henry, *207, 234*
Isbister, publishers, *74, 96*
"The Island of Doctor Moreau," *76*

Jaccaci, A. F., *21*
Jackson, Helen Hunt, *254*
Jacobus, R. P., *22*
James, Henry, 103; *22, 138, 159, 160*
"James; or, Virtue Rewarded," *100*
Jarboe, Kathryn, *22*
Jenks, Tudor, *22*
Jensen type, *56*
Jerrold, Laurence, *22*
"The Jessamy Bride," *126, 267*
"The Jew, the Gypsy and El Islam," *163*
Bright, John, *149*
"John Gabriel Borkman," 104
Johnson, Basil, *23*
Johnson, Charles Howard, 27
Johnson, Hilda, *22*
Johnson, Janey, *22*
Johnson, Ralph, *22*
Johnson, Samuel, *71*
Johnston, R. M., *358*
Joliquet, *22*
Jones, Myrta Leonora, *108*
Jossot, *22*
Judah, Mary Jameson, *358*
"A June Romance," *23, 197*
"Just about a Boy," *222*

Kavanagh, F. Edge, *95*
Kay, J. Illingworth, *16*
Keays, Mrs. Hersilia A., *251*

Kemp-Welch, Lucy E., *213*
Kennedy, Bart, *240*
Kennerley, Mitchell, 88
Keppel, Frederick, *130*
Kernahan, Coulson, *203*
Kimball, Hannah Parker, 22
Kimball, Hannibal Ingalls, Sr., 6-7
Kimbrough, F. R., *121, 123*
King, Basil, *261*
Kingsley, Charles, *238*
Kinross, Albert, *111*
Kirk, Ellen Olney, *152*
Kirk, W. J., 75, 121; *280*
Klapp, Eugene, 111-12, 133; *130, 176, 289*
Knapp, Frances, *78*
The Knight Errant, 28-29
Kobbé, Gustav, 22
Krysher, Elizabeth, *298*

L. C. W., 22, *241*
"Lady Bramber's Ghost," *86, 87*
"The Lady of the Flag-Flowers," *198*
Laird & Lee, publishers, 116
Lakeside Press, 83, 153, 361; *22, 27, 34, 36, 38, 41, 42, 44, 50, 55-57, 62, 68, 77, 81, 99, 107, 109-113, 115, 117-121, 123-125, 128-130, 132-136, 138, 139, 141-144, 146, 150, 152, 155, 159-161, 164-170, 176-179, 181-193, 196-201, 203-206, 209-212, 214-221, 223-226, 228-230, 232-236, 241-247, 249-252, 254, 256-263, 267, 268, 272-274, 276-279, 282, 283, 285, 289-294, 296-301, 303, 304, 308, 309*
Lampman, Archibald, 22
Lamson, Wolffe & Co., 28, 88; *12, 84*
"The Land of Heart's Desire," *25*
"The Land of the Castanet," *117*
Lane, John, 20, 52, 88; *6, 9, 21, 43, 56, 57, 58, 61, 66, 81, 85, 107, 297*
Lang, Andrew, 358; *22*
The Lark, 38
la Rose, Pierre, xi, xv; *14, 22*
Larremore, Thomas A., 66n
Larremore, Wilbur, 22
"The Last of the Knickerbockers," *262, 285*
Lathrop, George Parsons, 95
Laughlin, Clara E., 22
"Launcelot and Guenevere," *48*

Lawrence, Arthur, *228*
Lawrence and Bullen, publishers, 60
Lawson, Elsworth, *279*
Lee, Agnes, 22
Lee, Gerald Stanley, 22
Lee-Hamilton, Eugene, 26
Lee-Hamilton, Mrs. Eugene, *245*
Lefevre, Edwin, 22
Le Gallienne, Richard, 78; *107*
Leland, Anthony, 22
Leslie, Amy, 118; *234, 235*
Leslie's Weekly, 89
"Lesser Destinies," *211*
Lewes, George Henry, *207*
Lewis, Elizabeth Dike, 22
Life, 13, 89
"The Life of a Woman," *297*
Lighton, W. R., 22
Lincolniana, 117-18; *10, 225*
"Lincoln's Grave," *10*
Lindeberg, H., *130*
Lippincott, J. B., *133*
"Literary Statesmen and Others," *137*
"Little Eyolf," 33
"A Little Legacy," *185*
"Little Lords of Creation," *251*
'Little Magazines,' 42-44
"A Little Sister to the Wilderness," *42*
The Little Room Club, 64-65, 67
Lloyd, Beatrix Demarest, 22
Locke, William J., 22
"London in the Reign of Victoria," *175*
"The Londoners," *146*
Long, Birch Burdette, *130, 289*
Longmans Green & Company, *275*
"Love Among the Artists," *99; 260*
"The Love-Letters of Mr. H. & Miss R., 1775-1779," *46*
"Love Made Manifest," *213*
"The Love of an Uncrowned Queen," *268, 275*
"A Lover's Diary," *15*
"Love's Dilemmas," 69; xxix; *13, 180*
Lovett, Robert Morss, 5, 8, quoted 21, 22, 74
Low, Will H., *15*
"Low Tide on Grand Pré, xvi; *12*
Lowell, Orson, 103; *131*
"The Lower Slopes," *16*
"Lucifer," *11, 79, 201*
Lummis, Charles F., 358; *22*

Lummis, Harry B., *22*
Lungren, Fernand, *129*
Lusitania, 137
Lyde, Phoebe, *22*
Lydenberg, H. M., *277*
Lyendecker, J. C., 36, 118; xxxix; *22, 225*
Lynch, Gertrude F., *22*

Mabie, Hamilton Wright, 49; *22*
"Macaire," 61-62, 360; *24, 45*
McCabe, Joseph, *195*
McCarter, Henry, 49n; *31, 37*
McCarthy, Justin Huntley, *22, 196*
McChesney, Dora, *358*
McClure, Phillips & Company, *280*
McClure, Robert, 52, 76, 82-83, 95; *124*
McClure's Magazine, 29-30, 61; *24*
McClurg, A. C. & Co., 12-13, 116, 119, 122; *7, 134*
McCulloch, Hugh Jr., *14, 22*
McCutcheon, George Barr, 124, 127; *273, 296, 299*
McCutcheon, John Tinney, 10, 96; vii, xxxviii; *1, 3, 109, 112, 128, 130, 179, 296*
Macfall, Haldane, *359*
McIntyre, John T., *22*
Mackall, Leonard L., 15, 16n
Mackay, Eric, *59*
Mackaye, Percy Wallace, *249*
Mackeller, Smith & Jordan Foundry, *88*
MacLane, Mary, *295, 301*
Macleod, Fiona
  See Sharp, William
McManus, Blanche, xxxii; *93*
Macmillan, publishers, 116; *4, 15, 28, 80, 118, 190*
Macy, Arthur, *22*
Macy, John Albert, *22*
"Mademoiselle Blanche," *92*
"Madge o' the Pool," *50*
Maeterlinck, Maurice, 97-98; *32, 55, 70, 95*
Magazines, 139
Magazine circulation, 37, 44, 53-54, 134; *22, 130*
Magruder, Julia, *121, 141, 182*
The Mahogany Tree, 28-29

"The Maid He Married," *197*
"Main-Travelled Roads," 18; xi-xiii; *4*
Malet, Lucas, *116*
Mallarmé, Stéphané, 32; *22*
"A Man Adrift," *240*
"A Man and a Woman," *191*
Mansfield, Richard, 154
Marholm, Laura, *193*
"The Marriage of Guenevere," *48*
"Marshfield the Observer," *248*
Martyn, Edward, *243*
Mason, Edward G., 125; *272*
"The Massacre of the Innocents and other Tales," *55*
Masters, Edgar Lee, 67, 114
Mathews, Elkin, *9*
Mathews, Elkin & John Lane, 19-20; *9, 16-18, 21, 85*
Matthews, Brander, 35n, 49; *22*
"Maude," 103; *127*
"Mazel," *294*
"The Meddling Hussy," *106*
Melcher, Frederic G., 28, 71, 74, 75, 150
Melville, Lewis, *223*
Mendoza, Isaac, 58, 80
"Menticulture," 102-3; *134, 135*
"The Merchant Prince of Cornville," 153, 361
Merrick, Leonard, 103; *124*
Merrill, Stuart, 32-33
Merriman, Henry Seton, *188*
Merryweather, George, 65
Metcalf, Keyes D., 92n
Meteyard, T. B., 69; xvii; *22, 24, 48*
Methuen & Company, *15, 28, 39, 40, 44, 47, 49, 54, 64, 65, 71, 72, 76, 80, 113, 115, 122, 209, 215*
Metropolitan Magazine, 106-8; *140*
"Mexico City," *275*
Meynell, Alice, *18*
Millard, George M., 12-13, 65
Millard, Gertrude B., *22*
Miller, Henry, *190*
Miller, Joaquin, 18-19; *6*
Miller & Richards' Old Style type, *88*
Miller, J. & Son, printers, *66*
Mills, Rose Edith, *22*
Miln, Louise Jordan, *266*
"Miracle Plays," *56*
"Miss Armstrong's and Other Circum-

372

stances," *17, 72*
"Miss Ayr of Virginia," *121*
Mitchell, Langdon, *210*
Modern Art, 26
"A Modern Reader and Speaker," *230*
Monarch Book Company, *187, 191*
"The Money Captain," 113; *157*
"The Monk Wins," *265*
Monroe, Harriet, quoted 47, 63; *130, 289*
Monroe, Lucy, quoted 8-9, 20n, 63, 117, 120, quoted 121, quoted 127, quoted 130-31, 142; *273, 299*
Moody, William Vaughn, 21-22, 47
Moore, Dorothea Lummis, 22
Moore, F. Frankfort, 46, 360; *22, 125, 126, 267*
Moore, George, 118-19, 122; *199, 243*
Moore, Mrs. Augustus, *110, 186*
"More Fables in Slang," *258*
Morgan, Anna, 4, 65, 98, 104-5; *25, 130*
Morier, James, *47*
Morley, Christopher, quoted *126*
Morris, Governeur, 22
Morris, Harrison S., 22
Morris, William, 100, 357; *56*
The Morris Bookshop, *8*
Morrison, Arthur, 52, 360; *22, 113, 209*
Mosher, Thomas Bird, 26, 40
"Mother Goose in Prose," 357
Moulton, Louise Chandler, 23; *21, 22, 281*
"A Mountain Woman," *183*
Mower, Martin, xvi; *12, 22*
Mullin, E. H., 22
Mumford, A. W., *282*
Munkittrick, R. K., *358*
Munn, George Frederick, 22
Murfree, Mary Noailles, *204*
Murray, Frank, publishers, *31, 67*
Murray, John, publishers, *211, 262*
"My Father and I," *136, 218*
"My Friend Annabel Lee," 131; *301*

Naguchi, Yone, 22
The Nation, *108*
"Nature's Food Filter," *236*
"Nell Gwyn," *125*
New, E. H., 22

"The New Economy," *154*
New Review, *61*
"New Stories from the Chap-Book," *168*
Newberry Library, *244*
Newbolt, Henry, 360; *22*
Newman, Clyde J., *219, 258, 259*
Nicholson, Meredith, 22
"A Night in Acadie," 357; *192*
Noel, Roden, *358*
"Noll and the Fairies," *298*
Nordau, Max, 50
Nordhoff, Evelyn Hunter, 22
Norton, Charles Eliot, 2-3
Norwood Press, 83; *45*
Noxon, Frank W., 22
"Nude Souls," *255, 256*
Nugent, Claud, *171*
Nutt, David, publishers, 30

Oakley, Violet, *156, 185, 189, 197, 202*
"An Odd Situation," *191*
Offices
   Brewer's Block, Cambridge, 27-28
   Caxton Building, Chicago, 62-63, 74, 84
   Constable Building, New York, 74, 84, 86, 120-21
   Eldridge Court, Chicago, 111-12; vi
   Republic Building, Chicago, *130*
"Old Pictures of Life," *34*
"Old Wine; A Comedy in One Act," 4, *65*
"Oliver Iverson," *189*
Omar Khayyám, *264*
"One Forty-Two," 96, *284*
"One Man's View," *124*
Orcutt, William Dana, 115, 151
Osborne, Duffield, 22
Osbourne, Lloyd, *24*
Ostertag, Blanche, *182*
O'Shaughnessy, Arthur, *21*
Over, G. E., printer and publisher, 23
Overton, J. H., *148*
Overton, Robert, *90*

Packard, Winthrop, 22
"Pagan Papers," xiv; *9*
Paginations, description, 147
Paine, Albert Bigelow, 22
"Painters Since Leonardo," *306*

373

Palmer, A. M., 153-54
Palmer, John Williamson, 22
"The Palmy Days of Nance Oldfield," *173*
'Pamphlet Period,' 37-44
Paper, 57, 150
Paper Books, 121, 123
Parker, Donn, *130*
Parker, Gilbert, 23, 87-88; *15, 28, 44, 80, 97*
Parrington, Vernon Louis, *130*
Parry, Albert, quoted *131*
Partnership problems, 59-60, 62, 74-75, 103-4, 142
Pasolini, Count Pier Desiderio, *172*
"The Passion of Rosamund Keith," *186*
Paterson, William Romaine, 255, 256
Pattison, James William, 135; *130, 306*
Pawling, Sydney, 255, 256
Payne, Will, 65, 113; *157*
Peabody, Josephine Preston, 48; *22*
The Peacock Library, 73; *38, 41, 68*
Pearson, C. Arthur, publishers, *125, 219, 244, 257, 258, 264, 266, 267, 269, 270, 271*
Pearson, Charles William, *292*
Peattie, Elia W., 118, 358; *22, 183*
Peck, Harry Thurston, 48-49
Pegram, Fred, *269*
Pell, William B., *22*
"The Penalties of Taste," *170*
Penfield, Edward, 35-36; *22, 130*
Pennell, Joseph, *22*
Percival, Olive, *275*
Pereira, Lyndwode, *22*
"The Perfect Wagnerite," *169*
"The Perils of Josephine," *208*
Perry, Jeannette Barbour, *22*
Persigny, Comte de, *242*
Pewter Mug Associates, 28
"Pharais," *53, 67*
Phemister, Alexander C., *88*
Phillips, Roland Edward, *22*
Phillips, Walter S., *222*
"Phyllis in Bohemia," *131*
Piatt, John James, *22*
Pickering, Theodosia, *22*
Pickering, William, 150
"The Picture Book of Becky Sharp," *210*

"Pierre and His People," *28, 80, 97*
"Pilgrim's Progress," *270*
"Pink Marsh," xxxviii; *128, 219*
"Pippins and Cheese," *183*
Piracy, 125
Pissaro, Georges, 34; *22*
"Plays: Pleasant and Unpleasant," 102; *150*
La Plume, 31, 34n
Plymouth Rock Pants Company, 10; *1*
"Po' White Trash," *249*
Podmore, Periwinkle, *22*
Poe edition, 31, 56-58, 87; *35, 287*
"Poems of the Day and Year," *66*
Pollard, Percival, 26, 30, 358; *22*
Pool, Maria Louise, *22, 83, 93, 115, 158, 181, 216, 281*
"Popular Guide to Chicago and the World's Fair," 5; *1*
Posters, 34-37; *3, 13, 22, 24, 25, 31, 41, 61, 69, 74, 112, 128, 131, 168, 219*
Potts, William, *22*
Powell, Richard Stillman, 103; *131*
Power, Tyrone, *210*
"Prairie Folks," *4, 63*
"Prairie Songs," xi; *4, 5*
Pratt, Charles Stuart, *22*
Press Club, 65, 67
"Pretty Pierre," *80, 97*
Prince, Helen Choate, *22*
Prindiville, Mary L., *22, 130, 262*
"Priscilla's Love Story," *142*
Pritchard, Martin J., *110, 186*
Procrastinatorium, 28
"Prose Fancies," *107*
Publication defined, 147-48
Publicity, 139-40
Publishers' Weekly, 19, 148-49
Publishing history, 138-43
Pugh, Edwin, 360; *22*
Puliga, Countess, *136, 218*
"The Puppet," *99*
"The Purple East," *81*

"The Quest of Heracles," xi, xv; *14*
Quiller-Couch, Arthur, *22*

Raffaëlli, J. F., 34; *22*
Ragsdale, Lulah, *22*

374

Raimond, C. E., *114*
"The Rainbow's End: Alaska," *153*
Rand, Edward Kennard, 6
Rand, McNally Co., 116
Rankin, Daniel S., 115; *192*
Rarities, 154-55
Rayner, Emma, *205*
Read, Opie, 65, 358
Readers, 67-68
"A Realized Ideal," *141*
"Recent Advances in Astronomy," *237*
"The Red Room," 360; *76*
Reed, Helen Leah, 22
Regional publishing, 116-17
Regnault, John, 22
"The Religion of To-Morrow," *224*
Remainders
  See Editions
Reprints
  See Editions
"Resolved to Be Rich," *214*
"A Revolutionary Love-Story," *152*
"The Rewards of Taste," *291*
Rhead, Louis J., 35, 49n; *8*
Rhodes, Harrison Garfield, 4, 27, 31-32, 95-96, 117, 120, 143; *22, 130, 255*
Rhys, Ernest, 22
Rice, Wallace, 127; *22, 179, 273, 282, 304*
Richards, Grant, 99-100; *84, 124, 150, 169, 193, 227, 263, 273, 283, 288, 290, 295, 296*
Richardson, Fred, v; *22, 130*
Richardson, Mrs. Aubrey, *231*
Richmond, George H. & Co., publishers, *108*
Ricketts, Charles S., 22
Riddle, George, *230*
Rimbaud, Arthur, 32
Rimpled type, *88*
Rinder, Edith Wingate, 55
Rinehart, F. A., *244*
"Ring o' Rushes," *101*
"The Rise and Growth of Democracy in Great Britain," *147*
Risley, Richard Voorhees, 22, *297*
"Rob Roy," 27
"The Robb's Island Wreck," *20*
Roberts Brothers, publishers, 23
Roberts, Charles G. D., 26-27; *22*

Roberts, Theodore, 22
Roberts, William Carman, 22
Robie, Virginia, quoted 111-12, 120-21, 134-45, 137; *130, 176, 289, 309*
Robins, Edward, *173*
Robins, Elizabeth, *114*
Rogers, A. P., *101*
Rogers, Bruce, 26, 28, 114, 357, 358; xxiii; *42, 44, 183*
Rogers, W. A., *202*
"Roland of Altenburg," 135; *307*
"The Romance of a Rogue," *293*
"A Romany of the Snows," *80, 97*
Rook, Clarence, 52, 98; *22*
Robespierre, Maximilien, *207*
Rose, J. Holland, *147*
"Rose Island," *233*
"Rose of Dutcher's Coolly," *4, 62, 63, 192*
Roseboro', Viola, 22
Rosenthal, Beatrice, 22
Ross, Clinton, 46; *22, 98, 99, 106*
Rossetti, Christina, 103; *127*
Rossetti, Dante Gabriel, *18*
Rossetti, William, *127*
Rostand, Edmond, 153
Routledge, publishers, *207*
Royalties
  See Authors; Sales of books
"Rubaiyat," *264*
The Rugby Press, *23*
Rule, Lucien V., 361
"Running the Cuban Blockade," *229*
"Ruskin's Principles of Art Criticism," *286*
Russell, Robert H., publishers, *258*
Russell, W. Clark, *233*
Ryan & Hart Co., printers, *130*
Ryland, Hobart, 154

Sabin, Edwin L., *22*
Saddle & Cycle Club, 65
Sadleir, Michael, *147*
"St. Ives," 62, 81
St. Louis Post Dispatch, *192*
St. Nicholas, 183
"Saints and Sinners Corner," 12, 62
Sales of books, *3, 22, 36, 49, 69, 98, 109, 112, 118, 126, 128, 130, 132, 134, 135, 140, 178, 188, 202, 219, 273, 283, 284, 295*

See also Best-sellers
Salvini, Alexander, 249
"San Isidro," 221
Sanborn, Alvan F., 22
"Sand 'N' Bushes," 181
Sansom, Charles, 218
Santayana, George, 21, 22, 47, 84; xvi; 11, 79, 201
Sarony, Napoleon, 210
Sauber, Robert, 125, 188
Savage, P. H., 22
"Sawdust & Spangles," 278
"A Sawdust Doll," 38
"The Scarlet Coat," 98
Schmedtgen, William, 179, 259
Scholl, Walter, 278
Schulte, F. J., 18-19, 116-17; 63
"The Science of Life," 147, 239
Scollard, Clinton, 22, 95
Scott, Hugh Stowell, 188
Scott, Walter, publishers, 199, 283
Scott, Mary McNeil, 22
"Scoundrels & Co.," 203
Scribner's, Charles, Sons, 58, 82-84, 116; 8, 15, 24, 35, 36, 49, 79, 163, 169, 207
Scribner's Magazine, 156
"The Seats of the Mighty," 44
Sedgwick, Ellery, 137
"The Seekers," 191, 232
"A Sentimental Life of Horace," 17; 8
Seon, Alexandre, 34; 22
Sforza, Catherine of, 172
Sharp, Evelyn, 360; 22
Sharp, William, 76-81, 88, 144; iv; 22, 31, 50, 53, 67, 75, 84
Sharts, Joseph, 125; 277, 293
Shaw, George Bernard, 52, 98-102, 122, 125-26, 136; xxxiii-v; 150, 159, 260, 263, 283
Sheffield, A. D., 22
Shelby, Annie Blanche, 220
Sheldon, Charles, 91
Sheridan-Fry, Mrs. Emma, 249
Sherman, Francis, 22
Sherman, Frank Dempster, 22
Sherwood, M. E. W., 22, 143
Shipman, Louis Evan, 89, 190
"A Short History of the United States," 196
Sigerson, Dora, 22

Simpson, Eve Blantyre, 22
"The Sin Eater," 53
Singleton, Esther, 95
"The Sister of a Saint," 51
"The Slave," 217
"A Slave to Duty and Other Women," 156
Sloan, John, 42; 22
Small, Herbert, 22
Small, Maynard & Co., 28, 115, 136; 12, 48
The Smart Set, 250
"The Smart Set: Correspondence and Conversations," 139
Smith, F. Berkley, 74
Smith, G. Armitage, 174
Smith, Gertrude, 226
Smith, Harry B., 27
Snow, Florence, 358
"Some Correspondence and Six Conversations," 77
"Some Players," 234, 235
"The Son of Perdition," 162
Sons of the Revolution, 361
"A Song of the Sea," 59
"Sonnets of the Wingless Hours," 26, 245
Sothern, E. A., 190
"A Soul in Bronze," 254
Sources, 142-48
Southall, Joseph E., 22, 60
Southey, Robert, 65
"The Spanish-American War," 179
"Spanish Peggy," 117-18; 225
Spencer, Robert, 130
"The Splendid Shilling," 101
Spofford, Harriet Prescott, 142, 197
Sprague, A. A., quoted 109-110
"Standard Whist," 220
Stannard, Mrs. Henrietta E. V., 88
Stearns, Fred, 130
Stedman, Edmund Clarence, 23, 48, 57, 88-89; 22, 35
Steffens, Lincoln, 22
Sterne, Laurence, 39
Sterner, Albert Edward, 57; 22, 35
Stetson, Charlotte Perkins, 22
Stetson, Grace Ellery Channing, 22, 51, 253
Stevens, B. F., publishers, 166
Stevenson, Nathaniel, 22

376

Stevenson, Robert Louis, 52, 58-62, 81-84, 144, 360; *22, 24, 36, 45, 49, 281*
Stock, Elliott, printer and publisher, *26*
Stoddard, Richard Henry, *22*
Stoddard, William O., *164, 229*
Stokes, Frederick A., 113, 139; *13, 103*
Stone, Melville E., Jr., 5, 13, 103-110, 127, 131; *1, 123, 130, 139, 140, 188, 277, 290, 299, 303*
Stone, Melville E., Sr., 1, 4, 60, 74, quoted 137, 177
Stone's Monthly Library, 69, *110*
Stone's Paper Library, 114; *38, 63, 68, 69, 73, 75, 76, 90, 91, 97, 100, 110, 112, 113, 115, 120-124, 128, 131-133, 136, 144, 151, 157, 161, 162, 187, 195, 214, 215*
Stone's Quarterly Series, *112*
"Stories from the Chap-Book," *120*
"Stories from the Old Testament for Children," *177*
"The Story of Ab," *191*
"The Story of Blue-Beard," *60*
"The Story of Mary MacLane," 124, 129-32, 136; *295*
Stowe, Harriet Beecher, *271*
Strang, William, *49*
Strange, E. F., *90*
"The Strange Adventures of Mr. Middleton," 135; xxxvii; *302*
Street, Ida M., *286*
Stromberg, Allen & Co., printers, *116, 122, 126, 130, 140, 151-153, 156, 158, 162, 181, 306*
Stuart, Ruth McEnery, *22*
Stubbs, Charles William, *238*
"Studies in the Psychology of Woman," *193*
Studio, 90
"A Sturdy Beggar," *86, 87*
"Successful Houses," *176*
Sudbury, Richard, *242*
Sullivan, Sir Arthur, *228*
Sutherland, Evelyn Greenleaf, *249*
Swift, Benjamin, *255, 256*
Swift, Ivan, *130*
Swing, David, *34*
Sylvester, Paul, *172*

Tabb, John B., 48; *22*
Taber, I. W., *106*
Taber, Robert, *190*
Tait, J. Selwin, & Sons, publishers, 76; *96*
"The Tale of a Town," *243*
"Tales of Mean Streets," *209*
"Tales of the West," *184*
Tarkington, Booth, 42, quoted 73-74
Tarver, John Charles, *100*
Tassin, Algernon, quoted 30
Taupin, René, quoted 33-34, 50
"Tawny Spain," *117*
Taylor, J. Russell, *22*
Taylor, Winnie Louise, *7*
Teall, Gardner C., *22*
Tennyson, Frederick, 66
"The Terra Cotta Guide," 10; *3*
Terry, Ellen, *207, 234, 235a, 263*
Thackeray, William Makepeace, *223*
Thanet, Octave
  See Alice French
"That Last Waif; or, Social Quarantine," *166*
"This Little Pig, His Picture Book," *58*
"The Thlinkets of South Eastern Alaska," *78*
Thompson, Charles Miner, *22*
Thompson, John Stuart, *22*
Thompson, Maurice, 49-50; *10, 22, 281*
Thompson, Vance, *22*
Thomson, Sir J. Arthur, *147, 239*
Thomson, J. S., *22*
"Three Plays for Puritans," *263*
"Three Weeks in Europe," *308*
Thwaites, Reuben Gold, *358*
Ticknor & Fields, 139
"To London Town," *209*
Today, 24, 283
Tolstoi, Leo, *192*
Toulouse-Lautrec, Henri de, 34-35; xl; *22*
Townsend, Edward W., 96
Townsend, F. H., *267*
Traver, C. W., *22*
Trent, W. P., *62*
"The Tribulations of a Princess," *145*
Triggs, O. L., *22*
"The Triumph of Death," *108*
"Truth and a Woman," *300*

Turnbull & Spears, printers, *59, 194*
Turner, G. K., *22*
Twachtman, J. H., *69, 74, 96*
Twain, Mark, *128*
"Two Gentlemen in Touraine," *242*
"Two Women & a Fool," *41*
Types, 90-92, 150; *56, 88*
Typesetting, 150
Typography, 68-70, 76, 90, 97, 121, 133, 140, 149, 150

"Uncle Tom's Cabin," *257, 271*
United States Book Company, *48*
University Press, Cambridge, 13, 85, 87, 151, 153; *2, 4-8, 10-13, 15, 19, 20, 24, 25, 28, 29, 31-33, 35, 37, 43, 48, 49, 61, 63, 67-70, 72-76, 78-80, 82-84, 86, 87, 89, 91, 92, 94, 97, 98, 102-6, 108, 115, 137, 138, 145, 180*
"An Unsocial Socialist," *260*
Unwin, T. Fisher, publishers, *4, 25, 208*
Updike, D. B., 26
"Urban Dialogues," *89*

"Vailima Letters," 62, 83; *24, 49*
"Valley of the Great Shadow," *245*
Vallotton, F., 34; *22*
Van Doren, Carl, *62*
Van Vechten, Carl, *70-71*
"Vengeance of the Female," *200*
Verbeek, Gustave, *278*
Verlaine, Paul, 31, 32; *14, 22, 37*
"The Vice of Fools," *132*
Victorian Era Series, 112, 122; *147, 148, 149, 174, 175, 237, 238, 239*
Vielé, Herman Knickerbocker, 122, 125; *262, 285*
Vielé-Griffin, Francis, *262*
Vince, C. A., *149*
Virtue, J. S. and Company, printers, *231*
Visionists, 27-28
"Vistas," *31, 32*

"W. V. Her Book," *74, 96*
Wagner, Rob, *22*
Walford, L. B., *185*
Walker, John Brisben, *165*
Wallace Elizabeth, *22*
Walsh, Thomas, *22*

Walton, Izaak, *64*
Ward and Locke, publishers, *213*
Warner, Susan, *269*
Warren, Donald, *22*
Warren, S. D., & Company, 57, 75, 87
"Was It Right to Forgive?," *212*
"The Washer of the Ford," 79; *75*
Waterbury, Jennie Bullard, *22*
Waterloo, Stanley, 65, 117, 358; *191, 232*
Watermarks, *22, 25, 27, 106, 110, 138*
Watson, Dawson, ii; *22*
Watson, H. B. Marriott, *22, 61*
Watson, William, 360; *22, 57, 81*
Waugh, Arthur, *22*
Way, W. Irving, 16, 65, 68; *22, 130*
Way & Williams, 67, 114-15, 357-58; *157, 183, 184, 187, 191, 192*
Webster, Charles and Co., publishers, *12*
Weed, Clarence Moores, *130*
Weed, Raphael A., *22*
"Weekly Record of New Publications," 148
"Weir of Hermiston," 62, 81-84, 360; *24*
Wellford, Clarence, *22, 241*
Wells, Carolyn, 84, quoted 85-86; *22, 94, 95, 130*
Wells, Geoffrey H., *260, 263*
Wells, H. G., 52, 84, 360; *22, 76*
Wendell, Barrett, 4
Wendell, Everts, 144
Wenzloff, G. G., *361*
Westley, Hembert G., *22*
Wetherald, Ethelwyn, *22*
Wharton, Anne Hollingsworth, *22*
"What Maisie Knew," 103; *138*
"What Sense? or, Economic Nutrition," *167, 236*
"When Hearts Are Trumps," 69; *13*
"When Valmond Came to Pontiac," *44*
"When We Dead Awaken," 98, 122; *247*
Whigham, H. J., 112; *140, 179*
"The Whisperer," *31*
White, Eugene R., *22*
White, Gleeson, *18*
White, Herbert, 85
White, Hervey, *298*
White, Luther C., 75, 85; *72*

378

White, Norman H., 87
White, Stewart Edward, *22*
White William Allen, 67-68, *358*
Whitney, Caspar, *140*
"The Wide, Wide World," *269*
"A Widower & Some Spinsters," *216*
Whitechapel Club, 67
Wiggin, Kate Douglas, *22*
Wilcox, Ella Wheeler, 48; *22, 281*
Wilcox, Marrion, *200*
Wilde, Oscar, 31, 50-51
Wildman, L. D., *22*
Wilkins, W. H., *163, 268, 274*
Wilkinson, Florence, *198*
Wilkinson, William Cleaver, *198*
Williams, Chauncey L., 16, 65
Williams, H. M., *22*
Wilson, Frances, *12, 17*
Wilson, John, & Son
   See University Press, Cambridge
Wilson, Patten, *56, 66*
Wilson, Richard A., *294*
Winter, John Strange, *88*
"With the Band," *102*
"Without Sin," *110*
Witte, Beatrice, *22*
"Wives in Exile," 77, 88; *84*
Wolf, Alice, *38, 68*
"The Wolf's Long Howl," *191*
"A Woman's Courier," *73*

"The Wonderful Stories of Jane and John," *226*
Woodberry, George Edward, 57, 88-89; *22, 35*
Woodruff, Henry, *249*
Woods, Alice, *226*
"Wooings and Weddings in Many Climes," *266*
Woolley, Edward Mott, *135; 307*
Wratislaw, Theodore, *22*
Wrenn, John H., 65
Wright, Charles, *95*
Wright, Jean, *22*
Wyatt, Edith Franklin, *64; 22*
Wynne, Madeline Yale, *358; 130*

Yale, Catherine Brooks, *358*
"The Yankees of the East," *82*
Yeats, S. Levett, *22*
Yeats, William Butler, 20, 360; *22, 25, 243*
The Yellow Book, 30-31, 51
Yeoman, William Joseph, *73*
Yohn, Frederic, *90*
Young, F., *284*
"Young Man's Literature," *45*
The Youth's Companion, *183*

Zangwill, Israel, *22, 281*
Zimmerman, H. P., *273, 295*
"Ziska," *103*

The typefaces for this volume have been composed in Linotype Caslon 137 and Ludlow True-cut Caslon by the Norman Press. 1000 copies have been printed on Laid Ivory paper and 500 copies on a special rag-content paper by Louis Graf at the Black Cat Press. The illustrations have been reproduced by the Advance Lithograph Company. Bound under the supervision of James Blaine at the John F. Cuneo Company. The title page device used here for the first time is from the hand of Paul Hazelrigg. Completed at Chicago, Illinois, March, 1940

*Design & Typography by
Norman W Forgue*

Sidney Kramer